Literary Studies

Literary Studies: A Practical Guide provides a comprehensive foundation for the study of English, American, and world literatures, giving students the critical skills they need to best develop and apply their knowledge. Designed for use in all literature courses, *Literary Studies* begins by outlining the history of literary movements, enabling students to contextualize a given work within its cultural and historical moment. Specific focus is then given to the analysis of:

- Poetry
- Prose fiction
- Plays
- Films

A detailed unit offers clear and concise introductions to literary criticism and theory, encouraging students to nurture their unique insights into a range of texts with these critical tools. Finally, students are guided through the process of generating ideas for essays, considering the role of secondary criticism in their writing, and formulating literary arguments. This practical volume is an invaluable resource for students, giving them the tools to succeed in a range of English courses.

Tison Pugh is Professor of English at the University of Central Florida, USA.

Margaret E. Johnson is Professor of English at Idaho State University, USA.

Literary Studies
A Practical Guide

Tison Pugh and Margaret E. Johnson

Routledge
Taylor & Francis Group

LONDON AND NEW YORK

First published 2014
by Routledge
2 Park Square, Milton Park, Abingdon, Oxon OX14 4RN

Simultaneously published in the USA and Canada
by Routledge
711 Third Avenue, New York, NY 10017

*Routledge is an imprint of the Taylor & Francis Group,
an informa business*

British Library Cataloguing in Publication Data
A catalogue record for this book is available from the British Library

Library of Congress Cataloging in Publication Data
Pugh, Tison.
Literary studies : a practical guide / Tison Pugh and Margaret E.
Johnson.
pages cm
Includes bibliographical references and index.
1. English literature—Study and teaching. 2. American
literature—Study and teaching. I. Johnson, Margaret E. II. Title.
PR33.P84 2014
820.71′1—dc23
2013026370

ISBN: 978-0-415-53691-2 (hbk)
ISBN: 978-0-415-53692-9 (pbk)
ISBN: 978-1-315-85601-8 (ebk)

Typeset in Sabon
by Swales & Willis Ltd, Exeter, Devon, UK

Contents

Introduction   ix

UNIT 1
A Practical Guide to Linguistic and Literary History   1

1.1   A Brief Linguistic History of English and England   3

1.2   A Brief History of English Literature   13

The Middle Ages (731 CE–1485) 13
Renaissance (1485–1660) 16
The Long Eighteenth Century (1660–1785) 21
Romanticism (1785–1837) 25
The Victorian Era (1837–1901) 29
Modernism to the Present (1901–Present) 33

1.3   A Brief History of American Literature   38

Pre-colonial and Colonial Era (Pre-Columbian–1720) 38
Revolutionary and Early American Era (1720–1820) 42
Romanticism (1820–1865) 45
Realism and Naturalism (1865–1910) 49
Modernism (1910–1945) 52
Postmodernism (1945–Present) 56

1.4   A Brief History of World Literature   64

Pre-classical and Classical Greek Literature
  (c. 750–350 BCE) 65
Classical Chinese Literature (c. 1000–200 BCE) 68
Arabic and Persian Literature from the Middle Ages
  (c. 500 CE–1400) 70

Literature of the European Renaissance (1350–1650) 73
Nineteenth-Century Russian Literature (1820–1910) 76
Literature of European Modernism (1910–1945) 79
Postcolonial African Literature (1950–Present) 83
Twentieth-Century Latin American Literature
(1940–Present) 87

UNIT 2
**A Practical Guide to Major Literary Modes and
Cinematic Adaptations**   **91**

2.1 Poetry   **93**

Sound 93
Accent, Rhythm, Meter, and the Poetic Line 97
Images, Symbols, Allusions, and Figurative Language 106
Voice and Genre 111

2.2 Prose Fiction   **129**

Plot Structure 129
Point of View 132
Characters and Characterization 137
Setting 139
Theme 141
Style and Tone 142
The Novel and Its Genres 146

2.3 Plays   **155**

Structure, Plot, and Theme 155
Character and Dialogue 158
The Physical Stage: Mise-en-Scène and Lighting 162
Major Theatrical Genres: Tragedy, Comedy, Drama 163

2.4 Cinematic Adaptations of Literature   **178**

From Page to Screen: An Overview of Cinematic
Adaptations of Literature 178
Cinematic Vocabulary 182
Film Theories: Auteurs, Stars, and Spectators 190
Film Genres 197

UNIT 3
**A Practical Guide to Literary Criticism and
Literary Theory**   209

3.1   A Brief Historical Overview of Literary Criticism   211

3.2   Literary Theories and Their Applications   223

*Close Reading and New Criticism 224
Semiotic and Deconstructive Approaches 227
(New) Historicist and Cultural Studies Approaches 230
Theories of Social Class and Ideology 234
Psychoanalytic Approaches 237
Gender and Feminist Theories 240
Queer Theories 243
Postcolonial and Critical Race Theories 246
Rhetorical Analysis 249
Genre Theories 252
A Final Note on Literary Theories 256*

UNIT 4
A Practical Guide to Writing a Research Essay   257

4.1   The Research Essay   259

*The Core Elements of an Essay 259
Research 263
Building the Essay: Thesis, Research, Outline 265
Documenting Sources 267
Plagiarism 273
Presentations in New Media 275*

4.2   Revising the Research Essay   277

*All Writers Revise 277
Case Study: Revising an Essay 277
Tips for Self-Editing and Improving Academic Prose 288*

Works Cited   297
Index   312

Introduction

In *Literary Studies: A Practical Guide*, we offer students a unique and compact resource for reading and interpreting literature, one that they can carry with them throughout their undergraduate careers. This volume contains concise overviews of literary history, of literary modes (poetry, prose fiction, plays, and cinematic adaptations), of literary criticism and theory, and of research essays—all of which can facilitate study in a wide range of courses. Instructors often presume students have engaged with these topics prior to entering their classrooms, but each student takes a unique path through literary studies and may have not yet encountered one or more of them. Thus, such students will benefit from succinct introductions to these fundamental topics in literary studies. In a complementary fashion, we hope that this book will also be of service to instructors, who can use it to quickly review topics of deep complexity in their classes. Many literature departments offer, and many literature students take, entire courses—if not sequences of courses—addressing the various chapters and subchapters of *Literary Studies: A Practical Guide*. With this text, our goal is not to supplant these courses but to complement their efforts in a wide range of additional situations.

We developed this book from our experiences as instructors of various literary courses. Our fields of specialty diverge temporally: Tison is a medievalist, concentrating on Chaucer and the Arthurian tradition, and teaching additional courses in such fields as literature of the Bible, queer theory, and pedagogy. Margaret focuses on twentieth-century American literature, film, and writing and literature pedagogy, and she teaches courses in postmodern literature, film studies, and advanced composition. Despite the fact that we specialize in fields separated by centuries and an ocean, we realized through our conversations about teaching that we faced similar challenges. Due to the ways in which the curricula at our respective institutions are organized, we could not assume students entering our classes had taken a survey course providing foundational knowledge of the history of English or American literature, and so they might not have a clear sense of their historical trajectories. Many students had succeeded in their courses prior to joining our classrooms, yet prior academic success did not ensure that they had studied poetry's meter, or narrative structure, or film terminology. With such issues in mind, we decided to create a handbook that students could use to fill the gaps in their literary knowledge without losing sight of the overarching goal of each class.

The first unit of *Literary Studies: A Practical Guide* covers four histories: a history of the English language, a history of English literature, a history of American literature, and a history of world literature. Collectively, these chapters address how a language spoken on an isolated island during the Middle Ages became the world's most common modern tongue and how it became a literary force in Great Britain and in the United States of America. English and American literature does not exist in a vacuum, however, and the history of world literature explores literary epochs of various cultures to map out affinities and disjunctions among a range of disparate traditions.

The subsequent unit of *Literary Studies: A Practical Guide* addresses four predominant literary modes: poetry, prose fiction, plays, and cinematic adaptations. Poetry creates unique aesthetic experiences, asking readers to contemplate words and images combined in fresh ways. As such, it requires a unique vocabulary to analyze verse effectively, and this chapter explores poetic sound; accent, rhythm, and meter; images, symbols, and other forms of figurative language; and voice and genre. The chapter on prose fiction examines the basic tools of narratology, including issues concerning plot structure, point of view, characters and characterization, setting, theme, and style and tone, as well as an overview of the novels' historical development and key genres. Most plays share the same fundamental narrative structure as prose fiction, but theater also requires a separate set of conventions reflective of the translation from words on a page to actions and dialogue on a stage. This chapter also defines the genres of tragedy, comedy, and drama, exploring their development over time. This unit's final chapter, "Cinematic Adaptations of Literature," discusses the transition of literary texts into films, as well as including sections on cinematic vocabulary, film theories (including those of auteurs, stars, and spectators), and film genres. A primary theme running throughout these four chapters addresses the necessity of apt critical vocabularies for analyzing literary texts effectively. We also pay keen attention to various literary and cinematic genres, for these interpretive tools are essential for understanding how a given work fits within a larger literary tradition.

The third unit, "A Practical Guide to Literary Criticism and Literary Theory," begins with a brief history of literary criticism that explores how great literature generates perceptive analyses and discussions of its meaning, form, and function. Students are joining this critical conversation through their studies, and so it is useful to consider how this conversation has shifted over the centuries to provide a foundation for their own work in the field. In conjunction with literary criticism, literary theories assist readers in developing their own unique interpretations of texts. As surgeons use scalpels and painters use perspective, readers employ literary theories to assist them in constructing their interpretations of texts. This chapter reviews dominant literary theories beginning with close reading and new criticism and including semiotic and deconstructive approaches; (new) historicist and cultural studies approaches; theories of social class and ideology; psychoanalytic approaches; gender and feminist theories; queer theories; postcolonial and critical race theories; rhetorical analysis; and genre theories. Our hope with this section is that students will see literary theory not as an esoteric and disjointing field but as one that enlivens the experience of analyzing texts, for it gives readers avenues of access to develop critical insights.

To share one's interpretation of literature, one must be able to write logically and lucidly, and the fourth unit, "A Practical Guide to Writing a Research Essay," offers advice on how to develop a topic for a research essay, how to conduct research effectively, and how to document one's sources. The unit's second chapter addresses how to revise a draft and edit one's writing, for editing skills are essential for crafting precise and elegant prose.

We offer *Literary Studies: A Practical Guide* not as the final word on any of these subjects but as first steps. Literary studies is a vast, exciting, and ever-changing field. Even the oldest texts and genres delight new generations of readers with their wonders: Chaucer shows no signs of growing old, and James Joyce, a whippersnapper in comparison, looks like he too will engross readers for centuries to come—as will Shakespeare, Austen, Woolf, García Márquez, Morrison, and so many others. The newest texts and genres push our understanding of the literary arts in unexpected directions, and our objective with this book is to assist both students and instructors in being able to work from a shared foundation of knowledge. Also, *Literary Studies: A Practical Guide* is organized so that it can serve both as the primary text for an introductory course in literary studies and as a handbook for reviewing critical issues in various classes. It need not be read in order from first page to last, but it might well be, depending on the unique circumstances of the students and instructors who find it a helpful companion for facilitating their study—and their enjoyment—of literature.

Finally, we would like to thank our students, who have consistently challenged us to think through our pedagogical strategies to increase their effectiveness. Special thanks are due to Devin Snyder who kindly allowed us to use her writing as the sample essay in this book. We also thank Elizabeth Levine, Ruth Moody, and Polly Dodson for their generous editorial assistance with this project. Margaret appreciates the Humanities and Social Science Research Grant she received from Idaho State University to assist with this project, and Tison thanks the University of Central Florida College of Arts and Humanities for continued support.

Tison Pugh
Margaret E. Johnson

Unit 1

A Practical Guide to Linguistic and Literary History

1.1 A Brief Linguistic History of English and England

If, as the old axiom proclaims, history is written by the winners, so too is linguistic history affected by the conquests, migrations, and other cultural shifts among various cultures. In this light, it is critical to realize that, despite substantial overlap, a linguistic history of the English language differs from a linguistic history of England, for numerous languages have been spoken in the land known as Brittania to the Romans, and then as England after the Anglo-Saxon migrations, as Great Britain in recognition of the unions of England with Wales and Scotland, and also as the United Kingdom due to the union with Northern Ireland. The English language was born in England but not without various linguistic skirmishes and struggles along the way, with many tongues contributing to its present structure and content.

Prior to the Roman invasions of the first century BCE, Celtic languages were spoken across the British Isles. These tongues survive today in Irish, Scottish Gaelic, and Welsh, as well as in Manx (spoken on the Isle of Man), Breton (Brittany, France), and Cornish (Cornwall). Perhaps surprisingly, given their proximity to English-speaking peoples, Celtic languages influenced the birth and development of English only tangentially. An excerpt from the medieval Welsh masterpiece *Pwyll Pendeuic Dyuet*, the manuscript of which is dated circa 1230 CE (although the oral narrative dates significantly earlier), highlights the dissimilarities between Celtic languages and English:

> Pwyll Pendeuic Dyuet a oed yn arglywyd ar seith cantref Dyuet. A threi-gylgweith yd oed yn Arberth, prif lys idaw, a dyuot yn y uryt ac yn y uedwl uynet y hela.
>
> (Thomson 1)

> Pwyll, Prince of Dyfed was lord over the seven cantrefs of Dyfed. One time he was in Arberth, his principal court, and it came into his head and mind to go hunting.
>
> (Ford 37)

Unless trained in Welsh or other Celtic languages, most English speakers can discern no linguistic connections between this passage and Modern

English. Indeed, relatively few Celtic words have entered the English lexicon. Those that have often focus on landscapes or other culturally specific terms, a phenomenon evident in the Welsh-derived words *crag, corgi,* and *flannel*; the Scottish-derived words *bog, glen,* and *loch*; and the Irish-derived words *whiskey, colleen, shamrock,* and *leprechaun.*

With no rivals challenging their supremacy, Celtic languages flourished in the British Isles until 55 BCE, when Julius Caesar led a military invasion of Roman soldiers and a linguistic invasion of the Latin language. This initial excursion brought Britain to Rome's attention, and in 43 CE, during the reign of Claudius, the Romans established a province in Britain, thereby cementing Latin's role in the region. Furthermore, the Roman invaders pushed the island's Celtic speakers to geographically remote areas such as Cornwall, Wales, Cumbria, and Scotland. With the Celtic peoples and their languages marginalized during this period of occupation, Latin served as the preferred language for the Romans ruling England for approximately 500 years; indeed, it continued its role as the preferred tongue for ecclesiastical and political administration well past the Middle Ages.

Latin is linguistically distinct from English, a language, like Danish and Dutch, with Germanic roots; nonetheless, its influence on Modern English shines through in the vast number of words with Latin roots. In his *Ecclesiastical History of the English People* (731 CE), the Venerable Bede describes Britain's geographical location, and even if one has never studied Latin, the similarities between many Latin words and their English descendants require little decoding:

> Brittania oceani insula, cui quondam Albion nomen fuit, inter septentrionem et occidentem locata est, Germaniae, Galliae, Hispaniae, maximis Europae partibus multo intervallo adversa.

> Britain, an island of the ocean, which formerly was called Albion, stands between the north and the west, right over against Germany, Gaul, and Spain, three of the greatest countries of Europe, although divided from them by a far gap.
> (Bede 1.10–11, with modernizations of King's translation)

Beyond the similarities of place names (*Brittania* for Britain; *Germaniae* for Germany; *Galliae* for France, which was known as Gaul; and *Hispaniae* for Spain), several other Latin words in this passage clearly reveal their kinship to their English cognates: *oceani* to *ocean, insula* to *island* and *peninsula, locata* to *locate* and *location, maximis* to *maximum,* and *partibus* to *parts.* The Latin word *quondam,* although archaic today, was widely used by such great English writers as William Shakespeare in its original Latin meaning as *once* or *formerly.*

The emergence of English in England began circa 450 CE when the northern European tribes of the Angles, Saxons, and Jutes migrated to Britain, bringing with them Germanic languages previously alien to the islands. This segment of English linguistic history, which is roughly dated between 500 and 1100 CE, witnesses the rise of Old English. The masterpiece *Beowulf*, written circa 800 CE, proves the artistry of the language, as it also showcases its striking dissimilarity from Latin:

Hwaet, we Gar-Dena in geardagum,
theodcyninga, thrym gefrunon,
hu tha aethelingas ellen fremedon.
. . . .
weox under wolcnum, weorthmyndum thah,
othaet him aeghwylc thar ymbsittendra
ofer hronrade hyran scolde,
gomban gyldan. thaet waes god cyning.

(Klaeber, lines 1–3, 8–11)[1]

Listen! We have heard of the glory in bygone days
of the folk-kings of the spear-Danes,
how those noble lords did lofty deeds.
. . . .
[The king Shield Sheafson] grew under heaven and prospered in honor
until every one of the encircling nations
over the whale's riding had to obey him,
grant him tribute. That was a good king!

(Liuzza, lines 1–11)

Ironically, most contemporary English speakers find Old English, the earliest incarnation of Modern English, more difficult to decipher than Bede's Latin. Nonetheless, when one examines this passage from *Beowulf*, certain linguistic elements common to Modern English are apparent. Primarily, the pronouns of Old English are recognizable in their modern descendants: *we*, *he*, *him*, and *thaet* (for *that*) denote the same meaning today as they did in *Beowulf*. One also sees overlap between various conjunctions (*hu* for *how*) and prepositions (*in*, *under*, *ofer* for *over*). Even the opening word of this excerpt, *hwaet*, is recognizable in its Modern English descendant *what*, when one realizes that *h* and *w* transposed their positions in various common pronouns, conjunctions, and adverbs: Old English *hwa* became Modern English *who*; *hwaether* became *whether*; and *hwile* became *while*. As challenging as reading Old English can be, an occasional passage readily reveals its Modern English translations. The Old English "thaet waes god cyning," the final half-line of *Beowulf* quoted above, translates into Modern English simply as "That was [a] good king."

After approximately 600 years during which Old English served as the land's primary vernacular language, the French Normans invaded England in 1066. In the famed Battle of Hastings, William the Conqueror defeated the English king Harold II, and the Normans' victory brought French to the conquered land as the language of the ruling class. This era of English linguistic history, dated between 1100 and 1500 CE, is referred to as Middle English. Because French is a Romance language (that is, it descends directly from Latin, as do Spanish, Portuguese, Italian, and Romanian), Latin influenced the development of English both in itself, as the Christian Church's preferred language, and in its descendant tongue of French as the Norman aristocracy's *lingua franca*. Post-Conquest England, a polyglot land, was populated with an aristocracy speaking French, with commoners speaking Middle English, and with many educated persons, particularly those engaged in ecclesiastical and administrative functions, speaking Latin as well. In 1325 CE, the poet William of Nassyngton advocated that English should be the land's prevailing language:

> In ynglych [English] tonge I sale [shall] yow telle,
> If ye with me so lang [long] wille dwelle;
> Na latyn will I spek na wast,
> Bot in ynglych that men vses mast [use must],
> . . . .
> That cane ilk man vndirstand,
> That is born in ynglande.
>
> (lines 62–65, 68–69)

This defense of English argues for the necessity of a common tongue for a multilingual land, as it also recognizes the simple fact that the majority of English people speak English.

As a vernacular language, Middle English lacked cultural prestige, but in the late 1300s Geoffrey Chaucer transformed it from a language of the common people into a language of poetry. His most famous work, *The Canterbury Tales*, begins with an ode to spring declaimed in the Middle English vernacular:

> Whan that Aprill with his shoures soote
> The droghte of March hath perced to the roote,
> And bathed every veyne in swich licour
> Of which vertu engendred is the flour.
>
> (lines 1–4)

While occasional words of Chaucer's Middle English vocabulary appear unrecognizable to most speakers of Modern English, such as *soote* for *sweet*, many initially unfamiliar words become recognizable through their modern descendants—*shoures* for *showers*, *droghte* for *drought*, and *flour* for *flower*. When one learns a few basic rules of Middle English pronunciation, many words sharpen into focus as ancestors of their Modern English kin.

Chaucer's Middle English was spoken in London, and Modern English descends from this dialect. In linguistic terms, *dialect* refers to a variant of a common language, with dialects often used to distinguish between and among various peoples. Chaucer's English contrasts sharply with other regional dialects in the land; had one of these variants of Middle English flourished equally to Chaucer's London English, Modern English would likely sound remarkably different than it does today, or at least enjoy an even greater variety of words and pronunciations. For example, *Sir Gawain and the Green Knight*, an Arthurian romance recounting Gawain's quest to defeat a monstrous adversary menacing Camelot, is more difficult for most speakers of Modern English to decipher, as the following passage demonstrates:

> Gawan glyght on the gome that godly hym gret,
> And thought hit a bolde burne that the burgh aghte;
> A hoge hathel for the nonez, and of hyghe eldee;
> Brode, bryght, watz his berde, and al beuer-hwed.
> (Tolkien and Gordon, lines 842–45)

> Gawain studied the man who greeted him courteously,
> And thought him a bold one who governed the castle,
> A great-sized knight indeed, in the prime of life;
> Broad and glossy was his beard, all reddish-brown.
> (Winny, lines 842–45)

Some words in this passage are evident in their Modern English descendants, such as *brode* for *broad*, *bryght* for *bright*, and *berde* for *beard*; even *beuer-hwed* is recognizable as *beaver-hued* (that is to say, in the color of a beaver, or reddish-brown). For the most part, though, readers of Modern English find this northwestern dialect of Middle English challenging to comprehend, in contrast to Chaucer's Middle English with its more obvious parallels to Modern English.

With the close of the Middle Ages and the advent of the Renaissance, the English language entered the phase known as Early Modern English, which ranges between 1500 and 1800 CE. The Great Vowel Shift marks the transition from Middle English to Early Modern English, and as a result of this linguistic metamorphosis, Chaucer's fourteenth-century English sounds vastly different from Shakespeare's seventeenth-century tongue. Scholars continue to debate the causes of the Great Vowel Shift, yet it is clear that English long vowels changed their pronunciations, although the distinction between each vowel and its neighbors remained. (Long vowels sound like the vowels' names—*a, e, i, o* and *u*, whereas short vowels are the sounds of *pat, pet, pit, pot*, and *put*.) For example, Middle English long *e* was pronounced like Modern English long *a*, and Middle English long *i* was pronounced like Modern English long *e*. After the Great Vowel Shift, however, these vowels assumed their current intonations. For the most part, short Middle English vowels were pronounced similarly to their Modern English equivalents, with short *a* registering the greatest degree of variation from its former sound as if in *hot* and *pot* to its current sound as in *man* and *can*. Despite slight variations in stress or vocalization, consonants remain mostly consistent in their pronunciation between Middle and Early Modern English. Chaucer's Wife of Bath opens her Prologue with a cry to understand women's experience of medieval life, but her words also illustrate the shifts in pronunciation between the Middle Ages and today:

> Experience, though noon auctoritee
> Were in this world, is right ynogh for me
> To speke of wo that is in mariage.
>
> (lines 1–3)

Many words of this passage, including *experience*, *were*, and *world*, are pronounced similarly whether in Middle or Modern English. The vowel shifts are most evident in Middle English *right*, which would be pronounced with the vowel sound of Modern English long *e*, and Middle English *me* and *speke*, which would be pronounced like Modern English *may* and *spake*. The causes behind the Great Vowel Shift notwithstanding, it dramatically affected the sounds and tones of the language, such that, as for readers of Middle English today, many Renaissance readers found this earlier version of their language challenging to decipher.

The striking shifts in English—particularly those of vocabulary and pronunciation—that were evident from its beginnings as Old English through its transition into Chaucer's Middle English and then in its transition into Early Modern English, have since slowed remarkably. Despite their many differences, Modern English of the twenty-first century is much closer to Shakespeare's Early Modern English of the early 1600s than Chaucer's Middle English is to the Old English spoken 400 years before him. The invention of the printing press in the mid-1400s slowed such linguistic changes. Although languages are forever in flux as new words enter their vocabularies and outdated words fade into obsolescence, the printing press codified words and pronunciations in a manner hitherto unachieved in the language's history. In a similar manner, Samuel Johnson's *Dictionary of the English Language*, completed in 1755, helped to establish various preferred spellings and usages. Johnson's *Dictionary*, a truly magnificent achievement, compiles the definitions of over forty thousand words that he illustrated with over 114,000 quotations. As Johnson declares in the preface to this tome, "tongues, like governments, have a natural tendency to degeneration" (*Samuel Johnson* 326–27), and he aimed through his dictionary to preserve the English language from a decay feared to be inevitable.

Following Johnson's lexicographical achievements, Noah Webster published *An American Dictionary of the English Language* in 1828. While Webster's dictionary shares many features and definitions with Johnson's, it reflects as well the simple fact that different peoples experiencing different cultures in different geographies, no matter their common linguistic histories, will adapt languages to their unique needs. American English soon incorporated words indicative of its unique cultures and history, such as those with Native American roots (*moccasin, wigwam, tomahawk*) or those that arose from the Western expansion (*bronco, corral, lasso*). (As Oscar Wilde wrote in "The Canterville Ghost," with tongue firmly in cheek, the British "have really everything in common with America nowadays, except, of course, language" [*Complete Works* 194].) Today, the premier English dictionary is the *Oxford English Dictionary*. Mounting dissatisfaction with Johnson's, Webster's, and other dictionaries led members of the Philological Society of London in 1857 to undertake an ambitious endeavor of compiling the definitions of all English words. Realizing the vast scope of the project, the society, under the editorial guidance of James A. H. Murray, in 1879 enlisted the general public's assistance, advertising an "Appeal to the English-Speaking and the English-Reading Public to Read Books and Make Extracts for the Philological Society's New Dictionary" (Lerer 236). The resulting dictionary was first published as a series of booklets from the late nineteenth into the early twentieth centuries. In a prefatory essay entitled "The History of the *Oxford English Dictionary*: The First Edition, 1857–1928," the editors of the second edition wittily introduce their accomplishments by acknowledging the volume's size in contrast to its predecessors:

> If there is any truth in the old Greek maxim that a large book is a great evil, English dictionaries have been steadily growing worse ever since their inception nearly four centuries ago. To set Cawdrey's slim small volume of 1604 beside the completed Oxford English Dictionary is like placing the original acorn beside the oak that has grown out of it.
>
> (xxxv)

Cawdrey's *A Table Alphabeticall* defined 3,000 words, whereas today the *Oxford English Dictionary* defines over 600,000 words and illustrates their meaning with over three million quotations. Moreover, it shows no sign of slowing, for it can never succeed in its goal of comprehensively defining English, a language forever in flux.

Corollary to the fact that no dictionary can capture a language in its full complexity is the question of whether these tomes should be *prescriptive* or *descriptive*: that is, should dictionaries prescribe how words are to be used in an attempt to pin down their meanings and usages, or should they describe how words are used both formally and informally, whether correctly or incorrectly? Lexicographers must balance between these conflicting impulses, arguing for a word's denotative meaning while also alerting readers to its connotative usages. Denotations and connotations often overlap, but for many words the grey area between these two senses can obscure their meanings. For example, the word *enormity* denotes evil, horror, and monstrousness; it is derived from the Latin roots of *ex* and *norm*, which suggests that the word refers to an entity or action grossly divergent from cultural norms. In many instances, however, *enormity* is used simply to connote an object of large proportions. If *enormity* is consistently used—incorrectly, according to many experts—as a synonym of *enormousness*, at what point does its meaning nonetheless include this usage?

Over the course of the eighteenth century and continuing into the nineteenth, Early Modern English gradually became Modern English, with the basic forms of the language—including spelling, punctuation, and grammar—mirroring our contemporary structures. When reading a novel from the eighteenth and nineteenth centuries, one may occasionally encounter an odd word, archaic usage, or variant spelling, but, for the most part, the novels of Henry Fielding, Jane Austen, and Charles Dickens present few linguistic difficulties to hinder one's enjoyment. One might disagree with the sentiment expressed by Austen in the opening line of *Pride and Prejudice*— "It is a truth universally acknowledged, that a single man in possession of a good fortune, must be in want of a wife" (3)—viewing it as a benighted expression of archaic gender roles, but the language Austen uses to express this opinion remains fresh and clear despite the centuries between her penning it and her current readers enjoying it.

As England grew into an imperial power from the seventeenth through nineteenth centuries, various international dialects developed, each with their unique pronunciations, idioms, and coinages. The United States of America, Canada, Australia, India, South Africa, and other imperial outposts all fostered idiosyncratic variants of words and expressions. Such variability among dialects allows speakers to modulate their word choice for particular audiences. For example, the poet Paul Laurence Dunbar writes some of his poems in an African-American dialect, as evident in his "Little Brown Baby": "Little brown baby wif spa'klin' eyes, / Come to yo' pappy an' set on his knee" (lines 1–2). For other poems, Dunbar switches voices, such as in his poem "Emancipation," which he wrote in standard American English: "Fling out your banners, your honors be bringing, / Raise to the ether your paeans of praise" (lines 1–2). Linguists refer to speakers' fluency in various dialects, and their ability to select among them, as *code-switching*. This technique allows speakers to adapt their words to the rhetorical situations at hand. Dunbar's poems capture the variability possible in one person's voice, and this mutability and adaptability of English is one reason that it is increasingly becoming an international language. Dictionaries such as Johnson's, Webster's, and the *Oxford English Dictionary* may be seen as tools to staunch English's potential degeneration, yet the mutability of a language can also be seen as its life blood: all languages continually evolve, and it is only possible to imagine a truly unchanging and forever fixed language as a dead one.[2]

It may be tempting to think of today's modern English as the language at its apex, but it will undoubtedly continue to adapt to new conditions. Virtually every corner of the globe speaks a unique version of English, with nations as varied as Australia, Belize, Canada, Ethiopia, Kenya, New

Zealand, South Africa, and Zimbabwe, among many others, endorsing it as an official language. Furthermore, English's status as the world's preferred international language is increasing because of the vast number of people studying and speaking it as a second (or third, or fourth) language. As Salman Rushdie opines in an essay provocatively entitled "'Commonwealth Literature' Does Not Exist," "The English language ceased to be the sole possession of the English some time ago" (70). Some new English words, which are today considered slang and denigrated as examples of such linguistic hybrids as Chinglish, Japlish, Spanglish, Franglish, and Denglish (German and English), simply reflect the fact that English continues to infiltrate various tongues, and the corollary fact that these languages reciprocally affect the scope of English. For example, Junot Díaz begins his short story "Ysrael" mostly in English, yet switches to Spanish to communicate his narrator's bilingual voice: "We were on our way to the colmado for an errand, a beer for my tío, when Rafa stood still and tilted his head, as if listening to a message I couldn't hear, something beamed in from afar" (3). Only two Spanish words are included in this passage—*colmado*, meaning *grocery store*, and *tío*, meaning *uncle*—and, even if one does not speak Spanish, Diaz's meaning is mostly clear. Is this passage nonetheless an example of Spanglish? Would it need three, four, or ten more Spanish words to be considered Spanglish? The goal of all uses of language is to communicate, and usually to communicate to as wide an audience as possible. Authors must find the best words to accomplish this goal whether, in this instance, in English, Spanish, or a mixture of the two.

It is quite possible that, in the near future, English will be spoken by as many or more people as a second language than as a first language, and so it will by necessity incorporate loan words that these speakers bring into English's domain. David Crystal describes this linguistic tension as modulating between internationalism and identity: as an international language, English promises to enable speakers from various cultures to communicate with one another, yet this promise of cross-cultural contact is simultaneously handicapped by the fact that the various dialects of English reflect many nations' unique identities and cultures, even if English is not their official language (110). In a similar vein, Robert McCrum details the rise of "Globish," which he defines as a "highly simplified form of English, without grammar or structure," yet one that is "perfectly comprehensible" to speakers of varied fluencies in English (11). As much as the printing press and such efforts as Johnson's and Webster's dictionaries slowed the linguistic shifts of English, the increasing globalization of communication and commerce could well accelerate its shifts once more, perhaps dramatically. Languages constantly metamorphose and adapt to new conditions and new environments, and the one certainty of English's future is that tomorrow it will be different than it is today. Not so many years ago such mainstream English words as *ring tone*, *drama queen*, *manga*, *bling*, and *sexting* did not exist, and it is impossible to predict what neologisms will be part of the English lexicon only a few years into the future.

Notes

1 Archaic letters of Old and Middle English have been modernized in this and subsequent citations.
2 Latin, for example, can no longer change because it is not a spoken language. Even dead languages retain their allure for many modern English readers, as is evident in such modern texts translated into Latin as Peter Needham's *Harry Potter et Philosophi Lapis* (J. K. Rowling's *Harry Potter and the Philosopher's Stone*) and Mark Walker's *Hobbitus Ille* (J. R. R. Tolkien's *The Hobbit*).

1.2 A Brief History of English Literature

From its medieval roots on a remote island to its international reach today, English literature speaks to the history of the English language and its lands, as well as their joint expansion across the globe. The primary eras of English literature—medieval, Renaissance, long eighteenth century, romanticism, Victorian, and modern—capture the zeitgeist of these times through their most popular forms, including medieval Arthurian romances, Renaissance theater, eighteenth-century wit and satire, Victorian novels, and modernist reimaginings of previous forms. The breadth of English literature also expands beyond these dominant tropes, with a panoply of contrasting voices challenging the prevailing modes of the day. Also, no literary era ends on a certain day, at a certain hour, and so the following categories reflect general trends and possibilities, with an understanding of the limits of categorizing the human imagination to specific years, decades, or even centuries.

The Middle Ages (731 CE–1485)

Given the overarching Christianity of the European Middle Ages, it is surely no coincidence that, like Jesus, English literature was born in a manger. According to the Venerable Bede's *Ecclesiastical History of the English People* (731 CE), the poet Caedmon "received the gift [of poetry] by the aid of God" after fleeing a feast and falling asleep in a cattle shed. His dream miraculously inspires him to sing:

Nu sculon herigean	heofonrices weard
meotodes meahte	and his modgethanc.

(O'Donnell 208)

Now ought we to praise	the Maker of the heavenly kingdom,
The power of the Creator	and his counsel.

(Bede 2.143)

Like much of Anglo-Saxon poetry, *Caedmon's Hymn*, as this poem is known, is alliterative, with the half-lines linked together through the repetition of consonants. Although this is a poem praising God, Caedmon employs Old English, the vernacular tongue of the common folk, rather than Latin, the preferred language for matters both poetic and prayerful throughout much of the Middle Ages. Caedmon's poem, merely nine lines in its entirety, also illustrates the oral-formulaic qualities of much Old English poetry, in which certain patterns and phrasings of verse are reconstituted in new combinations.

The corpus of Anglo-Saxon poetry is scant, with the majority of works surviving in four manuscripts—the Junius manuscript, the Exeter Book, the Vercelli Book, and the Nowell Codex. Much of Old English poetry illustrates the unlikely intersection of a warrior ethos reflective of England's Anglo-Saxon invaders with Christian themes reflective of their proselytizers. Pope Gregory the Great sent Augustine of Canterbury to convert the Anglo-Saxons to Christianity in the late sixth century, and many Old English poems depict the cultural and moral tensions as a society based on revenge and blood feud slowly embraced a new religion emphasizing mercy and forgiveness. Thus "The Dream of the Rood" tells the story of Jesus's crucifixion from the perspective of the cross, while casting Jesus not as a humble man suffering for the sins of humanity but as a warrior embracing death in defiance of his enemies after a harrowing battle, as evidenced by the arrows that remain affixed in his cross after a climactic battle. Likewise, *Judith* retells the biblical account of the Jewish heroine's execution of Holofernes, the Babylonian general threatening the Israelites with their imminent slaughter, as a celebration of her daring bravery. Other religious poems of the Old English tradition include *Genesis, Exodus, Daniel,* and *Christ and Satan,* each of which vividly reimagines biblical narratives through an Anglo-Saxon cultural perspective. This intermingling of heroic and Christian values also influences *Beowulf,* the Anglo-Saxon epic recounting a great warrior's battles against three terrifying monsters—Grendel, Grendel's mother, and a dragon. Beowulf's bravery allows the poet to pay homage to the warriors of the past while also considering the relevance of Christianity to his changing culture.

Beowulf ends with his people mourning his death, and such a haunting air pervades one of the most common genres of Old English poetry— elegies. In such works as "The Wanderer," "The Seafarer," and "The Wife's Lament," the lyric speakers bewail their status as exiles from their communities. Riddles are another common genre of Old English literature, in which, often through a first-person self-description, the speaker poetically presents itself and demands readers to solve its mysteries.

Prominent genres of Old English prose literature include hagiographies (also known as saints' lives) and sermons. The tenth-century abbot Aelfric wrote various works in these genres, as well as his *Colloquy,* a didactic lesson in the form of a dialogue between a teacher and his students. Wulfstan, an eleventh-century English bishop, is remembered for such hortatory works as "The Sermon of 'Wolf' to the English When the Danes Persecuted Them Most, Which Was in the Year 1014" and "Sermon on False Gods." In these tracts he encourages his audience to retain their Christian faith despite the many trials confronting them. Aelfric and Wulfstan aside, the names of most Anglo-Saxon authors have not survived, yet the period's preeminent man of letters is undoubtedly the ninth-century monarch Alfred, who, in the Preface to the *Pastoral Care*, discusses the necessity of translating Latin texts into English to enhance literacy and education throughout England.

The Norman Invasion of 1066 brought a French-speaking aristocracy to England for several hundred years, and this linguistic shift coincided with a literary shift as well, in which the heroic and elegiac ethos of much Anglo-Saxon literature ceded to a celebration of courtliness and chivalry in the nascent genre of Arthurian romance. From the pseudohistory of Geoffrey of Monmouth's *History of the Kings of Britain* (written in Latin, c. 1135–1139), which the Norman cleric Wace translated into French verse as *Le Roman de Brut* (c. 1155), and which the English priest Layamon then retold in Middle English alliterative verse in his *Brut* (c. 1190), England's legendary history, as well as its preeminent legendary ruler, King Arthur, emerged as one of the defining literary topics of the Middle Ages. As this material shifted from the realm of Geoffrey's pseudohistory to literature, poets created the genre of romance, in which knights undertake quests to win the love of their ladies, or to find the lost Holy Grail, or merely to adventure in honor of their king. Also in the twelfth century, Marie de France wrote a series of short romances known as lais, several of which, such as "Lanval" and "Chevrefoil," address Arthurian themes. Interest in the Arthurian tradition extended beyond England, and continental authors, including the French poet Chrétien de Troyes (*Lancelot*, c. 1177–1181) and the German poets Wolfram von Eschenbach (*Parzival*, c. 1200) and Gottfried von Strassburg (*Tristan*, c. 1210), ensured that the Arthurian tradition would flourish throughout the Middle Ages. Other masterworks of the English Arthurian tradition include the anonymously penned *Sir Gawain and the Green Knight* (c. 1375) and Thomas Malory's *Le Morte D'Arthur* (c. 1470).

In the fourteenth century, Geoffrey Chaucer elevated Middle English from a disdained vernacular, one seen as aesthetically inferior to Italian, French, and Latin, into a truly literary language with *The Canterbury Tales*, *Troilus and Criseyde*, and other masterpieces. With Chaucer's meter and poetic magic, *The Canterbury Tales* presents portraits of various members of English society on a pilgrimage, capturing slices of life in a variety of literary genres, including romance, epic, tragedy, fabliau, saint's life, dream vision, and exemplum. As much as Chaucer was indebted to various classical, Italian, and French sources (especially Ovid, Virgil, and Statius; Dante, Petrarch, and Boccaccio; Guillaume de Lorris, Jean de Meun, and Jean Froissart), he innovated from these traditions, such as in his decision to use a frame narrative similar to Boccaccio's *The Decameron* for *The Canterbury Tales* but to populate it with characters of various social classes and sensibilities. Along with Chaucer, William Langland (*Piers Plowman*, c. 1360–1380), the anonymous *Gawain*-Poet (*Sir Gawain and the Green Knight* and *Pearl*, c. 1400), and John Lydgate (*The Fall of Princes*, c. 1431–1438) further cemented vernacular English as

England's preferred literary language. In a revealing contrast to these authors who committed themselves to the English vernacular, John Gower wrote his three primary works in three different tongues—*Mirour de l'omme* (Mirror of Man, c. 1374–1378) in Anglo-Norman, *Vox Clamatis* (Voice of the Crying One, c. 1385) in Latin, and *Confessio Amantis* (Confession of the Lover, c. 1386) in English—a testament both to his linguistic virtuosity and to the multilingual nature of fourteenth-century England.

Although the majority of poets and authors in the Middle Ages were men, women writers left a rich literary legacy as well, and these works were often imbued with themes of affective piety depicting the authors' relationship with the divine in highly emotional language. In *Showings* (c. 1413), Julian of Norwich ponders the humanity of Jesus, seeing her savior as a maternal figure irrespective of his physical gender—"And so Jesus is our true Mother in nature by our first creation, and he is our true Mother in grace by his taking our created nature" (296)—as she is also given to visions striking in their imagery, such as all of creation encapsulated in a hazelnut. *The Book of Margery Kempe* (c. 1436–1438), a spiritual autobiography, details author Margery's travails in expressing her deeply felt religious beliefs, which were so highly emotional as to annoy many members of her community, although she does so with an implacable determination. In one of her book's humorous passages, Margery's husband asks if she would "comown kindly" ("commune kindly," i.e., have intercourse) with him if he were to be decapitated, should they not do so; Margery refuses, and he glumly declares, "Ye arn no good wyfe" (23).

Medieval drama consists primarily of morality plays and mystery plays, which reached their height of popularity in the fourteenth and fifteenth centuries. Morality plays allegorically dramatize the journey of the soul to salvation. In such works as *Everyman*, *Wisdom*, and *Mankind*, these eponymous protagonists ward off temptations and other spiritual challenges as they model proper Christian virtue. Mystery plays enact biblical narratives in extended sequences, such as those of the York and Chester cycles. Vast in scope, these plays adapt the biblical story of humanity and Christianity from the creation of heaven and earth to the final judgment, and they required a day or more to perform in their entirety. The Wakefield Master's *Second Shepherds' Play* of the Towneley/Wakefield cycle stands as the undisputed apex of medieval drama, with its rowdy reinterpretation of Jesus's birth against the backdrop of the rakish thief Mak, his hungry wife Gil, and their plot to steal a sheep. From the beginnings of English literature in Caedmon's hymn to the farcical humor of the *Second Shepherds' Play* stretches a literary gap of centuries and sensibilities, yet both works employ the tableau of birth in a manger to elucidate the spiritual mysteries of their faith.

Renaissance (1485–1660)

The printing press, invented by Johann Gutenberg in Germany circa 1440 and introduced to England by William Caxton circa 1475, marks a major transition in literary history. Foremost, it heralds a shift between the Middle Ages and the Renaissance because it both accelerated the production of literature and codified various texts into a coherent, if eventually disputed, canon. Caxton published such masterpieces as Chaucer's *The Canterbury Tales* and Malory's *Le Morte D'Arthur*, cementing their positions as revered works. Also, because the printing press sparked wider dissemination of books, more people read and circulated them than ever before. Whereas the beginning of the Italian Renaissance is typically dated toward the start of the fourteenth century, the English Renaissance began toward the close of the fifteenth century, and the printing press played a pivotal role in this flourishing of learning. The printing revolution coincided with a renewed passion for classical texts, particularly those in Greek hitherto untranslated. With this infusion of interest in the arts and poetry, English writers looked to continental Europe and the classical past for exemplars of poetic excellence.

The fourteenth-century Italian poet Petrarch in many ways inspired England's Renaissance when, some two hundred years later, various poets began translating his sonnets into English. Sir Thomas Wyatt the Elder introduced the sonnet tradition to England with such poems as "The Long Love That in My Thought Doth Harbor," "Whoso List to Hunt," and "My Galley," all of which are translations of Petrarch's poems. Many of Wyatt's poems were published together with those of Henry Howard, Earl of Surrey, in an influential collection entitled *Tottel's Miscellany* (1557); Nicholas Grimald and various anonymous poets also contributed to this volume. With titles such as "Complaint of a Lover Rebuked," "Complaint of the Absence of His Love," and "Against an Unsteadfast Woman," these poems established many of the frequent themes of Renaissance amatory verse: the lover declares his affections, or rues that his desires find no succor. In his sonnets, Surrey developed what was to be called the Shakespearean, or English, sonnet. Surrey is also credited with the invention of blank verse, such as in his translation of Virgil's *Aeneid*.

The mid-years of the English Renaissance coincide with the Elizabethan era, so named for the long rule of Queen Elizabeth I (born 1533, reigned 1558–1603). Elizabeth enjoyed the literary pastimes of her court and participated in them, as author of such works as "The Doubt of Future Foes" and "On Monsieur's Departure." These poems are heavily influenced by the themes of Wyatt and Surrey's sonnet tradition, particularly through the use of oxymoron and paradox in their depiction of the lyric speaker's emotional anguish. Elizabeth's literary endeavors also include her many speeches, such as her famed "Speech to the Troops at Tilbury" (1588), in which she exhorts her soldiers to bravery before a feared invasion of Spain, and her "Golden Speech" (1601), her final address to Parliament.

Following the path trailblazed by Wyatt and Surrey, and recognizing their queen's appreciation of verse, numerous Renaissance courtiers pursued the pleasure and play of poetry. Prominent sonneteers and poets of the sixteenth century include Edmund Spenser, whose sonnet sequence *Amoretti* celebrates his love for his wife Elizabeth (as well as his admiration for his queen in sonnet 74); the *Amoretti* concludes with his *Epithalamion*, a wedding song. In addition to *Amoretti*, Spenser is acclaimed for his epic allegory *The Faerie Queen*, which depicts knights questing for earthly adventures and spiritual rewards; their actions allegorically comment on English politics of the day. In the 108 poems and sonnets collected in *Astrophil and Stella* (1582), Sir Philip Sidney recounts the challenges of courting an imperious beloved, and ends without resolution other than the paradoxical lament, "That in my woes for thee thou art my joy, / And in my joys for thee my only annoy" (sonnet 108, lines 13–14). Sidney also wrote the epic prose romance *Arcadia*, a work of immense complexity and delight that unites pastoral elements with those of adventure, politics, and intrigue. Sidney's niece Mary Wroth wrote her sonnet sequence *Pamphilia to Amphilanthus* (1621) from a woman's perspective. The title translates to "All-Loving to Double-Lover," and in these poems she questions conceptions of women's pleasure in courtship and concentrates as well on its pains.

The celebrated playwright William Shakespeare also wrote a sonnet sequence, with its latent plot detailing a love triangle among the lyric speaker, a mysterious dark lady, and an attractive young man. Along with his sonnets, Shakespeare is, of course, remembered for his plays, and the Renaissance marks the apex of English theater, a period simply stunning for an outpouring of drama unparalleled in its excellence. The roots of the Renaissance stage reach back to medieval morality and mystery plays, and nearer to Shakespeare's time, to the drama of Christopher Marlowe, the playwright of *Tamburlaine*, *The Jew of Malta*, and *Edward II*. Marlowe brought striking oratory and bold characters to the stage, such as in his *Doctor Faustus* (1604), in which the titular character resolves that "A sound magician is a mighty god" (A-Text, 1.1.64) as he turns from his Christian faith to the meretricious allure of sorcery. From this tradition Shakespeare emerges as the definitive voice of the English Renaissance with a strikingly diverse corpus of plays in a variety of genres, including tragedy (*King Lear*), comedy (*As You Like It*), history (*Richard II*), and romance (*The Winter's Tale*). The abundance of accomplished dramatists of the late sixteenth and early seventeenth century—including Thomas Kyd (*The Spanish Tragedy*), Francis Beaumont and John Fletcher (*Cupid's Revenge* and *The Maid's Tragedy*), Elizabeth Cary (*The Tragedy of Mariam, the Fair Queen of Jewry*), John Ford (*'Tis Pity She's a Whore*), and John Webster (*The White Devil* and *The Duchess of Malfi*)—testify to the popularity of the theater in Renaissance England as well as to its power, for these plays, through their soaring verse and lurid plotting, represent radical departures from the mystery and morality plays of the Middle Ages.

Despite Shakespeare's superior reputation today, Ben Jonson was acknowledged as the preeminent talent among his contemporary Renaissance literati. He penned a series of masques—performances that include music, dance, and acting—such as *The Masque of Blackness* and its sequel *The Masque of*

Beauty, for the court of Elizabeth's successor, King James I. These elaborately staged productions, many of which focus more on spectacle than on narrative, allowed the courtiers to participate in playmaking—often to the shock of the self-proclaimed virtuous. Jonson's plays, including *Bartholomew Fair*, *Every Man in His Humour*, and *Volpone, or The Fox*, evince a comic and satiric sensibility, skewering the opinions and pretensions of his day. His major collections of poems include *Epigrams*, *The Forest*, and *Underwood*. *Epigrams* showcases a striking variety of verse featuring disparate tones, moods, and genres, including the elegy "On My First Daughter," the short ode "To John Donne," and the marital satire "On Giles and Joan."

In the early years of the seventeenth century, many tropes of the sonnet tradition were becoming stale, with too many poets bemoaning their imperious beloveds in similar terms of oxymoron, paradox, and blazon. John Donne overturned the paradigms of this poetic tradition with his daring verse. His *Songs and Sonnets* (c. 1595–1615) addresses the vagaries of love with harsh diction and discordant images. "The Good Morrow" opens, "I wonder by my troth, what thou and I / Did, till we loved? were we not wean'd till then? / But suck'd on country pleasures, childishly?," with such words as "troth," "wean'd," and "suck'd" subverting expectations of poetic mellifluousness (*Complete English Poems* lines 1–3). Some of Donne's more memorable images, such as a fleabite as a prelude to seduction ("The Flea") and the sainthood of earthly lovers ("The Canonization"), similarly upend the expected iconography of poetic love. Donne's *Holy Sonnets* ponders the meaning of religious experience with images of graphically physical sexuality, with God depicted as a rapist ("Holy Sonnet 14") and the Christian Church as a prostitute ("Holy Sonnet 18"). In 1621 Donne was appointed dean of St. Paul's Cathedral in London, and he expresses a more somber side in such works as *Devotions upon Emergent Occasions* (1624). These tracts include his philosophical and theological reflections on life, religion, and community, famously encapsulated in his phrase, "No man is an island, entire of itself; every man is a piece of the continent, a part of the main" (98).

Cavalier poetry, one of the defining literary traditions of the seventeenth century, reflects the tensions and conflicting sensibilities of the English Civil Wars. After Elizabeth I died in 1603 without heirs, James VI of Scotland succeeded her to the throne and ruled as James I of England; James's reign marked the end of the Tudor dynasty and the beginning of the Stuart line. After James died in 1625, the reign of his son Charles I began, but turmoil ensued due to suspicions that Charles would reinstitute Catholicism as England's national religion. The following decades were marked by political and civil unrest: Charles was executed in 1649; England was then ruled between 1649 and 1660 successively by a Council of State, Oliver Cromwell, and Richard Cromwell; and in 1660 Charles's son Charles II was enthroned in an act known as the Restoration. Aligning themselves with Charles I and the rights of the monarchy, Cavalier poets such as Robert Herrick, Sir John Suckling, and Richard Lovelace express a *carpe diem* sensibility in which they profess both their desire to love lustily and their eagerness to defend Charles in his battles with Parliament. In Herrick's playfully erotic and decadent verse, which exemplifies the Cavaliers' amorous sensibility, he urges maidens to intercourse ("To the Virgins, to Make Much of Time"), irreverently mourns his abstention from alcohol ("His Farewell to Sack"), or rhapsodizes over his lover's nipples ("Upon the Nipples of Julia's Breast"). Suckling's "Out upon It!" (1659) encapsulates Cavalier poetry's stance on constancy in love, as evident in its opening stanza:

> OUT upon it, I have loved
> Three whole days together!
> And am like to love three more,
> If it hold fair weather.
>
> (lines 1–4)

Lovelace, in complementary fashion, rhapsodizes on the allure of love and on the honor of serving his king, particularly in his *Lucasta* poems (1649), including "To Lucasta, Going to the Wars," "The Grasshopper," and "To Althea, from Prison." Cavalier poets were a male tribe, many of whom referred to themselves as the Sons of Ben in honor of their esteemed forebear Ben Jonson, yet Katherine Philips evinces Cavalier sympathies in her poems as well, particularly in her defense of Charles I ("Upon the Double Murder of King Charles") and in her witty examination of the trials of marriage ("A Married State").

Contrasting with the rambunctious play of the Cavaliers, numerous Renaissance poets wrote deeply religious verse, and John Milton stands as the towering figure of this tradition, particularly with his epic *Paradise Lost* (1667). The poem tells of Adam and Eve's eviction from the Garden of Eden, as Satan, who in Milton's hands is a seductive figure of unmatched rhetorical eloquence, seeks revenge against God for his ignominious defeat and eviction to the bowels of Hell. In addition to his verse, which also includes "On the Morrow of Christ's Nativity," "Il Pensero," and "Lycidas," Milton wrote numerous prose tracts, including *Areopagitica*, his argument against censorship, and *The Divorce Tracts*, a controversial collection of essays arguing for the social benefits of dissolving unhappy marriages. Other esteemed religious poets of the seventeenth century include George Herbert, whose *The Temple* (1633) passionately tackles the challenges and rewards of faith; Henry Vaughan, whose *Silex Scintillans* (*The Scintillating Flint*, 1650) ponders the mysteries of the ineffable; and Richard Crashaw, whose *Steps to the Temple* (1646) and *Carmen Deo Nostro* (Song to Our God, 1652) anticipate union with the Divine, while his "To the Noblest and Best of Ladies, the Countess of Denbigh" proselytizes her to his Catholic faith. Religious poetry of the seventeenth century often grapples with the meaning of faith following Henry VIII's tumultuous break from the Catholic Church many decades earlier—and his declaration in 1534 that he was the head of the Church of

England—as Protestant and Catholic poets defend their respective doctrines while contemplating the call to unity with the divine.

Of all Renaissance poets, the most difficult to categorize is Andrew Marvell, a unique voice who conflates the erotic sensibility of the Cavaliers with a deep sense of religious devotion. His most famous poem, "To His Coy Mistress" (1681), possesses an exuberantly Cavalier sensibility, in which the lyric speaker urges his eponymous beloved to join him in sexual pleasures. This bounteous eroticism is counterbalanced by a looming morbidity in which the lovers' delayed consummation foreshadows the woman's consumption by worms in the grave: "then worms shall try / That long preserved virginity, / And your quaint honour turn to dust" (lines 27–29). Marvell's pastoral poems, including "The Mower against Gardens" and "Damon the Mower," replace the genre's standard figure of a shepherd with a mower, one who ponders the heat of love while peering at his image reflecting from his own scythe. In amatory musings which frankly confront the finality of death, Marvell rejects palliative paeans to love as resolving life's difficulties while also painting a picture of the emptiness of the grave. It is to his credit that he succeeds in these twin goals with poetry insistent in its pleasures. The accomplishments of the Renaissance are embodied in the mythical figure of the Renaissance man, a figure of piercing intellect and wide-ranging knowledge, and this image is embodied in the great poets and playwrights of the period, ranging from the queen on her throne to a man penning poems about a mower.

The Long Eighteenth Century (1660–1785)

No century is longer than any other, of course, but in English literary history, the period ranging from 1660 to 1785 is often referred to as the long eighteenth century, stretching from the Restoration of Charles II to the early stirrings of romanticism. This period is justly celebrated as both the Age of Reason and the Age of Wit, for both intellectual rigor and rapier-sharp wit define its zeitgeist. Toward the close of the seventeenth century, Sir Isaac Newton's scientific advances led to new understandings of the physical world. He also sparked a revolution in thought with his rigorous experimental methodology: "I shall not mingle conjectures with certainties" (57), Newton declares in his epistle explaining his theory of light and color. In the realm of philosophy, John Locke similarly posits in *An Essay Concerning Human Understanding* (1689) that, if one's ideas are merely taken from others, "*'tis no great Matter what they are, they not following Truth, but some meaner Consideration*" (7). Instead, Locke theorizes the necessity of "clear and distinct" ideas, with his philosophical views calling for empirical evidence to support one's claims. Such scientific and philosophical perspectives shifted humanity's relationship to nature, religion, and art, as they demand that one engage critically, objectively, and intellectually with one's milieu rather than accepting arguments based on faith and tradition.

Alongside this burgeoning interest in the scientific method, many eighteenth-century writers focused their talents on sparkling and, at times, ribald wit. One of wit's great theorists and practitioners, John Dryden peppers his sharp humor through his mock-epic poem "Mac Flecknoe" (c. 1679), in which he mercilessly ridicules the playwright Thomas Shadwell by using the structures of epic to depict his foe in "immortal War with Wit" (*Poetry, Prose* line 12). His many plays include *All for Love, Marriage à-la-Mode*, and *Troilus and Cressida, or, Truth Found Too Late*, and his wide-ranging aesthetic interests are also evident in his musically themed works, such as the poem "A Song for St. Cecilia's Day" and his libretto for the opera *King Arthur, or The British Worthy*, with music by Henry Purcell. In his literary criticism, including "An Essay of Dramatic Poesy," "A Discourse Concerning the Original and Progress of Satire," and the Preface to *Fables Ancient and Modern*, Dryden elucidates the techniques and skills of various writers such as Chaucer, Shakespeare, and Ben Jonson to theorize the foundations of their accomplishments.

Another great wit of the eighteenth century, Alexander Pope penned a comic masterpiece in *The Rape of the Lock* (1712), a mock epic poem that insouciantly details the repercussions of a slight social transgression—an amorous beau snipped a lock of a beauty's hair—that proves, in its invocation to its muse, "What mighty contests rise from trivial things" (line 2). Pope's wit and penchant for social satire shine through in such works as "Epistle to Dr. Arbuthnot" and *The Dunciad*, yet he also mulls with deep seriousness questions of philosophy, theology, and aesthetics in "An Essay on Man" and "An Essay on Criticism." Jonathan Swift is best remembered for *Gulliver's Travels* (1726), his allegorical tale of contemporary politics in which the eponymous protagonist encounters such memorable creatures as Lilliputians, Brobdingnagians, and Houyhnhnms. Swift's satiric masterpiece "A Modest Proposal" calls for the sale and consumption of infants to solve Ireland's economic problems in an ironic treatise designed to provoke readers into moral outrage—not over the proposed cannibalism but over the social and economic conditions facing Ireland. In *Hudibras* (1663–1678) Samuel Butler satirizes Presbyterians through the adventures encountered by the titular hero, a questing knight. Many eighteenth-century wits delighted in poems vulgar, scurrilous, and otherwise obscene: an infamous subgenre of verse, exemplified by Aphra Behn's "The Disappointment" and John Wilmot, Second Earl of Rochester's "The Imperfect Enjoyment," recounts the trauma of impotence with devastating humor. Lady Mary Wortley Montagu's poem "The Reasons That Induced Dr. Swift to Write a Poem Called the Lady's Dressing Room" employs this poetic subgenre to trumpet publicly her disdain for Jonathan Swift.

Undoubtedly, the great man of eighteenth-century English letters was Samuel Johnson, a towering figure among the nation's writers. A first-rate poet, as evidenced by his Juvenalian satire "The Vanity of Human Wishes" (1749), Johnson advocates that one should "Pour forth thy fervors for a healthful mind, / Obedient passions, and a will resigned" (lines 359–60), as his poem considers the folly of earthly desires and the necessity of transcendence over ephemeral concerns. His *History of Rasselas, Prince of Abyssinia* (1759) is a fable of philosophical depth, in which its titular prince seeks meaning in life. The novella ends inconclusively, with its final chapter titled "The Conclusion, in Which Nothing Is Concluded," but insights both comic and perceptive are gleaned along the way, such as the realizations that "Marriage has many pains, but celibacy has no pleasures" (377; ch. 26) and "Example is always more efficacious than precept" (385; ch. 30). (*For Johnson's* Dictionary of the English Language, *see p. 8; for his literary criticism, see pp. 215–16.*) James Boswell's *The Life of Samuel Johnson, L.L.D.* (1791) elevates biography into literary art, narrating the trajectory of Johnson's years in exhaustive yet energetic detail. Boswell's work ends hagiographically, showing his subject's sharp wit until the end of his days, such as when Johnson summarizes the comforts of a pillow: "That will do,—all that a pillow can do" (1388). Beyond such witty moments, Boswell depicts the various activities, from the mundane to the celebrated, that made Johnson's life both representative and transcendent of his era.

As Boswell's biography of Johnson attests, the eighteenth century also witnessed the rise of prose into an artistic medium commensurate with poetry and drama. The Spanish author Miguel de Cervantes is often credited with writing the first novel with his *Don Quixote* (1605), a parody of medieval romances featuring his eponymous protagonist questing to win the love of the peasant Dulcinea. Precursors to the novel in the English literary tradition include *The Pilgrim's Progress* (1678) by John Bunyan, whose allegory tells the story of an everyman character, appropriately named Christian, setting out for the Celestial City and encountering various obstacles on his path. Aphra Behn's novella *Oroonoko: or The Royal Slave* (1688), another precursor of the English novel, recounts the degradations inflicted upon the honorable African prince Oroonoko, who is kidnapped and sold into slavery in South America. The novel generally recognized as the first in the English literary tradition is Daniel Defoe's *Robinson Crusoe* (1719), an account of a shipwrecked man's twenty-eight-year struggle for survival on a deserted island. Defoe followed this work with *Moll Flanders* (1721), an account of the many crimes and sexual misadventures of his antiheroine, including her marriage to her brother.

As other novelists followed Defoe's lead, an explosive interest in this new prose genre developed. Samuel Richardson's *Pamela; or Virtue Rewarded* (1740) couples romance with melodrama in its tale of the virtuous Pamela Andrews resisting the Machiavellian seductions of her employer Mr. B., to be rewarded by marriage to this reformed scoundrel at the novel's end. In *Clarissa, or the History of a Young Lady* (1748), Richardson details the competing motivations surrounding the heroine's potential marriage, exposing the duplicities possible in amatory pursuits. Henry Fielding parodies Richardson's *Pamela* in his *An Apology for the Life of Mrs. Shamela*

Andrews (1741). His *Tom Jones* (1749), a picaresque novel, features the titular hero pursuing his wealthy love, Sophia Western, despite questions about his parentage and other obstacles to their union. Additional early novelists include Laurence Sterne (*Tristam Shandy*, 1759–1767), Tobias Smollett (*The Expedition of Humprey Clinker*, 1771), and Fanny Burney (*Evelina, or the History of a Young Lady's Entrance into the World*, 1778).

Periodical publications, another prose genre, also achieved prominence in the eighteenth century, most notably Joseph Addison and Sir Richard Steele's *The Tatler* and *The Spectator*, which featured essays ranging the spectrum of human interest. Addison outlines the aims of the *The Spectator*—"For which reasons I shall endeavor to enliven morality with wit, and to temper wit with morality, that my readers may, if possible, both ways find their account in the speculation of the day" (31)—a succinct statement of his aims that simultaneously captures the vast scope of his ambitions. *The Spectator* inspired Samuel Johnson's *Rambler* and other notable periodicals of the day, including Ambrose Philips's *The Free Thinker*, Eustace Budgell's *The Bee*, and Eliza Haywood's *Female Spectator*.

On the stage, wit, even when coupled with vice, triumphed as a character's defining virtue in the era's great comedies of manners, including William Wycherley's *The Country Wife* (1672), William Congreve's *The Way of the World* (1700), Oliver Goldsmith's *She Stoops to Conquer* (1773), and Richard Brinsley Sheridan's *The Rivals* (1775) and *The School for Scandal* (1777). Comedies of manners mercilessly expose the hypocrisy of society's rules of decorum, as the plays' protagonists seek love on their own terms, often in an amorously ruthless yet insistently comic fashion. The characters engage in *repartee*, the rapid-fire exchange of innuendo, insult, and irony in a verbal combat designed to exhibit their quick wits. (*For discussion of comedies of manners, see pp. 169–71.*) In contrast to the upper-class *milieu* typical of comedies of manners, John Gay's *The Beggar's Opera* (1728) begins with a vagrant stating, "If poverty be a title to poetry, I am sure nobody can dispute mine" (3), thus populating the stage with figures from the British underworld rather than its upper strata. In so doing, Gay comments on the depravities of London life, with these characters simply mirroring the duplicities of their supposed betters.

It would be remiss to leave the impression that all eighteenth-century poets and playwrights were equally invested in wit as were Pope, Swift, Congreve, Sheridan, and others. One can see the roots of romanticism and its celebration of nature in the poems of James Thomson, particularly *The Seasons* (1730). Likewise, William Collins rhapsodizes on the twilit beauties of the land in his "Ode to Evening" and probes the role of the poet in society in his "Ode on the Poetical Character." George Crabbe paints a harsher view of English life in *The Village* (1783), stating that his subject will be "What forms the real picture of the poor" (line 5). Thomas Gray chooses a tone somber and sincere for his ode "The Bard" and his masterpiece "Elegy Written in a Country Churchyard" (1751). Not immune to the charms of wit, Gray wrote humorous verse as well, such as his "Satire on the Heads of Houses," yet, in a self-description in "Sketch of His Own Character" that captures his exhaustion with the era's emphasis on sharp humor, he eulogizes himself as "NO VERY GREAT WIT, HE BELIEV'D IN A GOD" (line 4). Characterized by seismic shifts in scientific thought, by the zesty pleasures of wit, and by the rise of prose, the long eighteenth century stands as a vibrant period of English letters, one in which the human mind pursued the pleasures of the pen in creating new modes of thought and new forms of literary expression.

Romanticism (1785–1837)

The romantic period of English literature coincides with revolution: across the Atlantic Ocean, England's American colonies declared independence in 1776 with the Revolutionary War ensuing, and across the English Channel the French Revolution began with the storming of the Bastille in 1789. These wars signaled a new conception of the individual's relationship to governance, with the call of the U.S. Declaration of Independence ("We hold these truths to be self evident") and the rallying cry of the French Revolution ("Liberté, egalité, fraternité") asserting the autonomy of the citizen over the authority of the state. While some leading thinkers of the romantic era, such as Edmund Burke, were horrified by the violence of war, others espoused these radical views of the individual and endorsed the revolutions as necessary means to greater ends. In reply to Burke, Thomas Paine argues in *Rights of Man* (1791), "Every age and generation must be free to act for itself, *in all cases*, as the ages and generations which preceded it" (128). Mary Wollstonecraft, in *A Vindication of the Rights of Men* (1790) and *A Vindication of the Rights of Woman* (1792), argues with passion and rigor for the dignity of the individual and, particularly in the latter work, of women, with her words forcefully advancing arguments for female equality.

Such a revolutionary spirit brims throughout the works of William Blake. For Blake, poetry imbues human experience with meaning by breaking the grip of mechanistic thought, as he affirms in "There Is No Natural Religion" (1788): "If it were not for the Poetic or Prophetic character the Philosophic & Experimental would soon be at the ratio of all things, & stand still unable to do other than repeat the same dull round over again" (*Complete Poems* 75). His poems explore this need for such a prophetic voice. In *Songs of Innocence and Experience* (1790–1791), Blake limns the duality of human existence, pairing such poems as "Infant Joy" and "Infant Sorrow," "The Lamb" and "The Tyger," or separate poems of the same title, including "The Chimney Sweeper," "Nurse's Song," and "Holy Thursday," to counterbalance the ways in which innocence cannot resist experience and experience depends upon prior innocence. Blake's poetic vision unites with his religious and mythological perspectives in *The Four Zoas, Milton,* and *Jerusalem* (c. 1804–1820). In this last work he explains his philosophy of the individual and society through a unique cosmic mythology: "I must Create a System, or be enslav'd by another Man's. I will not Reason & Compare; my business is to Create" (10). With such declarations Blake affirms a break with prior traditions and thereby defines the energy of the romantic era as one of the individual unleashed.

Believing that his unfiltered voice freely sang the songs of Scotland, many of his contemporaries revered Robert Burns as a natural poet, one untainted by formal education and the literary tradition. Ironically, such an image of Burns envisions him as an ideal romantic poet but only by overlooking his detailed attention to his craft. Rejecting the polished diction of much eighteenth-century verse composed in heroic couplets, Burns employs Scottish dialect in such poems as "Auld Lang Syne," "To a Mouse," and "A Red, Red Rose" for phrasing, tonality, and acoustic effect. His "Tam o' Shanter" (1791) narrates in mock-heroic fashion the tale of Tam's journey home from drinking, during which he encounters a witches' dance and flees. His horse loses her tail in the chase, to which Burns appends the moral that, when one's thoughts turn to alcohol and sexual indulgence, "Think, ye may buy the joys o'er dear, / Remember Tam o' Shanter's mare" (lines 223–24). Burns's verse situates him both as uniquely Scottish and as a truly universal artist: his poems reflect his linguistic roots yet his themes speak to the spirit of the age as they urge resistance against the orthodoxies of society and religion.

A dominant theme of romanticism endorses the need to escape to nature, there to find a pure experience of the self. In "Lines Written a Few Miles above Tintern Abbey," William Wordsworth expresses his estrangement from the natural world—"Though absent long, / These forms of beauty have not been to me, / As is a landscape to a blind man's eye" (Wordsworth and Coleridge, lines 23–25)—which sparks his desire to return and relive the past, thereby to recapture the "sensations sweet, / Felt in the blood, and felt along the heart" (lines 28–29). Samuel Taylor Coleridge also extols the rejuvenating force of nature in such works as "The Eolian Harp," "The Nightingale," and "Frost at Midnight." He is best remembered for his "Rime of the Ancient Mariner," a ballad recounting the supernatural punishment meted out to a sailor who needlessly kills an albatross. Wordsworth and Coleridge's *Lyrical Ballads* (1798), which contains "Tintern Abbey," "Ancient Mariner," and such other poems as "We Are Seven," "A Slumber Did My Spirit Seal," and "Three Years She Grew in Sun and Shower," is considered the foundational text of romanticism, both for its themes of reflection in nature and for its diction approximating common idioms and speech, thus implicitly arguing for the essential dignity of all humanity. Along with Robert Southey and Wordsworth's sister Dorothy, Wordsworth and Coleridge are often referred to as the Lake Poets, as they lived and wrote much of their poetry in England's Lake District, a region of breathtaking natural beauty that enraptured these poets, as well as virtually all who ever find themselves there.

George Gordon, Lord Byron, and Percy Bysshe Shelley, in contrast to the Lake Poets, were dubbed the Satanic School for the radical themes and candid sexuality of their works. Byron's *Manfred* (1817), a dramatic poem, distills his ideas about the necessity of living truly to oneself, as his protagonist resists any blandishments to betray his core convictions: "*Thou* didst not tempt me, and thou couldst not tempt me; / I have not been thy dupe, nor am thy prey" (Act 3, lines 137–38), he proclaims defiantly while dismissing the fiend attempting to torment him at his death. Manfred models Byron's conception of the eponymously named Byronic hero, a larger-than-life figure who brooks no compromise of his beliefs and flagrantly defies social norms. In his semi-autobiographical *Childe Harold's Pilgrimage*, Byron recounts his travels throughout Europe, seeking remedy and repose for his disillusionment with life, and in his unfinished epic *Don Juan* the titular hero's many misadventures allow the poet to consider the tension between individual liberties and the demands of civilization. Along with his passionate sense of the individual's duty to be true to the self, Byron also penned with a lighter voice, celebrating love and its pursuits in poems such as "Written after Swimming from Sestos to Abydos," "She Walks in Beauty," and "So, we'll go no more a roving."

Shelley likewise believed in the necessity of defying social strictures to retain one's integrity. His lyrical drama *Prometheus Unbound* (1820) retells the legend of the titan eternally punished for sharing fire with humanity; for Shelley, this tale allegorizes the challenges of his era, which allows him to consider the relationship of the individual to the society that would punish him for following his core convictions. Similar to the Lake Poets in their joy in the outdoors, Shelley extols the virtues of nature in "The Cloud," "To a Skylark," and "Ode to the West Wind." His "Mont Blanc" considers the sublime aspect of nature and its ability to awe humanity through its grandeur: "The secret Strength of things / Which governs thought, and to the infinite dome / Of Heaven is as a law, inhabits thee!" (*Complete Poems* lines 139–40). In the ode "To Wordsworth," Shelley apostrophizes him as "Poet of Nature," and in the elegy "Adonais" Shelley honors John Keats and laments the untimely passing of his friend: "O, weep for Adonais!—The quick Dreams, / The passion-winged Ministers of thought, / Who were his flocks" (lines 73–75). These poems highlight Shelley's sense of the power of contemporary verse, seeing in the deaths of these two great poets a sign of the ephemerality of life—yet also the beauty of their legacy.

A contemporary reviewer derisively labeled John Keats a member of the "Cockney School of Poetry," dismissing him as a striver rather than an artist, but few have achieved more in such a brief lifetime. Keats's famous odes, including "Ode to a Nightingale," "Ode on a Grecian Urn," and "Ode on Melancholy," are masterworks of the form, inviting readers to luxuriate in the aesthetic and sensual texture of his words, as he couples these paeans with exquisite meditations on mortality. "Darkling, I listen: and, for many a time / I have been half in love with easeful Death" (lines 51–52), he muses in "Ode to a Nightingale" (1819), linking his appreciation for the nightingale with his sense of beauty's ultimate end. In "Eve of St. Agnes," "La Belle Dame sans

Merci: A Ballad," and "Lamia," lovers struggle to unite in hazily supernatural settings: Porphyro and Madeline become "like phantoms" (line 361) as they flee together; an enchanted knight, after encountering a "fairy's child" (line 14), stands alone in a desolate setting in "La Belle Dame sans Merci"; and Lamia and Lycius marry, only for Lamia to disappear and Lycius to die when a friend recognizes her as a sorceress. These poems exemplify Keats's interest in reaching beyond the everyday world to fathom the mysteries and dangers of love. As a whole, the poems of these seven writers—Blake, Burns, Wordsworth, Coleridge, Byron, Shelley, and Keats—characterize the romantic era as one celebrating the common individual, reposing in the bounty of nature, and luxuriating in the allure of beauty.

As romantic poets altered the course of English poetry, so too did contemporary novelists such as Horace Walpole, Anne Radcliffe, and Matthew Lewis alter the course of English prose. Beginning in the mid-eighteenth century, readers hungrily sought out gothic novels, a genre typically featuring musty castles, dark secrets, and supernatural events, with numerous thrilling and chilling plot points designed to keep readers in suspense. Walpole's *The Castle of Otranto* (1765) is credited as the foundational text of this genre, which was followed by his *The Mysterious Mother* (1768), Radcliffe's *The Mysteries of Udolpho* (1794) and *The Italian* (1797), and Lewis's *The Monk* (1796). The first science-fiction novel, Mary Shelley's *Frankenstein, or The Modern Prometheus* (1818), builds from a gothic foundation to probe with spine-chilling terror the dangers of human ambition, as Victor Frankenstein confronts the repercussions of his decision to create life.

Two of the greatest authors of the romantic era—Sir Walter Scott and Jane Austen—could not have been further apart in their sensibilities, yet they both profoundly influenced the history and development of the novel. Scott wrote a series of internationally popular adventure novels in various historical settings. Ranging from the Middle Ages to the nineteenth century, they are named the Waverley Novels in honor of the title of the first in the series (*Waverley*), which also includes *Guy Mannering, Rob Roy, Ivanhoe, Kenilworth, Quentin Durward*, and *Castle Dangerous*, all penned, with several others, between 1814 and 1831. (*For discussion of historical novels, see p. 149.*) Jane Austen wrote six masterpieces between 1811 and 1818: *Sense and Sensibility, Pride and Prejudice, Mansfield Park, Emma, Northanger Abbey*, and *Persuasion*. Austen focuses her attention on domestic matters of the English gentry. Contemplating her craft, she described her novels as detailing a small slice of English life while also documenting the attention necessary to achieve the proper aesthetic effect: "The little bit (two Inches wide) of Ivory on which I work with so fine a Brush, as produces little effect after much labour" ("Letter to James Edward Austen" 323). Austen's novels depict love, romance, and marriage among the gentry, and her *Northanger Abbey* gently satirizes the gothic tradition, which remained a popular genre. Despite the marked differences in styles, temperaments, and genres that characterize romanticism, the romantic spirit of the individual forging his or her own way in the world unites the era: the iconoclastic Byronic hero may appear to share little in common with Austen's female protagonists and their close-knit circles, yet they seek to live life according to their own terms, with their sense of individual honor and dignity intact.

The Victorian Era (1837–1901)

Under Queen Victoria's long reign, Great Britain achieved the height of its imperial ambitions during an era characterized by changes in prevailing beliefs and social structures. The Industrial Age, spanning roughly from 1750 to 1850, witnessed the transformation of English society, as a primarily agrarian and artisanal economy shifted rapidly into one based on nascent technologies. Unlike the United States and France, England did not undergo a revolution during this period, but this possibility simmered in its political tensions. In particular, mobs of Luddites, workers who destroyed the textile machines responsible for their unemployment, stoked fears of rebellion. The Reform Bills of 1832 and 1867 defused these tensions by extending voting rights to disenfranchised men. Political power was further recalibrated by diminishing the power of so-called "rotten boroughs," districts that wielded political clout disproportionate to their citizenry. It was not until 1928 that women over twenty-one were granted suffrage in Britain, but the "Woman Question" was vigorously debated throughout the Victorian era: were women destined to be "the Angel in the House," tending to the needs of their family and sheltering themselves in the domestic sphere, or should other, more independent opportunities be afforded them? In the realm of science, Charles Darwin's evolutionary theories in *The Origin of Species* (1859) radically reconceived views of human and planetary history, undermining certainties of faith and, to the mind of many, pitting science and religion against each other.

Of great concern to Victorian thinkers was the purpose of art and literature and its relationship to humanity's place in the world. John Henry, Cardinal Newman outlines the role of a liberal arts education in *The Idea of a University* (1852), advocating that one's intellect should be "disciplined for its own sake, for the perception of its own proper object, and for its own highest culture" (171). John Stuart Mill argues in *On Liberty* (1859) for the necessity of independent thought: "One whose desires and impulses are not his own, has no character, no more than a steam-engine has a character" (60–61). John Ruskin ponders the aesthetic nature of art in such works as *The Stones of Venice* (1851–1853) and *Modern Painters* (1843–1860), deciding in this latter work that "the art is greatest which conveys to the mind of the spectator, by any means whatsoever, the greatest number of the greatest ideas" (8). Newman, Mill, and Ruskin see education, learning, art, and poetry as defenses against a dehumanizing impulse in Victorian culture, in which industrial gains might cost too high a price to the fundamental dignity of the human spirit.

As Queen Victoria's reign defines the Victorian era politically, Alfred, Lord Tennyson, as England's poet laureate from 1850 until his death in 1892, presides over the period poetically. Tennyson's corpus includes "In Memoriam A. H. H.," an elegy lamenting the loss of his friend Arthur Hallam. The poem was written over a period of seventeen years, and it is prized for its slow revelation of despair moving through resignation to a muted consolation. Tennyson turned to the Middle Ages for many of his themes, primarily in his *Idylls of the King* (1859), but also in shorter works such as "The Lady of Shalott." In these works he retells the Arthurian legend to lament the passing of this idyllic former age, contrasting it implicitly with his contemporary Britain and its industrialism. "But man was less and less, till Arthur came" (*Idylls* line 12), Tennyson intones, and the glories of Arthur's reign are mirrored in his praise to Queen Victoria that ends this masterpiece.

Complementing Tennyson's medievalism as a subtle critique of Victorian culture and industrialism, additional authors responded to England's changing social conditions and their accompanying moral crises in their poems and novels. In "The Cry of the Children," Elizabeth Barrett Browning laments the exploitation of child labor, and "The Runaway Slave at Pilgrim's Point" argues passionately for the abolition of slavery. (The Slavery Abolition Act of 1833 outlawed slavery in the United Kingdom and most of its territories, but slavery remained a burning issue in the United States until it was outlawed through the Emancipation Proclamation of 1863.) Browning's heroine *Aurora Leigh* (1857) braves the challenges of writing a woman's poetic truth. "I choose to walk at all risks" (line 106), Aurora Leigh affirms, a simple yet powerful statement of a woman's right to self-determination. Browning's *Sonnets from the Portuguese* (1850) includes her famous amatory proclamation, "How do I love thee? Let me count the ways" (*Selected Poems*, Sonnet 43, line 1), as it also proves her skill with the sonnet tradition, probing the nature of love in verse brimming with emotion but never affectation.

Browning's husband Robert also achieved prominence as an esteemed poet, and an innovative one as well. In his dramatic monologues, including "My Last Duchess," "The Bishop Orders His Tomb at Saint Praxed's Church," and "Fra Lippo Lippi," Browning's speakers cloud their deeper motivations while nonetheless revealing themselves through their words. In this disjunction between the intentions of these speakers and their unintentional confessions, many literary critics have identified the seeds of modernism, for this stance extends beyond irony to explore more deeply the complexities of human thought. In "The Lost Leader," Browning's liberal political sympathies are evident as he excoriates Wordsworth, who grew increasingly conservative in his later years. Similar to Browning, Gerard Manley Hopkins is also claimed as a forerunner of modernism. Hopkins sought to capture in his verse the *inscape* of his subjects, which he describes as their distinctive and dynamic features reflective of their unique essence. In "The Windhover," his words tumble forth yet capture a striking vision of a falcon in flight: "I caught this morning morning's minion, king- / dom of daylight's dauphin, dapple-dáwn-drawn Falcon, in his riding / Of the rólling level únderneath him steady áir" (lines 1–3). (*For Hopkins's meter, referred to as sprung rhythm, see pp. 103–04.*) Identifying Browning's and Hopkins's poetry as forerunners of modernism rightfully acknowledges their innovative themes and techniques, yet erroneously casts the Victorian era as static or otherwise resistant to literary innovation.

As the medieval past animated much of Tennyson's finest verse, so too did this era inspire the members of the Pre-Raphaelite Brotherhood, a collection of poets and painters including Dante Gabriel Rossetti, William Holman Hunt, John Everett Millais, and William Morris. These artists looked to the Middle Ages for appropriate styles and subject matter for their artworks, in contrast to, from their perspective, the desiccated designs of their predecessors and contemporaries. They rejected neoclassicism, a style of art prevalent in Europe throughout the late eighteenth and early nineteenth centuries that favored recapturing the stark majesty of Greek and Roman art and architecture. Rossetti celebrates the spiritual force of eroticism in such poems as "The Blessed Damozel," "Jenny," and his sonnet sequence *The House of Life*. His sister Christina Rossetti's poems, particularly her collection *Goblin Market and Other Poems* (1862), use traditional forms, including folk tales and ballads, to startling effect, as evident in the lesbian undertones of "Goblin Market" and its eroticized treatment of temptation's dangers. William Morris's medieval interests are apparent in his poem "The Defence of Guinevere" and in his lavish edition of Chaucer's *The Canterbury Tales, Troilus and Criseyde*, and other works. Morris designed this volume, known as the Kelmscott Chaucer (1896), for which Edward Burne-Jones contributed eighty-seven illustrations.

In the early years of the nineteenth century and continuing throughout the Victorian era, the English novel became firmly entrenched as an artistic medium in which, with broad palettes, authors assemble a variety of characters to investigate with increasing psychological sophistication human desires and interactions. Charlotte Brontë, in *Jane Eyre* (1847) and *Villette* (1853), portrays determined young women striving to guide their own destinies, and her younger sister Emily Brontë paints with gothic undertones the doomed love affair of Catherine Earnshaw and Heathcliff in *Wuthering Heights* (1847). The Brontë sisters published under the pseudonyms Currer and Ellis Bell due to prejudices against female authors, as did Marian Evans, who, as George Eliot, wrote a string of classic novels including *Adam Bede* (1859), *The Mill on the Floss* (1860), *Silas Marner* (1861), and her masterpiece *Middlemarch* (1871–1872). Eliot's fiction addresses the often vexed interrelationships of life in English villages, in which social rituals inhibit an individual's pursuit of self-determination.

Many Victorian novelists satirized the foibles of the English people and their culture, with William Makepeace Thackeray, Charles Dickens, and Anthony Trollope reigning as the masters of this form. Thackeray's *Vanity Fair* (1847–1848), with its virtuous heroine Amelia Sedley contrasted against the social-climbing Becky Sharp, exposes the duplicities inherent in love, marriage, and courtship, especially when financial concerns trump romantic interests. Dickens's teeming novels, often populated with comic characters either virtuous or vicious, tackle the social concerns of his day, such as the plight of orphans in *Oliver Twist* (1839), England's byzantine legal system in *Bleak House* (1853), the disastrous social effects of the Industrial Revolution in *Hard Times* (1854), and the cruelty of debtors' prisons in *Little Dorrit* (1857). With *David Copperfield* (1850) and *Great Expectations* (1861), Dickens employs the genre of bildungsroman to explore his protagonists' lives and their maturation into adulthood, considering especially the ways in which, through the vagaries of love, one's amatory affections clarify one's sense of self. Due to the success of his Barsetshire Novels (including *Barchester Towers*, 1857) and his Palliser Novels (including *Can You Forgive Her?* 1865), Anthony Trollope was a celebrated and popular author of his day, exploring in numerous seriocomic narratives the responsibilities of the individual to his family and society.

Inspired by the thrills and chills of the gothic tradition, sensation novels arose as a popular subgenre of Victorian fiction. These narratives feature surprising plot twists, dark secrets, and exciting climaxes, and they also share many features of mystery novels. Wilkie Collins pioneered this form with *The Woman in White* (1860), *Armadale* (1866), and *The Moonstone* (1868). With *The Strange Case of Dr. Jekyll and Mr. Hyde* (1886), Robert Louis Stevenson employs the sensation novel to examine the depravity of his protagonist, who unleashes himself to perform unspeakable evil in the form of the terrible Mr. Hyde. In its treatment of men leading double lives, Stevenson's novel condemns the hypocrisies of his day. Alongside the narrative twists and turns of sensations novels, Britain's vast empire sparked literary interest in international settings and their peoples, with these subjects often treated as exotics. The definitive author of Victorian imperialism, Rudyard Kipling, with *Jungle Book* (1894) and *Kim* (1901), brought tales of India and empire back to Britain. His poem "The White Man's Burden" extols his nation's imperial reach and degrades the native citizens of these lands as "new-caught, sullen peoples, / Half-devil and half-child" (lines 7–8), yet, despite the bigotry of this statement, he is also capable of depicting the ignorance of the English and the wisdom of the indigenous cultures, such as in his short story "The Man Who Would Be King."

Toward the close of the nineteenth century emerged two men who forever changed the fashion and scope of English theater: Oscar Wilde and George Bernard Shaw. Wilde trumpeted a new interest in aestheticism, proclaiming the necessity of art for art's sake in the preface of *The Importance of Being Earnest* (1899): "[I]t has as its philosophy . . . [t]hat we should treat all the trivial things of life very seriously, and all the serious things of life with sincere and studied triviality" (95). Pitch-perfect satires of English manners, Wilde's plays, including *Lady Windermere's Fan* and *An Ideal Husband*, mock the affectations of polite society with a wit both deft and devastating. Shaw attacks the hypocrisies of Victorian culture in such works as *Mrs Warren's Profession* (1893), in which he criticizes the cultural degradation of women such that prostitution emerges as one of their few paths to financial independence. In *Major Barbara* (1905), Shaw condemns poverty, stating the play's theme that "poverty is an infectious pestilence to be prevented at all costs" (167), while depicting a controversial solution to this social ill. Using the theater as a means of social commentary and critique, Wilde and Shaw pilloried the affected manners of the English with their nonetheless insistently entertaining plays.

While the image of the Victorian era in the popular imagination stirs visions of stifling social decorum and repressed sexuality, this stereotype obscures the daring and provocative nature of much of its literature. In many ways continuing the romantic cultivation of the individual in their poems, novels, and plays, Victorian authors peered behind their culture's façade to question its values, to promote reforms, and to ask their readers to consider the relationship between English society and individual desires. The adjective *Victorian* should thus be applied carefully: it appropriately denotes all of the literature of the chronological period bearing the queen's name, yet it is less appropriate for many of these works if one focuses on its connotations of prudishness and exaggerated modesty.

Modernism to the Present (1901–Present)

As the Victorian era waned, modernism rose to challenge its sensibilities, with authors breaking with the literary forms and aesthetic sensibilities of the past. As the Victorian era witnessed the triumph of industrialism, the early years of the twentieth century similarly experienced increasing technological innovation. While some of these developments held great promise for the future, such as Orville and Wilbur Wright's air flight in 1903, the promise of such technological advances was undercut by the period's violence: the Second Boer War in South Africa (1899–1902), World War I (1914–1918), the Spanish Civil War (1936–1939), and World War II (1939–1945). With equally earthshaking implications, Sigmund Freud altered perceptions of the human mind with his theories of the subconscious in *The Interpretation of Dreams* (1899), *Totem and Taboo* (1913), and *Civilization and Its Discontents* (1930). By encouraging the investigation of subterranean desires, Freud framed one's individual consciousness as potentially alien and unsettling, a site of unresolved conflicts and desires. Gender roles shifted as well: English suffragettes including Emmeline and Sylvia Pankhurst succeeded in their ambitions, and in 1918 women over thirty were granted the vote if they met certain conditions. In 1928 the right was extended to all women over twenty-one. In 1929 the crash of the stock market heralded the Great Depression, a period of wrenching uncertainty that highlighted the fragility of a purportedly modern world.

Against the backdrop of these volatile changes, authors sought a style reflective of this changing world. The poems of William Butler Yeats showcase modernism's virtuosity, as he switches between voices and themes, celebrating a mythic vision of Ireland that he also subverts. "I wanted to write in whatever language comes most naturally when we soliloquise, as I do all day long, upon the events of our own lives or of any life where we can see ourselves for the moment," he mused (308). Yeats's poetic language illuminates images of life, such as in his haunting metaphor of humanity in "Sailing to Byzantium" (1926): "An aged man is but a paltry thing, / A tattered coat upon a stick" (lines 9–10). He queries in "The Circus Animals' Desertion" (1939) the source of poetry—"Those masterful images because complete / Grew in pure mind but out of what began?" (lines 33–34)—thereby undermining the certainty of artistic vision while capturing its force. Such contradictions run throughout modernist poetry, particularly through many poets' recognition of the conflicting impulses evident in human consciousness. The poems of A. E. Housman muse on life's ephemerality, counterbalancing visions of joy and humor ("When I Was One-and-Twenty") with those of loss and melancholy ("To an Athlete Dying Young"). Droll humor amidst alienation characterizes the work of Stevie Smith; her mordant title "Not Waving But Drowning" captures the ubiquitous potential for humans to miscommunicate despite dire circumstances. In his anthology *The Poet's Tongue* W. H. Auden defines poetry simply as "memorable speech"; it is that "to which in all its power of suggestion and incantation we must surrender, as we do when talking to an intimate friend" (Auden and Garrett v). In "As I Walked Out One Evening," "Musée des Beaux Arts," and "In Praise of Limestone," such a feeling of intimacy is coupled with the necessity to view life candidly, as the narrator of "In Praise of Limestone" (1948) states: "They were right, my dear, all those voices were right / And still are: this land is not the sweet home it looks" (*Collected Poems* lines 60–61). For Dylan Thomas, the business of life is coupled with the inevitability of death, famously expressed in his title "Do Not Go Gentle into That Good Night" but also in such works as "The Force That through the Green Fuse Drives the Flower" and "Poem in October."

Faced with worldwide conflicts of horrendous destruction, many twentieth-century poets grappled with the destructive force and human sacrifice of the World Wars. Poets of both conflicts—Rupert Brooke, Siegfried Sassoon, Ivor Gurney, Robert Graves, and Wilfred Owen for the first; Henry Reed, Keith Douglas, and Charles Causley for the second—ponder the suffering and cruelty generated by conflict. Owen summarizes this theme in "Dulce et Decorum Est" (1920) with agonizing accuracy:

> My friend, you would not tell with such high zest,
> To children ardent for some desperate glory,
> The old Lie: Dulce et decorum est
> Pro patria mori.
>
> (lines 25–28)

The Latin with which Owen concludes his poem translates as "It is sweet and proper to die for one's country," which he sees as a patriotic illusion inspiring young men to sacrifice themselves needlessly to the conflict. A mere twenty-five years later, Keith Douglas, who died during the D-Day campaigns on the Normandy beaches, personifies weaponry in his "Gallantry" (1943)—"the bullets cried with laughter, / the shells were overcome with mirth" (lines 21–22)—in contrast to the dead soldiers, ironically transposing life with death, animate weapons with inanimate corpses.

Mid- to late twentieth-century poets both continued and resisted modernist themes and structures. In returning to a more formal and metrical style, Philip Larkin rejects the tenets of modernism in many of his poems. In "Aubade" (1977) he reimagines this poetic genre, typically a love poem sung at dawn, into a dirge for the self: "Being brave / Lets no one off the grave" (lines 38–39). With Kingsley Amis and Thom Gunn, Larkin inaugurated a poetic school known as "the Movement," which rebutted many of the premises of modernism in favor of a simpler, sparer style. The poems of Ted Hughes evince a disjunctive tone and sharp diction. He rejects meter to stake out the rhythms of his voice, as in the discordant alliteration of "Pike" (1959), a poem that, in the terms of Gerard Manley Hopkins, captures its subject's inscape: "Pike, three inches long, perfect / Pike, in all parts, green tigering the gold" (lines 1–2). Poets such as Edwin Morgan, Douglas Dunn, Liz Lochhead, and Kathleen Jamie voice themes and images of Scotland, thereby further widening the parameters of the United Kingdom's sense of its poetic traditions, while across the Irish Sea, Seamus Heaney writes of the Republic of Ireland and family history, famously proclaiming in "Digging" (1966) his intention to explore his family and the world through verse: "Between my finger and my thumb / The squat pen rests. / I'll dig with it" (lines 29–31).

Finding the themes and narrative structures of Victorian fiction constrictive, modernist authors refashioned the scope and ambition of novels. Thomas Hardy, in *The Return of the Native* (1878), *The Mayor of Casterbridge* (1886), *Tess of the d'Urbervilles* (1891), and *Jude the Obscure* (1895), depicts his protagonists as hemmed in by the conformities of British culture and the cruel destiny of their fates. Whereas Hardy's novels maintain the expansive narrative style of his Victorian forebears, his refusal to grant his characters upbeat resolutions marks a profound disillusionment with the era. With *Heart of Darkness* (1899) and *Lord Jim* (1900), Joseph Conrad wrote of empire and its failings, using a structure of mediated narration to complicate the linearity of his tales, thus requiring readers to trace their truthfulness through their various tellers. In his plea that one should "Only connect" (3), as thematically expressed in *Howards End* (1910), E. M. Forster advocates human kinship and understanding as the necessary antidote to alienation, and *A Passage to India* (1924) depicts the necessity of cross-cultural communication for such harmony to be effected. Forster's *Maurice*, unpublished until 1971, addresses the subject of homosexuality, which was taboo for its time. Frankly tackling the subject of eroticism and its discontents, D. H. Lawrence argues for sexual honesty in *Sons and Lovers*

(1913), *The Rainbow* (1915), and *Lady Chatterley's Lover* (1928), celebrating in this infamous work that his protagonist Constance Chatterley and her gamekeeper Oliver Mellors "fucked a flame into being" (343), thus freeing themselves into a transcendent union irrespective of social repercussions.

Stream of consciousness, a narrative technique capturing the idiosyncratic and haphazard nature of human thought, characterizes the novels of Virginia Woolf and Irish author James Joyce, who both lived from 1882 to 1941. Woolf's masterpieces include *Mrs. Dalloway*, *Orlando*, and *Jacob's Room*, and her artistic sensibility is well summarized in the close of *To the Lighthouse* (1927) when the artist Lily Briscoe realizes with quiet triumph, "I have had my vision" (211)—a restrained yet joyful ode to the author's objective of capturing the artistic impulses inside her. Joyce's short-story collection *Dubliners* (1914) presents slices of Irish life culminating in "The Dead," a rich work probing Gabriel and Gretta Conroy's marriage and the ephemerality of love. *Ulysses* (1922) covers merely one day in Dublin, but Joyce gives his novel epic scope and complexity, plumbing through allusions and interior monologues the conflicting insights that constitute consciousness.

Major playwrights of the twentieth century sought to liberate the stage from its standard forms and themes, further disrupting the theatrical traditions that Wilde and Shaw undermined in the late Victorian era. The Republic of Ireland writer Sean O'Casey weds realism with mythology in *Juno and the Paycock* (1924), the second play of his Dublin Trilogy, in which he sets a family tragedy against the backdrop of the Irish civil war, probing the conflicting meanings of family, nation, and sacrifice. John Osborne's *Look Back in Anger* (1956) epitomizes the mid-century movement known as the Angry Young Men, a school of playwrights and filmmakers who exposed the middle-class hypocrisies of British life. Shelagh Delaney's *A Taste of Honey* (1958), often referred to as a "kitchen-sink" drama, tells the story of Jo, a working-class girl striving to create a sense of family with a self-preoccupied mother and a lover who deserts her despite her pregnancy. The plays of Irishman Samuel Beckett are characterized as Theater of the Absurd, with their plots undermining assumptions of humanity's rationality and purpose, as evidenced in the eternal waiting of Vladimir and Estragon for Godot in *Waiting for Godot* (1948–1949) and the comic bickering of Clov and Hamm in *Endgame* (1958). Another absurdist, Harold Pinter, depicts in *The Dumb Waiter* (1960) the hit men Ben and Gus awaiting their orders for a kill, as they come to realize that one of them may be the intended victim. (*For more on Theater of the Absurd, see p. 175.*) Tom Stoppard often finds inspiration from other authors— *Rosencrantz and Guildenstern Are Dead* (1966) blooms from Shakespeare's *Hamlet*, *The Real Inspector Hound* (1968) from Agatha Christie's *The Mousetrap*—while recasting these narratives to plumb questions of identity and the power of individuals to control their destinies. Caryl Churchill, with *Cloud Nine* (1979) and *Top Girls* (1982), brings a feminist sensibility to the stage, respectively exploring through farce and fantasy the challenges to women in asserting their identities against a patriarchal backdrop.

As English literature progressed into the twenty-first century, novelists advanced the traditions of the past while experimenting with new forms of engaging with their readers. Julian Barnes (*A History of the World in 10½ Chapters*, 1989), A. S. Byatt (*Possession*, 1990), Martin Amis (*Time's Arrow*, 1991), and Ian McEwan (*Atonement*, 2001) play with time and history, probing the various complexities of understanding the present through the past. Continuing the traditions of Jane Austen, the Brontë sisters, and George Eliot, female authors of the twentieth century often address the ways in which social conceptions of gender structure women's experiences and thus demand strategies of resistance, in such works as Doris Lessing's *The Golden Notebook* (1962), Muriel Spark's *The Prime of Miss Jean Brodie* (1961), Iris Murdoch's *The Black Prince* (1973), and in more comic works including Fay Weldon's *The Lives and Loves of a She-Devil* (1983) and Helen Fielding's *Bridget Jones's Diary* (1996). Lesbian and gay authors including Jeanette Winterson (*Oranges Are Not the Only Fruit*, 1985), Alan Hollinghurst (*The Swimming-Pool Library*, 1988), and Neil Bartlett (*To Catch Him Should He Fall*, 1990), address the intersection of homoerotic personal desires against the force of public stricture. Also, a growing diversity of voices speaks to the multicultural nature of modern-day Great Britain, its former empire, and its many peoples. Novels such as V. S. Naipaul's *The Mystic Masseur* (1957) and *A House for Mr Biswas* (1961), Chinua Achebe's *Things Fall Apart* (1958), Salman Rushdie's *The Satanic Verses* (1988), and Zadie Smith's *White Teeth* (2000) testify to the truly international scope of English-language literature and the varieties of landscapes, dialects, and peoples that contribute to its further growth and development.

In many ways, we are too close to the literature of the late twentieth century to determine which authors and texts will be deemed the canonical representatives of this period. Some critics identify a literary transition following World War II from modernism to postmodernism, with postmodernism employing such modes as pastiche and parody and a celebration of the absurd. It is nonetheless difficult to characterize many twentieth-century poets and authors under this rubric; such a distinction fits some authors better than others. Also, it is quite possible to imagine that some works currently denigrated as light fiction, such as J. R. R. Tolkien's *The Lord of the Rings* trilogy and J. K. Rowling's *Harry Potter* novels, may well pass the test of time. From the death of Queen Victoria in 1901 to the early twenty-first century ranges a wide variety of literary schools and sensibilities, of styles and voices, from the initial blast of modernism to its reimagining and refashioning both in and against postmodernism. In the growing diversity of authorial voices, as women, non-white, and gay and lesbian authors increasingly spoke their own truths, the twentieth century will be remembered as a time of liberation, if also of despair at humanity's endless ability to war with itself.

1.3 A Brief History of American Literature

The story of American literature reflects the vibrant and sometimes violent origins of the lands that formed the United States of America. American literature begins with narratives of indigenous Americans and international explorers, extending to the creative work of slaves and other disenfranchised people. Immigrants and their descendants, as well as the nation's continued influx of new immigrants, also contribute to the ongoing rebirth of the American character. Whether or not one adopts the metaphor of the United States as a melting pot, in which its citizens come together in the creation of a uniquely American ethos, its literary tradition speaks with diverse voices, and often with an eye to the land itself.

Pre-colonial and Colonial Era (Pre-Columbian–1720)

The literary heritage of the United States begins with the many indigenous communities of the Americas, whose stories, chants, and prayers came down from generation to generation through oral performances, which changed with each teller. For many years, these stories remained within individual tribal communities, though some Native American oral texts were eventually transcribed. Many Native American creation stories share common features, such as the importance of the natural world, yet each story offers unique insights into the history and beliefs of its people. Several creation stories, including those of the Creek, the Iroquois, the Cherokee, and the Lakota, depict a cataclysmic flood, after which the current world, populated with people and animals, comes forth. Numerous stories, including those of the Navajo and Lakota, discuss the role of a trickster figure who participates in the world's creation. North American creation stories unite the world of humanity with the natural world through such symbolically important animals as the wolf, turtle, and serpent.

Europeans traveling throughout the continent in voyages of discovery and acquisition produced the first major set of written texts coming from the Americas. The voyages of Christopher Columbus in 1492 inaugurated numerous exploratory trips authorized by Spain, Italy, England, and other European countries. Within fifty years after Columbus, Europeans had settled communities from the eastern coast of what is now Canada, along the eastern seaboard, and on throughout South America. Other explorers moved west through the interior of the continent. Throughout this period, explorers documented their experiences through a combination of travel journals and formal missives back to the governments sponsoring their travels. This literature of encounter records detailed information regarding the physical landscape, flora and fauna, and most importantly, the indigenous peoples of the Americas. Columbus's letters to King Ferdinand and Queen Isabella explain his early reactions to the New World, specifically to Hispaniola (comprised today of the Dominican Republic and Haiti). He describes the lush countryside ready for cultivation, as well as his plans to control the indigenous people if necessary. In his journal entry for October 15, 1492, Columbus notes that the Arawak Indians lack experience with fighting: "Your Highness will see from the seven whom I caused to be taken in order to carry them off that they may learn our language and return. However, when Your Highness so commands, they can all be carried off to Castile or held captive in the island itself, since with fifty men they would be all kept in subjection and forced to do whatever may be wished" (28). Columbus's journals convey his interest in the place and its people, but also his indifference to the Indians' welfare.

Other early explorers expressed a mix of emotions toward the New World. Bartolomé de las Casas, a Spaniard who traveled to America in 1502, criticized the ways the explorers treated indigenous peoples. For years Casas assisted in the settling of Hispaniola, work that included physical attacks on the Taino Indian community, supposedly undertaken as a defensive measure, although just as likely executed without provocation. Like other settlers, Casas conscripted slaves from among the indigenous people, taking their land and their liberty. After his ordination as a Roman Catholic priest in 1510, Casas realized that such violent measures for controlling the indigenous population were detrimental to the Indians and to his people. He released his slaves, and he also advocated for the rights of Native Americans, taking his argument to King Ferdinand. Although he initially failed to alter prevailing practices, he was appointed Protector of the Indians. In 1516 Casas presented to the King's regents his "Memorial de Remedios para Las Indias," which proposes methods for improving conditions in the West Indies, including ceasing the use of forced Indian labor and changing the economic system. Casas's "Brevísima Relacíon de la Destruccíon de las Indias" (1542), a tract detailing the violent treatment of the indigenous people, initiated changes in Spain's slavery laws. He also wrote *Historia de las Indias*, a three-volume work chronicling the history of the colonization of the West Indies, from 1492 through 1520.

La Relacíon de Alvar Núñez Cabeza de Vaca, originally published in Spain in 1542, recounts the adventures of Cabeza de Vaca throughout the American South and Southwest. Cabeza de Vaca traveled in 1527 as part of a large exploration to Hispaniola and then on to the Florida coast, surviving shipwrecks and other catastrophes. His *La Relacíon* describes the years he roamed the region, including his imprisonment by the Karankawa, his work as a healer and merchant, and his life among indigenous groups, including the Pimas, Coahuiltecans, and Conchos. His descriptions of these tribes' daily lives illuminate their customs and beliefs, including aspects of marriage, death rites, personal relationships, clothing, commerce, child-rearing, and other subjects. Although he struggled throughout his time in America, Cabeza de Vaca respected the indigenous people for their kindness to him.

Throughout the sixteenth and into the early seventeenth century, other explorers and settlers recorded their encounters with America. Such reports came from other Spaniards, such as Francisco Vásquez de Coronado, who traveled throughout the American Southwest, and Hernán Cortés, who traveled throughout Mexico, ultimately conquering the Aztec empire. Englishmen Arthur Barlowe described his voyage to Roanoke and John Smith wrote of his experiences in Jamestown, as well as other parts of the eastern coast. Frenchmen like Samuel de Champlain played an integral role in France's claims to land in what is now Canada and the northeast United States, and Robert de La Salle traveled the length of the Mississippi River and claimed the Mississippi River basin for France, naming it Louisiana.

By the seventeenth century, much of North America's eastern coast was being settled, with new immigrants creating communities or joining existing ones. These settlements fostered new publications, with some of the writing intended for people living in the colonies rather than for those living in Europe. Most of these nonfiction publications focused on issues important for people in these new towns and cities, including histories and religious tracts. One of the earliest and most important works from this period was William Bradford's *Of Plymouth Plantation*. A Puritan Separatist, Bradford came to North America on the Mayflower and settled in Plymouth, Massachusetts. His history of the region depicts the community's experiences from 1621 through the 1640s, and he also explains the religious reasons for the Puritans' exodus to North America.

John Winthrop, one of the founders and the first governor of the Massachusetts Bay Company, brought his Puritan beliefs to the colonies in 1630. On his voyage to America, he gave a speech, later published as *A Model of Christian Charity*, outlining his ideas about building a community based on religious responsibility. Like other Puritans, he believed that God creates roles for each human and that all people play a role in the community, whether as leader or follower, or as rich man or poor. Society, Winthrop argued, requires the cooperation of its members working together. Winthrop also kept a journal detailing his experiences in America, which was published as *The History of New England from 1630–1649*. After several generations of Puritans established colonies in North America, Cotton Mather, a Puritan minister in Boston, scripted his comprehensive work on the history of religion in New England. *Magnalia Christi Americana* (1702) tells of the hard work and dedication demonstrated by generations of New England settlers who established communities steeped in a Puritan sensibility.

An original member of the Massachusetts Bay Company like Winthrop, Anne Bradstreet wrote poetry as a child in England and continued in America. In addition to lyric poems such as "A Letter to Her Husband, Absent upon Public Employment," "The Author to Her Book," and poems in memory of her father, grandchildren, and others, Bradstreet also wrote a series of "Meditations." A collection of her work was first published in England in 1650, making Bradstreet the first published poet of the New World. Following Bradstreet's lead, Michael Wigglesworth, a Puritan minister, became the best-known poet of the age. "The Day of Doom" (1662) inspired a fervent readership, particularly among Puritan readers, due in part to the poem's graphic descriptions of the day when God returns to judge the wicked:

> Mean men lament, great men do rent
>   their robes and tear their hair:
> They do not spare their flesh to tear
>   through horrible despair.
> All kindreds wail, their hearts do fail:
>   horrour the world doth fill
> With weeping eyes, and loud out-cries,
>   yet knows not how to kill.
>   (stanza 11)

Such powerful religious language highlights the centrality of religious themes to the literatures of the British colonies. Not surprisingly, many colonists who fled England to escape religious persecution appreciated religious verse.

Although much of the writing from seventeenth-century America focuses on the establishment of colonies and religion in the New World, other publications accentuate the dangers of life in an apparently uncivilized land. On February 10, 1676, Mary Rowlandson, a minister's wife, was kidnapped along with her three children by members of the Wampanoag. A prisoner for eleven weeks and then ransomed for twenty pounds, Rowlandson records her experiences in *A Narrative of the Captivity and Restoration of Mrs. Mary Rowlandson* (1682). The narrative excited readers, and her religious devotion served as an example for others in duress. Rowlandson's *captivity narrative* is the most famous of this genre. Some stories of captivity recount not only captivity's dangers but also its positive features. In 1755, young Mary Jemison and her family were kidnapped by a group of Shawnee and Frenchmen during the French and Indian War. After many of her family died, Seneca Indians adopted her. Eventually she married a Delaware and, after he died, a Seneca. When Jemison had the opportunity to return to the colonies, she instead stayed and lived out her days among the Seneca. Her experiences were published in 1824 as *Narrative of the Life of Mrs. Mary Jemison*. The publication of these captivity narratives and of other stories of adventure, such as that of Cabeza de Vaca, started a long series of American adventure literature.

Revolutionary and Early American Era (1720–1820)

Throughout the eighteenth century, in the years leading up to the American Revolution, many colonists pondered issues related to independence and governance. Support for religious freedom played a role in the civic life of the colonies, and in the 1730s and 1740s a revival of religious faith known as the Great Awakening took hold. Jonathan Edwards, a Congregationalist minister, played a vital role in this movement, which deemphasized tradition and ritual in religion, focusing instead on helping believers to develop a personal connection with their faith: to feel emotionally attached to their beliefs rather than to experience them intellectually. In 1741 he delivered the sermon "Sinners in the Hands of an Angry God," which outlines the misery of hell awaiting those who ignore God's teaching. His sermon ends by summoning sinners to return to God while time remains to repent: "it is that natural men are held in the hand of God, over the pit of hell; they have deserved the fiery pit, and are already sentenced to it. . . . In short, they have no refuge, nothing to take hold of; all that preserves them every moment is the mere arbitrary will, and uncovenanted, unobliged forbearance of an incensed God" (156–57). In addition to the sermons of Edwards, George Whitefield, with his "Marks of a True Conversion" and "The Great Duty of Family Religion," and Gilbert Tennent, with "The Danger of an Unconverted Ministry," also participated in the Great Awakening, which likely influenced the coming American Revolution. The emphasis on personal, emotional experience rather than solely on churches' official positions, as well as the recognition that all people face the same possibilities of salvation or damnation, may have primed Americans for more revolutionary ideas in politics and governance.

Throughout the remainder of the eighteenth century, American literature developed a character based less on faith and more on intellect. Benjamin Franklin, one of the most famous figures in the American Revolution, published his *Poor Richard's Almanack* from 1733 through 1758, distributing useful information on such subjects as the weather, eclipses, and tides. More notably, Franklin's almanacs instruct their readers with maxims, many of which remain in currency today: "He that goes far to marry, will either deceive or be deceived" (6), "Humility makes great men twice honourable" (7), and "Early to bed and early to rise, makes a man healthy wealthy and wise" (9). Years later he co-authored the Declaration of Independence (1776). Franklin's *Autobiography* chronicles his rise from modest beginnings as the son of a candle maker, his training as a printer, and his success as a newspaper editor, leading to his position as a representative of the colonies. Franklin died before *The Autobiography* was completed, and so only events occurring prior to 1758 are depicted. An excellent example of autobiography, Franklin presents himself with refreshing candor.

A number of tracts criticizing colonial rule and promoting the establishment of the United States of America was published throughout the latter half of the eighteenth century. In *Common Sense*, published anonymously a few months before the start of the American Revolution in 1776, Thomas Paine articulates a "common sense" argument against British rule over America and for the development of an American government. Paine followed this publication with sixteen pamphlets collectively entitled *The Crisis*, published from 1776 through 1783. *The Crisis* inspired American readers, criticizing the tyranny of the English who, he believed, usurped powers that only God should have over men. He firmly believed that Americans were right to fight for independence.

Other authors focused on issues uniquely American in nature. J. Hector St. John de Crèvecoeur wrote *Letters from an American Farmer* (published 1782) prior to the American Revolution, while living on his farm, Pine Hill, in New York. In these letters, he discusses the animals, plants, and communities of America. For the most part, he idealizes the nation, discussing the multinational origins of Americans, their religious diversity, and the country's role as a refuge for the poor and disenfranchised. Crèvecoeur advances the idea of America as a melting pot: "Here individuals of all nations are melted into a new race of men, whose labours and posterity will one day cause great changes in the world" (70). Along with his positive representations of America, Crèvecoeur acknowledges the country's weaknesses, condemning slavery and the failure of Americans to recognize the suffering of enslaved men and women. In his letters Crèvecoeur discerns a distinctly American culture in this fledgling nation.

Thomas Jefferson's *Notes on the State of Virginia* (1785) discusses the colony's natural resources and influential social elements in America. Jefferson provides data about Virginia's land and resources and discusses its people, religions, and laws, among other subjects. In his discussion of slavery, Jefferson theorizes that, due to long-held prejudices and the effect of slavery, blacks and whites could not live together effectively in Virginia society. He therefore advocates relocating black men and women to Africa, after a period of education and work as slaves. Although *Notes on the State of Virginia* is among the most respected works of the eighteenth century, Jefferson's position on slavery continues to create debate and criticism among current readers, especially in light of his relationship with his slave Sally Hemmings.

True independence and the establishment of American citizenship did not extend to African Americans or American Indians. Even so, a number of these Americans played important roles in this period of American literary history. Among the many ministers publishing sermons, Samson Occom, a Mohegan and Presbyterian minister, penned his "Sermon Preached at the Execution of Moses Paul" in 1772, the first publication in English by an indigenous writer. This sermon was delivered in Connecticut at the execution of Moses Paul, a Mohegan who killed a white man. Occom, a skilled rhetorician, published his sermon soon after its delivery, and it went through nearly twenty editions into the nineteenth century. Olaudah Equiano, born in what is now Nigeria circa 1745, was captured as a slave in 1756, sent to Barbados, and eventually sold to a Pennsylvania merchant. After buying his freedom in 1766, he left for England, later traveling to many other countries, but never returning to America. Equiano strongly supported abolition and lectured on the subject in England. *The Interesting Narrative of the Life of Olaudah Equiano, or Gustavus Vassa, the African* (1789) details his childhood in Africa and his horrid experiences as a slave, although recent evidence suggests that Equiano may have been born in South Carolina, making some of his story a fabrication (Carretta 96–105). Nonetheless, his vivid and dramatic descriptions in this book advanced the abolitionist cause. Equiano's book represents a strong example of the *slave narrative*, a genre of autobiography common during the eighteenth and nineteenth centuries recounting a slave's life and mistreatment, including such later works as Frederick Douglass's *Narrative of the Life of Frederick Douglass, An American Slave* (1845) and Harriet Jacobs's *Incidents in the Life of a Slave Girl* (1861).

Of course, black Americans also wrote in genres other than slave narratives. The first published African-American poet, Phillis Wheatley was brought to Boston as a child in 1761 and sold to the wealthy Wheatley family, who educated her and encouraged her to write. In *Poems on Various Subjects, Religious and Moral* (1773), she pens verse in several genres, including elegies written on famous figures, such as minister George Whitefield; reflections on God and faith; and patriotic lyrics supporting America. "To His Excellency, George Washington" (1775) resulted in a meeting between the two. She enjoyed fame for a short time, but her success did not last. Soon after Wheatley was emancipated, she married, but her family succumbed to poverty and she died when approximately thirty-one years old, having lost two children before her and a third soon after.

Other prominent American poets during the revolutionary period include Philip Freneau, who supported and fought in the American Revolution. His poems include "On the Emigration to America and Peopling the Western Country" (1779), "The Indian Burying Ground" (1788), and "On Mr. Paine's Rights of Man" (1795). Joel Barlow's *The Vision of Columbus* (1787) and the later revised edition of the work titled *The Columbiad* (1807) pay a patriotic tribute to America and brought him much literary respect. More recently, the poem's critical reputation has fallen due to its rhetorical excesses. Of his poetry, "The Hasty Pudding" (1793) stands as his most lasting contribution to American literature.

Soon after American independence came the first American novels. During this period, the literacy rate improved, which increased readership for authors and booksellers. As the country was defining itself and its values, novels took up entertaining subjects that often intersected with social and political ideas. Recognized as the first American novel, William Hill Brown's *The Power of Sympathy* (1791) explores with sentiment and emotion a romantic relationship discovered to be incestuous. The novel was intended to be engaging for readers but also instructive for young women in their conduct. Susanna Rowson's *Charlotte Temple* (1794), the best-selling novel in America for approximately fifty years, tells of the seduction of Charlotte Temple, a teenager, who is impregnated but then deserted by her seducer. Rowson's sentimental novel warns young women to protect their honor and to avoid being led astray. Hannah Webster Foster's *The Coquette: Or, the History of Eliza Wharton* (1797) offers both entertainment and instruction for readers. This epistolary novel tells the story of Eliza Wharton, a young woman courted by two men: a clergyman and a libertine. After losing both men to marriage, she has an affair with Peter Sanford, the libertine, and finds herself pregnant. Alone and unmarried, Eliza gives birth, but her child dies, and Eliza dies soon after. Although the novel powerfully argues that feminine virtue is important above all else, the author also demonstrates great sympathy for Eliza and her struggles. *The Coquette*, like *Charlotte Temple* and *The Power of Sympathy*, is a *sentimental novel*, focusing on the realm of feelings rather than logic, and inviting readers to become emotionally invested in the characters' lives. These are merely three of numerous American novels in the sentimental tradition, an eighteenth-century English literary tradition as well that enjoyed continuing popularity in nineteenth-century America.

Romanticism (1820–1865)

As U.S. citizens were building a new nation, America's literary community was developing both the quality of its writing and its popularity, entering a period that would be known as the American Renaissance. Influenced by the revolutionary spirit of the war with Britain and the French Revolution (1789–1799), as well as by the English romantic literary movement, American writers in the first half of the nineteenth century drew on this romantic spirit while also creating a uniquely American voice. Much of this literature celebrates human emotion and the importance of freedom from governmental control, as it also praises the natural world for its beauty and power.

The first American authors to garner international acclaim for their work, Washington Irving and James Fenimore Cooper set their fiction in the United States. Irving enjoyed great success with *The Sketch Book of Geoffrey Crayon, Gent.* (1819–1820), which includes his most famous stories, "Rip Van Winkle" and "The Legend of Sleepy Hollow." His stories vary in subject and tone, with many employing elements of fantasy in their unfolding plots. "Rip Van Winkle" tells of a man who, in the years preceding the American Revolution, takes a nap and then wakes up after the war has ended, finding himself in a new America. In "The Legend of Sleepy Hollow," Ichabod Crane is chased by a headless horseman and disappears, leaving the girl he loves to marry another man. Irving's engaging stories, with their unique plots and wry humor, appealed to a wide range of readers. Cooper is recognized primarily for five novels known as the *Leatherstocking Tales* (1823 to 1841), each of which features the central character Natty Bumppo, a white man who grew up in proximity to Native Americans and shares their philosophical ideas. In addition, the character Chingachgook appears in the novels as a Mohican chief and Bumppo's friend. The most famous of these novels is *The Last of the Mohicans*, one of the best-selling novels of the nineteenth century. Cooper's literary works were unique in their time for depicting African American and Native American characters, although their stereotypical depictions are distasteful to many modern readers.

Although his writing evinces neither Irving's humor nor Cooper's adventuring, Nathaniel Hawthorne created a uniquely American narrative voice through his reconstruction of the genre of romance. *The Scarlet Letter* (1850), an immediate best-seller, tells the story of Hester Prynne, who has given birth to a daughter, Pearl, after an adulterous relationship with minister Arthur Dimmesdale. Hester withstands the scorn of her Puritan community, wearing a red "A" on her clothing as a sign of her transgression, but she keeps Dimmesdale's identity secret. This novel's attention to the pain brought about through sin builds sympathy for Prynne. Hawthorne's focus on the emotional worlds of his characters classifies this novel as a *romance*, although it is a much bleaker version of romance than some other works of the time. In addition to *The Scarlet Letter*, Hawthorne's major works include *The House of the Seven Gables* (1851), *The Blithedale Romance* (1852), and *The Marble Faun* (1860), and several short stories, such as "Young Goodman Brown" (1835) and "My Kinsman, Major Molineux" (1832). Hawthorne's insight into the dark elements of human psychology elevates his narratives into literary art, as he probes the ways in which his characters' transgressions affect their personal and their communities' sense of moral integrity. (*For Hawthorne's definition of romance, see p. 126.*)

During his life, Hawthorne inspired many writers, chief among them Herman Melville, who met Hawthorne while living in Massachusetts in the 1850s. In 1846, Melville published his first book, *Typee: A Peep at Polynesian Life*, which was informed by his experiences in the South Seas and filled with adventure and a romantic spirit; he followed it with *Omoo: A Narrative of Adventures in the South Seas* (1847). These proved to be his most successful books during his lifetime. Subsequent publications, including his masterpiece *Moby-Dick; or, The Whale* (1851), received mixed reviews and modest sales, and by the time of his death, he was no longer considered an important writer. *Moby-Dick* regained attention in the 1920s, resulting in his current status as one of the most important authors in American history. A romantic novel, *Moby-Dick* interweaves the adventure of a sea journey and the hunt for the whale with metaphysical considerations of life's meaning and purpose. Melville's artistry arises in his ability to engage readers philosophically while narrating riveting stories.

One of the country's most important short story writers, Edgar Allan Poe wrote tales of gothic terror, such as his compelling, clever, and frightening short stories "The Fall of the House of Usher" (1839), "The Cask of Amontillado" (1846), and "The Tell-Tale Heart" (1843). (*For a discussion* of *"The Cask of Amontillado," see p. 132.*) Poe's poem "The Raven" (1845) stages a forlorn lover's descent into madness as he talks with a raven, who responds to the speaker's questions about seeing his love in heaven with the bleak, "Nevermore," thus suggesting eternal loss and pain. Poe's "Annabel Lee" combines superb rhyme and rhythmic elements with bleak and forlorn imagery in its depiction of a haunting lost love. These poems' language, tone, and supernatural subjects place them, as well as much of Poe's other work, in the gothic literary tradition, a genre relying on literary devices both romantic and horrific.

Ralph Waldo Emerson, while influenced by romanticism, also pioneered the transcendental school of philosophy. In his essay "The Poet" (1844), he romanticizes the poetic calling as

> the true and only doctor; he knows and tells; he is the only teller of news, for he was present and privy to the appearance which he describes. He is a beholder of ideas, and an utterer of the necessary and casual. For we do not speak now of men of poetical talents, or of industry and skill in metre, but of the true poet.
>
> ("The Poet")

Although Emerson wrote poetry as well, he is best known for his work as an essayist, including "Nature" (1836), "The American Scholar" (1837), and "Self-Reliance" (1841). These tracts reflect his interest in American *transcendentalism*, a philosophical movement particularly significant in the 1830s and 1840s that rejects eighteenth-century rational thought and the belief that only empirical, physical information can lead to knowledge. Transcendentalism also emphasizes the value of the individual's inner spiritual experience. Emerson's writings influenced many writers throughout the nineteenth century, including Henry David Thoreau, Louisa May Alcott, Walt Whitman, and Emily Dickinson.

In *Walden* (1854), Emerson's fellow transcendentalist Henry David Thoreau recalls his experiences living humbly in a cabin near Walden Pond. Thoreau contemplates the value of solitude and living in accord with nature; he also discusses the ways in which he lived simply, spending little money, and understanding the true meaning of "economy." From this book, Thoreau gained a lasting reputation as a true naturalist, but he was also recognized for other literary works, including his famous essay "Resistance to Civil Government" (1849), in which he condemns slavery and American imperialism. Thoreau argues that when the government carries out unjust laws, such as slavery, citizens are obliged to oppose them. In the twentieth century this essay influenced such peace activists as Mahatma Gandhi and Martin Luther King, Jr.

During the middle of the nineteenth century many writers shared Thoreau's abolitionist stance, including Frederick Douglass, who escaped from slavery in 1838, when he was approximately twenty years old. After starting a new life in Massachusetts, Douglass began working for abolitionist organizations and giving speeches. His *Narrative of the Life of Frederick Douglass, An American Slave* (1845) argues passionately against the degradations of slavery. After slavery ended, Douglass continued to make public appearances, arguing for voting rights for African Americans. Harriet Beecher Stowe's *Uncle Tom's Cabin; or, Life among the Lowly* (1852), the best-selling novel of the nineteenth century, tells the story of several American slaves and depicts their lives while working for different slaveholders and while on the run. Stowe draws attention to the evils of slavery by depicting the black characters sympathetically. While of great political consequence in the nineteenth century, the novel's representations of black characters spawned long-lasting stereotypes, such as, most famously, an "uncle Tom." As a sentimental novel, *Uncle Tom's Cabin* elicits readers' sympathy, particularly white readers', for the degradations inflicted on slaves. Harriet Jacobs's *Incidents in the Life of a Slave Girl* (1861) also examines the personal and communal devastation caused by slavery, in an autobiographical narrative detailing the sexual abuse she endured, her escape from her abusive owner, and her years hiding in an attic before heading north. Her book addresses the ways in which slavery destroyed women's honor, an issue mostly overlooked in other slave narratives.

Because the issue of slavery in many ways defined the American character in the years preceding the U.S. Civil War, many other nineteenth century authors wrote about it as well. Henry Wadsworth Longfellow, an abolitionist, published *Poems on Slavery* in 1842, but he is better known for his verse on other themes. "Paul Revere's Ride" (1861), his account of Paul Revere's bravery during the Revolutionary War, suffers from historically inaccurate details, yet Longfellow's consistent meter, rhythm, and rhyme, along with the poem's themes, won many devoted readers. Longfellow's *The Song of Hiawatha* (1855) and *Evangeline: A Tale of Acadie* (1847) are epic works, translating the epic form to distinctly American storylines. He was certainly among the most famous poets of the nineteenth century, but in more recent years his work has often been treated as children's verse. Along with Longfellow, John Greenleaf Whittier, William Cullen Bryant, James Russell Lowell, and Oliver Wendell Holmes, Sr., have been labeled the Fireside Poets. These poets produced metered and rhymed verse, typically using traditional forms rather than experimental ones, making their work easy to memorize and recite (and resulting in their popularity in schools). Their poems incorporate images and subjects from American life, politics, and history.

Today, when looking back to the latter half of the nineteenth century, two poets stand above the others: Walt Whitman and Emily Dickinson. Whitman's groundbreaking *Leaves of Grass* was first published in 1855, although it went through many editions as he continued revising it. In the process it increased from twelve to nearly 400 poems in its 1892 edition, completed mere months before his death. Unlike other poetry of the time,

Whitman's poems were written in an early version of free verse, poetry without regular meter. The collection meditates on and celebrates the physical world, both nature and, more significantly, the human body and its senses, such as in this passage from "I Sing the Body Electric":

> The curious sympathy one feels when feeling with the hand the naked
>   meat of the body,
> The circling rivers the breath, and breathing it in and out,
> The beauty of the waist, and thence of the hips, and thence downward
>   toward the knees,
> The thin red jellies within you or within me, the bones and the marrow
>   in the bones,
> The exquisite realization of health;
> O I say these are not the parts and poems of the body only, but of
>   the soul,
> O I say now these are the soul!
>
> (*Leaves* lines 158–64)

Although some reviewers praised Whitman's poems, others accused him of crudity and offensiveness in his representations of sexuality, especially the indications of same-sex attraction. Whitman's validation of the ordinary individual's experiences and feelings offered a fresh perspective on American life, and this perspective profoundly influenced future generations of American poets, particularly Ezra Pound and Allen Ginsberg.

Emily Dickinson published only ten poems during her lifetime, mostly in small newspapers. After her death, her sister discovered over 1,700 of Dickinson's poems. The first collection of her poetry, published in 1890, was followed by other collections of her verse and letters. Dickinson's verse is unlike that of other poets of her time, particularly in style and form. She uses dashes instead of other types of punctuation, such as periods, as well as unique and peculiar capitalization. The meter of her poems is often irregular in presentation. She also regularly uses rhyme, but much of it is off-rhyme. Although her subjects are varied, many poems deal with death and dying, her most famous being "Because I could not stop for death—." Many images are strikingly unusual, such as when she writes, "The Brain—is wider than the Sky—" (poem 632, line 1). At first, her work met with mixed reviews, with some decrying the oddness in her style and form. However, as expectations regarding poetry changed during the modernist era, critics began praising her originality. Although a woman of the nineteenth century, in many ways Dickinson, like Whitman, feels perpetually contemporary.

Realism and Naturalism (1865–1910)

From the late nineteenth through the early twentieth century, a strong outpouring of realist and naturalist writings shifted the focus of American literature. In part as a reaction against romanticism, which revels in heightened versions of events and emotions, literary realism depicts characters, society, and experience faithfully. Authors describe characters and settings with an eye toward authentic detail. Although the characters come from all walks of life, from the wealthy and entitled to the poor and disenfranchised, realist literature portrays them with familiar and common behaviors rather than those which are heroic or moralistic. Also, realist authors depict situations more familiar to readers than those depicted in the adventure novels of Melville or the gothic stories of Poe. Literary naturalism relies on realistic descriptions and content, but authors writing in this genre also focus on the ways that humans are part of the natural/animal world. Darwin's theory of evolution influenced naturalist authors, who emphasize how environmental, physical, and hereditary elements control human behavior. Many of these novels describe characters who appear to lack free will and are guided by their nature.

At the heart of the realist movement is Mark Twain, the pen name of Samuel Langhorne Clemens, whose novels *The Adventures of Tom Sawyer* (1876) and *The Adventures of Huckleberry Finn* (1885), set in slavery-era Missouri, capture a unique yet recognizable version of American childhood. Twain couples his social critique with humor, most notably in *Huckleberry Finn*. His characters speak as real Americans speak, using regional words and dialects rather than a literary language. He draws his settings with particular attention to local details, which accounts for the high quality of his travel writing. *Roughing It* (1872) offers a comical version of Twain's travels in the American West, providing detailed stories about many subjects, including prospecting for silver and gold.

Sarah Orne Jewett's novella *The Country of the Pointed Firs* (1896) stands out as a superb example of *local color* literature, fiction focusing on the language, customs, and folkways of a particular region. Jewett sets most of her works in coastal Maine, and she features characters and situations distinctive to the landscape. Charles Chestnutt's *The Conjure Woman* (1899), set in North Carolina, compiles stories told by Uncle Julius McAdoo, a former slave. Chestnutt's stories, drawn from African-American folk tales, include elements of the supernatural, or "conjuring," ultimately criticizing the traditional American South. The book's regional dialects and folk tales place it amidst the local color tradition of the realist movement. Other writers linked with this movement include Mary E. Wilkins Freeman, Paul Laurence Dunbar, and Joel Chandler Harris.

Although the use of regional dialect and depictions of local traditions mark the local color strand of realist literature, other realist authors focus instead on the realism of psychology and emotion. Henry James's *The Portrait of a Lady* (1881) tells of Isabel Archer, whose vast inheritance makes her vulnerable to the dishonest manipulations of several people, including her eventual husband. Much of James's fiction grants readers access to a world of privilege, showing not only its benefits but also its failures and controls, offering readers *psychological realism* through the use of first-person narration from the point of view of a character in the narrative. This approach creates compelling narrative uncertainties, such as when the governess in the novella *The Turn of the Screw* (1898) tells a story of supernatural and terrifying events on the estate where she works, with readers asked to determine whether her story is true or the perception of an overly active imagination. (*For a discussion of* The Turn of the Screw *through psychoanalytic literary theory, see pp. 239–40.*) James's work with form elevates the use of realism to significant heights. Also contributing to the rise of American realism, novelist and literary critic William Dean Howells uses realist techniques to focus attention on issues of ethical behavior and social and economic inequalities in his novels *The Rise of Silas Lapham* (1885), *A Hazard of New Fortunes* (1890), and *The Landlord at Lion's Head* (1908). As editor of *Atlantic Monthly* magazine, Howells supported the work of other realist writers, such as Mary E. Wilkins Freeman, Paul Laurence Dunbar, Sarah Orne Jewett, and Charles W. Chestnutt, through his essays and by publishing their work.

Howells's advocacy extended to the branch of realism known as *naturalism*, supporting the work of such authors as Frank Norris and Stephen Crane. Much naturalist literature seems rather fatalistic, suggesting that, because human behavior is controlled by animal instinct and physical environment, a person's free will to make ethical or responsible choices is limited, which results in harsh outcomes. In *McTeague* (1899) Norris tells the story of a dentist, his miserly wife, and jealous friend, who are controlled by their physical desires and greed. One catastrophe follows another, as McTeague loses his business, then steals from and kills his wife, eventually becoming stranded, handcuffed to a dead man, without water, in the middle of Death Valley. As with novels in the realist vein, *McTeague* offers detailed insight into the lives of characters who are both ordinary and familiar; as with naturalist novels, it exposes how passion and instinct control humanity. Stephen Crane's novels and short stories also exemplify the naturalist tradition, particularly *Maggie: A Girl of the Streets* (1893) and *The Red Badge of Courage* (1895). *Maggie* features a working class New York family, in which a violent father and alcoholic mother traumatize their children. Their daughter Maggie, searching to escape them, begins a relationship with a young man who sees her as easy to manipulate. Eventually, Maggie's mother accuses her of promiscuity and ejects her from their home, and she is left by her boyfriend as well, abandoned on the streets of New York, where she dies. Crane suggests that poverty and violence trap Maggie, who cannot break free from the life she was born into. With a quite different setting, *The Red Badge of Courage* tells of a soldier whose emotions, especially fear, direct his actions as he deserts his regiment. These novels depict experiences of fear, violence, and need—all characteristics associated with naturalism.

Whereas Crane's and Norris's novels focus on gritty, physically difficult environments, Kate Chopin's novella *The Awakening* (1899) uses naturalism to depict the life of its central character, Edna Pontellier, and thereby offers insight into the experiences of wealthy Southern society. In this early feminist work, Edna questions her expected roles as mother and wife and pulls away from these responsibilities. As she allows her desire for freedom in love to guide her, she rejects social expectations for women's behavior. While addressing modern feminist issues, the novella aligns with the naturalist movement as Edna feels physically compelled to make choices that she knows may be destructive.

The power of realist and naturalist fiction affected literature well into the twentieth century. Both Theodore Dreiser's *Sister Carrie* (1900) and Edith Wharton's *The House of Mirth* (1905) are set in urban environments (Chicago and New York respectively) and detail the conflicts arising between human desire and free will, demonstrating that physical desires lead humans to wretchedness. Other works, such as Jack London's *The Call of the Wild* (1903), set in the Yukon, and Willa Cather's *My Ántonia* (1918), set in Nebraska, provide American readers with a vision of wilderness and rural environments. Although the modernist movement came to prominence in the early part of the twentieth century, realism continued to play a part in literature throughout this century.

Modernism (1910–1945)

As the United States entered the twentieth century, its authors began challenging both literary and social norms. From approximately 1910 through 1945, American modernist authors created literature experimental in both form and theme. Modern poetry rejects the traditional forms and meters of most nineteenth-century verse, embracing free verse and discarding formal meter. Much modern fiction experiments with narrative point of view, sometimes incorporating new techniques such as stream of consciousness and fragmentation. Influenced by important thinkers such as Sigmund Freud and Albert Einstein, modernist authors incorporated contemporary ideas about consciousness and the nature of reality in their work. Much modernist literature also addresses larger social concerns, such as the widespread emotional and physical alienation of contemporary society, the challenges to social expectations and norms, and frustrations over the impacts of the Great Depression and World Wars I and II on American culture and family.

Imagism exemplifies the shifting expectations of modernist literature. Beginning in 1912, this literary movement advocates focusing on a particular image with clear, precise language and rejecting traditional meter in favor of more natural, musical rhythms. Pound's poem "In a Station of the Metro" (1913) exemplifies the aesthetic goals of imagism:

> The apparition of these faces in the crowd;
> Petals on a wet, black bough.
>
> *(Selected Poems)*

This poem focuses entirely on a specific moment and elicits a precise feeling from a pared-down image. (*For Pound's tenets of imagism, see pp. 104–05.*) William Carlos Williams also advocated focusing on distinct images with verbal economy. His most famous poems—"The Red Wheelbarrow" (1923) and "This Is Just to Say" (1934)—paint simple images that resonate with extraordinary power. Both Pound and Williams later moved beyond imagism, experimenting with poetry in a range of other forms, but their imagist poems serve as hallmarks of the modernist rejection of previous styles.

Pound also advanced the tenets of modernism through his editorial work. While working for *Poetry* magazine, he advocated publishing T. S. Eliot's "The Love Song of J. Alfred Prufrock" (1915), the first of the poet's famous works. The poem's speaker, Prufrock, voices his feelings of longing, sexual frustration, and exhaustion, with stream of consciousness capturing his disjointed yet poignant musings. With its distinctive and unusual images, such as "I have measured out my life with coffee spoons," this poem established the combination of artistic and thematic issues central to modernism (*Collected Poems* line 51). "Prufrock" cemented Eliot's place as a major American poet—and a major British poet as well, as he took British citizenship in 1927—and his later works confirmed his role as one of the twentieth century's most important authors. Most notably, "The Wasteland" (1922), in many ways the definitive modernist poem, considers the modern condition through disjunction and fragmentation in its use of multiple voices. "The Wasteland" also creates another challenge for readers in its numerous allusions to and quotations from other works of art, anticipating well-educated readers of serious poetry.

While many modern poets, like Eliot, Pound, Marianne Moore, Wallace Stevens, and Gertrude Stein, experimented with poetic structures, others created poetry traditional in form yet capturing the concerns of modern society. Robert Frost uses meter and standard stanzaic forms to communicate feelings of isolation and uncertainty, such as in his poem "Desert Places" (1936). The poem's speaker notes the desolation of the landscape on a winter evening and connects his sense of emptiness to the place: "And lonely as it is that loneliness / Will be more lonely ere it will be less—" (lines 9–10). Frost wrote numerous poems about the natural world, linking him thematically to the romantics of the nineteenth century. In poems like "Nothing Gold Can Stay" (1923) and "A Prayer in Spring" (1913), he reflects on nature and its changes.

Traditional verse forms, including rhyme and meter, were also popular among writers of the Harlem Renaissance, also known as the New Negro Renaissance, a movement roughly spanning the years 1918 through 1929. During this period, African-American authors created a collective voice marking the twentieth century as a new era for artistic expression. In 1925 Alain Locke published *The New Negro: An Interpretation*, an anthology of works by such artists as Countee Cullen, Claude McKay, Langston Hughes, and Zora Neale Hurston. Both Countee Cullen and Claude McKay wrote in traditional literary forms. Cullen's "Incident" (1924) uses ballad stanzas, offering a light sing-song rhythm to narrate a story of childhood racism. His use of the sonnet form and classical allusions in "Yet Do I Marvel" (1925) informs his theme of bigotry against African Americans. Through these traditional forms and allusions, Cullen reveals his place in a long history of lyric poetry, yet the manner in which he incorporates these traditional poetic elements emphasizes his modernity. In "Yet Do I Marvel," the poem's final couplet underscores his ironic theme: "Yet do I marvel at this curious thing: / To make a poet black, and bid him sing!" (lines 13–14). While demonstrating a poet's artistry, he criticizes social biases resulting from race. Claude McKay similarly combines traditional form and meter with social critique and representations of contemporary life. Many of his sonnets take racial bigotry as their subject, which is not a traditional theme for this lyric genre. In "The Lynching," McKay describes the scene as a crowd gathers around the remains of the body, including "little lads, lynchers that were to be" (line 13). His alliteration, which adds a lilting quality to the line, underscores the way that hatred can be hidden in the seemingly innocent parts of our culture. Both McKay and Cullen created fascinating new uses for older forms of literature, revealing their distinctly modern sensibilities.

Other writers from the Harlem Renaissance embraced more contemporary forms of free verse in their work. Langston Hughes innovated fresh forms of poetic expression with the rhythms of jazz and blues. Like Cullen and McKay, Hughes addresses racial bigotry and the struggles of African Americans, but his work often expresses hopefulness and pride. In "I, Too," the speaker laments society's rejection of him as a black man but looks to the future when, stronger, "Nobody'll dare / Say to me, / 'Eat in the kitchen'" (lines 11–13). Instead, he continues, "They'll see how beautiful I am / And be ashamed— / I, too, am America" (lines 16–18). His music-inspired rhythms and colloquial language make his poetry both new in approach and accessible to a wide variety of readers. Although many of Hughes's poems have become American classics—such as "Harlem," "The Negro Speaks of Rivers," and "Dream Boogie"—he is also well known for his autobiography *The Big Sea* (1940), which chronicles his childhood in Kansas and his young adulthood in Paris and New York, and his novel *Not without Laughter* (1930), which depicts his life in semi-autobiographical terms.

Zora Neale Hurston collaborated with Hughes and other black writers on the publication of *Fire!!* (1926), a literary magazine featuring the work of Harlem Renaissance writers. Particularly interested in African-American folklore, Hurston uses regional African-American dialects in her fiction to build her local color settings. In *Their Eyes Were Watching God* (1937), the narrator Janie Crawford tells her life story, one that includes relationships with several different men, all of whom attempted to control her. Janie's narrative informs readers of the difficulties she withstood, as she also leads them to appreciate her journey to self-fulfillment. Today, Hurston is acclaimed as one of the most prominent figures of the Harlem Renaissance, and her narrative voice and focus on women's issues stand out as her strongest contributions.

Other fiction writers, each with a unique voice and narrative structure, contributed to the multiplicity of modernism's styles and forms. In particular, the works of Ernest Hemingway, F. Scott Fitzgerald, and William Faulkner define the era. Hemingway enlisted in the military and served as an ambulance driver in World War I, and *A Farewell to Arms* (1929) fictionalizes his experiences during this time. His influential novel *The Sun Also Rises* (1926), set primarily in Paris and Pamplona, Spain, is based in part on his experiences as an expatriate living and traveling in Europe. It focuses on the World War I generation, the Lost Generation, particularly returning soldiers who were disillusioned and psychologically lost. These novels, along with *To Have and Have Not* (1937), *For Whom the Bell Tolls* (1940), and *The Old Man and the Sea* (1962), showcase Hemingway's minimalist and direct style, often using simple sentence constructions rather than more complex syntax to avoid sentimentality and excessive explanation.

Unlike Hemingway, F. Scott Fitzgerald writes with a lush style, although his characters, like Hemingway's, find themselves disillusioned in the postwar era. *The Great Gatsby* (1925), told from the point of view of Nick Carraway, a World War I veteran, records Nick's relationships with his wealthy and mysterious neighbor Jay Gatsby, Nick's cousin Daisy Buchanan, and her husband Tom. As deceit and lies lead to tragedy, Nick finds the world around him unpalatable. The novel's themes, including the desire for wealth, the possibility of reinventing oneself, and the underlying importance of social class, put forth a pessimistic view of modern American life as a state of decaying morality. *Tender Is the Night* (1934) also reflects a world of moral failures, specifically relating to power and the seduction of youth, as well as the role of sexuality, highlighting some of the ways that modern morality is challenged.

While Fitzgerald's characters move among the upper classes, William Faulkner's fiction is often set in Yoknapatawpha County, a Southern location based on his life in Mississippi. His characters represent a range of people from a small-town community who embody various social mores and attitudes, and economic, racial, and educational classes. In *The Sound and the Fury* (1929), *As I Lay Dying* (1930), *Light in August* (1932), and *Absalom, Absalom!* (1936), Faulkner experiments with new styles, including stream-of-conscious and non-chronological narration. He uses fifteen distinct points of view in *As I Lay Dying*, including that of Addie Bundren, who dies during the novel but continues to narrate its events. Throughout the novel, stream of consciousness illuminates the characters' feelings and thoughts, sometimes blending the past and present together. Such narrative techniques create a literary world that replicates the uncertainty and unknowability of modern life.

Other novelists such as Djuna Barnes, John Steinbeck, and John Dos Passos also shaped the contours of modernist literature. In *Nightwood* (1936), Barnes tells the story of Robin Vote, who leaves her husband for Nora Flood, only to leave Nora for another woman. The novel's thematic interest in lesbian relationships made it unique in its time, and its depiction of the struggles of the characters to find lasting relationships imbues it with themes of alienation found in other modern novels. Barnes's stream-of-conscious narration links her with the experimental style of Eliot and the British writer Virginia Woolf. John Steinbeck's novels stylistically adhere to realist traditions while tackling political and economic themes. *The Grapes of Wrath* (1939) portrays with great sympathy the agricultural workers hit hard by the Dust Bowl—the agricultural decline brought on by devastating dust storms during the 1930s—and interweaves a critique of capitalism, which Steinbeck believed to be responsible for the Great Depression. Steinbeck continued publishing notable fiction and nonfiction well into the latter half of the twentieth century, but his early work—including *Tortilla Flat* (1935), *Of Mice and Men* (1937), and *Cannery Row* (1945)—remains his most influential. Dos Passos shared Steinbeck's concerns with the country's economic problems, and his trilogy *U. S. A.*, consisting of *The 42nd Parallel* (1930), *1919* (1932), and *The Big Money* (1936), are fictionalized accounts of the economic realities facing different classes in the country. In addition to traditional narrative structures, Dos Passos includes experimental techniques such as newsreels (montages of song lyrics and headlines from newspapers), biographies of famous figures, and stream-of-conscious passages.

The most significant playwrights of the era are Eugene O'Neill and Thornton Wilder. O'Neill's early plays, such as *Anna Christie* (1920) and *The Hairy Ape* (1922), depict the experiences of the oppressed classes, and a later work, *Long Day's Journey into Night* (completed in 1942, but not published until 1956), focuses on one day in the lives of a dysfunctional, alcohol- and drug-addicted family, which O'Neill based on his own experiences. O'Neill's plays address sexuality, abuse, and loss, reflecting a psychological interest in the lives of his characters, and he uses experimental techniques, such as stream-of-conscious sections in *Strange Interlude* (1928). Wilder is best known for his plays *Our Town* (1938) and *The Skin of Our Teeth* (1942), and the novel *The Bridge of San Luis Rey* (1927). In *Our Town*, Wilder uses a variety of inventive techniques, including having only minor elements of a set, made up of ordinary objects such as tables, chairs, and ladders, and few props for actors to employ. This stripped down approach draws attention to the play as an artificial construction, reflecting both the modern rejection of artistic traditions and a leaning toward aesthetic approaches common during the postmodern period.

Postmodernism (1945–Present)

The term *postmodern* applies both to the literary period running approximately from the end of World War II in 1945 to the current day, and to a set of aesthetic principles and styles describing particular elements of literature. Consequently, a book might be from the postmodern era without being stylistically or thematically postmodern. This taxonomic uncertainty means that some literary works from this period adopt, for instance, realist or romantic sensibilities, among others. Regardless of specific artistic styles, the literature of the postmodern period responds to contemporary society and culture and addresses current ideas and experiences. Among subjects common in literature of the latter half of the twentieth century, issues of gender and sexuality, race and ethnicity, and truth and history evince an interest in understanding the individual's place in a society of rapidly shifting values. Also, fragmentation, pastiche, irony, intertextuality, and other types of formal experimentation can be seen in much postmodern literature. While such elements can be found in modernist work as well, the purposes for which these techniques are used are different in the latter half of the century. For example, some modern authors use fragmentation as reflective of the confusion and pain of modern life; postmodern authors are more accepting of such fragmentation as a regular state of existence. Postmodern literature embraces fragmentary styles and experiences in playful ways. Rather than bemoaning the isolation and loss of faith in the world around them as many modernists do, postmodernists find ways to exist within, and sometimes even celebrate, a disorienting and meaningless world.

An early school of the postmodern era, the Beats addressed social and political issues in their works. This group of writers, including Allen Ginsberg, Jack Kerouac, Michael McClure, William S. Burroughs, Lawrence Ferlinghetti, Gregory Corso, and Gary Snyder, probed issues of freedom and sexuality (and often drug use) at the center of their writings. Much of their literature reflects a romantic sensibility through its embrace of emotion and physical experience, and stylistically contrasts with much modernist literature. The most influential works of the Beats come from Ginsberg and Kerouac. Ginsberg's poem "Howl" (1956) is angry and political, reflecting his frustration with the U.S. government's treatment of nonconformists during the Cold War:

> I saw the best minds of my generation destroyed by madness, starving
>   hysterical naked,
> dragging themselves through the negro streets at dawn looking for an
>   angry fix . . .

(lines 1–2)

The poem describes scenes of the disenfranchised, images taken from Ginsberg's experiences with political radicals, homosexuals, drug users, and the mentally ill. Due to its graphic images and language, *"Howl" and Other Poems* was banned for obscenity, and its publisher, poet Lawrence Ferlinghetti, was arrested. In the 1957 court case *California v. Ferlinghetti*, the book was determined not to be obscene by virtue of its social merit. Although Kerouac also penned verse, he is most well-known for his novel *On the Road* (1957), which tells the story of friends Sal Paradise and Dean Moriarty as they travel around the United States and into Mexico in search of discovery and meaning. The novel chronicles their sexual encounters and their drug experiences, as they rhapsodize about the beauty of the world and look for greater significance in their lives. Stylistically, the rhythms of jazz influence Kerouac's prose, and he often uses long, nearly breathless sentences to underscore the characters' passion for life. Published during the height of the Cold War, when the nation was suspicious of and resistant to outsiders, this semi-autobiographical novel countered the social and political climate of the U.S. to welcome new experiences and change.

In addition to Beat literature's romantic leanings, the 1950s and 1960s saw several other poetic movements also evincing a romantic and anti-modernist sensibility. Confessional poets wrote about intimate details of their lives, often detailing unappealing events that cast the writers in a poor light. In her collection *Ariel* (1965, published posthumously), which contains the famous poems "Lady Lazarus," "Daddy," and "Cut," Sylvia Plath describes her emotional and mental struggles with disconcerting language and details. In "Daddy" Plath pictures her father and her husband by invoking images of a Nazi and a vampire, among others. She also refers to a failed suicide attempt when she was twenty years old, bemoaning that "they pulled me out of the sack, / And they stuck me together with glue" (lines 61–62). Other important confessional poets include Anne Sexton, John Berryman, and Robert Lowell. The Black Mountain poets, including Charles Olson, Denise Levertov, Robert Duncan, and Robert Creeley, voiced anti-establishment views in their poetry, focusing on the use of the poetic line as a way to communicate one's emotion. The New York School, including Frank O'Hara, John Ashbery, and James Schuyler, wrote poetry highly influenced by abstract art and that generally focuses on urban life.

The Black Arts Movement also addressed the challenges and possibilities of urban life. After the 1965 assassination of Malcolm X, a group of black writers headed by Amiri Baraka (previously known as LeRoi Jones) joined forces in New York City under the banner of the Black Arts Movement. This collective of writers advocated for the importance of African-American literature, and also, in the spirit of Malcolm X and the Black Power movement of the 1960s, for taking action to ensure that their voices and those of other black Americans were valued. Black Arts members created both poetry venues and theater groups for black writers to disseminate their work (Martin 119–22). Baraka's poem "Black Art" proclaims a manifesto for these writers:

> We want a black poem. And a
> Black World.
> Let the world be a Black Poem.
> And Let All Black People Speak This Poem
> Silently
> or LOUD.
>
>   (lines 50–55)

The poem reflects both the passion and the purpose of the movement. Nikki Giovanni, Etheridge Knight, Ron Milner, Sonia Sanchez, and Michael S. Harper advanced the aesthetic objectives of the Black Arts Movements in their writing. The Black Arts Movement brought attention to African-American writers, as its artists ushered in a new era of racially and ethnically diverse creative writing.

Since the 1970s, American poets have continued experimenting with form and content while probing the conditions of life in the United States. Audre Lorde's poems address gender, race, and sexuality in collections such as *From a Land Where Other People Live* (1973) and *Our Dead behind Us* (1986). Noted especially for engaging with politics and feminism, Adrienne Rich draws unforgettable images that resonate with power in her books *Diving into the Wreck: Poems, 1971–1972* (1973) and *The Dream of a Common Language: Poems, 1974–1977* (1978). Sharon Olds's poetry chronicles her life as child and adult, with specific focus on emotion and sexuality. In addition, she addresses in striking detail her experiences in an abusive household, and their long-term effects on her family, in works such as *The Dead and the Living* (1984) and *The Father* (1992). In "Late Speech with My Brother," she pleads with him to break free of the trauma of childhood: "don't produce a stopped life like some / work of art, the bottle fallen / away from your open hand" (lines 19–21). Her direct style underscores the pain of her past experience. Poets from this era powerfully explore personal identity and social concerns, and they are joined in their work by postmodern prose writers.

The earliest novelists of the postmodern era showcase the move from modernism to postmodernism, with works increasingly interested in newer styles of narration and expression. The fiction and nonfiction of Richard Wright, including his novel *Native Son* (1940) and his autobiography *Black Boy* (1945), employ a realist approach to expose the heinousness of racism in American society, while subsequent works experimented more with style and structure. Ralph Ellison's experimental novel *Invisible Man* (1952) questions the place of black men in American society. Told from the perspective of an unnamed but self-aware African-American man, born and raised in the South and later living in New York, *Invisible Man* recounts the experience of being "invisible" and unimportant in society. In relaying his narrator's life story, Ellison is creative with his narrative style, telling the first part of the story with a naturalist style, while using more expressionistic and surrealistic approaches in later sections. Ellison's book dramatically differs from other literary works about the impact of race on individuals and society written at the time.

Complementing Faulkner's efforts, additional Southern authors brought the region's literature to national attention in a movement known as the Southern Renaissance. Among these are Flannery O'Connor, Eudora Welty, Carson McCullers, Harper Lee, and Truman Capote, who can be characterized as writing in the *southern gothic* tradition, a particularly American subset of gothic fiction. These authors tell stories of ordinary people who find themselves in extraordinary circumstances. O'Connor's prose fiction, such as "Everything That Rises Must Converge" (1965), "A Good Man Is Hard to Find" (1955), and *Wise Blood* (1952), describe a grotesque and comical society bound by generations of racism and entrenched values. Informed by her Catholicism and her belief in the possibility of redemption, O'Connor's morally vacuous characters find salvation brought on by violence or pain. In Welty's "A Worn Path" (1940), an elderly African-American woman walks a long distance to a doctor's office to pick up her grandson's medicine, dealing with obstacles throughout the trek that are reflective of the travels of Odysseus for a woman of her age and infirmity. Only an act of great love could carry her through. Carson McCullers's *The Heart Is a Lonely Hunter* (1940) focuses on the experiences of a deaf man in a small town and its citizens, including males and females, white-collar and blue-collar workers, white and black characters, and younger and older characters. Harper Lee's instant classic *To Kill a Mockingbird* (1960) depicts racial conflict engulfing a community when white attorney Atticus Finch defends black defendant Tom Robinson against the charge of raping a white woman. The novel's candid and compassionate representation of the horrors of racial bigotry influenced perceptions of racial difference during pivotal years of the U.S. Civil Rights Movement. Lee's childhood friend Truman Capote also blazed a successful literary path, beginning with his gothic bildungsroman *Other Voices, Other Rooms* and continuing to his creation of the genre of nonfiction novel with *In Cold Blood*, a horrifying account of the slaughter of a Kansas family.

Other novelists in the 1950s, 1960s, and 1970s focus more on language and form—on literature as an artificial construction—than on emotional connections among characters. These authors, whose output reflects postmodern artistic elements, include Kurt Vonnegut, Vladimir Nabokov, John Barth, Ishmael Reed, Robert Coover, Donald Barthelme, and Thomas Pynchon. As a group, they foreground elements of comic irony, pastiche, and *metafiction*—writing about fiction as fiction, or drawing attention to the artificial qualities of a literary work. In addition to telling a story about a family's trip to Ocean City in "Lost in the Funhouse" (1967), Barth also tells the story of writing the story "Lost in the Funhouse." Early in the story, the narrator pauses in the story of the family trip to consider the structure of the tale:

> Actually, if one imagines a story called "The Funhouse," or "Lost in the Funhouse," the details of the drive to Ocean City don't seem especially relevant. . . . Then the *ending* would tell what Ambrose does while he's lost, how he finally finds his way out, and what everybody makes of the experience. So far there's been no real dialogue, very little sensory detail, and nothing in the way of a *theme*. And a long time has gone by already without anything happening; it makes a person wonder. We haven't even reached Ocean City yet: we will never get out of the funhouse.
>
> (77)

By drawing attention to the construction of literary texts, these authors point out the artificiality of art and also of any narrative readers might be told. They encourage readers to think critically when consuming texts.

In the latter part of the twentieth century, postmodern aesthetics combined with political themes, addressing gender, race, and ethnicity in numerous novels. Toni Morrison comments on both gender and race in her novels, including *The Bluest Eye* (1970), *Song of Solomon* (1977), and *Beloved* (1987). In telling the story of Sethe, an escaped slave who kills her daughter to save her from returning to slavery, and Beloved, the woman Sethe believes is her daughter's ghost, the novel explores both the extraordinary ties between mother and child and the horrid disenfranchisement of women and black Americans. Morrison's social commentary connects her to the political writing of many authors of the late twentieth century, and her experimental style connects her with postmodern authors. In *Tripmaster Monkey: His Fake Book* (1989), Maxine Hong Kingston addresses Asian-American identity by drawing on a range of postmodern elements, including a fragmented storyline and lack of clarity regarding which events actually occur and which unfold in the protagonist's mind. Similarly, Tim O'Brien has written impressively about the Vietnam War: *Going after Cacciato* (1978) and *The Things They Carried* (1990) meditate on the experience of war on soldiers, both the horrors and the monotony, offering an alternative to the patriotic literature of past centuries. Leslie Marmon Silko's *Ceremony* (1977) responds to post-war trauma as she describes the experiences of a man returning home to the Laguna Pueblo. Traumatized by his experiences in World War II, he seeks healing through traditional spiritual ceremonies. In *Maus* (1991), the first graphic novel to be awarded the Pulitzer Prize, graphic novelist Art Spiegelman relates the experiences of his father, who survived the Holocaust, using a variety of animals (such as mice and pigs) to represent different groups of humans (such as Jews and Poles). *Tracks* (1988), a novel by Louise Erdrich, relies on multiple narrative voices to relate the lives of several Anishinaabe families living on a North Dakota reservation. Her novel offers a rich understanding of reservation life as well as exploring the conflicts between traditional Indian culture and white, Christian culture. These are just a few of many contemporary works of fiction addressing political issues while incorporating a variety of postmodern artistic techniques.

The theatrical world similarly experienced a move from modernism to more postmodern themes. During the late years of modernism and the early years of postmodernism, a period when American attitudes were undergoing change, playwrights William Inge, Lillian Hellman, Clifford Odets, Lorraine Hansberry, and others wrote about contemporary issues such as sexual identity, class, and ethnicity and race. In addition, the dramatists Arthur Miller and Tennessee Williams, who published their plays during the war years, as had Hellman and Odets, ushered in the postmodern era with some of their most significant work. Miller's most famous plays undermine the idea of the American Dream by showing the destructive force of superficial desires. In

All My Sons (1947), the Keller family apparently embodies the best of the United States' national values—both sons fought in the war and the father supplied parts to the military, hoping to pass on his business to his offspring. By selling broken cylinder heads to the military during World War II, Keller caused the crashes of twenty-one planes and the deaths of their crews, along with the ultimate destruction of his family. *Death of a Salesman* (1949) similarly reveals the ways in which a desire for the wealth and importance promised by the American Dream can destroy a family. (*For Miller's* Death of a Salesman, *see pp. 166–67.*) *The Crucible* (1953) uses the seventeenth-century Salem witch trials to criticize the fanaticism and intolerance of the 1950s Communist hunt. Collectively, these plays demonstrate Miller's inter-est in using the stage to criticize the social and political problems he wit-nessed in the country. Tennessee Williams's most significant plays dramatize the desperation of characters struggling to overcome loneliness. *The Glass Menagerie* (1944) and *A Streetcar Named Desire* (1947) depict women who, for very different reasons, become isolated and out of step with their times. In *Cat on a Hot Tin Roof* (1955), much of the isolation of the characters results from their lies, or, as the alcoholic Brick says repeatedly, their "men-dacity" (940). This play, along with many of Williams's other works, such as *Suddenly, Last Summer* (1958), addresses the ways in which the rejection of one's sexual identity, in this case homosexuality, leads to isolation and tragedy.

Williams' sympathetic view of homosexuality was a harbinger of increas-ing theatrical depictions of gay life. In the 1980s and 1990s, playwrights increasingly began to address homosexual storylines and, more specifically, the AIDS crisis in their work. In *The Baltimore Waltz* (1992), Paula Vogel comically examines the public rejection of people with AIDS in the early years. Her play incorporates a variety of techniques that help audiences dis-tance themselves from the subject to gain perspective; for example, she uses intertextuality, referencing Orson Welles's film *The Third Man* (1949) and creating parallel scenes to those in the film, as well as elements of the absurd, such as a stuffed rabbit that the characters take with them throughout the play. Tony Kushner's *Angels in America: A Gay Fantasia on National Themes* (1993) also approaches AIDS in a nonrealist manner. The play calls for actors to perform multiple roles, regardless of sex; this approach under-mines conceptions of gender and sexuality as stable referents of a person's identity. Other plays, such as Larry Kramer's *The Normal Heart* (1985), David Henry Hwang's *M. Butterfly* (1988), and Terrence McNally's *Love! Valour! Compassion!* (1994), tackle the challenges of queer love in a straight society.

During the early years of the twenty-first century, a new strand of lit-erature has focused on 9/11 and post-9/11 life in the United States. John Updike's *Terrorist* (2006) follows an American teenager who plots a terror-ist attack on the Lincoln Tunnel; in part, the novel investigates the impact of religious fanaticism on its central character. Don DeLillo's *Falling Man*

(2008) follows the experiences of a man who survives the collapse of the World Trade Center to find himself lost in his own life as he tries to move forward. Jay McInerney focuses on two privileged New York couples and the ways their lives change on 9/11—the way that the ordinary elements in life, such as love and family, become more important—in *The Good Life* (2006). Neil LaBute's play *The Mercy Seat* (2002) depicts a married man and his mistress who work in the World Trade Center but are away from the buildings during the attack, as they consider running off together to start a new life. Numerous poets have written pieces about life after the attacks as well. These include Lawrence Ferlinghetti's "History of the Airplane" and David Lehman's "9/14/01." As this new century continues, it becomes difficult to determine which current writers will enjoy the most lasting impact. American writers continue to take on subjects as varied as war and terrorism, gender and sexuality, and ethnicity and race, all with an eye toward adding to the rich literary heritage that reflects the diversity and ideals of the nation.

1.4 A Brief History of World Literature

The Epic of Gilgamesh, one of the earliest surviving works of world literature, ponders themes—love, loss, life, and death—found in the writings of various countries over millennia. Gilgamesh, the king of Uruk around 2700 BCE, inspired myths that circulated for centuries and were compiled into *The Epic of Gilgamesh* (c. 2100–1000 BCE). It tells of Gilgamesh's brutality as a king and his friendship with Enkidu, a wild man. The two embark on adventures together, at one point cutting down trees in a forest that the gods have forbidden humans to enter. Enkidu's life is taken as punishment, and Gilgamesh, terrified of death, seeks eternal life. Along his journey, he encounters Siduri, a barkeeper and winemaker, who advises him with words still relevant these many centuries later:

> "Gilgamesh, where are you hurrying to? You will never find that life for which you are looking. When the gods created man they allotted to him death, but life they retained in their own keeping. . . . Let your clothes be fresh, bathe yourself in water, cherish the little child that holds your hand, and make your wife happy in your embrace; for this too is the lot of man."
>
> (102; chapter 4)

Although Gilgamesh does not immediately accept Siduri's counsel, he eventually returns to Uruk to rule as a wise king who will live in his subjects' memory for generations. The messages from this early text, along with its sense of adventure and emotional power, have resonated throughout literary history. *The Epic of Gilgamesh* is but one of countless examples from world literature that offers readers insight into specific times and places, but also into a shared humanity spanning eras and cultures. This chapter offers brief examinations of some of the more influential eras of world literature, including pre-classical and classical Greek literature, classical Chinese literature, Arabic and Persian literature from the Middle Ages, European Renaissance literature, nineteenth-century Russian literature, European modernist literature, postcolonial African literature, and twentieth-century Latin American literature.

Pre-classical and Classical Greek Literature
(c. 750–350 BCE)

The early achievements of Greek literature are evident in two epic poems, Homer's *The Iliad* and *The Odyssey* (c. eighth century BCE). *The Iliad* relates the story of the Trojan War fought between Troy and Greece, focusing primarily on Achilles, the mightiest Greek warrior. Along with powerful descriptions of battles and deaths, the epic contains deep emotional content, particularly in the grief Achilles feels after Hector, the Trojan king's eldest son, kills his friend Patroclus. Struggling with his loss, Achilles avenges Patroclus's death by stabbing Hector through the neck with a spear. Hector pleads with him to return his dead body to his family for burial rather than to leave him on the battlefield, but Achilles furiously responds,

> "No more entreating of me, you dog, by knees or parents.
> I wish only that my spirit and fury would drive me
> to hack your meat away and eat it raw for the things that
> you have done to me. So there is no one who can hold the dogs off
> from your head, not if they bring here and set before me ten times
> and twenty times the ransom, and promise more in addition."
> (22.345–50)

Achilles eventually relents, but the power of his emotions raises a story of battle into a deep exploration of human suffering and forgiveness. *The Odyssey*, a sequel to *The Iliad*, narrates the trials of the Greek hero Odysseus during his ten-year journey home after the Trojan War. Unlike *The Iliad*, which focuses on the trials of war, *The Odyssey* includes many elements of an adventure story. In part it depicts the challenges faced by Odysseus's wife Penelope and son Telemachus, who must contend with the many dissolute suitors wooing her. Odysseus's adventures during this time consistently hinder him from returning home. Captured by the Cyclops Polyphemos, he and his men blind the monster to escape; they stay on the island of Circe, a sorceress, and Odysseus travels to the land of the dead. Eventually, after a shipwreck drowns all but Odysseus, Calypso holds him captive for seven years, hoping to marry him. Only when the gods intervene is Odysseus freed, eventually finding his way home and slaughtering Penelope's suitors. With their stories of heroism and the challenges of defending one's nation and family, *The Iliad* and *The Odyssey* testify to the emotional appeal of the epic tradition as well as to its broad scope of action and setting. (*For a discussion of literary epics, see pp. 118–20.*)

As Homer developed the epic tradition, Hesiod innovated in the traditions of didactic poetry, which teaches readers important lessons. His most famous texts, *Theogony* and *Works and Days*, date from around the eighth century BCE. *Theogony* presents the history of the gods in the Greek pantheon, including stories of Zeus, Hera, Aphrodite, Gaia, and Demeter.

He presents their origins and their interrelationships, starting with the creation of the Earth: "First of all, Chaos came into existence; thereafter, however, / Broad-bosomed earth took form, the forever immovable seat of / All of the deathless gods who inhabit the heights of Olympus" (lines 112–14). Hesiod dedicates *Works and Days* to his brother Perses, advising him about agriculture. In some ways, this publication resembles modern farmers' almanacs, providing advice such as "Every year when you hear the shrill din of the cranes from the clouds, take / Note, for it signals the season to plow, indicating the rainy / Wintertime, gnawing the heart of the man who possesses no oxen" (lines 441–43). This work also advises Perses to accept the lot of humans through references to stories of the gods, such as the legend of Pandora and the suffering resulting from her curiosity. Together, Hesiod and Homer established key foundations for Western literature through their interest in epics, didactic poetry, and the Greek pantheon.

Writing circa 600 BCE, Sappho lyrically captures the delights and jealousies of love in her verse. Her poems sing of passionate feelings for both men and women, and due to the romantic feelings expressed for women in some poems, the term *Sapphic* describes lesbian relationships. Fragment 1 of her work is a rare complete poem, for most of her writings have been lost. It depicts Sappho (the speaker) beseeching Aphrodite, the goddess of love, for help with heartbreak. Aphrodite, speaking of Sappho's lover, reassures her that

> If she balks, I promise, soon she'll chase,
> If she's turned from gifts, now she'll give them.
> And if she does not love you, she will love,
> Helpless, she will love.
>
> (lines 21–24)

Sappho's writing, direct yet passionate, captures love's contradictions and longing, as evident in her ability to articulate deep feelings through Aphrodite's words. With lines like "My tongue sticks to my dry mouth, / Thin fire spreads beneath my skin" (fragment 20, lines 9–10), she captures the physicality of sexual desire.

Pindar, also a lyric poet, is remembered for his victory odes for athletic competitions, which appear in four collections respectively named after the Olympian, Pythian, Isthmian, and Nemean Games. These odes praise the victors in competitions such as wrestling, boxing, and horse races, while also addressing such subjects as the role of the gods in human success and the hard work necessary for victory. In *Olympian IV* (c. 452 BCE), Pindar acknowledges the dedication and goodness of a chariot race's winner:

For I praise him, ready indeed to train horses,
Glad to entertain all strangers,
With his pure heart turned
To Quiet who loves his city.
With no lie shall I stain the saying:
"Trial is the test of men."

> (lines 18–22, numbering
> provided by translator)

Pindar's attention to the effort involved in success speaks to the values celebrated in his poems. It is not enough to win, for victors must demonstrate goodness in their whole person. (*For further discussion of Pindaric odes, see pp. 123–24.*)

Classical Greek drama has profoundly affected European and American theater. The playwrights Aristophanes, Aeschylus, Sophocles, and Euripides wrote plays that define the contours of comedy and tragedy. Aristophanes's comic plays include *The Frogs*, *The Clouds*, and *Lysistrata* (c. 411 BCE), which tells of its title character's attempts to end the Peloponnesian War by convincing Greek women not to have sex with their husbands, hoping that their boycott will force men to choose peace. Among the tragedians, Aeschylus is known best for his plays *The Persians* and *Agamemnon*. Sophocles's *Oedipus Rex* (c. 429 BCE) tells the story of King Oedipus, who unknowingly kills his father and marries his mother, and the tragic events that ensue. Equal disaster comes to pass in *Antigone* (c. 441 BCE), in which King Creon demands that the body of Antigone's brother Polyneices, who lost his life in battle, be denied burial. This decision catalyzes a series of events resulting in the death of the heroine Antigone as well as the deaths of the king's son and wife. Few Greek tragedies inspire such horror as Euripides's *Medea* (c. 431 BCE), in which Medea's husband Jason leaves her for another woman, Glauce. In anger, she kills Glauce by sending poisoned golden robes, and in irrational fury she also murders her two children, taking their bodies with her and leaving Jason without even the solace of burying them. She explains her reasons to Jason, expressing her hatred for him one last time:

MEDEA. . . . You, as you deserve,
   Shall die an unheroic death, your head shattered
   By a timber from the Argo's hull. Thus wretchedly
   Your fate shall end the story of your love for me.
JASON. The curse of children's blood be on you!
   Avenging Justice blast your being!
MEDEA. What god will hear your imprecation,
   Oath-breaker, guest-deceiver, liar?

(60)

Medea's cruel desire for revenge blinds her to the horror of killing her children. A fascinating character, she behaves horrifically, yet she completes her plans with little sense that the gods frown on her actions. Many Greek tragedies resist endings that might imply an overarching justice guides the universe, interrogating instead humanity's limited understanding of the world.

Classical Greece's rich theatrical world also includes the beginnings of literary criticism and philosophy. In his *Poetics* (c. 335 BCE), Aristotle discusses tragedy in depth, offering definitions of the genre and theorizing about its effects. His *Rhetoric* focuses on the art of persuasion. (*For more on Aristotle and tragedy, see pp. 164–65; for Aristotle and rhetoric, see pp. 249–50.*) Aristotle's mentor Plato wrote a series of dialogues between his teacher Socrates and a variety of interlocutors on issues related to morality and ethics. These exchanges feature Socrates asking a series of questions to expose the weaknesses in others' thinking. In the dialogue "Crito," Socrates awaits his execution in jail when Crito, who wants to liberate Socrates by bribing the guards, visits. Socrates engages Crito in a discussion regarding the ethics of such an escape, leading Crito to recognize that Socrates must live by the laws of Athens. The Socratic method of questioning established a pedagogical approach to critical thinking that has lasted for centuries. It is, however, only through the writings of others, such as Plato's dialogues, that Socrates's ideas remain. The impact of these and other writers from the pre-classical and classical Greek era on Western literature cannot be overstated, for they established foundational principles of poetry, drama, and philosophy that remain in effect today, and were particularly influential on the many masterful Roman writers in the centuries that followed, including Virgil, Ovid, and Seneca.

Classical Chinese Literature (c. 1000–200 BCE)

The first great period of Chinese literature came during the Zhou dynasty, which ruled from about 1045 to 221 BCE. *The Book of Songs* (also known as *Classic of Poetry*) collects approximately 300 poems whose authors are mostly unknown. These lyric poems focus on a range of subjects including love, friendship, children, sacrifice, war, and admiration for the dynastic rulers. For many years, it was suggested that Confucius compiled an edition of *The Book of Songs* but no evidence proves his involvement. The poems speak simply yet directly, reflecting the concerns of the people at that time. In a poem celebrating the Duke of Zhou, the speaker proclaims:

> Broken were our axes
> And chipped our hatchets.
> But since the Duke of [Z]hou came to the East
> Throughout the kingdoms all is well.
> He has shown compassion to us people,
> He has greatly helped us.
>   (de Grazia 40; song 232, lines 1–6)

This poem's simplicity strengthens its message of appreciation, and such a straightforward approach characterizes poems addressing other subjects. In a poem about serving the king during wartime, the speaker tells of his difficulties:

> Now that we are on the march again
> Snow falls upon the mire.
> The king's service brings many hardships.
> We have no time to rest or bide.
> We do indeed long to return.
>   (de Grazia 43; song 132, lines 27–31)

Although speaking respectfully of the king, the poem presents the struggles of a soldier—the physical work, the challenges of weather, and the longing for home. *The Book of Songs* demonstrates both the personal and social concerns of people from this era while also displaying delicacy and artistry in writing.

The classical Chinese era also witnessed the birth of major sacred and philosophical works. The *I Ching*, also known as *Book of Changes* (c. 1000–200 BCE), is a book of divination and philosophy compiling sixty-four hexagrams for divining the future. The book's readers, traditionally using plant stalks or similar items, distribute them according to detailed guidelines. Based on a complex system of determination, users are directed to specific hexagrams, which enlighten them to particular understandings of their meaning. In one configuration of the Sun Hexagram (hexagram 41), the interpretation suggests that "if there be sincerity (in him who employs it), there will be great good fortune:—freedom from error; firmness and correctness that can be maintained; and advantage in every movement that shall be made" (146–47). This oracle was used during the classical era as a guide for decision-making. Although the *I Ching* functions more as a code book than traditional literature, its interest in signs influenced philosophies such as Taoism, which advocates opening oneself up to the world to be guided along the path that is offered.

The *Analects* of Confucius, the central document of the philosophical movement Confucianism, was written by Confucius's followers, most likely during the century following his death in 479 BCE. The *Analects* collects sayings, anecdotes, and other brief texts explaining Confucius's beliefs about ethical conduct. Confucius advocated an orderly society, encouraging respect for parents and elders. Although some think of Confucianism as a religion, it is more a code of behavior for maintaining a humane, ethical society. Confucius's writings stress the necessity of civility and modesty with phrasings pithy yet dense, such as in his musings over one's personal failings: "The Master said: 'Your faults define you. From your very faults one can know your quality'" (4.7). He also expounds on one's potential propensity to conceit: "The Master said: 'Clever talk and affected manners are seldom signs of goodness'" (1.3). These examples emphasize the importance of self-reflection and respectfulness, and, taken together, the maxims of the *Analects* offer a comprehensive guide to ethical behavior.

   Tao Te Ching (c. sixth to fourth century BCE), the best-known work of Taoist philosophy, is a compilation of philosophical poems pondering numerous themes important in Taoism. Lao Tzu (also spelled Lao Tsu) is credited as the author, although nothing definitive is known about his life. The term *Tao Te Ching* translates into *"the Book (ching) of the Way (tao) and the Power (tê)"* (de Grazia 247). The Way of Taoism outlines the path of nature that allows one to live simply and reflectively. Taoists emphasize the value of passivity—letting oneself be guided by silence and nature rather than forcing one's life through artificial steps—as expressed in poem 48:

> In the pursuit of learning, every day something is acquired.
> In pursuit of Tao, every day something is dropped.
>
> Less and less is done
> Until non-action is achieved.
> When nothing is done, nothing is left undone.
>
> The world is ruled by letting things take their course.
> It cannot be ruled by interfering.
>
> (Lao Tsu 50)

In addition to the virtue of non-action, the *Tao Te Ching* advocates in poem 67 the three treasures—mercy, economy, and humility—that serve as the core values of Taoism (69). Building the foundational principles of Confucianism and Taoism, the *Analects* of Confucius and the *Tao Te Ching*, along with the *I Ching*, continue to inspire countless people to reflect on the goals of earthly existence, through literature elegantly mixing simplicity with profundity.

Arabic and Persian Literature from the Middle Ages (c. 500 CE–1400)

Although writers living in the area of current-day Iran (the historic Persia) from the sixth through the fourteenth centuries CE wrote in a variety of literary genres, the height of literary artistry was found in their poetry. During the pre-Islamic era (c. 500–620), a rich tradition of oral poetry addressed a range of subjects including love, praise, and sorrow. The *qasīdahs*, or odes, are perhaps the most well-known type of Persian poetry. In Al-Shanfarā's *qasīdah* "*Lâmîyat al-'Arab*," the speaker tells of being rejected by his family and going into the wilds where "a sleek leopard, and a fell hyena with shaggy mane [are] / True comrades" (Lichtenstadter 150; lines 6–7). As an outcast, he is alone, yet achieves a sense of independence with his

. . . companions three at last: an intrepid soul,
A glittering trenchant blade, a tough bow of ample size,
Loud-twanging, the sides thereof smooth-polished, a handsome bow
Hung down from the shoulder-belt by thongs in a comely wise,
That groans, when the arrow slips away, like a woman crushed
By losses, bereaved of all her children, who wails and cries.

(lines 17–22)

The speaker's rejection by his family sends him into physical and emotional desolation. His comparison of the sound of his bow to a grieving woman's sobs indicates his deep pain at living in this place far beyond the world he knows. The poem's imagery vibrantly depicts the world at that time, a poetic strategy also apparent in "Rain" by Imra' al-Qays. This speaker describes a rainstorm through a series of vivid similes: rain is compared to the beating wings of a bird, clouds are compared to clothing falling over the earth, and the storm pounding through the trees makes them "look as if headless but covered with veils" (Lichtenstadter 151; line 4). Poets writing in Arabic shared similar concerns to the Persian poets. One of the better known female poets from the era, Al-Khansā', wrote "Lament for a Brother," in which she angrily addresses and personifies death because of her brother's passing: "What have we done to you, death / that you treat us so, / with always another catch" (Pound, *Arabic* 33; lines 1–3). Her anger over her brother's early passing is tempered only by her wish for him to have comfort: "Peace / be upon him and Spring / rains water his tomb" (lines 21–23). These poets create lyrics uniting human passion and artistic skill, meditating on the potential pain of the human condition.

Persian and Arabic literature changed with the birth of Islam and the writing of the *Qur'an*, which shares Allah's revelations to Muhammad from 609–632. Written in Arabic, the *Qur'an* employs many poetic devices that have brought it attention as a literary, as well as a spiritual, work. The *Qur'an* dramatically shifted the focus of much literature of the period to religious themes. During this era, fiction was largely discouraged, but poetry maintained its prestige. From approximately 750 through 1400, as the larger society adopted Islam as its faith and cultural expectations changed, a new golden age of Persian literature, largely focused on religious content, arose. *The Ruba'iyat* of Omar Khayyam, composed throughout his lifetime (c. 1048–1131), is a collection of quatrains, four-line poems. Khayyam's poems are varied, although they consistently evince an appreciation of life, nature, and spirituality. In one poem he writes, "Since no one can Tomorrow guarantee / Enjoy the moment, let your heart be free" (Khayyam 66; poem 15, lines 1–2). Many of his poems express a desire for living for the moment and enjoying life, but these messages reflect his belief that living in the present allows one to connect with the divine. He depicts his passion for life with a variety of images of sensuality and robustness, including references to drinking wine. In the following poem, he connects such images to his religious beliefs:

Deliver me, O Lord, from prayer and plea,
Rid me of *self* and let me be with THEE:
When sober, good and bad engage my mind;
Let me be drunk—of good and bad be free.

(233; poem 165)

In Khayyam's poetry, drunkenness is not simply physical intoxication; instead, his plea for drunkenness seeks the elation of union with Allah. This combination of physical and spiritual ecstasy inspires many of his poems.

Sufism, a practice of mysticism within Islam, arose during this period, and much Persian poetry reflects this tradition. Among other elements that define Sufism is the belief that one may find Allah and grow close to Him while living in this world, rather than waiting until death. Sufi poets emphasize the need to appreciate life in its present moment and to let go of the distractions of the world to achieve spiritual wholeness. The most famous Sufi poet from this era is Jalāl al-Dīn Rūmī (also spelled Rúmí), whose major works include *Masnavi*, a six-book religious poem combined with brief stories, and *Divan-I Shams-I Tabriz*, a collection of short lyric poems. In this passage from *Masnavi* (c. 1258–1273), Rūmī delights in the love of Allah:

Thou art as joy, and we are laughing;
The laughter is the consequence of the joy.
Our every motion every moment testifies,
For it proves the presence of the Everlasting God.

(Rúmí 263; bk. 5, story 8)

The poem depicts a deep pleasure in the simplicity of the connection between the physical world and the spiritual world, recognizing the power of Allah in everyday life.

The lyric poetry of Hāfiz of Shiraz emerges from the mystic traditions of the Sufis, with his many love poems suggesting passion for both the spiritual and the physical world. Some of his works muse on secular understandings of love, while others express devotion to Allah. In many cases the poems can be read as simultaneously addressing both aspects of life. In his religious poem "Revelation," he begins, "My soul is the veil of his love, / Mine eye is the glass of his grace" (Arberry 77; lines 1–2). The language conjures images of romance while expressing devout sensibilities. Even as much of his poetry tackles the subject of faith, he also writes sensual poetry. In this passage from "Desire," Hāfiz writes:

I cease not from desire till my desire
Is satisfied; or let my mouth attain
My love's red mouth, or let my soul expire,
Sighed from those lips that sought her lips in vain.

(Arberry 69; lines 1–4)

Hāfiz presents the passion of religious ecstasy and physical sensuality. While Hāfiz, Rūmī, and Khayyam are only a few of the many talented poets of this era, they illustrate the mixture of religious and secular themes characterizing much literary art during the centuries after Islam's birth.

Poetry served as the primary literary form during this period, yet the story collection *The Thousand and One Nights* is likely its best-known work. Ironically, because its prose resembles spoken Arabic and its stories are fantastical, the work was considered unworthy of serious literary attention in its day. The stories were likely collected over centuries, with the earliest written extant version from the fourteenth century. Perhaps the most famous stories for modern Western audiences detail the exploits of the sailor Sinbad, who travels to magical lands and experiences incredible adventures. The stories themselves are engaging, but the frame story holds the complete work together. King Shahrayar, angry over his wife's infidelity, kills her. He then marries a new woman each night and murders her the following morning to prevent any possibility of unfaithfulness. Shahrazad volunteers to marry him, with a plan to stop the slaughter. An excellent storyteller, Shahrazad stays up each night narrating a story to Shahrayar, only to stop before a climactic moment as the sun rises in the morning. Because Shahrayar wants to hear each story's end, he delays her execution for another day, until, after 1,001 nights, he cancels his plans entirely. The variety of Arabic and Persian literature reflects the vast changes occurring in religion and culture during these centuries.

Literature of the European Renaissance (1350–1650)

The Renaissance is generally dated from fourteenth-century Italy to the middle of the seventeenth century. The term *renaissance* literally means rebirth, and the writers of the Renaissance presented it as an era of new beginnings. Christopher Columbus traveled across the Atlantic Ocean from Spain and landed in the Americas. In astronomy, Nicolaus Copernicus and Galileo Galilei determined that the Earth revolves around the Sun, which altered Europeans' understanding of the cosmos. Such discoveries called for a new era of curiosity and creativity. Like great medieval thinkers before them, Renaissance writers engaged with and imitated works from antiquity, specifically works from the classical Greek and Roman eras. Writers believed that ancient texts could give new life to their own work and that the study of classical texts could help their communities become more broadly educated and more capable of diverse and rational thought. They advocated a broad range of learning reflective of antiquity's influence, including the fields of literature, philosophy, rhetoric, and history.

A medieval writer credited with beginning the Renaissance, the Italian Francesco Petrarch is best known for his collection of love poems celebrating Laura, *Il Canzoniere* (or *Song Book*, c. 1360), written in contemporary Italian vernacular rather than Latin. The poems in this collection recount the speaker's undying love for Laura but also his agony because he cannot have her. In sonnet 269, he invokes several figures from Greek and Roman mythology to capture the vastness of his love. He notes that "Jove exults in Venus' prospering. / Love is in all the water, earth, and air, / And love possesses every living thing," before bemoaning his own lack of love (lines 6–8). Petrarch draws on these classical images to demonstrate his immense suffering without Laura, which he considers in sonnet 126:

> Who knows her not can never realize
> How beauty may the heart of man beguile,
> And who looks not upon my Laura's eyes
> Knows not how love can kill and otherwhile
> May heal us; let him hear how soft she sighs
> And gently speaks, oh, let him see her smile!
>
> (lines 9–14)

Petrarch distills the paradoxical concept of the pain of love in this passage. Along with Petrarch, Dante (*The Divine Comedy*) and Boccaccio (*The Decameron*) wrote their own masterpieces, making fourteenth-century Italy one of the most scintillating periods in all of world literature.

Nearly 200 years after Petrarch's work, Baldesar Castiglione, in *The Book of the Courtier* (1528), describes the customs and decorum of courtiers, those who regularly attend the court of a king or other member of royalty. Castiglione's book records fictional conversations among a group of courtiers in which they comment on such subjects as appearance, speech, physical ability, and the arts. Many of the recommendations proffered in the book are superficial yet practical, such as that a courtier should take care with his physical appearance and dress (123). The book also addresses acts of physical bravery, such as fighting in battle. Castiglione recommends that, if possible, the courtier should perform his actions to win the admiration of his social betters, and he should do this

> in as small a company as possible and in the sight of all the noblest and most respected men in the army, and especially in the presence of and, if possible, before the very eyes of his king or the prince he is serving; for it is well indeed to make all one can of the things well done.
>
> (99)

Although the true worth of heroic action rests in the action itself, the courtier's need for recognition demonstrates the public nature of this role. The effective courtier seeks respect in the court, which depends on his social betters appreciating his contributions.

Soon after *The Book of the Courtier*, Niccolò Machiavelli wrote *The Prince* (1532), a political discourse on gaining and maintaining power. Like *The Book of the Courtier*, *The Prince* advises readers on court life but focuses instead on the strategies necessary to reign. This work advocates force when necessary to meet one's ends, to "know well how to imitate beasts as well as employing properly human means" (61; chapter 18). Furthermore, while Machiavelli asserts that "every ruler should want to be thought merciful," he also advises strategic deployments of cruelty:

> If a ruler can keep his subjects united and loyal, he should not worry about incurring a reputation for cruelty; for by punishing a very few he will really be more merciful than those who over-indulgently permit disorders to develop, with resultant killings and plunderings. For the latter usually harm a whole community, whereas the executions ordered by a ruler harm only specific individuals.
>
> (58; chapter 17)

Machiavelli seeks to establish and maintain an orderly, efficient society under the effective control of a prince. The means may be manipulative and sometimes brutal, but Machiavelli believes that the achievement of the goals justifies the ways in which one attains them.

Frenchman Michel de Montaigne developed a new approach to nonfiction writing with his *Essays*. Collected in three volumes and published between 1580 and 1595, Montaigne's essays allow readers to follow him on self-reflective journeys concerning such topics as the imagination, friendship, repentance, and education. His essays adopt a personal tone, reflecting his observations and experiences, as he affirms in the preface:

> Had it been my purpose to seek the world's favour, I should have put on finer clothes, and have presented myself in a studied attitude. But I want to appear in my simple, natural, and everyday dress, without stain or artifice; for it is myself that I portray.
>
> (23)

Montaigne's essays cite a range of sources from the Greco-Roman classical era, including those of Cicero, Seneca, and Quintilian, as well as more contemporary sources, such as Castiglione's *The Book of the Courtier*. Despite his erudition, he adopts a humble persona, as evidenced in "On Books," when he writes, "I have no doubt that I often speak of things which are better treated by the masters of the craft, and with more truth. This is simply a trial of my natural faculties, and not of my acquired ones," after which he quotes Catullus, Horace, and Virgil (159). Renaissance authors placed great value on classical learning, and Montaigne's essays capture the Renaissance spirit of intellectual curiosity.

One of the great masterworks of the Renaissance and the first European novel, Miguel de Cervantes's *Don Quixote*, published in two volumes in 1605 and 1615, satirizes chivalric romances such as *Sir Gawain and the Green Knight* and *Le Morte D'Arthur*, which tell of heroic knights-errant undertaking quests in pursuit of worthy causes. Don Quixote, so obsessed with romances that he believes he is a knight, begins his quest to reawaken the chivalric spirit. Throughout his journey, he consistently misunderstands the world, and his absolute belief in his own interpretations sparks much of the novel's comedy and pathos. His romantic, misguided view of the world is offset by that of his "squire," the farmer Sancho Panza, whose witty reactions ironically comment on Don Quixote's misinterpretations. In one of the novel's most memorable passages, the men see a group of windmills, which Don Quixote believes to be giants. Sancho explains his error:

> "Those over there are not giants but windmills, and those things that seem to be arms are their sails, which when they are whirled around by the wind turn the millstone."
>
> "It is clear," replied Don Quixote, "that you are not experienced in adventures. Those are giants, and if you are afraid, turn aside and pray whilst I enter into the fierce and unequal battle with them."
>
> (98; part 1, chapter 8)

After Don Quixote races to battle, his lance is caught in a windmill's arms, throwing him and his horse to the ground. Throughout the book, Don Quixote's fanciful beliefs lead him both to express buoyant optimism regarding his quest and to suffer repeated failures. Apart from its satiric elements, *Don Quixote* stands as a classic of Renaissance literature for the inventive metatextual strategies used in its sequel. Published ten years after the popular first part of the book, the second part begins with Don Quixote's discovery that his adventures have been published in the book *Don Quixote*: "He could not convince himself that such a history could exist, for the blood of the enemies he had slain was hardly dry on the blade of his sword, yet they were already saying that his high deeds of chivalry were in print" (544; part 2, chapter 3). By referring to the novel *Don Quixote* in its continuation, Cervantes challenges the boundaries between fiction and reality. As Renaissance ideals and literary art spread throughout Europe, artists of each nation jointly looked to the past and to the future in creating new ways to express the human condition.

Nineteenth-Century Russian Literature (1820–1910)

The Golden Age of Russian literature arose during the nineteenth century, with authors penning masterworks of romanticism and realism, as well as innovating narrative strategies hailed as hallmarks of modern literature. Alexander Pushkin's verse, fiction, and plays established him as the father of modern Russian literature, with his works capturing a romantic sensibility that spread from Western Europe into Russia at the start of the nineteenth century. His great masterpiece *Eugene Onegin*, a novel in verse (1825–1832), covers the life of its eponymous protagonist, who inherits a country estate. A young woman, Tattiana, falls in love with Eugene and writes him a letter expressing her feelings. But Eugene, a self-involved, insensitive man, rejects her, despite his feelings for her:

And honestly 'tis my belief
Our union would produce but grief.
Though now my love might be intense,
Habit would bring indifference.
I see you weep. Those tears of yours
Tend not my heart to mitigate,
But merely to exasperate.

(4.8.5–11)

Eugene's harsh rejection of Tattiana's affections reflects poorly on him, for his life lacks real depth. St. Petersburg's extravagant social life shapes his behavior, and his general disdain for the genuine, if humble, people in the country controls his attitudes. Years later, he again meets Tattiana, now married, and vows his love to her. Although she still loves Eugene, she rejects his advances, remaining faithful to her husband. *Eugene Onegin* condemns the artificiality of Eugene's urban lifestyle and celebrates the genuine feelings of Tattiana and others in the country. Eugene eventually redeems himself as he allows himself to accept and express his love. The intense emotional content of the novel— love, pain, fear—establishes this as the cornerstone of Russian romanticism and cemented Pushkin's status as the father of Russian literature.

Another Romanticist, Mikhail Lermontov wrote both poetry and prose in this tradition. Although he published little of his poetry during his life (he died from a duel at age 26), his work, including the famous novel *A Hero of Our Time* (1840), has been influential since that time, reflecting interests in the natural world, the challenges of emotion, and patriotic attitudes.

Building on yet innovating from Pushkin's and Lermontov's romanticism, a new crop of writers worked within the realist tradition, depicting the ordinary world rather than a romantic one. Russia's preeminent satirist, Nikolai Gogol unites comic and absurdist elements in such short stories as "Diary of a Madman," "The Nose," and "The Overcoat," and the novel *Dead Souls*. His fiction is characterized by a sense of ordinariness and descriptive detail common to realist works, which he often couples with unbelievable situations. In "The Nose" (1836) a man awakens to discover his nose is missing, and another man finds a nose in the bread he is preparing for breakfast. As Ivan Yakovlevich sits down to eat, he

> ... sprinkled some salt, peeled two onions, picked up a knife, and, assuming a solemn expression, began cutting the bread. Having cut it in two, he had a look into the middle of one of the halves and, to his astonishment, noticed some white object there. Ivan Yakovlevich prodded it carefully with the knife and felt it with a finger. "It's solid," he said to himself. "What on earth can it be?"
>
> He dug his fingers into the bread and pulled out—a nose! Ivan Yakovlevich's heart sank: he rubbed his eyes and felt it again: a nose!

(203–04)

Gogol presents this fantastical and grotesque discovery with the same direct style used in describing the onions, salt, and bread. Such a realistic depiction of an unrealistic situation infuses Gogol's literature with a satiric sense of play that attempts to distill meaning from life's meaninglessness.

Ivan Turgenev and Leo Tolstoy, the most highly regarded realists of nineteenth-century Russian literature, depict their characters' challenges in stark, clear prose. Turgenev's most influential works include the short-story collection *Sketches from a Hunter's Album* (1852) and the novel *Fathers and Sons* (1862). In *Sketches* he realistically portrays the lives of peasants, narrating the struggles and restrictions they face, including illiteracy, violence, and poverty. *Fathers and Sons* explores the conflicts arising among different generations and the changes in behavior and ideology that the younger generation advocates. In *War and Peace* (1869), Tolstoy narrates the events surrounding the Napoleonic invasion of Russia at the start of the nineteenth century, focusing with extraordinary historical detail on the lives of five aristocratic families. *Anna Karenina* (1873–77) foreshadows its themes in its famous opening sentence: "Happy families are all alike; every unhappy family is unhappy in its own way" (part 1, chapter 1). In the central storyline, Anna Karenina, a married woman, falls in love with Count Vronsky, a single military man. She leaves her husband for Vronsky after learning of her pregnancy, and she falls into a desperate state when she suspects Vronsky is cheating on her and she is socially shunned. Her desperation leads to a tragic suicide. The novel slowly develops Anna's story and others, detailing the many conflicting thoughts of its central characters, presenting their daily lives—the conversations, travels, social events, and work—in great detail. The novels of Tolstoy offer grand stories of love and family, while also considering issues of politics, economics, religion, and nation.

While Tolstoy's novels are sweeping in scope, those of Fyodor Dostoevsky are intensely intimate, examining events through the psychological perspectives of his compelling characters. His most famous works, the novels *Notes from Underground* (1864), *Crime and Punishment* (1866), *The Idiot* (1869), and *The Brothers Karamazov* (1880), feature characters of impressive psychological depth—and often mental instability. In *Crime and Punishment,* the former student Raskolnikov, finding himself isolated, destitute, and desperate, decides to kill and rob a manipulative pawnbroker to whom he pawned his possessions. Although he justifies the action as freeing the world of a bad person while providing him the financial means to do good, he battles with conflicting emotions—the horror of murder against the apparent reasonableness of his decision. Upon leaving the pawnbroker's establishment, he walks to the street and exclaims:

> "Oh God, how repulsive! Can I possibly, can I possibly . . . no, that's nonsense, it's ridiculous!" he broke off decisively. "How could such a horrible idea enter my mind? What vileness my heart seems capable of!
> . . . "

But words and exclamations were not a sufficient outlet for his agitation. The feeling of infinite loathing that had begun to burden and torment him while he was on his way to the old woman's had now reached such a pitch that he did not know what to do with himself in his anguish.

(6)

Raskolnikov's ethical dilemma forms the core of the novel, both before and after he kills the pawnbroker. Dostoevsky allows readers to perceive these struggles through Raskolnikov's point of view, experiencing for themselves his psychological and moral vacillations. This novel and the rest of Dostoevsky's corpus anticipated the psychological novels of the modern era.

The nineteenth century's final great Russian writer is Anton Chekhov, whose plays and fiction frequently blend realism and comedy. His best-known works were produced at the turn of the century: *The Seagull* (1896), *Uncle Vanya* (1897), *Three Sisters* (1901), and *The Cherry Orchard* (1904); and his short stories "The Darling" (1899) and "The Lady with the Dog" (1899). (*For Chekhov as a dramatist, see pp. 157, 172–73.*) This pre-Soviet literature reflects a culture that experienced massive changes in the nineteenth and early twentieth century, engendering a legacy of some of the finest fiction in literary history.

Literature of European Modernism (1910–1945)

The start of modernism in Europe is generally dated to the onset of World War I, but important artistic developments preceding this date influenced its development. Modern art rejects realistic approaches to literature, questions the idea of a divine creator and an orderly world, plumbs human psychology, and reinvents and sometimes parodies older literary forms. (*For more on modernism, see pp. 33–37 and 52–56.*) The most notable precursor to the modern era, the Symbolist movement reacted against realism and its representation of the world through ordinary details. Symbolism began in France during the 1850s with the belief that the truth of the world could not be expressed through "realistic" accounts but only through suggestive descriptions including symbols, metaphors, and other indirect language. Symbolism rebelled against the "kind of realism that is but the description of things, feelings and people" and "re-create[d] through their words a state of being, a feeling, a glimmer, a vision. They want the reader to sense, and to react to, the experience itself" (Peschel 2). Charles Baudelaire, Stèphane Mallarmé, Paul Valéry, Arthur Rimbaud, and Paul Verlaine inaugurated the Symbolist movement. Verlaine's poem "Moonlight" (c. 1869) dramatically captures its subject through symbolic and evocative imagery:

Your soul is like a painter's landscape where
charming masks in shepherd mummeries
are playing lutes and dancing with an air
of being sad in their fantastic guise.

(MacIntyre 29; lines 1–4)

This poem rejects any semblance of a realistic portrayal. In describing a person's soul, Verlaine evokes an image of a painting of a festival—chaotic, festive, but also sad. The soul appears light yet weighted down, quiet yet noisy. For Verlaine, the soul cannot be understood in its own terms but only through powerful images evoking a range of emotions.

Surrealism, another key aspect of modernist literature yet primarily a movement in the visual arts, explores the unconscious and engages with the relationship between reality and dreams. Surrealist writing "does not look back to traditional forms or themes: it finds its only stability in what is to come. . . . The nature of the human mind, open to all possibilities however strange, *unconditioned* and unlimited, forms the ground of surrealist hope" (Caws 78). André Breton and Guillaume Apollinaire, two of the more influential surrealist authors, explore in their literature the ways the human mind works. In Breton's novel *Nadja* (1928), the narrator discusses his relationship with the titular character, a young Parisian, but the novel also includes non-narrative elements such as photographs of people, places, and objects, which serve as the narrator's touchstones for linking together different feelings and experiences. He explains his interest in facts as a way to understand the world:

> I am concerned, I say, with facts which may belong to the order of pure observation, but which on each occasion present all the appearances of a signal, without our being able to say precisely which signal, and of what; facts which when I am alone permit me to enjoy unlikely complicities, which convince me of my error in occasionally presuming I stand at the helm alone.
>
> (19–20)

Breton portrays the ways that people react to objects without understanding why, knowing that they experience in their subconscious powerful connections resulting in unexpected feelings. The surrealists' focus on the subconscious serves as one example of modern authors' engagement with the psychological conditions of life.

One of the most significant figures of French modernism, Marcel Proust published his novel *Remembrance of Things Past* (also known as *In Search of Lost Time*) in seven volumes between 1913 and 1927. This momentous work, pushing against the traditions of realism, introspectively presents the narrator's life. The novel is driven more by his contemplation of experience than by his actions, more by rumination than by plot. In a celebrated passage from the section entitled "Swann's Way," the narrator considers the power of memory when, after many years with no recollections of Combray, a village from his childhood, he drinks some tea into which he dipped a small cake—a "petite madeleine." A flood of sensation washes over him:

> An exquisite pleasure had invaded my senses, something isolated, detached, with no suggestion of its origin. And at once the vicissitudes of life had

become indifferent to me, its disasters innocuous, its brevity illusory—
this new sensation having had on me the effect which love has of filling
me with a precious essence; or rather this essence was not in me, it *was*
me. . . . Whence could it have come to me, this all-powerful joy? I sensed
that it was connected with the taste of tea and the cake, but that it infinitely
transcended those savours, could not, indeed, be of the same nature.

(48)

He eventually remembers his Sunday morning teas as a child. The associations among a scent, a flavor, and the feelings caused by his past permeate
his present. Proust's combination of rich detail with emotional and psychological insight enables readers to learn about the narrator through his experiences and memories, through his sensations and emotions, providing a new
approach to the novel.

Simone de Beauvoir, Jean-Paul Sartre, and Albert Camus wrote works
of *existentialism*, another branch of French modernism. Existentialism
assumes that human existence bears no inherent meaning, but that conscious
thought and decisions create the world as we know it, including its absurdity. De Beauvoir wrote existential philosophical tracts such as *The Ethics of
Ambiguity* (1947), and she is best known for her nonfiction volumet *The
Second Sex* (1949), in which she examines the history of women in society,
thereby establishing the foundation for later feminist authors. Sartre, with
the novel *Nausea* (1938) and the play *No Exit* (1944), and Camus, with
the novels *The Stranger* (1942) and *The Plague* (1947), ponder the vagaries
and limitations of human life through their existential themes. *The Stranger*
opens with a famous passage foregrounding life's meaninglessness:

> Mother died today. Or, maybe, yesterday; I can't be sure. The telegram
> from the Home says: YOUR MOTHER PASSED AWAY. FUNERAL
> TOMORROW. DEEP SYMPATHY. Which leaves the matter doubtful;
> it could have been yesterday.

(1)

Such emotional indifference reflects the tenor of the entire work. Rather than
grieving for his mother's death, the narrator Meursault appears more caught
up in the irrelevant details of which specific day she died. Meursault remains
detached from the death, his mother's funeral, and even a murder he commits later in the novel; all of these actions reflect his perspective that life holds
no true meaning.

German modernism speaks to the absence of an orderly and meaningful
world, particularly in the works of Franz Kafka, Bertolt Brecht, and Thomas
Mann. Kafka's major works include the novella *The Metamorphosis* (1915),
the short story collection *A Hunger Artist* (1922), and the novel *The Trial*
(1925). Kafka frequently presents disoriented and powerless characters
caught up in circumstances beyond their control, such as in *The Trial* when a

man is prosecuted for a crime that is never explained to him. Bertolt Brecht's plays, including *The Threepenny Opera* (1928), *Mother Courage and Her Children* (1939), and *The Good Person of Szechwan* (1943), exemplify the subgenre of epic theater. These plays demand that audiences think rationally about their subjects rather than react emotionally, with the goal of prompting them to political action. *The Good Person of Szechwan* stages the difficult life of a prostitute whose efforts to live as a good citizen fail, as the play reveals its theme that morality depends on a society's economic systems. (*For more on epic theater, see pp. 174–75.*) Thomas Mann's prose fiction includes *Tonio Kröger* (1903), *Death in Venice* (1912), and *The Magic Mountain* (1924), in which he muses on the relationship between art and life and incorporates psychological influences into his work. In *Death in Venice*, Gustav Aschenbach, a writer, vacations in Venice to reinvigorate himself. During his trip he encounters a teen boy, Tadzio, traveling with his family, and the boy's beauty inspires and excites him. Although Aschenbach never talks to Tadzio, he watches him closely, studying his beauty. As Aschenbach obsesses over this boy, he falls into a state of ruin. The novella ends with Aschenbach on the beach, watching Tadzio:

> It seemed to him, though, as if the pale and charming psychagogue out there were smiling at him, beckoning to him; as if, lifting his hand from his hip, he were pointing outwards, hovering before him in an immensity full of promise. And, as so often before, he arose to follow him.
>
> (63)

But Aschenbach never makes his way to Tadzio, instead falling dead in his chair. This passage reveals Aschenbach's romantic vision of the boy "beckoning to him" across the sand, as his death also posits that the pursuit of beauty can lead one to ruin, that the relationship between art and life is fraught with loss. With unique visions and styles, these German modernists explore how one confronts a fragmented world through a fragmented consciousness.

Questioning the purpose and meaning of the world also extended to Italy during the modern era. The author of *Six Characters in Search of an Author* (1921), *The Man with the Flower in His Mouth* (1922), and *One, No One and One Hundred Thousand* (1926), Luigi Pirandello questions in his fiction and drama how humans distinguish between reality and illusion. In *Six Characters in Search of an Author*, six unfinished characters interrupt the rehearsal of a play (Pirandello's *The Rules of the Game*) to ask the director and actors for help completing the play in which they are cast. The play creates an absurdist world like that of Kafka, as it questions the relationship between life and art, reality and fiction. The Father speaks to these conflicts:

> We are one thing for this person, another for that! Already *two* utterly different things! And with it all, the illusion of being always one thing for all men, and always this one thing when, by some unfortunate chance, in

one or another of our acts, we find ourselves suspended, hooked. We see, I mean, that we are not wholly in that act, and that therefore it would be abominably unjust to judge us by that act alone, to hold us suspended, hooked, in the pillory, our whole life long, as if our life were summed up in that act.

(84)

The Father sums up not only the situation of characters but the situation of humans: are we one unchangeable essence, or are we different things in different situations, or are we unknowable? With questions such as these, modernist writers searched for new ways to understand the world and people in it.

Along with Pirandello, poet F. T. Marinetti advanced modernist themes in Italian literature. Marinetti founded futurism, including writing the "Futurist Manifesto" (1909), which advocates art celebrating the future and rejecting the past. This manifesto includes a list of eleven goals, including the desire to "sing the love of danger, the habit of energy and fearlessness." Marinetti also affirms, "Courage, audacity, and revolt will be essential elements of our poetry." The manifesto advocates struggle, war, speed, industry, nationalism, arguing that "Poetry must be conceived as a violent attack on unknown forces" (Marinetti). Although futurism did not enjoy a long life, coming to an end around the time of World War I, its energy ignited the arts during the modern era. This vibrant approach can be traced back to the influences of the Symbolists, whose pre-modern poetry opened up the genre for experimentation.

Postcolonial African Literature (1950–Present)

During the nineteenth century and the first half of the twentieth, much of Africa remained under the colonial rule of countries such as Great Britain, France, Belgium, and Portugal. The colonial powers controlled the legal, political, and economic systems of these nations. When African nations began emancipating themselves from colonial rule, a rich array of literature, often depicting the experience of colonial and postcolonial life, established the continent's literature as among the world's most eloquent. The most acclaimed author from this period, Chinua Achebe placed African literature on a world stage with *Things Fall Apart* (1958). Published before Nigerian independence from Great Britain, the novel details the life of an Igbo family as the British are colonizing the country. Okonkwo, a strong, stoic man with traditional Igbo values, sees his world come apart as his culture clashes with the colonists and Christian missionaries. Okonkwo also clashes with members of his own community because his interpretation of their laws differs with theirs. Indeed, his son Nwoye is attracted to the Christian missionaries because they offer a compassionate alternative to the hard laws of the community, such as leaving twins, a bad omen, in the forest to die. Nwoye, like his grandfather, seeks a world of love and music:

It was not the mad logic of the Trinity that captivated him. He did not understand it. It was the poetry of the new religion, something felt in the marrow. The hymn about the brothers who sat in darkness and in fear seemed to answer a vague and persistent question that haunted his young soul. . . . He felt a relief within as the hymn poured into his parched soul.

(147)

Nwoye's struggle with the laws of his community leads him to consider other options, but Okonkwo's inflexibility ends his relationship with his son. The novel's groundbreaking depiction of colonialism and of the Igbo community in its depth and complexity shook the foundations of the colonialist project by dramatizing its pains. Because Achebe wrote the novel in English it has enjoyed an international impact, presenting a multifaceted depiction of life in Nigeria and the many influences on its people during and after colonization.

Whereas Achebe wrote in English in recognition of its role in Nigerian life, other African authors advocate writing in a historically African language. Kenyan author Ngũgĩ wa Thiong'o, after writing earlier works in English, including *Weep Not Child* (1964) and *Petals of Blood* (1977), began writing in Gĩkũyũ, the language of one of Kenya's largest ethnic groups. He explains the importance of writing in the traditional languages of African communities:

Values are the basis of a people's identity, their sense of particularity as members of the human race. All this is carried by language. Language as culture is the collective memory bank of a people's experience in history. Culture is almost indistinguishable from the language that makes possible its genesis, growth, banking, articulation and indeed its transmission from one generation to the next.

(14–15)

To communicate the culture and beliefs of a people, Ngũgĩ argues, one must use the language of those people. In *Devil on the Cross* (1982), written in Gĩkũyũ, Ngũgĩ tells a modern-day parable about Warĩĩnga, a woman fleeing postcolonial city life in Kenya but finding continued problems along the way. She has lost her job for rejecting her supervisor's advances, has been broken up with by her boyfriend who suspects she is having an affair, and has been evicted from her miserable home because she would not pay more rent. Through her life story, the novel criticizes colonialism's impact on Kenya. Ngũgĩ's literature mixes art with politics, drawing attention to the ongoing struggles of postcolonial nations.

Nigerian author Wole Soyinka, the first African author awarded the Nobel Prize in Literature, is best known for his plays, including *A Dance of the Forest* (1963), *The Bacchae of Euripides: A Communion Rite* (1973), and *Death and the King's Horseman* (1975), which address the effects of colonialism on the lives of indigenous Africans. *Death and the King's Horseman* dramatizes an event that occurred in 1946 in a Yoruba city in Nigeria. The Yoruba believe that, upon a king's death, his horseman must commit ritual suicide to assist the king on his journey to the afterlife. As Elesin prepares for this ritual, Simon Pilkings, a district officer who wants to avoid the problems of a suicide and does not understand the event's importance to the community, stops him. While held by the police, Elesin converses with Pilkings about their differing world views:

> ELESIN. The night is not at peace, ghostly one. The world is not at peace. You have shattered the peace of the world for ever. There is no sleep in the world tonight.
> PILKINGS. It is still a good bargain if the world should lose one night's sleep as the price of saving a man's life.
> ELESIN. You did not save my life, District Officer. You destroyed it.
> PILKINGS. Now come on . . .
> ELESIN. And not merely my life but the lives of many. The end of the night's work is not over. Neither this year nor the next will see it. If I wished you well, I would pray that you do not stay long enough on our land to see the disaster that you have brought upon us.
>
> (50)

This misunderstanding sets off chaos among the Yoruba, who see their world and the afterlife in turmoil due to Pilkings's intervention. When Elesin's son kills himself in place of his father, he restores his family's reputation, but he also interferes with traditional customs; ultimately, his death leads to his father's suicide as well. Soyinka's play considers the ways that colonialism alters everyone involved, leading to misunderstandings with disastrous consequences.

In addition to Achebe, Ngũgĩ, and Soyinka, African authors who are descendants of European immigrants settling in the continent have also written notable African literature. The fiction of South African authors Nadine Gordimer, Alan Paton, and J. M. Coetzee addresses issues of politics and race in their homeland. Coetzee, in *Waiting for the Barbarians* (1980), depicts the story of a magistrate in a small colonial town. When the Empire warns that the "barbarians," or the indigenous people, will attack, a violent crackdown begins, shaking the magistrate's attitudes toward colonialism. As he watches the vicious Colonel Joll investigate the attack, the magistrate sympathizes with the tortured prisoners, particularly a severely injured girl. After tending to her and returning her to her people, he is imprisoned for abetting the enemy. Throughout this ordeal, he contemplates the behavior of the colonizers, including himself, and realizes that their depravity makes them the true barbarians. While jailed, he reflects that

I cannot save the prisoners, therefore let me save myself. Let it at the very least be said, if it ever comes to be said, if there is ever anyone in some remote future interested to know the way we lived, that in this farthest outpost of the Empire of light there existed one man who in his heart was not a barbarian.

(104)

The theme he points out in this passage, that the "Empire of light" in fact practices barbarity, infuses the novel with a biting irony, as Coetzee ponders the thin line between civilization and savagery. Coetzee, Gordimer, and Paton began writing before the end of Apartheid in South Africa, and through their novels' themes they criticize the system that denied equal rights to black and other nonwhite South Africans.

Arab-African writers have created another major strand of African literature. Naguib Mahfouz of Egypt, Hisham Matar of Libya, and Tayeb Salih of Sudan depict the Arab-African world, often in light of colonialism and its aftermath. Salih's novel *Season of Migration to the North* (1966) tells the story of a young man, the narrator, who returns to his Sudanese village after studying in England and encounters a new member of the community, Mustafa Sa'eed, who remains remote and secretive. The narrator learns that Mustafa lived abroad but endured violent and unhappy experiences before returning to Sudan. As the narrator adjusts to life in his home village, he struggles between his village's culture and the Western ideas he has adopted, carrying himself passively, unable to make decisions. Through this character, Salih examines the social and cultural impacts of colonialism. The novel ends after great tragedy befalls the community, and the narrator is on the verge of giving up. While floating in a river, wanting to let the river pull him down, he undergoes a change of heart:

I thought that if I died at that moment, I would have died as I was born—without any volition of mine. All my life I had not chosen, had not decided. Now I am making a decision. I choose life. I shall live because there are a few people I want to stay with for the longest possible time and because I have duties to discharge. It is not my concern whether or not life has meaning. If I am unable to forgive, then I shall try to forget. I shall live by force and cunning.

(139)

The narrator's decision to take part in his world and not to be led along by forces other than himself—tradition, colonial force, education—reflects a positive outlook for the future of postcolonial nations. Although the past may be lost forever, people and communities may thrive as they adopt new attitudes respecting the hybrid nature of twentieth-century Africa. African literature presents the stories and people of a culturally diverse set of nations and smaller communities, revealing the ongoing search for identity and control during the postcolonial era.

Twentieth-Century Latin American Literature (1940–Present)

During the latter half of the twentieth century, many Latin American authors reached international audiences with literature of inventive styles, emotional storylines, and political resonance. Argentine author Jorge Luis Borges, whose publications began in the early part of the century, profoundly influenced writers in the latter half of the twentieth century during an explosion of Latin American literature. His story collection *Ficciones* (1944) includes an array of fantastical stories that challenge linear conceptions of time and reality. In "Pierre Menard, Author of Don Quixote," the narrator sums up the written work of fictitious author Menard, focusing on Menard's plan to create the original *Don Quixote*. He aims not to copy it; rather, as Borges explains, "His admirable ambition was to produce pages which would coincide—word for word and line for line—with those of Miguel de Cervantes" (49). Much of Borges's writing is metatextual, making the texts themselves the focus of his stories and challenging readers' understanding of both reality and time. Such approaches deeply influenced postmodern writers from Latin America and from other parts of the world.

Fantastical elements permeate the work of Colombian author Gabriel García Márquez, who penned *One Hundred Years of Solitude* (1967) and *Love in the Time of Cholera* (1985). His writing is known for its *magical realism*, the inclusion of magical or supernatural elements presented in a realistic, ordinary style as if they form a regular part of the environment. In his masterwork *One Hundred Years of Solitude*, García Márquez employs tropes of magical realism to tell the story of several generations of the Buendía family and their lives in the fictional town of Macondo. At first they live in isolation, but as the years pass, the people in Macondo interact more with the rest of the world, which brings many changes in economics, politics, and the social order. Considered a fictional representation of Colombian history, the novel depicts a community struggling as the world around them changes, placing traditional values at odds with modernization. At one point, as the town experiences the arrival of new technologies—movies, telephones, electric lights, phonographs—the people question their reality:

> It was as if God had decided to put to the test every capacity for surprise and was keeping the inhabitants of Macondo in a permanent alternation between excitement and disappointment, doubt and revelation, to such an extreme that no one knew for certain where the limits of reality lay. It was an intricate stew of truths and mirages that convulsed the ghost of José Arcadio Buendía under the chestnut tree with impatience and made him wander all through the house even in broad daylight.
>
> (212)

García Márquez's magical realism treats ordinary aspects of life—movies and electric lights—as unreal and magical while depicting supernatural elements such as ghosts as integrated into reality. Magical realism effectively contributes to the novel's thematic consideration of the challenges of a changing world where tradition and modernity collide. This novel and other texts of magical realism reassess reality and question apparently empirical truths.

The novels of Chilean author Isabel Allende also employ magical realism to address the changes unfolding in Latin America. Allende's work, including *Eva Luna* (1987), *Daughter of Fortune* (1999), and her most famous, *The House of the Spirits* (1982), addresses the place of women in society and the effects of changing political and social spheres. Chronicling the experiences of the Trueba family over several generations, *The House of the Spirits* depicts political and class conflicts between the peasants/socialists and the upper classes/conservatives. Like García Márquez, Allende tells the stories of several generations of a family in order to investigate larger cultural forces at play in Latin America, and both authors also employ magical realism to address the state of flux in society. For these authors, time is flexible, as the deeply connected relationships among past, present, and future prove the impossibility of experiencing life as if it were linear. As *The House of the Spirits* concludes, Alba García, who struggles throughout her life and tells the multigenerational story of her family, comments on this element of time:

> I write, she wrote, that memory is fragile and the space of a single life is brief, passing so quickly that we never get a chance to see the relationship between events; we cannot gauge the consequences of our acts, and we believe in the fiction of past, present, and future, but it may also be true that everything happens simultaneously—as the three Mora sisters said, who could see the spirits of all eras mingled in space.
>
> (432)

Alba García sees time as an artificial construct, suggesting instead that the world circumscribes all times simultaneously. Allende draws readers' attention to the living role of the past in the present and to the ever-changing reality of the world.

Other Latin American novelists whose work enjoys international acclaim include Argentine Julio Cortázar (*Hopscotch* and *62: A Model Kit*), Mexican Carlos Fuentes (*The Death of Artemio Cruz* and *The Old Gringo*), Peruvian Mario Vargas Llosa (*Aunt Julia and the Scriptwriter*, *The War at the End of the World*, and *The Storyteller*), Brazilian Jorge Amado (*Dona Flor and Her Two Husbands* and *Tent of Miracles*), and Argentine Manuel Puig (*Betrayed by Rita Hayworth* and *Kiss of the Spiderwoman*).

In addition to these Latin American masterpieces from the realm of prose fiction, the twentieth century also witnessed a great flourishing of poetry, especially from Chileans Gabriela Mistral and Pablo Neruda, and Mexican Octavio Paz. These authors respond to different concerns in their verse, yet they are particularly attentive to issues of love and identity in Latin America. In "Sun Stone" (1957), Paz ponders the symbolism of the Aztec sun stone, which is an Aztec calendar marking 584 days (the time it takes for Venus to be in inferior conjunction between Earth and the sun); the poem itself consists of 584 lines. The poem's speaker meditates on life's meaning, both through images of the natural world and through human relationships. Paz alludes to Aztec figures such as Moctezuma and to classical Greek figures such as Agamemnon and Cassandra, as well as to more recent historical figures such as Leon Trotsky and Maximilien de Robespierre. Combining past and present, indigenous and international, Paz's poem reflects a contemporary world informed by a dense and hybrid identity. The poem's speaker also addresses his loneliness and desire for connection in passionate, evocative language:

> you write a red and indecipherable
> writing upon my skin and these open wounds
> cover my body, a burning suit of flame,
> I burn and am not consumed, I long for water,
> and in your eyes there is no water, but stone,
> your breasts are made of stone, your mouth has the taste of dust,
> your mouth tastes to me of an envenomed time,
> your body has the taste of a pit without
> any exit, a hall of mirrors reflecting
> the eyes of one thirsty man.
>
> (Paz 13)

Paz weaves together erotic images of desire with the longing for a cultural identity and larger purpose in life. And Paz shares these interests not only with other Latin American poets but with many fiction writers as well. In the latter part of the twentieth century, concerns with distinct national identities, indigenous American identities, and more regional Latin American identities fused together to provide the source for much of the impressive literature of the region. As with so many of the masterpieces of world literature, the works reflect a unique culture experiencing timeless challenges: to work, to love, and simply to be, in a world where one's desires run against those of the culture, the gods, and sometimes, one's very self.

Unit 2

A Practical Guide to Major Literary Modes and Cinematic Adaptations

2.1 Poetry

Poetry invites readers to revel in the inherent beauty of language, to luxuriate in its rhythm and flow while pondering the author's themes and insights. Poems often challenge readers as well, asking them to interpret words, phrases, images, and symbols conjoined in striking ways. Whereas one might think that the goal of language is to communicate simply and directly, to express ideas with as little ambiguity as possible, the goal of poetry is also to communicate—but to do so with keen attention to the nuances and aesthetic qualities of language through sound, meter, images, voice, and genre. Poets remove words from their everyday milieu, encouraging readers to enjoy the play of language and the rewards of immersing oneself in its cadences.

Sound

Poetic language erupts from the ordinary to create art: the words themselves need not be esoteric as much as they must conjure vivid images, arouse fresh emotions, and spark new insights. To achieve these aims, poets employ various techniques, particularly those focusing on the sounds and acoustics of language. Common techniques of poetic sound include rhyme, assonance, consonance, alliteration, and onomatopoeia, which build aural patterns into a poem's lines.

Rhyming words, regardless of spelling, share vowel sounds and closing consonant sounds: for example, *bite*, *site*, *right*, *bright*, and *height*. As one of the most recognizable acoustic effects, rhymes are easily identifiable, yet they achieve powerful aesthetic results through their resonance. Phillis Wheatley concludes each line of her "An Hymn to the Evening" (c. 1771) with a rhyme:

> SOON as the sun forsook the eastern main
> The pealing thunder shook the heav'nly plain;
> Majestic grandeur! From the zephyr's wing,
> Exhales the incense of the blooming spring.
>
> (lines 1–4)

Due to their overlap of vowel and consonant sounds, rhymes sound with a clarion effect in a poem, as readers anticipate the closing term of the pair. When used effectively, rhymes echo off each other in both sound and sense, such as in Wheatley's pairing of *wing* and *spring*.

Many poets employ rhymes in their verse, but this strategy constrains their vocabularies. In contrast to languages such as French, whose verb endings create a plenitude of rhymes, English offers poets significantly fewer rhyming words. In his "Complaint to Venus," Geoffrey Chaucer complains that "rym in Englissh hath such skarsete [scarcity]" (line 80), and many poets, agreeing with this assessment, disavowed rhyme due to these limitations. For example, John Milton chose blank verse, unrhymed lines of metered poetry, for his *Paradise Lost* (1667), and in describing this decision in the Preface to its second edition, he concomitantly berated rhyme:

> The measure is *English* Heroic Verse without Rime, as that of *Homer* in *Greek* and of *Virgil* in *Latin*; Rime being no necessary Adjunct or true Ornament of Poem or good Verse, in longer Works especially, but the Invention of a barbarous Age, to set off wretched matter and lame Meeter.
>
> (10)

(It should be noted that, despite these words, Milton employs rhyme in many other poems, such as his sonnets.) Rhyme's scarcity in English carries with it a positive consequence, however, in that it compels poets to think creatively to overcome these limitations. The humorist Florence King, when imagining an appropriate fate for a foe, simultaneously confronts rhyme's inherent challenge:

> It's awfully hard to rhyme it—
> After all, I'm not a Horace—
> But I'd love to see him buggered
> By a Rex Tyrannosaurus.
> (186; lines 9–12)

King overcomes the difficulty of finding a rhyme for *Horace*, but only by inverting the typical word order of *Tyrannosaurus Rex*. Her grotesquely whimsical satire succeeds in its aim of debasing her antagonist, as she also proves her corollary argument of rhyme's challenges.

Like rhyme, assonance and consonance link words together, but they do so more subtly. *Assonance* describes the repetition of vowel sounds in words, particularly in their stressed syllables, but without the repetition of a closing consonant sound as well. For example, *hope*, *rope*, and *dope* rhyme, while *hope*, *road*, and *dough* share assonance. In Emily Dickinson's "We never know how high we are" (c. 1870), she first links words through assonance and then switches to rhyme:

> We never know how high we are
> Till we are called to rise;
> And then, if we are true to plan,
> Our statures touch the skies—
> (lines 1–4)

The assonance of *high* and *rise* links the words together both in their pronunciation and in their imagery, and Dickinson thereby prepares her reader for the final ascent afforded in the rhyme of *rise* and *skies*. As assonance may be thought of as a half-rhyme that matches vowel sounds without corresponding final consonant sounds, so too does consonance acoustically register as nearly a rhyme. *Consonance* repeats one or more consonant sounds in words, typically their medial or final consonants, without matching vowels. Irregular verbs often display consonance: *arise, arose; grind, ground; hang, hung; write, wrote; ring, rang, rung*. Consonance also includes so-called eye-rhymes, words that look like they should rhyme but do not, such as *height* and *weight; brown* and *grown; sound* and *wound; shear* and *wear*. Christina Rossetti's "Song" (1848) urges a celebration of her passing—"When I am dead, my dearest, / Sing no sad songs for me" (lines 1–2)—with the consonance of *sing* and *songs* harmonizing her exhortation. The title of Langston Hughes's memoir *I Wonder as I Wander* features the consonance of *wonder* and *wander*. If one is truly wandering, one is likely wondering what the future holds in store, and through this consonance Hughes's title harmonizes these activities and encourages readers to consider their relevance to his life story.

Alliteration refers to the repetition of initial consonant sounds in a line or lines of poetry. Alliteration is occasionally (and incorrectly) dismissed as a juvenile poetic technique, perhaps because of its use in nursery rhymes ("Baa-baa black sheep") and tongue-twisters ("rubber baby buggy bumpers"), as well as the many cartoon and comic characters with alliterative names: Daffy Duck, Mickey Mouse, Bugs Bunny, Porky Pig, Roger Rabbit. Poems featuring alliteration as their defining feature are referred to as *alliterative verse*. Much Old and Middle English poetry was written with alliteration as its primary poetic structure, including such masterworks as *Beowulf, Sir Gawain and the Green Knight*, and William Langland's *Piers Plowman*. Langland's poem opens, "In a somer seson, whan softe was the sonne" (line 1), with the repetition of the *s*'s in *summer, season, soft*, and *sun* linking these words together and building a harmonious image from them. In "Shiloh," his requiem for the April 1862 battle of the U.S. Civil War, Herman Melville uses alliteration to connect sounds and concepts together:

Over the field where April rain
Solaced the parched one stretched in pain
Through the pause of night
That followed the Sunday fight
    Around the church of Shiloh—
The church so lone, the log-built one,
That echoed to many a parting groan
      And natural prayer
    Of dying foemen mingled there—
Foemen at morn, but friends at eve.
(lines 5–14)

The pairing of *solaced* and *stretched*, *parched* and *pain*, *lone* and *log-built*, and, most tragically, *foemen* and *friends* imbues Melville's poem with heightened emotions and imagery, for these words accentuate and complement one another. Alliteration's simplicity belies its power in the poet's toolkit, as linking words together through initial consonants creates a deeper sense of their thematic echoes, thereby enhancing the poem's aural treatment of its subject.

At its simplest, *onomatopoeia* refers to words that sound like their meaning: the word *hiss* virtually hisses at readers, and *buzz* captures the hum of buzzing. Comic books frequently feature onomatopoeic words in their depictions of violence—*pow, wham, whack, zap*—and most words associated with animal noises are onomatopoeic: *bark, meow, bray, roar, screech, cheep, hoot, moo, cluck, whinny*. In his *Parliament of Fowls* (c. 1382), Chaucer dreams of an avian mating ritual that, he confesses, gives him a headache:

The goos, the cokkow [cuckoo], and the doke [duck] also
So cryede, "Kek kek! Kokkow, quek quek!" hye,
That thurgh myne eres [ears] the noyse wente tho.
(lines 498–500)

One can hear the birds screeching in this onomatopoeic play, through which Chaucer builds humor into his celebration of amatory fowls. Often, however, onomatopoeia operates more subtly, and one must listen to the words and phrases for how their pronunciations connect to their meaning. The phrase *puncture wound* captures a nuanced form of onomatopoeia, in which the opening *punct-* suggests a popping that is then followed by the openness of the vowel sound of *wound*. In "A Song for St. Cecilia's Day" (1687), John Dryden pays homage to the patron saint of music and seeks to capture the sounds of various instruments with his words. The poem begins with a universal (and alliterative) acclaim of music's power—"From Harmony, from Heav'nly Harmony / This Universal Frame began" (*Poetry, Prose* lines 1–2)—as Dryden then records the sounds of various musical instruments: "The TRUMPETS loud Clangor / Excites us to Arms" (lines 25–26), with *clangor* capturing the brassy exuberance of the instrument. He then describes

"The double double double beat / Of the thundring DRUM" (lines 29–30) with the onomatopoeic repetition of *double* mimicking a drum. Dryden's description of the flute—"The soft complaining FLUTE / In dying Notes discovers / The Woes of hopeless Lovers" (lines 33–35)—likewise captures its sonorous soundings, with its soft, warbling tones; additionally, the assonance of the *hopeless* lovers' *woes* echoes the instrument's lower registers. Edgar Allan Poe's "The Bells" (1848) exhibits such virtuoso and daring onomatopoeia as well, in which in four stanzas he captures distinct sounds of bells, from "the jingling and the tinkling" (*Collected Tales* line 14), to "the rhyming and the chiming" (line 35), to "the clamor and the clanging" (line 69), and then to "the moaning and the groaning of the bells" (line 113). The poem builds its melancholy meaning as the bells move from light pealing to dark knells, with Poe's onomatopoeia tracking the speaker's increasingly panicked consciousness.

Accent, Rhythm, Meter, and the Poetic Line

Poets pay keen attention to accent and meter, which unite to form the rhythmic patterns in a poetic line. *Accent* refers to the stresses used in pronouncing a word. Humans do not speak in a monotone; on the contrary, we articulate words in ways reflective of their common pronunciations, as well as of regional variations. The alternations of accented and unaccented syllables build rhythms into words and phrases, which are combined in distinct patterns to create the poem's meter. The five basic units of rhythm in English poetry are iambs, trochees, anapests, dactyls, and spondees:

- An *iamb*, or an iambic foot, consists of an unstressed syllable followed by a stressed syllable, such as in the words *giraffe* (gĭ-ráffe), *baboon* (bă-bóon), and *raccoon* (răc-cóon). *Orangutan* consists of two iambs: ŏ-ráng-ŭ-tán.
- A *trochee*, or a trochaic foot, is the opposite of an iamb. It consists of a stressed syllable followed by an unstressed syllable, such as in the words *badger* (bádge-r̆), *walrus* (wál-r̆us), *tiger* (tí-gĕr), and *jackal* (jáck-ăl). The word *trochee* is itself trochaic.
- An *anapest*, or an anapestic foot, consists of two unstressed syllables followed by a stressed syllable, such as in the words *chimpanzee* (chĭm-păn-zée), *silver fox* (sĭl-vĕr fóx), and *kangaroo* (kăn-gă-róo). Although most pronunciations of *anapest* stress the first syllable, the adjective *anapestic* switches the stress to the third syllable, which serves as an apt mnemonic for this term.
- A *dactyl*, or a dactylic foot, consists of a stressed syllable followed by two unstressed syllables, such as in the words *centipede* (cén-tĭ-pĕde), *elephant* (él-ĕ-phănt), *unicorn* (ú-nĭ-cŏrn), *buffalo* (búff-ă-lŏ), and *rattlesnake* (rát-tlĕ-snăke).
- A *spondee*, or a spondaic foot, consists of two equally stressed syllables, such as in **góod dóg**, **réd fóx**, and **bláck cát**.

Of these units of rhythm, the iamb is the most common, as it provides a steady heartbeat to a poem: dŭh **dúm**, dŭh **dúm**, dŭh **dúm**. Trochees, anapests, dactyls, and spondees, although less frequently employed than iambs, bring their unique pulses to poetry: the syncopation of the trochee, the rush of the anapest, the stop and flow of the dactyl, and the sharp emphasis of the spondee.

A line of metrical poetry consists of a certain number of iambs, trochees, anapests, dactyls, or spondees, and the seven basic lengths of meter are *monometer, dimeter, trimeter, tetrameter, pentameter, hexameter,* and *heptameter.* If a poetic line has one foot, it is referred to as monometer, and so on with dimeter (two feet), trimeter (three feet), tetrameter (four feet), pentameter (five feet), hexameter (six feet), and heptameter (seven feet). Lines longer than heptameters are rare, but octometers, nonometers, decimeters, and so on, are possible as well. To describe a line of poetry, one must determine its combination of poetic feet with its meter. Robert Herrick's "Upon His Departure Hence" (1648) is likely the most famous poem written in iambic monometer, which means that each line consists of a single foot of one iamb:

> Thŭs Í
> Passe bý,
> Aňd díe:
> Aš Ońe
> Ŭnknówn
> Aňd gón:
> I'ḿ máde
> Ă sháde
> Aňd laíd
> I'ťh gráve:
> Thĕse háve
> My Cáve.
> Whĕre téll
> Ĭ dwéll
> *Fărewéll.*

Herrick builds stark simplicity into his poem through this iambic monometer, thereby emphasizing the speaker's isolation. No lines are adorned with excess, as they pass fleetingly to narrate the speaker's loneliness, death, and valediction. Notwithstanding the poem's overarching iambic structure, performers should not feel chained to this rhythm when reciting the poem; on the contrary, recitalists could enhance their performances of "Upon His Departure Hence" by reading such lines as "These have" and "Farewell" as spondees, thus modulating the poem's meter to avoid falling into a rigid rhythm.

As iambs echo the normal rhythms of speech, trochees, anapests, dactyls, and spondees establish a wide variety of metrical rhythms from which poets may select. Poets need a range of rhythms for their verse to create appropriate and unique patterns reflective of their subject matter. For example, the witches in William Shakespeare's *Macbeth* (1606) speak in trochaic tetrameter. This rhythmic structure distinguishes their voices from those of the play's other characters:

> Dóublĕ, | dóublĕ, | tóil aňd | tróublĕ
> Fírĕ | búrn aňd | cáuldrŏn | búbblĕ.
> (4.1.10–11)

By comparing the witches' lines to a sample passage spoken by Macbeth in iambic pentameter—"Šo fóul | aňd fáir | ă dáy | Ĭ háve | nŏt séen" (1.3.38)— it is apparent that Shakespeare uses shifts in meter and rhythm to capture aspects of his characters' dispositions. As inversions of iambs, trochees can slow a poem's pace, as they can also provide it with an appropriate majesty. In "Queen and Huntress" (1600), Ben Jonson honors Queen Elizabeth I through the stately unfolding of his trochees:

> Queéne aňd | *Huńtreés*, | cháste, aňd | fáire,
> Nów thĕ | *Súnne* ĭs | láid tŏ | sléepe,
> Séatĕd | in thy | silvĕr | cháire,
> Státe in | wóntĕd | mánnĕr | kéep.
> (*Complete Poetry* lines 1–4)

Jonson's trochaic tetrameter achieves a stately effect, prodding his auditors to stand in awe before their queen. Because he omits the final unstressed syllable of his trochaic lines, his poem also exemplifies lines with *masculine endings*, in which the final syllable is stressed. (By definition, iambic meters feature masculine endings, but poets may vary this form by adding an unstressed syllable, which is referred to as a *feminine ending*.)

Anapests frequently sport a rolling and accelerating rhythm with one cadence leading into another. Clement Moore employs anapestic tetrameter in his holiday classic "A Visit from St. Nicholas" (1823):

> 'Twas thĕ níght | bĕfŏre Chríst | măs, whĕn áll | thrŏugh thĕ hóuse
> Nŏt ă créa | tŭre wăs stír | rĭng, nŏt é | vĕn ă móuse.
> (lines 1–2)

Edgar Allan Poe's "Annabel Lee" (1849) likewise employs anapests, as the lyric speaker rhapsodizes over his lost beloved:

> Fŏr thĕ móon | nĕvĕr beáms | wĭthŏut bríng | ĭng mĕ dréams
> Ŏf thĕ beáu | tĭfŭl Ańn | ăbĕl Lée;
> Aňd thĕ stárs | nĕvĕr ríse | bŭt Ĭ féel | thĕ bright eýes
> Ŏf thĕ beáu | tĭfŭl Ańn | ăbĕl Lée.
> (lines 34–37)

By alternating lines of anapestic tetrameter with anapestic trimeter, Poe's lines measure the speaker's mourning. The shorter line elegizes the lost Annabel Lee, capturing within the poem's structure the brevity of her life that leaves the speaker eternally bereaving her loss.

The strong opening stresses of dactyls can be used to create dramatic emphasis that then relaxes with two subsequent unstressed syllables. In "The Charge of the Light Brigade" (1854), which commemorates a battle of the Crimean War, Alfred, Lord Tennyson, writes in dactylic dimeter, a meter with a disorienting effect in his hands, as he captures the chaos of war:

> Cánnŏn tŏ | ríght ŏf thĕm,
> Cánnŏn tŏ | léft ŏf thĕm,
> Cánnŏn ĭn | frónt ŏf thĕm
>   Vólleў'd aňd | thúndĕr'd.
>   (*Selected Poems* lines 18–21)

Henry Wadsworth Longfellow employs dactylic hexameter to achieve a soothing yet majestic effect in his *Evangeline* (1847):

> THÍS iš thĕ | fórĕst prĭ | mévăl. Thĕ | múrmŭriňg | pínes aňd thĕ | hémlŏčks . . .
>
>   (line 1)

Although a popular verse form of Greek poets, dactylic hexameter is rarely chosen by poets in the English tradition. Longfellow's use of it reveals his attempt to elevate his romantic subject matter—Evangeline's quest for her beloved Gabriel—into the matter of epic.

Spondees are rarely used for an entire line of verse, for they have a halting effect. Similar to a car's brakes, spondees decelerate a poem, and if used excessively, they create a jarring sense of excessive emphasis. When used effectively, they shift a poem's tempo to register a climactic or otherwise noteworthy moment, such as in Oscar Wilde's "The Ballad of Reading Gaol" (1897):

> Hé díd | nŏt wéar | hĭs scár | lĕt cóat,
> Fŏr blóod | aňd wiņe | ăre réd,
> Aňd blóod | aňd wiņe | wĕre ón | hĭs hánds
> Whĕn théy | fóund hĭm | wĭth thĕ déad,
> Thĕ póor | dĕad wó | man whóm | hĕ lóved,
> Aňd múr | dĕred ĭn | hĕr béd.
>   (*Complete Works* lines 1–6)

The majority of these lines are written in iambs, but the fourth begins with two spondees so that Wilde can slow his readers down as he brings them to this climactic moment. As these examples of trochees, anapests, dactyls, and spondees show, varying acoustic and thematic effects are achievable through poetic feet and meter. In the best metrical poetry, authors unite their rhythms with their themes, allowing them to complement each other in a harmonious union of sense and sound.

As the excerpts from Poe's "Annabel Lee" and Wilde's "Ballad of Reading Gaol" demonstrate, poets often vary the length of their lines. Another example of this poetic strategy appears in George Herbert's "Easter Wings" (1633), a prayerful poem detailing a spiritual crisis:

> My tender age in sorrow did beginne;
> And still with sicknesses and shame
> Thou didst so punish sinne,
> That I became
> Most thinne.
> With Thee
> Let me combine,
> And feel this day Thy victorie;
> For, if I imp my wing on Thine,
> Affliction shall advance the flight in me.
> (lines 11–20)[1]

Herbert's poem is a *carmen figuratum*, a shaped poem. By shrinking his iambic lines from pentameter to tetrameter to trimeter to dimeter to monometer, the poem enacts the constriction of spirit that the lyric speaker recalls. When he is at his smallest—"Most thinne"—he unites with his God in the following line—"With Thee"—as the poem itself grows through longer lines until the poem ends as it begins with a line of iambic pentameter. As "Easter Wings" demonstrates, a poet's choice of metrical lines gives both form and freedom, for the form must be followed yet ample freedom can nonetheless be found.

The defining metrical line of much English poetry, and the preferred form for such great poets as Chaucer, Shakespeare, Milton, Dryden, Pope, and Barrett Browning, is iambic pentameter. A line of iambic pentameter is composed of five iambic feet, and, like the iamb itself, this form approximates the rhythms of speech. Chaucer's description of the Knight in the *General Prologue* of *The Canterbury Tales* models iambic pentameter—"Ă knýght | thĕr wás, | ănd that | ă wórth | ў mán" (line 43)—as do the opening lines of many of Shakespeare's plays:

THE MERCHANT OF VENICE: "Ĭn sóoth, | I Ĭ knów | nŏt why | Ĭ ám | sŏ sád."
THE TWO NOBLE KINSMEN: "Nĕw plays | ănd máid | ĕn héads | ăre néar | ăkín."
THE THIRD PART OF HENRY VI: "Ĭ wón | dĕr hów | the Kíng | ĕscáp'd | oŭr hánds."
TWELFTH NIGHT: "Ĭf mú | sĭc bé | the fóod | ŏf lóve, | plăy ón."

One of the most apt uses of iambic pentameter is spoken by Shakespeare's Richard III: "Ă hórse! | ă hórse! | my kíng | dŏm fór | ă hórse!" (5.4.13). It is virtually impossible to imagine this line being read other than as standard iambic pentameter, with Richard's desperation mirrored by the line's natural iambic acceleration. When reciting iambic pentameter and other poetic rhythms, speakers need to parse each line carefully, selecting which syllables should be emphasized and for what effect. Although iambic pentameter echoes natural speech patterns, overusing it risks the poetry becoming mired in rhythmic ruts. Poets therefore vary their meter frequently, a poetic technique evident in Elizabeth Bishop's "One Art" (1976):

> Thĕ árt | ŏf lós | ĭng ís | n'̆t hárd | tŏ más | tĕr;
> sŏ mán | y̆ thíngs | sĕem filléd | wĭth thĕ | ĭntént
> tŏ bĕ lóst | thăt thĕir lóss | ĭs nó | dĭsást | ĕr.
>
> (lines 1–3)

The basic rhythm of these lines is iambic pentameter, but with many striking modulations of the form. The first and third lines of this poem have feminine, or unstressed, final syllables, while the second has a masculine, or stressed, final syllable. The feminine ending of the first line breaks the structure of iambic pentameter, which returns in the second line. The third line, however, begins with two anapests before returning to two iambs with a feminine ending to the line, such that the lost items seem virtually to lose themselves in its quicker pace.

Poets writing in iambic pentameter and other metrical forms must determine whether to employ or eschew rhyme at the end of their lines. Although some verse forms, such as sonnets, require rhyme for their cadences, other forms allow poets to forgo rhyme altogether. Paired lines of rhyming iambic pentameter are referred to as *heroic couplets*, which can enhance a poem's rhythm and sense, such as in William Congreve's heroic couplets in the prologue to his comedy of manners *The Way of the World* (1700):

> Of those few fools, who with ill stars are curst,
> Sure scribbling fools, called poets, fare the worst:
> For they're a sort of fools which Fortune makes,
> And, after she has made 'em fools, forsakes.
> With Nature's oafs 'tis quite a diff'rent case,
> For Fortune favours all her idiot-race.
>
> (lines 1–6)

Congreve's heroic couplets maintain his poetic prologue's flow and pulse, and in many instances the first word foreshadows its rhyme: *curst* and *worst*, *makes* and *forsakes*, and *case* and *race*. In contrast to heroic couplets, *blank verse* consists of unrhymed lines of regularly metered poetry, particularly those in iambic pentameter. Forfeiting rhyme as a poetic technique, blank verse relies solely on meter's pulse for its rhythm. Henry Howard, Earl of

Surrey, is credited with inventing blank verse in his translation of Virgil's *Aeneid* (1554). The following excerpt, in which Aeneas describes to Dido the fall of Troy, would register a different tone if expressed in rhyme: "Who can expresse the slaughter of that night, / Or tell the nomber of the corpses slaine, / Or can in teres bewaile them worthely?" (lines 463–65). From this beginning, blank verse blossomed on the Renaissance stage, particularly from the dramas of Christopher Marlowe. The playwright of *Tamburlaine*, *The Jew of Malta*, and *Doctor Faustus*, Marlowe revolutionized English theater with his soaring blank verse, such as in Faustus's closing words as he is damned for eternity: "All beasts are happy, for when they die, / Their souls are soon dissolved in elements; / But mine must live still to be plagued in hell" (5.2.102–04). Although Marlowe was not the first to sound blank verse on the stage, Ben Jonson praised him for the majesty of his meter, referring to it as "*Marlowes* mighty line" and thereby recognizing the strength and power of this form ("To the Memory of My Beloved, the Author, Mr. William Shakespeare, and What He Hath Left Us," *Complete Poetry* line 30).

Despite the disjunction between them, heroic couplets and blank verse are often used complementarily. Many Renaissance playwrights employ blank verse for much of their dialogue but then close a scene or the entire play with heroic couplets. In John Webster's *The Duchess of Malfi* (c. 1612), Bosola waxes eloquently in poetry and prose. When this reformed villain plots his murderous revenge, he envisions himself as an instrument of justice in blank verse but closes the scene with rhyme:

> The weakest Arme is strong enough, that strikes
> With the sword of Justice. Still methinkes the Dutchesse
> Haunts me: there, there: 'tis nothing but my mellancholy.
> O Penitence, let me truely taste thy Cup,
> That throwes men down onely to raise them up.
>
> (5.2.335–39)

Such variation in poetic lines cues the audience that the scene is concluding. This technique further exemplifies how such apparently simple decisions—to rhyme or not to rhyme—achieve significant artistic effects.

Not all verse adheres to the rhythms of iambs, trochees, anapests, dactyls, and spondees, and some poets, chafing against meter's restrictions, have innovated new paradigms of rhythm. Gerard Manley Hopkins dubbed the meter of his poetry *sprung rhythm*, which he describes as "the echo of a new rhythm" that liberates poetic feet from a certain number of stresses, so that, as Hopkins states, "a foot may be one strong syllable or it may be many light and one strong" (Mariani 144–45). Hopkins's sprung rhythm requires a certain number of stressed syllables in each line of a poem yet without regard for the corresponding number of unstressed syllables. He believed this strategy allows his verse to mimic the natural rhythms of speech. Hopkins's "Pied

Beauty" (1877) exemplifies this technique, as it also illuminates his consideration of God's place in the world:

> Glŏr̆y bé tŏ Gód fŏr dáppl̆ed thíngs—
>   Fŏr skíes ŏf cóupl̆e-cóloŭr ăs ă brínded ców.
>   Fŏr róse-móles ăll ĭn stípl̆e ŭpŏn tróut thăt swím;
> Frésh-fírecŏal chéstnŭt-fálls; fínches' wĭngs.

(lines 1–4)

Each line features five stressed syllables, but the first line contains four
unstressed syllables, the second line has seven, the third line has seven, and
the fourth line has four. With its free-floating accents, Hopkins's sprung
rhythm resists meter's potential monotony, in which the patterns of verse
might degrade into a singsong style.

The poetic genre referred to as *free verse* likewise rejects traditional
form and meter as defining principles; in contrast, the lines and stanzas
of free verse poetry vary in length. Free verse emerged as a major poetic
tradition in the twentieth century, but precursors of the form are evident in William Blake's prophetic books and in Walt Whitman's poems.
Whitman's "The Sleepers" (1855) exemplifies the break with meter that
characterizes free verse:

> I wander all night in my vision,
> Stepping with light feet, swiftly and noiselessly stepping and stopping,
> Bending with open eyes over the shut eyes of sleepers,
> Wandering and confused, lost to myself, ill-assorted, contradictory,
> Pausing, gazing, bending, and stopping.

(*Leaves of Grass* lines 1–5)

A free-verse poem does not depend on the rhythms of iambs, trochees, anapests, dactyls, and spondees, for it eschews an overarching structure from line
to line. Still, free verse need not be entirely devoid of metrical effects. In the
final line of this excerpt, Whitman uses four trochaic words—páusĭng, gázĭng,
béndĭng, and stóppĭng—and the syncopated rhythms of these trochees acoustically mimics the actions the speaker describes. This pattern, however, was
not established by the previous line.

As free verse blossomed, various poets of the early twentieth century theorized its advantages over meter. Ezra Pound, a fervent proselytizer of this
new poetic tradition, fostered a school of free verse known as imagism. With
his collaborators H. D. and Richard Aldington, Pound outlined its tenets in
the essay "A Retrospect," advocating that poetry should involve:

1   Direct treatment of the "thing" whether subjective or objective.
2   To use absolutely no word that does not contribute to the presentation.

3   As regarding rhythm: to compose in the sequence of the musical phrase,
      not in sequence of a metronome. (3)

Not all poets of free verse would agree with each of these prescriptions, but
the sense that rhythm should capture a musical phrase rather than measure
iambs, trochees, anapests, dactyls, and spondees applies to many poems of
the genre. The comparison of metrical verse to a tick-tocking metronome
disparages the illustrious achievements of metrical poets, yet it is nonetheless
a clarion call for free verse over metered lines.
    When reading poetry, whether metrical or free form, it is essential that
readers pay close attention to the phrasing of each line and how it should
be recited. Novice readers often err by pausing at the end of each line;
however, to recite poems fluently, readers must determine when pauses
effectively contribute to the poem's meaning by noting whether each line is
end-stopped or *enjambed*, and whether it contains a *caesura*. End-stopped
lines require a pause at their conclusions, and these pauses are typically
signaled by commas, periods, or other punctuation marks. In enjambed
lines, the meaning carries forward from one line to the next, and so no
pause should be registered. Caesuras are medial breaks within a given line
of poetry. Like end-stopped lines, they are often indicated by punctuation
marks. The following speech from Shakespeare's *King Lear* (c. 1603), as
Lear rages over his daughter Cordelia's dead body, illustrates these various strategies:

> Howl, howl, howl! O, you are men of stones:
> Had I your tongues and eyes, I'd use them so
> That heaven's vault should crack. She's gone forever!
> I know when one is dead, and when one lives;
> She's dead as earth. Lend me a looking-glass;
> If that her breath will mist or stain the stone,
> Why then she lives.
>
> (5.3.258–64)

The first, third, fourth, fifth, sixth, and seventh lines are end-stopped, and so
the performer playing Lear should pause at the end of each of them to better
capture Shakespeare's phrasings. The second line, however, is enjambed. If
an actor paused here, he would disrupt the flow of Lear's grief. The first, second, third, fourth, and fifth lines contain caesuras, which are clearly marked
by commas, periods, and an exclamation point. These moments allow the
speaker to modulate the flow and expression of Shakespeare's words. All
poetry, not merely dramatic works, is meant to be spoken aloud so that one
may experience its acoustic effects. Articulating the silences of end-stops
and caesuras—as paradoxical as such a practice may be—is a key feature of
reciting poetry effectively.

Images, Symbols, Allusions, and Figurative Language

Poetry invigorates language so that readers can consider life's beauty and complexity through comparisons daringly fresh and unexpected. For poets, language can never be trite or banal; rather, they seek to infuse their subjects with unexpected meaning by recalibrating their essences. Indeed, even when poets play with the banality of language, they do so to refocus our attention on its conflicting senses and interpretations. In Stevie Smith's meditation on the overused word "pretty" in her poem of the same name (1966), she repeats the word frequently to defamiliarize it:

> Cry pretty, pretty, pretty and you'll be able
> Very soon not even to cry pretty
> And so be delivered entirely from humanity
> This is prettiest of all, it is very pretty.
>
> (lines 33–36)

Smith's repetition of "pretty" compels readers to ponder its meaning and its limitations, as she refigures death as the desired epitome of all prettiness. By examining one word so exhaustively, by repeating it to the extent that readers must confront its overuse and thus see it anew, Smith exhibits the poet's power to reinvigorate even the tritest of words. Other versatile tools for this task of refocusing words and their significations include images, symbols, allusions, and figurative language (including similes, metaphors, and paradoxes, among others).

Images appeal to the senses. The pictures that poets draw with words, images invite readers to experience them primarily through their visual cues but also through their acoustic, olfactory, gustatory, and tactile qualities. Amy Lowell's poem "Autumn" (1919) captures the beauty of a single flower:

> They brought me a quilled, yellow dahlia,
> Opulent, flaunting.
> Round gold
> Flung out of a pale green stalk.
> Round, ripe gold
> Of maturity,
> Meticulously frilled and flaming,
> A fire-ball of proclamation:
> Fecundity decked in staring yellow
> For all the world to see.
> They brought a quilled, yellow dahlia,
> To me who am barren.
> Shall I send it to you,
> You who have taken with you
> All I once possessed?
>
> (lines 1–15)

The majesty of Lowell's poem is its simplicity—the purity of the image she creates that leaves readers' imaginations seared with the flower's beauty. As the poem closes, its lyric speaker hints at an untold story—her barrenness and heartbreak over her lost love—and her loneliness is magnified by the loss of this last image, blazing in her recollection in all of its splendor.

Although visual imagery is most common in poems, appeals to other senses likewise capture the fine details of an object or experience. Galway Kinnell uses tactile images to describe collecting berries from a bush in "Blackberry Eating" (1980), noting that "the stalks [are] very prickly" (line 4). The speaker indicates that "as I stand among them / lifting the stalks to my mouth, the ripest berries / fall almost unbidden to my tongue" (lines 6–8). Kinnell conjures up the physical sensation of picking and tasting this luscious fruit, "the fat, overripe, icy, black blackberries" (line 2) through a rich combination of sultry images. Also compelling are acoustic images, such as those in Brigit Pegeen Kelly's "Song" (1995), in which she describes the strange killing of a goat, the pet of a girl who often "heard the trains passing, the sweet sound of the train's horn / Pouring softly over her bed, and each morning she woke / To give the bleating goat his pail of warm milk" (lines 27–29). The comforting whine of the passing trains combines with the welcoming calls of the goat to underscore the girl's peaceful life, which will be ruptured once she learns of the goat's death. Drawing on a variety of senses allows poets to create images fostering aesthetic beauty and experiential resonance.

Whereas an image need only represent itself—in Kelly's poem, the goat is simply a goat—a *symbol* represents both itself and another entity. In its most basic sense, all language is symbolic, for readers must extrapolate from the letters *c-a-t* to determine their meaning and thus to understand that they refer to a four-legged mammalian quadruped, although they would likely need more information to know whether, in each particular instance, the letters *c-a-t* refer to a house cat, a lion, an ocelot, an alley cat, or some other feline creature. Numerous symbols are encountered in everyone's daily lives—corporate logos, university mascots, religious icons—each of which represents an entity other than itself. In his cheekily lascivious poem "The Vine" (1648), Robert Herrick writes, "I Dream'd this mortal part of mine / Was Metamorphoz'd to a Vine" (lines 1–2) with the vine symbolizing and enacting the sexual desires imputed to his penis. The sexual symbolism is also quite clear in Bessie Smith's song "Empty Bed Blues" (1928): "He boiled my first cabbage, and he made it awful hot, / When he put in the bacon, it overflowed the pot." George Herbert's "The Collar" (1633), in which the lyric speaker rages during a spiritual crisis, showcases the multiple registers one symbol may encode. The titular collar symbolizes a clerical collar, indicative of the speaker's spiritual vocation, but because the word *collar* is a homophone of *choler*, or anger, the speaker simultaneously expresses his disenchantment and rage with religion. The poem's final lines—"But as I raved and grew more fierce and wild / At every word, / Methoughts I heard one calling, *Child!* / And I replied, *My Lord*" (lines 33–36)—suggest another homophonic symbol in the divine *caller* who succeeds in calming him. By embedding symbols in their poems, poets play with multiple levels of signification, and readers must decipher these multiple meanings to understand fully the poet's themes.

As symbols must be decoded if one is to understand the poet's purpose in employing them, so too must allusions. At their simplest, *allusions* refer to a person, a text, a historical moment, or some other such culturally recognized entity or event, whether fictitious or factual. The poet expects his reader to grasp the relevance of the allusion and to contemplate its resonance to the poem at hand. T. S. Eliot's *The Wasteland* (1922) encodes so many allusions that Eliot himself footnoted the poem, an apparatus to which subsequent editors have appended many additional explanations. Some of the poem's passages clearly register as allusions, such as in its closing lines, when Eliot writes, "These fragments I have shored against my ruin / Why then Ile fit you Hieronymo's mad againe" (*Collected Poems* lines 431–32). The second of these two lines cites the subtitle and a passage from Thomas Kyd's *The Spanish Tragedy* (4.1.68). In other instances readers must determine whether an allusion is in play. For instance, it seems reasonable to infer that Eliot alludes to Chaucer's *The Canterbury Tales* in the opening lines of *The Wasteland*, with his "April is the cruelest month, breeding / Lilacs out of the dead land" (lines 1–2) echoing Chaucer's "Whan that Aprill with his shoures soote / The droghte of March hath perced to the roote" (lines 1–2). Still, not every reference to April constitutes an allusion to Chaucer's *The Canterbury Tales* (or to Eliot's *The Wasteland*), and readers must determine through their understanding of both poems—the alluding poem and the poem alluded to—whether the latter contributes to a deeper understanding of the former.

Figurative language, including similes, metaphors, and other symbolic and comparative forms, juxtaposes two or more concepts. By allowing these multiple senses to intertwine, poets illuminate their subjects through fresh new perspectives linking like and unlike together. *Similes* frame their comparisons with *like* or *as*, while *metaphors* frame their comparisons implicitly. Clichéd similes such as *crazy like a fox*, *busy as a bee*, and *mad as a wet hen* exemplify the form, yet similes are rich and varied in their adaptability, as evidenced by the countless attempts of poets and musicians to define love through simile: it is like a fever (William Shakespeare); like a red, red rose (Robert Burns); like a heat wave (Martha and the Vandellas); and like a butterfly (Dolly Parton). Metaphors similarly enlighten the latent relationship between two entities, yet without the prepositions *like* or *as* structuring the comparison. So whereas Burns uses a simile to compare his love to a red, red rose, Robert Southwell achieves a similar effect with metaphor in his "The Burning Babe" (1602):

> My faultless breast the furnace is,
>   The fuell wounding thornes;
> Love is the fire, and sighs the smoake,
>   The ashes, shame and scornes.
>   (lines 17–20)

Southwell builds a series of metaphors in these lines: his heart burns as a furnace, one whose fire is stoked by the pains and fire of love; his sighs are the smoke escaping the pit, with his amatory despair rendered as the ashes. Like the many similes attempting to capture the essence of love, memorable metaphors of love compare it to a sickness full of woes (Samuel Daniel), a mischievous devil (Samuel Butler), a dog from hell (Charles Bukowski), and a battlefield (Pat Benatar).

Additional comparative and imagistic forms include synecdoches and metonymies. In a *synecdoche*, part of an entity represents its entirety, or conversely, the entirety of an entity represents one of its parts. (This latter usage is decidedly rarer.) The nautical synecdoche "all hands on deck" does not imply that the sailors should lop off their hands and deposit them atop the ship; instead, the sailors are to decode the figurative meaning of the phrase and to report to their captain in their complete persons. In another such instance of synecdoche, Dylan Thomas focuses on hands and their symbolic meaning in his "The Hand That Signed the Paper" (1936): "The hand that signed the paper felled a city; / Five sovereign fingers taxed the breath, / Doubled the globe of dead and halved a country" (lines 1–3). Obviously, hands are indeed used to sign papers, but this synecdoche obscures the person who unleashes such calamity through this document. The poem concludes "Hands have no tears to flow" (line 16) to underscore the connection between the hand and the person who should be shaken to the core by his or her acts but who remains invisible to readers, who can only see this hand as it unleashes such carnage.

In *metonymy*, an entity significantly related to another comes to represent it. For example, rulers of state are often associated with their residences (the White House for the U.S. President, 10 Downing Street for the British Prime Minister, Kirribilli House for the Australian Prime Minister), and a press release may be described as coming from these addresses. The residence itself did not write and release these announcements, of course, and in this metonymic use of language, the address represents its inhabitant and his or her advisors. Readers frequently speak of authors metonymically. If one says, "I love to read Jane Austen," it is clear that the author's name metonymically represents her literature, for—with apologies for the gruesome image—one does not read Austen's deceased corpse. John Milton begins his pastoral elegy *Lycidas* (1638) with an image both symbolic and metonymic:

> YET once more, O ye Laurels, and once more
> Ye Myrtles brown, with Ivy never sear,
> I com to pluck your Berries harsh and crude.
>
> (lines 1–3)

The image depicts the lyric speaker plucking laurels, myrtles, and ivy, which metonymically denote Apollo (the god of poetry), Venus (the goddess of love), and Bacchus (the god of wine) due to these divinities' association with the respective vegetation. Through these metonymies, Milton encodes an invocation to his muses while focusing primarily on the loss structuring his elegy. Metonymies, as with other figurative language, may be elliptical. When Yeats writes in "The Second Coming" (1919), "The darkness drops again but now I know / That twenty centuries of stony sleep / Were vexed to nightmare by a rocking cradle" (lines 18–20), readers must decipher that the rocking cradle metonymically refers to Jesus in the manger, which requires a deep understanding and contextualization of Yeats's symbolism and themes.

Paradoxes and *oxymorons* expose the inherent contradiction possible in thought and language. These terms are synonymous in describing seemingly impossible and self-negating contradictions, with their primary distinction arising in the fact that paradoxes are more extended and oxymorons more compact. Queen Elizabeth I strings together paradoxes in her poetic lament "On Monsieur's Departure" (c. 1582) to capture the conflicting feelings of love:

> I grieve and dare not show my discontent;
> I love, and yet am forced to seem to hate;
> I do, yet dare not say I ever meant;
> I seem stark mute, but inwardly do prate.
>   I am, and not; I freeze and yet am burned,
>   Since from myself another self I turned.
>   (lines 1–6)

These paradoxes capture Elizabeth's disequilibrium following the collapse of negotiations that were to result in her marriage to a French duke. Many Renaissance poets employed paradoxes to capture love's disorienting effects, and in Elizabeth's account of her broken heart, she illustrates the pains of love by focusing on its ability to render a logical account of one's emotions impossible. *Oxymorons* encode such paradoxical sentiments in two paired words, such as *wise fool, sweet sorrow, open secret,* and *deafening silence.* Much like Queen Elizabeth I in "On Monsieur's Departure" with her numerous paradoxes, Shakespeare's Romeo expresses his love for Juliet by stringing together a litany of oxymorons, limning it as a "heavy lightness" and a "serious vanity" and comparing it to "bright smoke, cold fire, sick health" (1.1.178–80). Similarly, in Shakespeare's *Timon of Athens* (c. 1605), Timon castigates his former friends as "Courteous destroyers, affable wolves, meek bears" (3.6.95), with these collapsed contradictions pithily summarizing his sense of stunned betrayal. Through their economy of words, oxymorons compel readers to hold two contradictory ideas simultaneously and to decipher which sense best reveals the author's meaning.

Finally, it should be noted that images, symbols, and figurative language overlap considerably. In "The Love Song of J. Alfred Prufrock" (1911),

T. S. Eliot describes the setting sun, but is the picture he paints an image, a symbol, or a simile?

> Let us go then, you and I,
> When the evening is spread out against the sky
> Like a patient etherized upon a table.
>
> (lines 1–3)

This passage contains a simile—"Like a patient etherized upon a table"—but this simile captures an image as well. Readers can visualize the sun setting in the sky, filling the horizon flatly as the day descends into darkness. The image is melancholy, if not foreboding, and it thus appears to symbolize as well humanity's inherent isolation. When reading poetry, one must be attuned to the multiplicity of images, symbols, and figurative language, seeking ways in which poets construct multiple levels of meaning often by signifying across various poetic strategies.

Voice and Genre

When interpreting a poem, readers must consider the identity of its speaker and the stance that this voice takes in relation to the poem's themes. Many poems employ a first-person speaker who details the circumstances that motivate his or her unburdening of feeling through verse, but one cannot assume that this "I" reflects the desires and experiences of the poet. Also, the voice of a poem may speak sincerely or ironically, objectively or passionately, truly or falsely, and so readers must accurately gauge the speaker's character if they are to understand the poem's meanings. If readers fail to comprehend a poetic speaker's ironic stance to the matters described in the poem, they will misread its surface meaning for its deeper significations.

When poets speak sincerely, their words reflect their feelings (or the feelings of their poems' speakers). Readers have little reason to doubt, for instance, that in Thomas Carew's "An Elegy upon the Death of the Dean of Paul's Dr. John Donne" (1633), the speaker's words, while somewhat effusive, sincerely capture his grief for Donne's passing. It also appears that the "I" of the poem represents Carew himself:

> I will not draw the envy to engrosse
> All thy perfections, or weepe all our losse;
> Those are too numerous for an Elegie,
> And this too great, to be express'd by mee.
>
> (lines 87–90)

Elegies express the lyric speaker's anguished sense of loss, and in this instance the speaker's sincerity matches that of the author. Carew's speaker employs a modesty topos—"And this too great to be express'd by me"—so that he may elevate Donne further by contrasting himself as the weaker artist. In these humble yet heartfelt words, Carew's praise of Donne exemplifies the ways in which a poet's speaker may align with his or her understanding of the poem's subject.

Frequently, however, it is difficult to connect the "I" of a poem to its author, for the "I" represents all of humanity and the totality of human experience. When a poem's voice treats universal subjects and emotions, those from which all readers should be able to find relevance, it is often unclear whether the poet's musings reflect a personal experience. In Alfred, Lord Tennyson's "Break, Break, Break" (1834), the lyric speaker finds himself transfixed by the beauty and wonder of nature while contemplating the transience of life:

> Break, break, break,
> On thy cold gray stones, O Sea!
> And I would that my tongue could utter
> The thoughts that arise in me.
>
> (lines 1–4)

Likewise, in Emily Brontë's "I'm Happiest When Most Away" (1838), the lyric speaker details the freedom she finds through her imagination. Escaping the constraints of her mortal body enlivens her:

> I'm happiest when most away
> I can bear my soul from its home of clay
> On a windy night when the moon is bright
> And the eye can wander through worlds of light.
>
> (lines 1–4)

This analysis refers to Tennyson's lyric speaker as a "he" and to Brontë's lyric speaker as a "she," but the poems make no definitive claims about their speakers' genders. Should one therefore consider Tennyson's lyric speaker a "she" and Brontë's a "he"? Rather than conclusively answering this question, it is often better for readers to consider the interplay between the poet's voice and that of the lyric speaker, as well as what type of person this speaker represents. Gender, in itself, may not be as interesting a question to pursue as the poet's play between a speaker representing him- or herself and a universal representation of humanity.

In judging the voice of a poem, the tension between sincerity and irony provides an effective guidepost, yet it is essential to remember that sincerity and irony can overlap, particularly in scenes characterized by *situational irony*, in which expectations and events do not cohere. In the first sonnet of Mary Wroth's *Pamphilia to Amphilanthus* (1621), the lyric speaker describes her plight when Cupid obeys his mother Venus and conscripts her (the speaker) unwillingly into the game of love:

Hee her obay'd, and martir'd my poore hart.
I, waking hop'd as dreames itt would depart,
Yett since: O mee, a lover I have binn.

(lines 12–14)

Readers have little reason to doubt the truthfulness of the speaker's words—
she faithfully recounts her experiences and her hesitations with love—yet
the poem features the situational irony of a sonnet sequence's lover resisting
the throes of passion. Wroth's artistry effectively melds her speaker's sincerity with the irony of her circumstances, as she confronts the amatory travails of loving the fickle Amphilanthus, whose name means "lover of two."
(In contrast, and further heightening the poem's situational irony, the name
Pamphilia means *all-loving*.) Likewise, when Richard Lovelace describes his
freedom while incarcerated in "To Althea, from Prison" (1649), the situation
is ironic yet his words are sincere:

Stone Walls doe not a Prison make,
    Nor I'ron bars a Cage;
Mindes innocent and quiet take
    That for an Hermitage;
If I have freedome in my Love,
    And in my soule am free,
Angels alone that sore above,
    Injoy such liberty.

(lines 25–32)

The speaker's voice may sound overly romantic as he rhapsodizes over the
freedom of love rather than concentrating on the physical condition of his
incarceration. An excessively romantic voice, however, is not an insincere
one, and so, when interpreting Lovelace's poems, readers must take into
account the disjunction between his speaker's lofty sentiments and his incarceration. The poem's situational irony infuses it with a deeper meaning
through its consideration of freedom's meaning to a lover.

A poem's voice is often related to its genre. As in the example of Carew's
"An Elegy upon the Death of the Dean of Paul's Dr. John Donne," an elegy
is likely to be sincere, while a dramatic monologue is more likely to unfold
ironically. Many poems belong to certain aesthetic traditions and adhere to
the overarching rules of these genres. However, as expressions of the human
imagination, poems cannot be circumscribed by rules, and many of the greatest poems subvert, ignore, enhance, or innovate beyond such structural paradigms. Poetic genres do not share the taxonomical certainty of kingdom,
phylum, class, order, family, genus, and species that guides biologists and
zoologists; consequently, the line dividing one genre of poetry from another
can be slight. For example, an ode—a poem of praise—and an elegy—a poem
lamenting the loss of a beloved or respected figure, often by praising him or

her—might overlap in their themes, thereby blurring their distinctions. Some rules of genre are more rigid: a sonnet is defined as having fourteen lines, and so could a poem of thirteen or fifteen lines ever be considered a sonnet? Despite the inconsistencies that may arise when interpreting a poem in light of its genre, it is helpful to consider how poets view their work in terms of the traditions that precede them. The following brief introductions to poetic genres provide a foundation for understanding their place in the English literary tradition.

Aubade

Aubades are lyric dawn songs, in which the speaker regrets the rising sun because it signals the end of the lovers' rapturous night together. Famous aubades include Troilus's words after consummating his love for Criseyde in Chaucer's *Troilus and Criseyde* (3.1422–91), Robert Browning's "The Year's at the Spring," Philip Larkin's "Aubade," Stevie Smith's "Aubade," and Allen Ginsberg's "My Alba." Shakespeare uses aubades for dramatic effect in his plays, such as the song "Hark, hark, the lark at heaven's gate sings" in *Cymbeline* (2.3.20–26) and Romeo and Juliet's post-coital discussion of nightingales and larks (3.5.1–36). Most aubades sincerely express the speaker's emotional commitment to his or her beloved, but the genre invites a variety of tones, such as in John Donne's "The Sunne Rising," in which the lyric speaker petulantly expresses his discontent with the dawning day: "Busy old foole, unruly sun, / Why dost thou thus, / Through windows, and through curtains call on us?" (*Complete English Poems* lines 1–3). Edith Sitwell takes an insouciant tone in her "Aubade," stating "Jane, Jane, / Tall as a crane, / The morning light creaks down again" (lines 1–3). Aubades are also known as *albas* and *aubes*, although these French terms more correctly refer to Provençal poems featuring these sentiments.

Ballad

Ballads are poetic folk narratives, often songs, that tell a story in verse. They primarily focus on common folk or the lower nobility, with the narrative climaxing on a fateful or tragic event central to the characters' lives. Ballads concentrate on plot over characterization and setting, paying little attention to these latter elements beyond the broadest of strokes. Because ballads arise from folk culture, the original authors are unknown. Instead, as we know the identities of Charles Perrault and Jacob and Wilhelm Grimm for the fairy and folk tales they collected, the anthologizers of various English ballads are remembered for disseminating these tales to a wider audience, including Bishop Percy for his *Reliques of Ancient English Poetry* (1765), Sir Walter Scott for his *Minstrelsy of the Scottish Border* (1802–1803), and Francis James Child for *The English and Scottish Popular Ballads* (1882–1898).

Hundreds and hundreds of ballads survive in the anthologies of Percy, Scott, Child, and others, with the legends of Robin Hood among the most popular of this genre. Additional noteworthy ballads include "Bonny Barbara Allan," which tells of the unrequited love that brings both the lordly Sir John Graeme and his beloved Barbara Allan to their premature graves; "Lord Randall," which tells of a huntsman returning home to his mother after being poisoned by his true love; and "Sir Patrick Spens," which tells of this sailor's tragic death at sea. With their spare storylines, ballads relay the general outline of their plots yet withhold key details. No explanation elucidates why Sir John Graeme initially slights Barbara Allen and thus alienates her affections, or why Lord Randall's beloved poisons him. In "Sir Patrick Spens," it is unclear why the protagonist, "the best sailor / That sails upon the sea," is sent on his mission when the weather assures his death, as Sir Patrick wonders:

> "O wha [who] is this has don this deid [deed],
> This ill deid don to me,
> To send me out this time o' the yeir,
> To sail upon the se!"
> (Child, 2.17–32, stanza 5)

The stanzas of "Sir Patrick Spens," with four lines of alternating iambic tetrameter and trimeter, illustrate the standard meter form of ballads, which is called the *ballad stanza*. Numerous variations alter or expand on this meter.

Although the ballad tradition is rooted in folklore, individual poets also write in this genre, and this tension subverts the purported boundaries between low and high culture. By titling their poetry collection *Lyrical Ballads*, William Wordsworth and Samuel Taylor Coleridge implicitly argue for the artistry of the form. While many of the poems in *Lyrical Ballads* do not conform to the basic parameters of the ballad tradition, Wordsworth's "We Are Seven" and Coleridge's "The Rime of the Ancient Mariner" employ the same stanzaic structure of such folk ballads as "Sir Patrick Spens." Additional ballads by esteemed poets include John Keats's "La Belle Dame sans Merci: A Ballad," which tells the story of a mysteriously cursed knight, and Christina Rossetti's "No, Thank You, John," which depicts a woman rejecting her suitor. Ballads with religious themes include William Butler Yeats's "The Ballad of Father Gilligan," in which the titular priest confronts the despair of death, and Ezra Pound's "Ballad of the Goodly Fere," in which the narrator retells the story of Jesus's crucifixion from Simon the Zealot's perspective while giving him the voice of an English countryman. Langston Hughes wrote several ballads, including "Ballad of the Gypsy," "Ballad of the Fortune Teller," and "Ballad of the Girl Whose Name Is Mud." Despite their many differences, these poems illustrate the utility of the ballad tradition for poets seeking to tell stories reflective of common people, even in Pound's retelling of the Christian gospels.

In the United States, ballads still flourish in the southern Appalachians, a region heavily influenced by British folkways. The ballad tradition is evident in much of the nation's country music, such as in the songs of Loretta Lynn ("One's on the Way"), Johnny Cash ("A Boy Named Sue"), Tammy Wynette ("D-I-V-O-R-C-E"), and Reba McEntire ("Fancy"). Indeed, Dolly Parton, with such ballads as "Kentucky Gambler," "Mountain Angel," "These Old Bones," and "Me and Little Andy," is one of the preeminent balladeers of modern times. A continuing interest in the ballad tradition is also discernable in narrative songs of popular culture, such as The Temptations' "Poppa Was a Rolling Stone," Janis Joplin's "Me and Bobbie McGee," Jeannie C. Reilly's "Harper Valley P.T.A.," and Vicki Lawrence's "The Night the Lights Went Out in Georgia." In popular parlance, the definition of *ballad* is shifting in response to pop music, in which the term refers to a love song or to a song with a slower tempo than the standard quick beats of most modern music.

Dramatic Monologue

A *dramatic monologue* may be thought of as a one-act play with a single speaker. The poet sets a scene in which the speaker expostulates on a subject to a voiceless character (or characters), who serves as the speaker's audience but not his interlocutor; indeed, readers can only know that any secondary characters exist from the speaker's words. As the speaker talks, he reveals deeper complexities of intention and meaning than likely intended. Robert Browning is credited with creating the dramatic monologue with "My Last Duchess," "The Bishop Orders His Tomb," and "Andrea del Sarto," but precursors of this genre are evident in the speeches of the dead souls in Dante's *Inferno*, in John Donne's "The Flea," and in Alexander Pope's "Eloisa to Abelard." Additional noteworthy dramatic monologues include Elizabeth Barrett Browning's "The Runaway Slave at Pilgrim's Point," Alfred, Lord Tennyson's "Ulysses," Rudyard Kipling's "The 'Mary Gloster,'" Ezra Pound's "Hugh Selwyn Mauberley," T. S. Eliot's "The Love Song of J. Alfred Prufrock," Robert Lowell's "Mr. Edwards and the Spider," Langston Hughes's *Madam to You*, and Carol Ann Duffy's "The Dummy."

Alan Sinfield provocatively argues that "all first-person poems where the speaker is indicated not to be the poet [are] dramatic monologues" (42). While some might consider this definition of the term too expansive, through it Sinfield asks readers to consider the ways in which many poetic utterances contain a latent dramatic structure. Indeed, the dividing line between dramatic monologues and lyrics is often slight, as some lyrics have a subtle dramatic quality in which the poet paints the scene provoking the speaker's reveries. In Matthew Arnold's "Dover Beach," the poem opens as the lyric speaker declares, "The sea is calm to-night. / The tide is full, the moon lies fair / Upon the straits" (*Matthew Arnold* lines 1–3). It appears that Arnold's speaker imparts this information to his readers, detailing the setting that sparks his musings. The final stanza, however, addresses a beloved—"Ah, love, let us be true / To one another!" (lines 29–30)—as he then limns the confused state of human perception: "we are here as on a darkling plain / Swept with confused alarms of struggle and flight, / Where ignorant armies clash by night" (lines 35–37). By blurring the borders between lyric reverie and dramatic monologue, Arnold pulls readers deeper into the poem: if the poem is a dramatic monologue, it makes little sense for the speaker to describe the setting to his beloved, who would herself see the sea's calmness. Instead, it is readers who benefit from the speaker's explication of the setting, for they are thereby invited to meditate on this serene image. By combining lyric with dramatic monologue, Arnold's speaker merges his reader with his beloved, creating a dramatic ending to a lyric structure. The dramatic structure of poems may be latent or explicit, and so readers must evaluate how the speaker's words engage them and the characters to whom they are speaking within the poem's fictions.

Elegy

In its most common usage, an elegy is a poem lamenting the death of a beloved. The Greek word *elegos* means "mournful song." Classical Greek elegies were highly structured poems, featuring couplets of dactylic hexameters and pentameters. English elegies, in contrast, do not share a common meter. Of central concern in an elegy, in some instances more important than the loss that provokes the grief serving as the poem's subject, is the psychological condition of the poem's speaker. As Samuel Taylor Coleridge observes, elegies invite readers to assess the poet's understanding of sorrow:

> Elegy is the form of poetry natural to the reflective mind. It *may* treat of any subject, but it must treat of no subject *for itself*; but always and exclusively with reference to the poet himself. As he will feel regret for the past or desire for the future, so sorrow and love become the principal themes of the elegy. Elegy presents every thing as lost and gone, or absent and future.
>
> (*Collected Works*, 2.266; italics in original)

The artistic force of elegies arises in their ability to capture a person's experience of loss and bereavement. In a sense, the poem's subject becomes a means of learning about the speaker's subjectivity through mourning.

Esteemed elegies in the English literary tradition date back to the Anglo-Saxon era and include "The Wanderer," "The Seafarer," and "The Wife's Lament." In these poems, the speakers mourn their exile from their communities, presenting themselves as bereft of fellowship and affection. In *Book of the Duchess* (ca. 1368), Geoffrey Chaucer portrays himself as narrator of this dream vision, in which he encounters the enigmatic Man in Black mourning the loss of his beloved. The anonymously penned *Pearl*, by the same author as the Arthurian romance *Sir Gawain and the Green*

Knight, depicts a dream vision in which a father mourns the loss of his infant daughter, who comforts him and teaches him of her place in heaven. Alfred, Lord Tennyson's *In Memoriam A. H. H.* (1850) is a monumental elegiac achievement. Written over a period of seventeen years to honor his deceased friend Arthur Henry Hallam, Tennyson's poem achieves a deeper realization of life's purpose through loss: "But trust that those we call the dead / Are breathers of an ampler day / For ever nobler ends" (*Selected Poems*, canto 118, lines 5–7). Some elegies, such as Thomas Gray's "Elegy Written in a Country Churchyard," do not focus on a specific deceased loved one but instead meditate on the transience and ephemerality of the human condition. John Donne's elegies, such as "On His Mistress" and "To His Mistress Going to Bed," demonstrate the elasticity of the genre, for they look back to the Latin models of Ovid's *Amores*, which bear the term due to their meter rather than their subject matter and evince a witty rather than a sorrowful tone.

A noted subgenre of elegy is the *pastoral elegy*, in which a shepherd mourns the loss of his beloved. In the "November" section of Edmund Spenser's *The Shepheardes Calendar* (1579), the shepherd Colin mourns the love of his beloved Dido: "*Dido* is gone afore (whose turne shall be the next?) / There liues shee with the blessed Gods in blisse" (*Shorter Poems*, "November," lines 193–94). John Milton's *Lycidas* (1638), which he wrote to commemorate the death of his friend Edward King, is the crowning jewel of this tradition in English literature. In another subgenre of the elegy, poets dedicate poems to their friends and fellow authors, including Thomas Carew's "An Elegy upon the Death of the Dean of Paul's Dr. John Donne"; Percy Shelley's "Adonais," in honor of John Keats; Thomas Hardy's "A Singer Asleep," in honor of Algernon Charles Swinburne; W. H. Auden's "In Memory of W. B. Yeats"; Elizabeth Bishop's "North Haven," in honor of Robert Lowell; and Ted Hughes's "Emily Brontë" (1979), which plaintively ends, "Her death is a baby-cry on the moor" (line 12). As long as humanity suffers loss, poets will write elegies, a genre attuned to the pains of privation and the work of mourning that the lyric speaker must undertake.

Epic

Few poems merit the designation *epic*, and defining examples in the Western literary tradition include *Gilgamesh*; Homer's *The Iliad* and *The Odyssey*; Virgil's *Aeneid*; *Beowulf*; *Song of Roland*; and Milton's *Paradise Lost*. Highly structured narrative poems, epics detail the deeds of a heroic figure of central importance to a people—in the examples above, Gilgamesh, Achilles, Ulysses, Aeneas, Beowulf, Roland, and Adam and Eve respectively. Across a vast setting, these heroes undertake a battle, adventure, or journey, and the results of their experiences affect the future of their people, if not of all humanity. The gods play a part in the unfolding action, favoring some characters while disfavoring others. An epic's elevated tone reflects the seriousness of the events unfolding.

Most epics share numerous structural elements as well. In the invocation to the Muse, the poet requests divine assistance for the daunting task ahead. In *The Faerie Queene* (c. 1600), which blends epic with romance, Edmund Spenser invokes Calliope, the muse of epic poetry, to guide his unfolding narrative:

> Helpe then, ô holy Virgin chiefe of nine,
> Thy weaker Nouice [novice] to performe thy will,
> Lay forth out of thine euerlasting scryne [chest, repository]
> The antique rolles, which there lye hidden still.
>
> (stanza 2)

Following the invocation, most epics pose an epic question to the Muse, such as Milton's query in *Paradise Lost* (1677): "say first what cause / Moved our grand parents in that happy state, / Favored of Heav'n so highly to fall . . . ?" (book 1, lines 28–30). Epics begin *in medias res* (in the middle of things), with preceding events related in flashback. Epic catalogs, which list characters, armies, or other important entities, extend the scope of the narrative by detailing its vast array of actors and their equipment. In *epic similes*, the poet constructs extended comparisons that often appear to digress from the narrative action, yet powerfully develop characterizations or other poetic points.

Beyond this formal definition, the term *epic* denotes a wide range of forms ample in scope yet variable in style and sensibility. Henry Fielding refers to his novel *Joseph Andrews* (1742) as a "comic Epic-Poem in Prose" (4), despite the fact that epics are traditionally neither comic nor written in prose. Alexander Pope's *The Rape of the Lock* (1714) employs the standard features of epic, but in comic form, resulting in the definitive mock-epic of the English literary tradition, as evident in the trivial sentiments expressed in his epic questions:

> Say what strange Motive, Goddess! could compel
> A well-bred lord t'assault a gentle belle?
> Oh say what stranger cause, yet unexplored,
> Could make a gentle belle reject a lord?
> In tasks so bold, can little men engage,
> And in soft bosoms dwell such mighty rage?
>
> (lines 7–12)

Hardly an epic subject of the same level as Ulysses's long voyage home in Homer's *The Odyssey*, *The Rape of the Lock* instead treats a minor social transgression as if it were of earth-shaking importance. Pope's interest in the epic tradition is also evident in his translations of *The Iliad* and *The Odyssey*. George Gordon, Lord Byron, describes his *Don Juan* (c. 1823) as an epic, but, in this instance as well, the ensuing verse does not adhere to the traditional parameters of the genre:

> My poem's epic, and is meant to be
> Divided in twelve books; each book containing,
> With love, and war, a heavy gale at sea,
> A list of ships, and captains, and kings reigning
> New characters; the episodes are three:
> A panorama view of hell's in training,
> After the style of Virgil and of Homer,
> So that my name of Epic's no misnomer.
>
> (canto 1, stanza 200)

Byron's poem, however, with its satiric perspective on its titular lover, is modeled more on medieval chivalric romances than on epic. His allusions to various aspects of the epic tradition—twelve books, a catalog of ships and characters, citations of Virgil and Homer—imbue his poem with an epic gravitas that Don Juan's rakish adventures undercut, thus building an ironic subtext throughout. Fielding's, Pope's, and Byron's "epics" exemplify both the strictures and the suppleness of the epic tradition, for although their works do not adhere to its standard requirements, they embellish from an epic foundation to create works vast in scope yet comic in tone. Philip Pullman's *His Dark Materials* trilogy unites the epic tradition with fantasy and children's literature, with his protagonists Lyra and Will inversely retelling Milton's *Paradise Lost*. (*For the meaning of "epic," in film terminology, see pp. 199–201.*)

Epithalamion

Epithalamia celebrate weddings. Their typical features include praise of the bride and her beauty, a description of the marriage ceremony, an account of the marriage feast, and anticipation of the spouses' union. Edmund Spenser's *Epithalamion* (1595), which he wrote for his bride Elizabeth Boyle, exemplifies this genre in the English tradition. In it, the speaker beseeches night to hide him and his beloved—"Spread thy broad wing ouer my loue and me, / That no man may vs see, / And in thy sable mantle vs enwrap" (*Shorter Poems* lines 319–21)—a delicate phrasing requesting privacy for the pleasures of consummation. In "Epithalamion Made at Lincolnes Inne," John Donne urges the bride to leave her bed for the last time as a virgin and to anticipate union with her spouse:

The sun-beams in the east are spread,
Leave, leave, fair Bride, your solitary bed,
   No more shall you return to it alone,
It nurseth sadness, and your body's print,
Like to a grave, the yielding down doth dint;
      You and your other you meet there anon;
      Put forth, put forth that warm balm-breathing thigh,
Which when next time you in these sheets will smother
    There it must meet another,
          Which never was, but must be, oft, more nigh;
Come glad from thence, go gladder than you came,
To day put on perfection, and a woman's name.
          (*Complete English Poems* lines 1–12)

Donne also wrote "An Epithalamion, or Marriage Song on the Lady Elizabeth and Count Palatine Being Married on St. Valentine's Day." Other notable epithalamia include Hymen's Song in Shakespeare's *As You Like It* as Rosalind and Orlando, Celia and Oliver, and Audrey and Touchstone marry (5.4.141–46), Ben Jonson's epithalamion concluding his *Masque of Hymen*, and Robert Herrick's "An Epithalamium to Sir Thomas Southwell and His Lady." In a surprising twist to the genre, Gerard Manley Hopkins's "Epithalamion" reimagines the form as a song of praise to nature. John Suckling's "A Ballad upon a Wedding" parodies the epithalamion in its depiction of the marriage of commoners, and e e cummings' "Epithalamion" updates the form by celebrating the perpetual rejuvenation of earth and nature.

Lyric

A *lyric* expresses the subjective musings of its first-person speaker, inviting readers to ponder the perceptions and emotions expressed. The word *lyric* derives from the Greek word for *lyre*, which indicates that the earliest lyrics were performed with musical accompaniment. (This aspect of the word's derivation is also evident in its contemporary usage referring to song lyrics.) Lyric poets typically write shorter verses, although some poets extend their length significantly. In contrast to narrative verse, a lyric typically describes a state of mind rather than an action, as Felix Schelling summarizes: "dramatic poetry is dynamic; lyric poetry is static. Hence the simplicity, the brevity, and the intensity of the finest lyrical poetry" (2). Commenting on the static nature of lyric verse, Northrop Frye similarly observes, "The private poem often takes off from something that blocks normal activity, something a poet has to write poetry about instead of carrying on with ordinary experience" ("Approaching" 32). From this perspective, lyrics transcend history and the passage of time, yet they also respond to the circumstances necessitating that their speakers unload their burdens through poetry.

Lyrics often blur the distinction between the poet and the poem's speaker, particularly when the author's autobiography coincides with the feelings expressed in the poem. Poems such as Anne Finch, Countess of Winchilsea's "A Nocturnal Reverie" (1713) exemplify the play of the lyric voice, as she establishes a setting familiar to anyone facing a sleepless night:

> In such a *Night*, when every louder Wind
> Is to its distant Cavern safe confin'd;
> And only gentle *Zephyr* fans his wings,
> And lonely *Philomel* [nightingale], still waking, sings.
>
> (lines 1–4)

Attuned to the natural world around her, Finch's lyric speaker then muses over the night and her restless thoughts until she concludes:

> In such a *Night* let Me abroad remain,
> Till Morning breaks, and All's confus'd again;
> Our Cares, our Toils, our Clamors are renew'd,
> Or Pleasures, seldom reach'd, again pursu'd.
>
> (lines 47–50)

Finch's lyric speaker could represent Finch herself, but the creation of such a lyric voice also merges the universality of this experience with a potential fictional construct. By mixing the individual with the universal, lyric poets create scenarios with which many readers can readily identify.

In describing her play with lyric voice, Anne Sexton asserts the necessity of mingling fact and fiction: "I use the personal when I am applying a mask to my face . . . I fake it up with the truth" (Brewster 104). By merging fiction with a deeper truth, Sexton outlines the inherent paradox of writing poetry through the figure of an "I" who embodies the poet herself while also representing a fictionalized self necessary for the truth of the poem to cohere. In "Her Kind" (1959), Sexton's lyric speaker imagines herself as a witch—"I have gone out, a possessed witch, / haunting the black air, braver at night"—and she concludes each stanza of the poem by declaring, "I have been her kind" (lines 1–2, 7). A slight discrepancy thus arises in these voices, in that one describes actions she has undertaken while the other sees herself in these actions. In other lyrics, the speaker may be a conventional figure, such as the many disappointed lovers of the sonnet tradition, or the speaker may reflect the poet's play with form by reimagining the identity of the lyric voice. The speaker's identity is key to understanding all lyrics, and so readers must determine how each lyric voice is scripted to unfold a deeper understanding of the poem's tone and themes.

Lyrics pervade the English literary tradition, and it is difficult to name a major poet who did not write a lyric. Furthermore, many common genres of poetry, including aubades, odes, elegies, epithalamions, and sonnets, are lyric in their expression.

Ode

The classical tradition established two models of odes: the Pindaric and the Horatian. In his odes, Pindar (c. 522–443 BCE) praises the winners of Greek athletic contests (including the Olympic games) in elaborate verse celebrating the victor, his family, and his city-state. Pindar's odes consist of stanzas referred to as strophes, antistrophes, and epodes, with these stanzas guiding the movement of the poem's performers: the strophe was recited moving to the left, the antistrophe to the right, and the epode while standing still. The odes of Horace (65–8 BCE) are more meditative and intimate in tone, and they evince a simpler structure of a single stanza form. Both forms of the ode incorporate an elevated style about a serious subject, and the ode is often directed to a specific person in honor of a particular event or experience.

During the Renaissance, as English poets looked to the classical past for inspiration, the ode was rediscovered. Ben Jonson revived this poetic tradition with "To the Immortal Memory and Friendship of That Noble Pair, Sir Lucius Cary and Sir Henry Morison" (1629), in which he retitles strophe, antistrophe, and epode as "the turn," "the counterturn," and "the stand." In "Ode to Himself" (1629), Jonson maintains the trifold stanzaic structure of the ode without explicitly labeling his stanzas. Written in response to some disparaging theatrical reviews, the "Ode to Himself" rebuts his critics:

> Let their fastidious vaine
> Commission of the braine
> Run on, and rage, sweat, censure, and condemn:
> They were not made for thee, lesse thou for them.
> (*Complete Poetry* lines 7–10)

Jonson's ode illustrates the thematic looseness of the form, in which his desire to refute his critics matches his desire to celebrate his dramatic accomplishments. Abraham Cowley further popularized odes in the seventeenth century with such works as "Ode: Of Wit," "The Resurrection," and "To the Royal Society," which loosened the strict requirements of this genre. Frustrated by the freedoms some poets took with this genre, William Congreve criticizes, in his "Discourse on the Pindaric Ode," the use of the term *ode* for poems far removed from the Pindaric model:

> There is nothing more frequent among us, than a sort of Poems intitled Pindarique Odes; pretending to be written in the Imitation of the Manner and Stile of Pindar, and yet I do not know that there is to this Day extant in our Language, one Ode contriv'd after his Model.
> (Heath-Stubbs 49)

While the ode's form has indeed shifted markedly from Pindar's model, English poets have nonetheless achieved works of impressive majesty while reconceiving its form. In particular, the romantic era witnessed a resurgence of interest in odes, including William Wordsworth's "Ode on Intimations of Immortality from Recollections of Early Childhood," Samuel Taylor Coleridge's "Dejection: An Ode," and Percy Shelley's "Ode to the West Wind." The most celebrated odist in the English literary tradition is, without question, John Keats, with his many masterpieces of the genre: "Ode to Psyche," "Ode to a Nightingale," "Ode on a Grecian Urn," "Ode on Melancholy," and "Ode on Indolence." As a whole, these poems merge the poetic spirit of the Pindaric and Horatian models: like the Pindaric, they typically exemplify keen attention to meter and stanza, but, like the Horatian, they are often deeply felt and personal meditations rather than public exclamations.

Pastoral

The Latin word *pastor* translates into Modern English as *shepherd*, and thus it is not surprising to find that shepherds populate pastoral poems. In this genre, poets envision an ideal life of simplicity in the outdoors, with shepherds as the avatars of a wholesome connection to nature. The Greek poet Theocritus created the pastoral form in the third century BCE, with Virgil's *Eclogues* defining the form for the Western literary imagination. In pastoral poems the lyric speaker idealizes the bucolic life of shepherds, thereby implicitly (and sometimes explicitly) criticizing the pressures of urban life. In this respect pastoral poems bespeak an urban fantasy of the countryside, with poets waxing eloquently over the lives of impoverished shepherds.

Christopher Marlowe's "The Passionate Shepherd to His Love" (1599) is the defining pastoral poem of the English tradition. It sings of romance and love while celebrating the beauty of nature:

> Come live with me, and be my love,
> And we will all the pleasures prove
> That valleys, groves, hills and fields,
> Woods, or steepy mountain yields.
>
> And we will sit upon the rocks,
> Seeing the shepherds feed their flocks
> By shallow rivers, to whose falls
> Melodious birds sing madrigals.
>
> And I will make thee beds of roses
> And a thousand fragrant posies,
> A cap of flowers, and a kirtle
> Embroidered all with leaves of myrtle;
>
> A gown made of the finest wool
> Which from our pretty lambs we pull;
> Fair-linèd slippers for the cold,
> With buckles of the purest gold. . . .
>   (*Complete Poems* lines 1–16)

Painting a sensuous picture of the shepherd's devotion to his beloved, Marlowe's poem luxuriates in amatory pleasures. At the same time, the poem presents such an idealized version of love that readers are tempted to overlook its inherent fantasy: shepherds' beloveds do not sport slippers buckled with gold. Pastorals create a fantasy of shepherding life, one that few poets would willingly trade for its reality. Other famous pastorals include Edmund Spenser's *Shepheardes Calendar*, Andrew Marvell's mowing poems "The Mower against Gardens," "Damon the Mower," and "The Mower's Song," Alexander Pope's *Pastorals*, Oliver Goldsmith's "The Deserted Village," James Thomson's *The Seasons*, George Crabbe's *The Village*, and Wordsworth's "Michael: A Pastoral Poem."

Many notable pastorals extend their parameters beyond the lyric form, expanding the range of this genre. The Wakefield Master's *Second Shepherds Play* tells the story of Christ's nativity through the eyes of English shepherds, and Sir Philip Sidney's *Arcadia* unites pastoral themes with romance. Shakespeare's *As You Like It* (1599), in which Rosalind escapes from court intrigues to flirt in a forest with Orlando, combines romantic comedy with pastoral pleasure. As her companion Celia states, as they flee from court, "Now go we in content / To liberty, and not to banishment" (1.3.137–38), which optimistically expresses her hope that life in the forest will prove more liberating than at court. In some ways a silly genre—the shepherding profession is fairly grubby, and so very few people envy its practitioners of their vocation—pastorals speak to a recurring human longing for simplicity over complexity, for nature over civilization, and for the eternal belief that the grass is always greener somewhere close by but not quite here. (*See also* elegy *at p. 118, for a consideration of the pastoral elegy.*)

Romance (also known as Chivalric or Arthurian Romance)

A genre of narrative verse born in the Middle Ages, romances feature a knight on a quest, with this protagonist modeling the chivalric values of bravery, honor, and mercy. He is also an ideal courtly lover, one well-versed in amatory traditions, who fights to bring honor to his beloved and to his lord. The word *romance* originally referred to a poem written in French, which is a descendant of Latin, the language of Rome. Most medieval romances belong to one of four families: the Matter of Britain, which tells of King Arthur and his knights; the Matter of Rome, which tells of figures from the classical tradition; the Matter of France, which tells of Charlemagne and his men; and the Matter of England, which tells of such English heroes as Bevis of Hampton, King Horn, and Athelston. The first great romancer was not British but French: the twelfth-century poet Chrétien de Troyes, with his tales of the questing knights Lancelot, Cligés, Yvain, Erec, and Perceval. Esteemed English romances include *Sir Gawain and the Green Knight*, Chaucer's *Wife of Bath's Tale*, and Tennyson's *Idylls of the King*. The boundary between romance and epic is often slight: Chaucer's *Knight's Tale* and *Troilus and Criseyde*, and

Edmund Spenser's *The Faerie Queene*, play with both traditions, staging stories of adventure and courtship against epic backdrops.

While most early romances were written in poetry, the genre opened to prose accounts as well, including Thomas Malory's encyclopedic *Le Morte D'Arthur* in the fifteenth century and T. H. White's *The Once and Future King* in the twentieth. The term *romance* also designates prose works that are more imaginative and fanciful than standard novels, as evident in Nathaniel Hawthorne's use of the term. In his preface to *The House of the Seven Gables* (1851), Hawthorne explains the difference between romances and novels:

> When a writer calls his work a Romance, it need hardly be observed that he wishes to claim a certain latitude, both as to its fashion and material, which he would not have felt himself entitled to assume, had he professed to be writing a Novel. The latter form of composition is presumed to aim at a very minute fidelity, not merely to the possible, but to the probable and ordinary course of man's experience. The former—while, as a work of art, it must rigidly subject itself to laws, and while it sins unpardonably, so far as it may swerve aside from the truth of the human heart—has fairly a right to present that truth under circumstances, to a greater extent, of the writer's own choosing or creation.
>
> (1)

Mark Twain's satire of medieval romance, *A Connecticut Yankee in King Arthur's Court*, takes the subject matter of a chivalric quest and melds it with Hawthorne's idea of the form. Modern pulp romance novels, such as those published by Harlequin and Mills & Boon, both reveal and obscure their affinities with poetic romances of the past: love remains the narrative's chief focus, but without the emphasis of its chaste, and thus ennobling, spirit.

Sonnet

A subgenre of the lyric, *sonnets* consist of fourteen lines of rhymed iambic pentameter. The basic forms of sonnets are named in joint reference to their country of origin and to the author most associated with them: the Italian/Petrarchan sonnet and the English/Shakespearian sonnet. The Italian/Petrarchan sonnet consists of an octave (eight-line segment) and a sestet (six-line segment), with the octave rhyming *abbaabba* and the sestet rhyming *cdecde* (although such variants as *cddcee* and *cdccdc* are common). Sir Thomas Wyatt the Elder introduced the sonnet tradition to England by translating many of Petrarch's poems. Inspired by Petrarch's Rima 134, Wyatt's "I Find No Peace" (1557) models this form:

I find no peace, and all my war is done.	(a)
I fear and hope, I burn and freeze like ice,	(b)
I fly above the wind, yet can I not arise,	(b)
And naught I have, and all the world I seize on.	(a)
That looseth nor locketh holdeth me in prison.	(a)
And holdeth me not, yet can I scape no wise;	(b)
Nor letteth me live, nor die at my device,	(b)
And yet of death it giveth me occasion.	(a)
Without eyen [eyes] I see, and without tongue I plain.	(c)
I desire to perish, and yet I ask health.	(d)
I love another, and thus I hate myself.	(d)
I feed me in sorrow, and laugh in all my pain;	(c)
Likewise displeaseth me both life and death,	(e)
And my delight is causer of this strife.	(e)

Wyatt's sonnet employs paradoxes to capture the lover's agonies. Frequently, the octave of an Italian/Petrarchan sonnet outlines the lover's troubles and the sestet hints at their resolution, but in this poem Wyatt continues his litany of paradoxes to suggest his troubled state, revealing in the final line that his beloved causes him his pains. By concluding with the off-rhyme of *death* and *strife*, Wyatt encodes a closing note of disharmony, enhancing his treatment of love's discontents.

In contrast to the Italian/Petrarchan sonnet, the English/Shakespearian sonnet consists of three quatrains (four-line segments) and a concluding couplet (two-line segment), such as in the romantic poet Charlotte Smith's "To the Moon" (1789):

Queen of the silver bow!—by thy pale beam,	(a)
Alone and pensive, I delight to stray,	(b)
And watch thy shadow trembling in the stream,	(a)
Or mark the floating clouds that cross thy way.	(b)
And while I gaze, thy mild and placid light	(c)
Sheds a soft calm upon my troubled breast;	(d)
And oft I think—fair planet of the night,	(c)
That in thy orb, the wretched may have rest:	(d)
The sufferers of the earth perhaps may go,	(e)
Released by death—to thy benignant sphere;	(f)
And the sad children of Despair and Woe	(e)
Forget, in thee, their cup of sorrow here.	(f)
Oh! That I soon may reach thy world serene,	(g)
Poor wearied pilgrim—in this toiling scene!	(g)

The three quatrains read like small chapters in the unfolding narrative, with the concluding couplet offering the resolution. By paying attention to the rhyming structure of sonnets, readers discern the subtle interrelationships of their forms and their meanings.

In *sonnet sequences* (also known as *sonnet cycles*), poets reveal an implicit plot as the sonnets progress, allowing readers insight into the changing perceptions of the speaker to his or her subject matter. Noted sonnet sequences include Edmund Spenser's *Amoretti*, Sir Philip Sidney's *Astrophil and Stella*, Mary Wroth's *Pamphilia to Amphilanthus*, Elizabeth Barrett Browning's *Sonnets from the Portuguese*, George Meredith's *Modern Love*, Edna St. Vincent Millay's *Fatal Interview*, and W. H. Auden's *In Time of War*. As the poems of a sonnet sequence progress, readers witness the speaker's shifting sentiments, which may or may not culminate in a clear resolution.

* * *

As this survey of poetic structures and genres attests, poetry is a precise and demanding yet subtle and sympathetic art, in which authors distill the human condition into lyric reveries, narrative encounters, and other such moments, whether episodic or extended. From Shakespeare's sonnets to Keats's odes, from Tennyson's elegy for a friend to Stevie Smith's embrace of death through meditating on the meaning of the simple word "pretty," poets invite readers to see the world through their eyes or through the eyes of their fictional creations. In all instances of such shared vision, poets encourage their readers to see the ruts of human existence as vistas. Perhaps the greatest tribute to the human poetic imagination is that countless poets have written of love and death, of hope and despair, of loss and longing, and of the other banal and almost laughingly trite disappointments of humanity, and yet so much has been said so well, and so much remains still to be said. In "Eating Poetry" (1968), Mark Strand writes, "Ink runs from the corners of my mouth. / There is no happiness like mine. / I have been eating poetry" (lines 1–3)—a sentiment with which all devotees of the poetic arts enthusiastically agree.

Note

1 Herbert's poem is intended to be printed horizontally, not vertically, to capture better the image of wings.

2.2 Prose Fiction

The term *prose fiction* refers to a wide variety of literary forms relating imaginary events. The line between prose and poetry can be slight, for much prose brims with poetic potential; nonetheless, one can distinguish between them easily due to their formatting on a page. Prose in English runs from a text's left to right margins, whereas a poem's lines run according to the poet's meter and phrasings, typically with more white space remaining on the page. These visual cues alert readers to a text's primary identity as poetry or prose.

The realm of prose fiction extends to many subgenres. *Short stories* focus on a few characters, who, given the genre's compressed form, achieve a key, if partial, insight by the narrative's end. The vast scope of *novels* allows for more complex storylines and numerous rich, fully developed characters whose motivations readers come to understand. *Novellas* typically run about one hundred pages and feature deeper complexity than short stories but do not share the expansive scope of novels. Miscellaneous genres of prose fiction include anecdotes, jokes, and parables, which further illustrate that the basic requirements of prose fiction include characters undertaking actions and the ensuing consequences. Also, while the term *prose fiction* denotes the imaginative aspects of this genre, the oxymoronic conflation *nonfiction novel* highlights how some authors employ the narrative strategies of fiction for such forms as memoirs, biographies, and other accounts of real life. Despite the variety of these forms of prose fiction, they share numerous key features uniting them into a coherent subsection of literature, including plot structure, point of view, characters and characterization, setting, theme, and style and tone.

Plot Structure

When someone inquires what a story is about, its readers most often respond by summarizing the plot. The *plot* of a short story or novel entails its sequence of events, which are arranged in a purposeful and deliberate way to demonstrate their causal relationships. In explaining the difference between a story and a plot, English novelist E. M. Forster states:

> We have defined a story as a narrative of events arranged in their time-sequence. A plot is also a narrative of events, the emphasis falling on causality. "The king died and then the queen died," is a story. "The king died, and then the queen died of grief," is a plot. The time-sequence is preserved, but the sense of causality overshadows it. . . . Consider the death of the queen. If it is in a story we say "and then?" If it is in a plot we ask "why?"
>
> (*Aspects of the Novel* 86)

Any sequence of events might constitute a story, but a plot depends on causality and interconnection, with various narrative elements falling into their proper place. Plots require motivations, which introduce issues of character psychology into much narrative fiction.

In many literary works, authors present the events of their plot chronologically, which guides readers through the story in a linear fashion. Franz Kafka's novella *The Metamorphosis* (1915) begins as follows:

> When Gregor Samsa woke up one morning from unsettling dreams, he found himself changed in his bed into a monstrous vermin. He was lying on his back as hard as armor plate, and when he lifted his head a little, he saw his vaulted brown belly, sectioned by arch-shaped ribs, to whose dome the cover, about to slide off completely, could barely cling.
>
> (3)

Readers enter this story at its beginning, at the moment when Gregor finds himself transformed into a bug. The novella then details in chronological order Gregor's struggles to remain a member of his family once they discover that he is no longer recognizably human. The opening moment sparks a series of events to follow, and readers move through Gregor's life and experiences along with him. A simple yet effective plot structure, chronology guides readers from beginning to end as the story unfolds.

While chronology structures many narratives, some prose fiction reorders its events, beginning in the middle of the story or near its end. Emily Brontë's *Wuthering Heights* (1847) opens with the arrival of Lockwood at Wuthering Heights, the home of Heathcliff. Lockwood, who is renting Thrushcross Grange from Heathcliff, finds the inhabitants of Wuthering Heights peculiar, and, upon returning to his rental home, his housekeeper relays the tragic story of Heathcliff and his family. This novel uses a *frame tale* as its primary structure. A frame tale encompasses another story, providing two (and sometimes more) layers of the narrative. By creating a "present time" situation in the frame—Lockwood's rental of Thrushcross Grange as the novel begins—*Wuthering Heights* invites readers to learn about the novel's past events along with Lockwood. Thus, Brontë relies on several characters to fill in details about Heathcliff's tormented love for Catherine. Many narratives also use *flashbacks*, in which narrators or characters recall past events, those preceding the start of the plot. In many cases, authors introduce flashbacks through a device such as a character's memory being jogged by a conversation, sensory experience, or a chance element they encounter. In her *Harry Potter* series, J. K. Rowling employs the plot device of the pensieve, a magical device through which Dumbledore allows Harry to witness events prior to his birth. With this ingenious type of flashback, Rowling can stage key plot points rather than simply summarizing them.

Most fictional plots also rely on a particular event or sets of events that create *narrative conflict*, with this conflict serving as the plot's motivating factor. Conflict can result from either external or internal causes. *External conflicts* arise when the central character struggles with another character, an event, or some other outside force. *Internal conflicts* occur when the struggle exists inside the protagonist, such as a psychological conflict between a character's desires and morality. Internal and external conflicts may merge in a single plot, such as in Flannery O'Connor's "A Good Man Is Hard to Find" (1953). The story tells of the Grandmother's external conflict with the Misfit, a criminal who murders her family, but O'Connor explores more deeply the internal conflict that the Grandmother experiences over her self-satisfaction and spiritual complacency. O'Connor's darkly comic story concludes with the Misfit declaring of the Grandmother, "She would of been a good woman . . . if it had been somebody there to shoot her every minute of her life" (133), with his words pointing to her need to confront and overcome her spiritual sloth. Conflict provides the narrative's main tension, which sparks the story and keeps it moving forward, creating suspense along the way. Readers who recognize the central conflicts in literary works can better anticipate how they will unfold.

The plots of many fictional texts progress through a series of stages. In *Technique of the Drama* (1863), the literary critic Gustav Freytag developed a structure for analyzing plot known today as Freytag's Pyramid. Although designed to describe the structure of drama, this framework applies to novels, short stories, and other forms of prose fiction as well. Freytag identifies five stages in the development of plots: (1) introduction (or exposition), (2) rising action (or complication), (3) climax, (4) falling action (or return), and (5) catastrophe (or dénouement) (114–40). Narratives employ these stages in unique ways, with their inherent versatility allowing for endless permutations. In the first stage, the introduction, the author divulges foundational information, such as the identity of the central characters, the time and location of the action, and other aspects of the narrative's general context. After the introduction, as Freytag argues, the "excited action" is presented (121). This complication propels the remainder of the plot. In a romantic story, this moment might occur when a couple meets for the first time; in a mystery, it might be when a crime is committed. Whatever the event or set of events, the plot then moves forward through the rising action. Throughout this part of the narrative, readers learn more about the characters' personalities and objectives, and the events build on one another and lead to the climax. The *climax* serves as the pivotal point in a story's development, in which events build to a crisis and turning point. Following this moment, the literary work relates the falling action or reversal, in which the intensity of the narrative subsides and proceeds to its conclusion. The final stage, the catastrophe or dénouement, provides closure and resolution. This moment can be marked by joy, pain, ambivalence, or any other emotion that marks the plot's ending. Although these stages can be applied to many literary works, not all conform equally. Even when literary narratives evince such a structure, the amount of focus given to each stage might vary greatly. Some literary works set the climax in their middle, while others place it near the end. Some stories focus mostly on the falling action, while others might exclude it altogether.

Edgar Allan Poe's "The Cask of Amontillado" (1846) follows these traditional stages of plot, although the story ends almost immediately after the climax, mostly ignoring the falling action and encapsulating the dénouement into a mere two sentences. The story opens as the narrator, Montresor, expresses his anger toward Fortunato for past wrongs and states his desire for revenge. The introduction also establishes the story's setting in Italy and alerts readers to Fortunato's passion for fine wine. The complication that sets off the rising action occurs when the narrator meets Fortunato during a festival, when Fortunato is rather drunk. Montresor invites Fortunato to sample a fine cask of Amontillado sherry to determine its authenticity. By enticing the inebriated Fortunato away from the festival, Montresor creates the necessary motivation for the remainder of the action. While wandering through the vaults beneath his home, Montresor plies Fortunato with more wine to weaken his awareness and strength. The climax occurs when Montresor chains Fortunato in a small crypt and walls him in, ignoring Fortunato's clanking chains and screams. Poe needs only two sentences to detail the story's falling action and dénouement, in which he informs his reader that no one has found Fortunato's bones in the fifty years since the murder.

Some literary works, particularly novels, employ multiple or complex plots rather than a single and easily identifiable one. Others may be structured in a largely episodic fashion without providing obviously connected events. Recognizing the causal relationships among events in a work of prose fiction gives readers opportunities to analyze the development of ideas, meanings, and characters so that they better understand how the author unites these elements into a coherent whole. Also, readers should look for moments when narratives overlook any internal inconsistencies, as such holes in plots offer fertile material for considering how they construct multiple or contradictory meanings.

Point of View

Every novel or short story is told from a particular perspective or *point of view*. This point of view establishes a vantage point from which the author presents actions, characters, and settings, and so a story's point of view profoundly influences the way that readers understand the narrative and the significance of events. The two most common points of view are *third-person narration* and *first-person narration*. In third-person narration, the narrator exists outside of the story's actions and relates the events to readers, referring to the characters by their names or by third-person pronouns such as "he" and "she." In contrast, first-person narrations unfold from the perspective of a character involved in the story's action, and the narrator uses "I" when relating its events as he or she witnesses them. Regardless of whether a narrator stands outside of the story's action or participates in it, the narrator enjoys a wide range of knowledge or biases that affect how readers experience the story.

Many third-person narratives use an *omniscient point of view*. In these works, the narrator knows everything possible about the characters and events and shares information regarding the characters' private thoughts and feelings, their histories, and the places and events presented in the text. Omniscient narrators can sometimes be intrusive, subtly encouraging readers to accept particular interpretations of events, or they may be virtually invisible, relaying events objectively without interjecting opinions. Gabriel García Márquez begins his *Love in the Time of Cholera* (1985) with his omniscient third-person narrator's observations: "It was inevitable: the scent of bitter almonds always reminded him of the fate of unrequited love. Dr. Juvenal Urbino noticed it as soon as he entered the still darkened house where he had hurried on an urgent call to attend a case that for him had lost all urgency many years before" (3). One might reasonably ask, who is this disembodied voice that knows Dr. Urbino so intimately that he recognizes that the mere scent of almonds inevitably leads Urbino to ponder his lost loves? Asking such a question, however, undermines the *suspension of disbelief* necessary to enjoy much fiction. Readers must accept that, in many instances, narrators have access to information that elevates them into omniscience within the narrative's structure.

In a *limited omniscient point of view*, the narrator enjoys complete knowledge about one character (or sometimes several) but not about everyone. With this structure of narration, readers gain access to an individual character's feelings and experiences, seeing the world through his or her perspective. Such an approach allows for a clear focus on certain characters while other characters' motivations remain more opaque. In "Young Goodman Brown" (1835), Nathaniel Hawthorne uses a third-person limited omniscient point of view in telling the story of Brown's journey into a forest and the terrifying ceremony that he witnesses there. At the story's climax, the narrator reports only Brown's perspective, as he cries out to his wife, allegorically named "Faith," who is apparently taking part in a devilish ritual: "'Faith! Faith!' cried the husband, 'look up to heaven, and resist the wicked one.' Whether Faith obeyed, he knew not. Hardly had he spoken when he found himself amid calm night and solitude, listening to a roar of the wind which died heavily away through the forest" (*Nathaniel Hawthorne's Tales* 95).

Because Hawthorne's narrator focuses specifically on Brown, readers better understand his fear and spiritual crisis without creating conflicting impressions of the events. Also, by assuming Brown's viewpoint while recognizing its limitations, the narrator imbues the story with mystery. If Hawthorne's narrator were sufficiently omniscient to gauge all of the characters' motivations, he might explain Faith's thoughts during this portentous encounter. Because he does not do so, however, readers are left to grapple with the perplexing events, which resist a tidy moral conclusion.

In some works of prose fiction, the narrative method of *stream of consciousness* grants readers personal access to individual characters through their thought processes. Stream of consciousness relays the thoughts filtering through a character's mind, without apparent editing or interpretation. Critics trace the roots of stream of consciousness to such narratives as Laurence Sterne's *Tristam Shandy* (1759), Edgar Allan Poe's "The Tell-Tale Heart" (1843), and Henry James's *The Portrait of a Lady* (1881); it became a significant element of modern fiction during the early twentieth century when authors such as James Joyce and William Faulkner used it powerfully in their novels. In *To the Lighthouse* (1927), Virginia Woolf uses stream of consciousness to reveal her characters' thoughts as they spend time together at a summer house. As Mrs. Ramsay assists her daughter Rose with jewelry before dinner, the narrator discloses the mother's thoughts:

> [Rose] had some hidden reason of her own for attaching great importance to this choosing what her mother was to wear. What was the reason, Mrs. Ramsay wondered, standing still to let her clasp the necklace she had chosen, divining, through her own past, some deep, some buried, some quite speechless feeling that one had for one's mother at Rose's age. Like all feelings felt for oneself, Mrs. Ramsay thought, it made one sad. It was so inadequate, what one could give in return; and what Rose felt was quite out of proportion to anything she actually was. And Rose would grow up; and Rose would suffer, she supposed, with these deep feelings.
>
> (81)

The narrator enters into the immediate perceptions of Mrs. Ramsay as she moves from thinking about the present moment to pondering her daughter's opinion of her and then to considering Rose's future. Readers follow this thought process, as Mrs. Ramsay shares herself and her concerns through these musings.

In contrast to third-person points of view, first-person narrators use "I" to refer to themselves, and authors limit their narration to the information these characters would know. The first-person narrator can be a novel's central character, such as in Charles Dickens's *David Copperfield* (1850), which famously begins:

Whether I shall turn out to be the hero of my own life, or whether
that station will be held by anybody else, these pages must show. To
begin my life with the beginning of my life, I record that I was born
(as I have been informed and believe) on a Friday, at twelve o'clock at
night. It was remarked that the clock began to strike, and I began to cry,
simultaneously.

(1)

In this passage Dickens also hints at the difficulties of first-person narration
for authors, as David tells readers of events during his birth that he could not
possibly remember; Dickens thus explains that his protagonist reports these
details through other people's accounts. A first-person narrator can also be
a character who participates in a narrative's events but is not its focus, such
as Nick Carraway in F. Scott Fitzgerald's *The Great Gatsby* (1925). In some
works, the narrator might be entirely uninvolved in the story's central events,
as in Joseph Conrad's *Heart of Darkness* (1899), in which a first-person narrator gives way to the character Marlow, who then tells the ensuing narrative
in his own first-person narration. First-person point of view draws readers
into a relationship with the narrator, allowing them to feel the character's
emotions and to experience the same events as if alongside him. In a particularly striking use of first-person narration, Paul Auster opens his novel
Leviathan (1992) with FBI agents arriving at the home of the narrator, Peter
Aaron. When they interrogate him about a recent terrorist attack committed
by a friend, Aaron cannot fully assess his predicament because he knows only
his own experience:

I'm still their only lead, after all, and if they go on the assumption that I
lied to them, then they're not about to forget me. Beyond that, I haven't
the vaguest notion of what they're thinking. It seems unlikely that they
consider me a terrorist, but I say that only because I know I'm not. They
know nothing, and therefore they could be working on that premise,
furiously searching for something that would link me to the bomb that
went off in Wisconsin last week.

(8)

Such uncertainty about characters other than the narrator allows first-person
points of view to create conflict and suspense. Readers must, by necessity,
share the gaps in the narration that reflect the narrator's limited understanding of events.

First-person narration often employs *unreliable narrators*, whose presentation and interpretation of events cannot be fully trusted. Many reasons
might account for such unreliability: a narrator might suffer from mental illness, forgetfulness, or bias. Kazuo Ishiguro's *The Remains of the Day* (1989)
is narrated by Mr. Stevens, a butler driving across England to Cornwall to

meet with Miss Kenton, a former housekeeper with whom he worked at Darlington Hall. As the narrative progresses, it becomes increasingly clear, despite his protests otherwise, that Mr. Stevens loves Miss Kenton, that he desperately hopes she will return to Darlington Hall with him, and that his former employer, whom he reveres as a man of deep kindness and perception, sympathized with the Nazis during World War II. Readers see the world through Mr. Stevens's eyes, but his guarded descriptions of past events do not accurately convey them or his own feelings about them. Indeed, Mr. Stevens frequently corrects himself, and Ishiguro captures his protagonist's vacillations with such phrases as "But now that I think further about it" and "In fact, now that I come to think of it" (60) to alert readers that his narrator's memories do not depict the past accurately. By using this unreliable narrator, Ishiguro challenges readers to piece together the true contours of Stevens's life, rather than to accept the façade he mounts for the public.

While most stories and novels use either first- or third-person narration, authors occasionally use *second-person narration*. In telling a story to a "you," the narrator may address the reader, a character in the story or novel, the narrator herself, or the "you" may be undefined. Second-person point of view is commonly found in children's "choose your own adventure" stories, in which "you" turn to one page if "you" decide to fight a dragon but to a different page if "you" decide to flee. Second-person point of view also appears in some postmodern novels, those that draw attention to their literary devices. Italo Calvino uses second-person narration in *If on a Winter's Night a Traveler* (1979), in which he intersperses unrelated stories amid chapters focusing on the hunt for and creation of a particular book called *If on a Winter's Night a Traveler*. The novel opens as follows:

> You are about to begin reading Italo Calvino's new novel, *If on a winter's night a traveler*. Relax. Concentrate. Dispel every other thought. Let the world around you fade. Best to close the door: the TV is always on in the next room. Tell the others right away, "No, I don't want to watch TV!" Raise your voice—they won't hear you otherwise—"I'm reading! I don't want to be disturbed!" Maybe they haven't heard you, with all that racket. Speak louder, yell: "I'm beginning to read Italo Calvino's new novel!" Or if you prefer, don't say anything; just hope they'll leave you alone.
>
> (3)

With this second-person narration, Calvino directly addresses and draws in readers, as if they too populated the pages of his novel. While such an approach can feel somewhat jarring because it is used so infrequently, it can also create a feeling of intimacy for readers who associate themselves with the events of the unfolding narrative.

With each type of narration, authors face benefits and liabilities. Third-person narration allows for omniscience, so that narrators can explain each character's thoughts and feelings, whereas first-person narration puts readers in the position of the narrator. Second-person narration sports engaging and quirky charms, yet, at this stage of its development, it often feels forced and unnatural. After centuries in which first- and third-person narrations have reigned preeminent, the novelty of second-person narration still catches many readers by surprise.

Characters and Characterization

The charisma of various characters deeply affects readers' enjoyment of a narrative. To fully understand the plot and themes of a literary text, readers must perceive the reasons behind characters' actions, and, even if readers do not sympathize with their choices, they must understand what moves them to act as they do. In simple terms, a *character* refers to any individual—be it human, animal, or otherwise—that undertakes actions depicted in a narrative. The central or most important character serves as the *protagonist*. Most of the action of a literary work revolves around the protagonist, and readers often identify or sympathize with this character. Frequently, the protagonist's name serves as the title of a story or novel, such as with Jane Austen's *Emma*, Edith Wharton's *Ethan Frome*, and Virginia Woolf's *Mrs. Dalloway*. Many of Charles Dickens's novels are titled for their eponymous characters: *Oliver Twist, Martin Chuzzlewit, Nicholas Nickleby, David Copperfield*, and *Barnaby Rudge*. Regardless of the title, readers identify the protagonist through the author's focus on this character. Literary works may also have an *antagonist*, a character (or characters) against whom the protagonist struggles. Although antagonists are often exciting characters—such as Dickens's Madame Defarge in *A Tale of Two Cities*—not all literary works include them; instead, other circumstances, psychological conditions, or environments can serve as the central struggle for the protagonist to overcome.

Authors construct readers' understanding of their characters through several types of literary devices, including how characters are described, how they behave, and how they speak. When providing *characterization through description*, a narrator paints a character's appearance in words: the person's age, size, clothing, and hair color, among many other such factors, give insight into such matters as his health and economic status, or even his sense of style. In addition, a character's movements and facial expressions divulge her personality and psychological state. In *Ruth Hall* (1855), Fanny Fern describes how her protagonist has metamorphosed from an "ugly duckling" into a beauty:

> Simple child! She was unconscious that, in the freedom of that atmosphere where a "prophet out of his own country is honored," her lithe form had rounded into symmetry and grace, her slow step had become light and elastic, her eye bright, her smile winning, and her voice soft and melodious.

(15)

Fern describes Ruth not as the character sees herself, but as other characters, and thus as readers, view her. Through this disjunction between Ruth's
self-perception and her readily apparent beauty, readers also learn of her
modesty. Such details about a character's appearance contribute to our
understanding of who a character is and how that person fits into a story.

Readers also learn about characters by *characterization through action.*
How does a character behave? What does he do? How does she treat her
family? Is he assertive or passive, responsive or quiet? What actions does
she take that affect others? What sense of personal responsibility does he
take for these actions? By analyzing characters' actions, readers learn about
their motivations and personalities, which allows them to make sense of the
characters' pasts and to anticipate future behavior. In Monica Sone's *Nisei
Daughter* (1953), a memoir of her life in Seattle and her internment in a
World War II relocation camp, she recalls a humorous encounter with her
cousin Yoshiye:

> When Aunt suggested to Yoshiye that she give one of her pretty kimonos
> to me, Yoshiye refused. Her face white with alarm, she said, "But I don't
> want to give any of them away."
>
> Aunt Itoi look unhappy, "I insist you give one to your cousin right
> now."
>
> Yoshiye fled from the room weeping and stayed out of sight the rest
> of the day.
>
> (93)

Yoshiye's behavior illustrates her greed better than a simple description of
her social status could convey. Furthermore, characterization through action
allows authors opportunities to escalate narrative tension, for this technique
also involves, as in the example above, characterization through interaction, in which readers learn about the personalities of the various characters
involved in a particular exchange.

The words that characters speak also guide readers' interpretations. With
characterization through dialogue, readers learn about the relationships
among characters, their emotional reactions, what they think, and how they
fit into their fictional world. Readers must be attentive to characters' words,
for the simple reason that the ideas and opinions they express tell readers
their beliefs. Their tone of voice and inflections reveal additional information. Does a character seem to hold back, to be reticent? What might that
imply about her feelings? Is a character overflowing with words, demonstrating nervousness or excitement? Also, a character's accent or dialect indicates where he is from and his (dis)similarity to other characters, and his
vocabulary reveals such aspects as his education and profession. In Arthur
Conan Doyle's *A Study in Scarlet* (1887), Dr. Watson, stunned by Sherlock
Holmes's ability to deduce the occupation of a stranger on the street, asks
Holmes how he determined this information:

"How in the world did you deduce that?" I asked.

"Deduce what?" said he, petulantly.

"Why, that he was a retired sergeant of Marines."

"I have no time for trifles," he answered, brusquely; then with a smile: "Excuse my rudeness. You broke the thread of my thoughts; but perhaps it is as well. So you actually were not able to see that that man was a sergeant of Marines?"

"No, indeed."

"It was easier to know it than to explain why I know it. If you were asked to prove that two and two made four, you might find some difficulty, and yet you are quite sure of the fact."

(23)

In this brief exchange between Watson and Holmes, readers observe several aspects of their characters. Both men appear educated, as evidenced by their clear speech and complete sentences. Watson's words reveal his curiosity and openness. He readily acknowledges his inability to recognize the passerby as ex-military, wanting to know more about Holmes's deductive powers. Holmes displays an interesting combination of superiority and good breeding. He patronizes Watson for failing to realize the sergeant's past employment and responds abruptly when interrupted, but he recognizes that polite society expects certain pleasantries, and so he offers a brief apology. Not just a brilliant mind, Holmes is also a rude and self-indulgent man. Dialogue reveals characters to readers, with their words exposing their personalities and sometimes their duplicities. To this end, readers must always be alert for ironies, for, if a character says one thing but means another, they must peer below the surface meaning to catch the truth underneath.

Ultimately, the combination of these methods—characterizations through description, action, and dialogue—gives readers a rich understanding of characters and their complexities. By pulling together observations and analyzing them in detail, readers perceive the depth and contradictions of characters, just as occurs in real life.

Setting

All fiction involves characters moving through a plot in a *setting*—the specific locations and times of the narrative action. In some literary works, the setting may play a relatively minor role, serving mostly as a backdrop, but more often the setting plays a vital role for understanding a fictional world. For readers to fully imagine the events in a literary work, the setting should be vibrant and detailed, providing an immersive visual experience. At the most basic level, settings establish a background for events to help readers visualize them, as they also create an appropriate mood or atmosphere. In *The Mambo Kings Play Songs of Love* (1989), Oscar Hijuelos titled his fattest chapters "In the Hotel Splendour, 1980" and "Sometime Later in the Night in the Hotel Splendour," which notifies readers of the central importance of this location. The first of these chapters begins:

> Nearly twenty-five years ago after he and his brother had appeared on the *I Love Lucy* show, Cesar Castillo suffered in the terrible heat of a summer's night and poured himself another drink. He was in a room in the Hotel Splendour on 125 Street and Lenox Avenue, not far from the narrow stairway that led up to the recording studios of Orchestra Records, where his group, the Mambo Kings, made their fifteen black brittle 78s. In fact, it could have been the very room in which he had once bedded down a luscious and long-legged party girl by the name of Vanna Vane, Miss Mambo for the month of June 1954.
>
> (11)

Even if one knows little about the geography of New York City, one can conclude that, if Cesar suffers due to the "terrible heat," the hotel room is not air-conditioned, and thus that the Hotel Splendour's name ironically comments on its actuality. Hijuelos also establishes the novel's temporal setting: the year is 1980, but more importantly, it is a quarter-century after Cesar's heyday, and now he can only reminisce over his sexual conquests of the past—which may or may not have taken place in his current location.

A setting can also serve as the antagonist in prose fiction, providing the main conflict for the protagonist through a physical challenge that must be overcome. In "To Build a Fire" (1908), Jack London tells the story of a man walking the Yukon Trail to meet some friends. Along the way, he falls through ice. His lower body soaked in frigid water, he must light a fire to prevent frostbite, but after igniting it, snow and other elements extinguish it, resulting ultimately in his death. In this story, the weather—severe cold, ice, and snow—becomes more than simply the background for his experience. It is the source of the protagonist's conflict and vital to the story's plot.

Setting can also enhance characterization. In "The Yellow Wall-paper" (1892), Charlotte Perkins Gilman narrates the story of a woman who is prescribed rest while recovering after childbirth. Her husband, a doctor, believes a quiet life, without social interaction or intellectual stimulation, will assist her convalescence. While staying in a bleak room with bars on the windows, a bed nailed to the floor, and old, peeling, yellow wallpaper, the woman begins to believe that another woman, trapped inside the wallpaper, is struggling to emerge. As she falls into insanity, the room reflects her mental state and the woman in the wallpaper symbolizes her feelings of isolation. As she observes,

> On a pattern like this, by daylight, there is a lack of sequence, a defiance of law, that is a constant irritant to a normal mind.

The color is hideous enough, and unreliable enough, and infuriating enough, but the pattern is torturing. . . .

The outside pattern is a florid arabesque, reminding one of a fungus. If you can imagine a toadstool in joints, an interminable string of toadstools, budding and sprouting in endless convolutions—why, that is something like it.

(12)

The narrator's depiction of the revolting wallpaper parallels the way she feels toward her life: that it is controlled, miserable, and desperate. Readers learn about her emotional state, including her declining mental health, through the way she sees the room. Beyond helping readers to understand characters, setting illuminates themes in literary texts. The confined room and ugly wallpaper in Gilman's story also evince its larger concern: women's frustrations due to their limited freedoms in the late nineteenth century, in which they are metaphorically locked inside confining spaces.

Apart from the physical locations where stories occur, settings also include the time of the unfolding events. Time can refer to a period as narrow as the time of day, or it can focus more on a season, or even an era, such as the Middle Ages or the American Revolutionary War. Events taking place during a stormy winter evening, rather than a clear summer day, may carry with them a cozier, or perhaps a more ominous, feeling. Understanding when events take place also allows readers to better understand their social significance. A story depicting an unmarried woman giving birth bears vastly different meanings if the setting is during the late 1700s (as in George Eliot's *Adam Bede*, 1859) or the late 1900s (as in Ellen Gilchrist's *The Annunciation*, 1983). Careful readers must be attentive to all facets of setting, analyzing the ways in which it sheds light on the characters, the action, and the themes of a literary work.

Theme

The *theme* puts forth the message or deeper meaning of a fictional work; it reveals the author's impressions or ideas about the events depicted in the narrative. The subject of a literary work might be violence or love or growing up, but the theme would be the author's assertion about that idea: violence cannot solve conflict; romantic love fades quickly; growing up entails enduring a series of struggles. When identifying themes, readers unite their understanding of other aspects of literary analysis, including plot, characterization, and setting, to create a larger, comprehensive understanding of the work as a whole. Whereas a short story might express one primary theme, a novel might include several. By reviewing the work and looking for connections among its various structural elements and its narrative contents, readers can discover themes developed through the narrative.

Characters offer numerous clues for determining theme. By paying attention to how characters develop, to how their ideas change, and to how they see their world, a work's themes become evident. Similarly, the narrator of the work, even if not a character, guides readers to major themes. Sometimes titles of literary works hint at their themes, such as Bret Easton Ellis's *Less Than Zero* (1985), which focuses on a group of college-age friends in Los Angeles. For these young people, who spend their days using drugs and partying, life carries no significance. In essence, their lives mean "less than zero." Another such example is Harper Lee's *To Kill a Mockingbird* (1960), in which the title distills her thematic conviction that one should never purposefully harm another creature, particularly those that do no harm to others.

Motifs also guide readers to a literary work's most important themes. Motifs consist of recurring characters, objects, ideas, or other elements, and by noticing the repetition of particular motifs, readers can connect them to the theme of a work. In Julian Barnes's *A History of the World in 10½ Chapters* (1989), the image of Noah's Ark and the idea of history act as recurring motifs. Noah's Ark ties together the book's chapters, which include a retelling of the Noah story from the perspective of a woodworm, a story of a woman's trek up Mount Ararat in 1840 as she searches for the Ark's remains, and the hijacking of a cruise ship by political extremists who kill their hostages two by two (or two per hour). Barnes also includes the motif of history as he rewrites a judicial record from 1520 and describes the historical shipwreck that inspired Théodore Géricault's painting *The Raft of the Medusa* (1818–19). Among the possible themes for Barnes's novel is that history depends entirely on who tells a story, a theme reinforced by its title; thus, multiple histories, not just one, must be confronted when determining the truth of events.

Although many themes of a literary work express a moral stance, they need not be didactic in their aims. Often the theme of a work does not present an idea as right or wrong but instead allows readers to contemplate a position and to see the world from a new perspective. Moreover, to be an effective reader, it is important to recognize that literary works may encode themes with which readers may not agree. Whatever one's personal response to a book, its themes ask readers to consider new perspectives and their relationship to the narrative's events.

Style and Tone

Although readers usually pay more attention to a literary work's plot and characters, its style leaves a lasting impression and elevates a simple story into art. The style of prose fiction entails the language the author employs to narrate events in a particularly memorable way. Authors guide and control readers through their creative attention to language. To maintain a particular style, writers employ a variety of techniques, including diction, syntax, figurative language, symbolism, and allegory. Each choice impresses readers uniquely, thereby also affecting the tone of a work.

Diction refers to the selection of specific words in a literary text. Words give readers insight into characters' behaviors, socioeconomic backgrounds, educational levels, and work experiences, especially when used in their dialogue. The diction used in narration also informs readers about the narrator's or author's attitude toward the characters and events described. When analyzing diction, readers should consider the *denotative* and *connotative* meanings of words. A word's denotative meaning corresponds to its dictionary definition, but its connotative meaning entails what it suggests or implies in a particular usage. When Julian Barnes describes a group of terrorists hijacking a cruise ship in *A History of the World in 10½ Chapters*, he introduces them with the neutral term *visitors*: "While the passengers were ashore the *Santa Euphemia* took on fuel, vegetables, meat, and more wine. It also took on some visitors, although this did not become apparent until the following morning" (39). The term *visitors* indicates individuals with whom one might enjoy a casual acquaintance: denoting neither close friends nor adversaries, *visitors* implies neutrality. In introducing the terrorists with this word, as well as using it for the chapter's title, Barnes foreshadows the formal way with which the main character, Franklin Hughes, attempts to negotiate with these men, treating them as if they were engaged in a business relationship. By his word choice, Barnes contrasts Hughes's desire to forge a relationship with the men with the reality of their violence. By understanding the connotations of *visitors*, readers more fully observe the irony of its use.

A character's use of concrete or abstract diction further attunes readers to the ways in which he interacts with others. *Concrete words* impart a well-defined, often visual representation of objects and events: a frayed, beige cashmere scarf, for example, leaves little to the imagination. *Abstract words*—love, freedom, beauty—also evoke strong emotional responses or sensations. Between these two extremes stretches a continuum of concreteness and abstraction. In Toni Morrison's *Beloved* (1987), Beloved, who is believed to be the ghost of Sethe's murdered daughter, narrates a powerful section of the novel:

> in the beginning the women are away from the men and the men are away from the women   storms rock us and mix the men into the women and the women into the men   that is when I begin to be on the back of the man   for a long time I see only his neck and his wide shoulders above me   I am small   I love him because he has a song.
>
> (211, spacing in original)

The passage uses some words that are neither entirely concrete nor abstract, but that are, instead, very general. Words like *men*, *women*, and *small* escape the definitiveness of more concrete descriptions, but they are not as abstract as terms like *love*. In this excerpt, Morrison creates a dreaminess through her use of vague language while eliciting a strong sense of need and desire.

Readers should also be attentive to the use of *repetition* in a work of fiction. Authors use repetition to emphasize an idea, to draw attention to an event or a character, to demonstrate the emotional state of a character, or for a variety of other reasons. Donald Barthelme employs repetition in "Game" (1965) to reveal the mental state of his unnamed narrator, a member of the military. Isolated in an underground bunker for 133 days without hearing from anyone outside, the narrator and another man become increasingly unstable:

> Our behavior was painfully normal. Norms of politeness, considera-tion, speech, and personal habits were scrupulously observed. But then it became apparent that an error had been made, that our relief was not going to arrive. Owing to an oversight. Owing to an oversight we have been here for one hundred thirty-three days. When it became clear that an error had been made, that we were not to be relieved, the norms were relaxed.

> *(Sixty Stories* 64)

The repetition of "norms," "error," and "owing to an oversight" captures an obsessiveness in the narrator brought on by the isolation in the bunker and the lack of information. He has created a story to calm himself and only by repeating variations of the same words and ideas can he feel as if he is in control. In this case, repetition hints at the character's emotional state.

The structure of the author's sentences through the arrangement of phrases and clauses—their *syntax*—also constructs the style of a literary work. Unusual sentence structures alert readers to such issues as a character's mind-set, a moment of narrative significance, or the writer's artistic prose style. The opening sentence of J. D. Salinger's *The Catcher in the Rye* (1951) dis-closes the personality of the narrator Holden Caulfield from both its style and its syntax:

> If you really want to hear about it, the first thing you'll probably want to know is where I was born, and what my lousy childhood was like, and how my parents were occupied and all before they had me, and all that David Copperfield kind of crap, but I don't feel like going into it, if you want to know the truth.

> (3)

Holden's dismissive attitude toward life shines through in these words. He is unhappy, but he cannot be bothered to explain himself. Readers also learn about him from his style, both in terms of diction and syntax. Words like "lousy," "crap," and the contraction "you'll" indicate Holden's casual style of interacting with his audience, as well as his youth and rebelliousness nature. Furthermore, the syntax reinforces his disdain for formality and appropriate-ness. By connecting each segment of his sentence with "and"—rather than connecting each point with commas and using "and" only before the last item in the series, as a more elevated tone would require—Holden communicates his thoughts in casual and unplanned structures. With this run-on sentence, he simply blurts out his ideas without formally constructing them.

Figurative language deviates from daily speech and standard meanings to create literary effects. Commonly used in poetry, figurative language plays an important role in fiction by building insights into themes and characters. (*For more detailed examples of figurative language, see pp. 106–11.*) As they do in poetry, similes compare two unlike objects through the use of *like* or *as*, and in prose fiction they effectively enlighten characters' perspectives on their situations. In *Oliver Twist* (1838), Charles Dickens employs a simile when thieves Bill and Toby plan to rob a house and Bill says, "Toby and I were over the garden-wall the night afore last, sounding the panels of the doors and shutters. The crib's barred up at night like a jail; but there's one part we can crack, safe and softly" (135). Bill sees the world through the eyes of a criminal, and so a quaint country house metamorphoses into a confining and inaccessible prison. This simile also points to a later irony when the young orphan Oliver finds freedom and refuge from criminal life in this very home. Like similes, metaphors ask readers to consider an object in new terms. In Yann Martel's novel *Life of Pi* (2001), the narrator, Pi Patel, explains with a military metaphor how he attempts to counter his fear with reason:

> [Fear] is a clever, treacherous adversary, how well I know. . . . Then fear, disguised in the garb of mild-mannered doubt, slips into your mind like a spy. Doubt meets disbelief and disbelief tries to push it out. But disbelief is a poorly armed foot soldier. Doubt does away with it with little trouble. You become anxious. Reason comes to do battle for you. You are reassured. Reason is fully equipped with the latest weapons technology. But, to your amazement, despite superior tactics and a number of undeniable victories, reason is laid low.
>
> (161)

In using a metaphor of battle to explain how reason cannot conquer fear, the narrator emphasizes both the physicality and oppressiveness of fear, as well as the depth of the character's anxiety. Regardless of the advanced weaponry and methods for overcoming fear (one's logic and ability to reason away the panic), the emotion overwhelms and so resists such strategies.

Fiction, like poetry, also employs symbolism. *Symbols* in literature represent both their denotative meaning and an idea of deeper significance in the work. The meaning of symbols is often implied, and frequently one symbol can be interpreted in multiple ways. In Herman Melville's *Moby-Dick* (1851), Ahab, the captain of the ship *Pequod*, seeks to destroy the white whale Moby-Dick. Injured by the whale in the past, Captain Ahab single-mindedly pursues his quest. For Ahab and readers, Moby-Dick becomes more than a whale: the creature symbolizes several concepts, such as an evil that must be destroyed, the power—or callousness—of nature, and the dangers of obsession. Similarly, the green light at the end of Daisy's dock in *The Great Gatsby* (1925) symbolizes Gatsby's hopes and desires, and more generally represents the American Dream of prosperity and happiness. The novel closes as narrator Nick Carraway observes, "Gatsby believed in the green light, the orgiastic future that year by year recedes before us. It eluded us then, but that's no matter—tomorrow we will run faster, stretch out our arms farther. . . . And one fine morning—" (159). The fact that the green light is barely visible from Gatsby's home indicates that his hopes have been frustrated, yet that he still aspires to this dream.

Like symbols, *allegories* open up varying interpretations. In an *allegory*, characters, objects, and other elements represent other entities. A preferred genre of the Middle Ages, allegory structures such masterpieces as Guillaume de Lorris and Jean de Meun's *Roman de la Rose*, William Langland's *Piers Plowman*, Christine de Pizan's *Book of the City of Ladies*, and the morality plays *Everyman* and *Mankind*. George Orwell's *Animal Farm* (1945) allegorically retells the story of the Russian Revolution of 1917 as set on a country farm populated with speaking animals, and C. S. Lewis's *The Lion, the Witch and the Wardrobe* (1950) allegorizes aspects of Christian belief, with the lion Aslan symbolizing Jesus. Allegories build deep symbolic meanings into narratives, and the reader must be alert to the multiple levels of meaning each of the various symbols encodes.

The beauty and aesthetic pleasure of reading novels arises in the seamless combination of these many elements. While one may take precedence over another in a specific work, the unity of plot, points of view, characters and characterization, setting, theme, style, and tone elevates a given work into an organic whole. In interpreting novels, readers must pay keen attention to their interrelationships. Another key strategy for interpreting prose fiction asks readers to consider novels in relation to their various genres, which are discussed in this chapter's next section.

The Novel and Its Genres

The category of *novel* is comprised of a scintillating variety of works and has evolved markedly from its infancy. The first novel in the European tradition, Cervantes's *Don Quixote* (1605) inaugurated this literary tradition, with the earliest English-language novels published in England in the early 1700s and in the United States at the end of that century. (*For more on* Don Quixote, *see pp. 75–76.*) From these roots, the novel continues to reinvent itself in exciting ways. Mikhail Bakhtin argues that

> the novel is the sole genre that continues to develop, that is as yet uncompleted. The forces that define it as a genre are at work before our very eyes: the birth and development of the novel as a genre takes place in the full light of the historical day. The generic skeleton of the novel is still far from having hardened, and we cannot foresee all its plastic possibilities.
>
> (3)

Poets and playwrights might challenge Bakhtin's assertion, pointing to the ways in which these aesthetic forms continue to evolve as well, yet his point stresses the shifting historical contours of the novel and its adaptability to a range of cultural and aesthetic conditions.

The Epistolary Novel

In epistolary novels, the narrative is told through exchanges of letters among its characters. These novels detail characters' intimate thoughts, thereby providing an in-depth understanding of their actions and motivations. The content and style of these communications illuminate the various characters' personalities, for the author must effectively shift from one character's voice to another's for the letters to ring true. Also, readers must piece together the plot of an epistolary novel because, without the use of narrators, authors provide little guidance other than what the characters express of themselves and others. Among the most famous epistolary novels are Samuel Richardson's *Pamela: or, Virtue Rewarded* (1740) and *Clarissa: or, the History of a Young Lady* (1748), both of which depict young women hounded by rakish men. In the United States, Hannah Webster Foster's *The Coquette, or the History of Eliza Wharton* (1797), tells a similar story of a young woman whose virtue is compromised by treacherous suitors. Variations of the epistolary form include novels with letters, diary entries, and other correspondence, such as Bram Stoker's *Dracula* (1897). Although the epistolary novel has largely fallen out of favor, as has letter writing in general, some contemporary writers have reinvigorated the form. In *LETTERS* (1979), John Barth's postmodern novel, the Author (a fictional stand-in for Barth) exchanges letters with five characters from Barth's previous novels and one new character. In Alice Walker's novel *The Color Purple* (1982), the narrator Celie writes letters to God describing her life. Even as the popularity of the epistolary novel has waned, writers continue to create new uses for this genre, with email creating a subgenre of e-epistolary novels, such as David Llewellyn's *Eleven* (2006).

The Coming-of-Age Novel

Coming-of-age novels, or *bildungsromans*, depict the developments of their protagonists from youth to adulthood, focusing on the psychological, emotional, and moral changes these characters undergo. In general, the central characters of bildungsromans find themselves in conflict with some aspect of society and must learn to address this conflict; in so doing they mature into fully realized members of society. These novels do more than describe the experience of entering adulthood; their characters undergo a process of self-discovery, learning about themselves in profound ways. A famous and influential example of this genre, Johann Goethe's *Wilhelm Meister's Apprenticeship* (1795–1796) recounts the protagonist's struggles against society's expectations that he will be a traditional businessman; instead, he aspires to a more satisfying life in the theater. As Wilhelm gains experience with love and an intellectual life, he finds his way into the next stage of his life. Exemplary coming-of-age novels include Charlotte Brontë's *Jane Eyre*, Charles Dickens's *Great Expectations* and *David Copperfield*, Mark Twain's *The Adventures of Huckleberry Finn*, Jeanette Winterson's *Oranges Are Not the Only Fruit*, Khaled Hosseini's *The Kite Runner*, and J. K. Rowling's *Harry Potter* series.

A particular subset of bildungsromans, referred to as *künstlerromans*, narrates the maturation of artists as they grow into a deeper understanding of their culture—often in terms of its limitations—and their talents. In *A Portrait of the Artist as a Young Man* (1916), James Joyce narrates the growth of Stephen Dedalus, who pushes against the Irish Catholic traditions to which he is bound, ultimately leaving home to begin his life as an artist. Near the novel's end, as Stephen discovers his way in the world, he asserts,

> I will not serve that in which I no longer believe whether it call itself my home, my fatherland or my church: and I will try to express myself in some mode of life or art as freely as I can and as wholly as I can, using for my defence the only arms I allow myself to use—silence, exile, and cunning.
>
> (247)

This newfound confidence, after a long time of struggle, signifies Stephen's entry into the life of a mature artist. Writers' (auto)biographies, such as Rita Mae Brown's highly fictionalized *Rubyfruit Jungle* (1973), can also belong to the künstlerroman tradition.

The coming-of-age novel remains a popular and powerful genre. Stephen Chbosky's *The Perks of Being a Wallflower* (1999) uses an epistolary form to tell the story of how high-school student Charlie transforms from a "wallflower," someone who observes rather than participates, into a young man actively engaged in life. In the process, he confronts repressed memories of childhood abuse, guilt, and loss. As the novel ends when he and his friends are driving through a tunnel headed for the city, he experiences a moment of clarity:

> But mostly, I was crying because I was suddenly very aware of the fact that it was me standing up in that tunnel with the wind over my face. Not caring if I saw downtown. Not even thinking about it. Because I was standing in the tunnel. And I was really there. And that was enough to make me feel infinite.
>
> (213)

This first step of living in the moment, of not being controlled by his past, is Charlie's major breakthrough in his journey toward adulthood. In following their protagonists along their life stories, bildungsromans speak to a common human experience of transitioning from youth to maturity.

The Historical Novel

Historical novels entice readers to reimagine the past in their fictional representations of historical events or eras. Most authors of these works strive to create a rendering of a time and place as accurately as possible, reflecting a respect for the historical experience. Still, other authors in this tradition do not concern themselves as strenuously with the possibility of anachronism, and readers must determine for themselves whether a novel's emotional depth suffers from slips in historical authenticity. The characters in historical novels can be fictionalized versions of real people, characters invented for the novel, or a combination of both. Some historical novels dramatize famous events in history, while others use these events only as backdrops against which to tell a new story in an old setting.

Sir Walter Scott published several influential historical novels in the early nineteenth century. *Rob Roy* (1817), set in early eighteenth-century Scotland, focuses on the period before the Jacobite Risings, which were rebellions intended to return James VII of Scotland and II of England to the throne. Recreating Rob Roy, a historical figure, and incorporating authentic depictions of the miserable living conditions in part of Scotland, the novel combines dashing storytelling with a riveting re-creation of the past. Scott also penned several other historical novels, including *Waverley* (1814) and *Ivanhoe* (1819), that helped to make the historical novel a popular genre during the nineteenth century. Retelling history also involves questioning or buttressing the ideology of the period, and readers must assess how authors in this tradition objectively or subjectively reinterpret the people of the past.

The historical novel remains popular in the present, although it is increasingly used to question the very foundations of history and historical knowledge. Don DeLillo's novel *Libra* (1988) retells the story of Lee Harvey Oswald's assassination of U.S. President John F. Kennedy. DeLillo combines real events from Oswald's life with fictional events. His characters include numerous real-life people as well as his own creations. In his version of the assassination, DeLillo offers historical verisimilitude that allows his readers to question what they really know about this shared history. Additionally, DeLillo recounts the assassination from the viewpoints of several people, including Oswald, members of Kennedy's entourage, and observers on the street. Each perspective adds to and questions what readers think they know about that moment in Dallas in 1963. For historical novels, the re-creation of the past provides a foundation from which history's truths are retold and re-examined, often to comment, through parallel and intertextual allusion, on more current events.

The Novel of Manners

Novels of manners take as their subject the customs, behaviors, and cultural values of a group of people at a particular place and time. These narratives may be partly educational, as they reflect normative values, but many novels of manners depict characters at odds with social expectations. James Tuttleton defines the novel of manners as one

> in which the manners, social customs, folkways, conventions, traditions, and mores of a given social group at a given time and place play a dominant role in the lives of fictional characters, exert control over their thoughts and behavior, and constitute a determinant upon the actions in which they are engaged, and in which these manners and customs are detailed realistically.
>
> (10)

In the novel of manners tradition, central conflicts often arise between protagonists and their cultures, for the cultures are typically unsympathetic, if not hostile, to their unique ideas.

Novels of manners were quite popular during the nineteenth century, and among the most famous are those by Jane Austen. In *Pride and Prejudice* (1813), Austen illustrates the various social pressures surrounding marriage, particularly addressing the question of the qualities of a good marriage. Although the novel suggests that social and emotional compatibility makes the most harmonious unions, it is nonetheless true that the two oldest Bennet daughters, Jane and Elizabeth, marry wealthy men. While these novels usually include exemplary characters, those whose behavior is admired and respected, other characters often serve as foils to indicate contrasting possibilities. In *Pride and Prejudice*, the behavior of Lydia Bennet, the youngest of the daughters, demonstrates the disastrous consequences of ignoring social expectations. When Lydia runs off with George Wickham without benefit of marriage, they are saved from social ruin only by the financial support of Mr. Darcy and their unexpected marriage. By focusing attention on the often small aspects of proper social behavior, the novel of manners provides insight into the daily lives, communities, and values of its main characters.

While authors of novels of manners often indicate clearly the values that their protagonists should uphold, in other instances these lines are not as sharply delineated. In *Daisy Miller* (1878), Henry James portrays a brief episode in the life of an American girl traveling in Europe, following her through changes as she adapts to European customs and leaves behind her American moral values. Her decisions, often made in opposition to the opinions of other expatriates, ultimately bring her to ruin. Unlike the world of *Pride and Prejudice*, no one rescues Daisy from her missteps. Instead, even as she has been inattentive to her reputation, she has been inattentive to her physical well-being; the novella ends with her death from malaria. In

James's version of the novel of manners, competing cultural systems collide, and readers must determine which system best affords the various characters an avenue both to social respect and to personal happiness, if such a path is open to them at all.

The Realistic Novel

The realist movement in literature began in the nineteenth century with the work of French author Honoré de Balzac, with realism spreading throughout Europe and into the United States. Realist novels seek to represent life as it really occurs, without embellishment or artistic flourish. Most realist novels depict ordinary people, particularly of the middle and lower classes as their main characters, demonstrating the value in everyday life. In part a reaction against romanticism and its fascination with the ideal of nature and humanity, realism honors the ordinariness of the world. Realist novels pay keen attention to detail, portraying places and events with great precision. The plots in these novels tend to be believable, eschewing romantic or exceptional storylines. Characters emerge as complex individuals struggling with real problems that do not have simple solutions. Realist novels also employ vernacular language, the language of ordinary people, rather than more poetic or sophisticated diction.

Many realist authors believe that their novels reflect an unvarnished truth, one that might be uncomfortable for readers but which must nonetheless be expressed. Theodore Dreiser, author of *Sister Carrie* (1900) and *An American Tragedy* (1925), found inspiration for his novels in real-life events, seeing in them the possibility of capturing the truth of people's dreams and their actual circumstances. His words about truth and art capture much of the realist sensibility: "The sum and substance of literary as well as social morality may be expressed in three words—tell the truth. . . . [T]he business of the author . . . is to say what he knows to be true, and, having said as much, to abide the result with patience" (469). From this perspective, realist novels share the worlds of their characters, offering their experiences with as much detail and sense of the real world as possible. Among the most important realist novelists are Mark Twain, William Dean Howells, Leo Tolstoy, Fyodor Dostoyevsky, and Henry James. Notably, realism has maintained its importance throughout the twentieth and into the twenty-first century. The value placed on the stories of common people has continued to resonate with readers as it did in the nineteenth century. (*For the realist tradition in American literature, see pp. 49–52.*)

The Modern Novel

During the first half of the twentieth century, many novelists reacted against the literature of the nineteenth century, believing it failed to capture the unique experience of the modern era. David Daiches argues that the modern novel was born as a result of "the breakdown of public agreement about what is significant in experience and therefore about what the novelist ought to select, the new view of time, and the new view of the nature of consciousness" (10–11), referring to such events as World Wars I and II, scientific developments overturning previously held truths, and Sigmund Freud's theories of the unconscious. Thematically, modern novels ponder the emotional and physical alienation of the era, which arose from rapidly shifting social norms, including changes in relationships between women and men. Stylistically, modern novels experimented with a range of new approaches that reflect and reinforce these themes of alienation, such as stream-of-conscious narration. In *The Sound and the Fury* (1929), William Faulkner uses the character Benjy Compson, a developmentally disabled man, as one of his narrators, thereby blurring the narrative's chronology as present events mix together with past reflections. Such chronological uncertainty underscores the sense of loss and self-doubt experienced by characters as they navigate a world of changing and unclear values.

In *Ulysses* (1922), a daringly influential novel of the era that epitomizes modernist sensibilities, James Joyce tells the story of Leopold Bloom, an ordinary man, on an ordinary day. But Joyce creates his novel as a commentary on and revision of Homer's *The Odyssey*, turning the heroic Odysseus into the very common Bloom. Joyce divides the novel into sections titled after characters or locations in *The Odyssey*, such as "Proteus," "Hades," and "Cyclops," and he fills it with jokes, literary allusions, and much sexual detail and humor, thereby turning the heroic qualities of the epic tradition into a reflection on the impossibility of heroism in modern life. The novel also incorporates stream-of-conscious narration and, famously, its final chapter, "Penelope," includes very long, unpunctuated, run-on sentences as readers follow the roaming thoughts of Bloom's wife Molly.

While *Ulysses* may be the most powerful example of modernist technique, most modern novels incorporate a variety of stylistic and formal strategies that separate them from the linear narrative form typical of much realism. In addition, many modern novels demonstrate pessimism about the present and future, and a longing for the past. Written during a long period of world war and economic struggle, the challenges of modern life clearly resound in the literature of the time. (*For more on modernist literature, see pp. 33–37 and 52–56.*)

The Postmodern Novel

Postmodern novels, whose beginnings most critics date to the 1950s, both reflect and react against modernism. Like authors of modernist novels, postmodern authors recognize the disruption and alienation of contemporary society, but, unlike modern authors, the postmoderns express greater ambivalence about this state of society, finding ways to create new art with a sense of possibility. In general, postmodern fiction posits that no single version of

truth or of history captures the totality of human experience, that in reality
alternate versions of events arise from the many people telling their stories.
Similarly, postmoderns criticize the idea of art as inspired and fully unique.
Postmodern novels consider these ideas thematically, tonally, stylistically,
and formally.

Much postmodern fiction assumes an ironic sensibility, reflecting a significant change from the sense of nostalgia of much modern fiction and voicing
skepticism toward the subject matter. As Richard Bradford argues, postmodern authors address "the apparently unsteady relationship between linguistic
representation and actuality, what goes on within a text and what exists
outside it." He then explains, "their watchword, if they had one, would
have been self-referentiality: that the familiar cliché of 'suspending disbelief'
should be challenged, even forbidden, in the writing of fiction and replaced
with an engagement with the very nature of language and identity" (7). The
use of *pastiche*—an imitation of one or more other literary works—also characterizes postmodern fiction. Unlike parody, which mocks what it imitates,
pastiche presents its imitation without judgment. Pastiche reminds readers to
be skeptical of the idea of a true original, as the sources become reimagined
and reinvented for new artistic experiences. In addition, in opposition to the
serious "high art" of the modernists, much postmodern fiction engages with
"low art," the common aspects of popular culture. For example, Donald
Barthelme rewrites a famous fairy tale in *Snow White* (1967), with Snow
White as a seductress enjoying sexual encounters with the dwarves, thereby
criticizing gender expectations and social norms. Ishmael Reed incorporates
cartoons, handbills, and images of pageants, dances, and civil rights protests
into his novel *Mumbo Jumbo* (1972), which addresses the abuses of racism
and the joyful possibility of black empowerment.

Many postmodern novels are *metafiction*—fiction whose subject is fiction
or the writing of fiction itself. Midway through *Snow White*, Barthelme gives
his readers a survey about the book in their hands, drawing them out of the
action itself and into a reflective state:

1. Do you like the story so far? Yes ( ) No ( )
2. Does Snow White resemble the Snow White you remember? Yes ( )
   No ( )
3. Have you understood, in reading to this point, that Paul is the prince-
   figure? Yes ( ) No ( ). . .
9. Has the work, for you, a metaphysical dimension? Yes ( ) No ( )

(88)

By drawing attention to the novel *as* novel, postmodern fiction reminds readers that all stories are constructed in a specific way to achieve specific effects.
Even more powerfully, metafiction suggests that all narratives, fictional or
otherwise, organize their accounts in a particular manner, thereby encouraging readers to question stories and to recognize that they all rely on some

level of fabrication. This element of skepticism extends to numerous novels fictionalizing contemporary historical and political events, encouraging readers to question whether they can ever know the truth of a situation, as in Robert Coover's *The Public Burning* (1977), which fictionalizes the story of Julius and Ethel Rosenberg, U.S. citizens executed in the early 1950s for spying for the Soviet Union, and Italo Calvino's *Invisible Cities* (1972), which describes Marco Polo's travels. Overall, postmodern novels embrace the uncertainty and unknowability of contemporary life, making use of many artistic devises to spur fresh, new art.

The Graphic Novel

Stephen Tabachnick defines the genre of graphic novels as consisting of "extended comic book[s] that treat nonfictional as well as fictional plots and themes with the depth and subtlety that we have come to expect of traditional novels and extended nonfictional texts" (2). An unwarranted prejudice against illustrations seems to account for the prior critical dismissal of graphic novels, despite that many great literary works have included illustrations, perhaps most notably those of Charles Dickens, who collaborated with such artists as George Cruikshank and Hablot Knight Browne (known as "Phiz"). Also, current graphic novels evolved from comic books; this links them to ostensibly puerile interests. Graphic novels such as Art Spiegelman's *Maus* (1985), Marjane Satrapi's *Persepolis* (2000), and Jason Lutes's *Berlin: City of Stones* (2000) indicate the power of this popular culture genre to address serious social and political issues. Like postmodern novels, graphic novels blur distinctions between high and low art, embracing both as valid avenues for understanding culture. While the various techniques of narrative analysis apply equally well to graphic novels, readers must also take into account their visual elements. To read graphic novels in depth, one must examine their combinations of text and image, particularly the ways in which the "gutters," the sections between illustrations, move the story along.

* * * * *

Understanding the primary subjects and themes of these major genres gives readers useful methods to frame their interpretations of prose fiction. Whether reading centuries-old historical novels or the most recent graphic text, fiction continues to transport readers to previously unknown places and times, or to bring readers to a better understanding of the world close to home. Through all of these imaginary journeys, readers who put to use the elements of literary analysis will find that fiction opens up extraordinary new experiences and opportunities to explore further the human condition.

2.3 Plays

Unlike novels and other forms of prose fiction, plays must be performed in front of audiences to achieve their artistic potential. As Tennessee Williams passionately stated, "a play in a book is only the shadow of a play and not even a clear shadow of it. . . . The printed script of a play is hardly more than an architect's blueprint of a house not yet built or built and destroyed" (747). The performative aspect of plays, in that a director, actors, and crew must bring to life the playwright's vision, separates the theater from other literary forms, which do not require intermediaries between author and reader. Indeed, the necessity of performing theatrical works is encoded etymologically in its terminology: the word *theater* derives from the Greek word meaning *to behold* or *to view*, and the word *audience* hails from the Latin word meaning *listening*. When plays are performed in a theater, the audience engages through multiple senses as the story comes alive before them. At the same time, plays include similar narrative and aesthetic elements as fiction and poetry: like fiction, plays need characters, settings, and plots. Like poetry, plays pay detailed attention to language and its oral presentation. Like both poetry and fiction, plays employ symbols and themes to communicate the deeper significance of their storylines.

Structure, Plot, and Theme

Just as novels may be divided into chapters and poems into stanzas, most plays are divided into *acts*, the major organizational unit of drama. Until the nineteenth century, many plays employed a five-act structure, but the three-act structure has become increasingly common. One-act plays compress their narratives into a single unit and thus depict relatively brief storylines. The acts of a play establish its major divisions, and they are often comprised of multiple *scenes*. Both acts and scenes call attention to changes in location, time, or another dramatic development. Moving beyond the standard forms of five-, three-, or one-act dramas, playwrights frequently experiment with the overarching structure of acts and scenes, such as in Edward Albee's *The Zoo Story*, which is not a one-act but a one-scene play, and his *The Death of Bessie Smith*, which he describes as "a play in eight scenes" (41). The arrangement of a play with acts and scenes or some other permutation of this standard form influences audiences' perceptions of its meaning, for these divisions structure the presentation of characters and their storylines.

Whether the audience views a play in a theater or reads the text at home, the story should enthrall them. Effective plays spellbind their audiences as events unfold, with one action carrying forward to the next. As noted in the previous chapter, a story consists of a series of events occurring in a particular order; a plot, on the other hand, tells the audience not just what happens but why, and consists of the sequence of events arranged so that they demonstrate the causal relationships among events. As with much prose fiction, the plots of plays typically follow the order of Freytag's pyramid: (1) introduction (or exposition), (2) rising action (or complication), (3) climax, (4) falling action (or return), and (5) catastrophe (or dénouement) (114–40). In some plays the five elements of Freytag's pyramid correspond respectively to the play's five acts.

During the exposition, the playwright provides vital background information, introduces the characters, clarifies their relationships with one another, and commences the play's main action. Like epics, many plays begin *in medias res*, or in the midst of the action. The audience may overhear characters conversing without any explanatory introductions to guide them in understanding who is speaking to whom. Such an opening engages the audience immediately because they need not wait through introductory material before being immersed in the action. Molière's *Tartuffe* (1664) begins as Madame Pernelle, the mother of Orgon, prepares to leave his home out of frustration:

MADAME PERNELLE. Come, come, Flipote; it's time I left this place.
ELMIRE. I can't keep up, you walk at such a pace.
MADAME PERNELLE. Don't trouble child; no need to show me out.
     It's not your manners I'm concerned about.
ELMIRE. We merely pay you the respect we owe.
     But, Mother, why this hurry? Must you go?
MADAME PERNELLE. I must. This house appalls me. No one in it
     Will pay attention for a single minute.

(11)

Through this abrupt beginning, the audience understands that Madame Pernelle feels unwelcome and leaves because she believes no one pays her any attention. Before the audience is fully introduced to the play's characters or dramatic scenario, they are drawn into this argument and see Madame Pernelle as a disgruntled and critical woman. As the scene proceeds, Molière shares more information, but the audience becomes connected to the play's energy from the very beginning.

As part of the exposition, plays often introduce *antecedent actions*, events that precede their beginnings. In *Tartuffe*, the audience quickly learns that the central character, Tartuffe, a deceitful man pretending to be good and holy, has moved into the house of Orgon's family prior to the play's commencement. Similarly, in the opening act of William Shakespeare's *Hamlet* (c. 1601), the audience learns that Hamlet's father died recently; questions about his death spark all future events in the play. Although works of prose fiction often incorporate flashbacks to provide information about events preceding the main timelines of their narratives, plays rely more often on the introduction of antecedent actions as part of their expositions.

Playwrights may also use *foreshadowing* during the exposition to prepare audiences for later events. When playwrights introduce an idea or object early in their narratives, they often do so to indicate its future importance. Anton Chekhov famously describes the structure of theatrical foreshadowing: "If in the first act you hang a pistol on the wall, then in the last act it must be shot off. Otherwise you do not hang it there" (Simmons 190). The audience must be especially vigilant not only to the characters' words, but also to the objects they see on stage. In general, the exposition, which can vary in length but usually lasts no longer than the first act in a five-act play, prepares the audience to recognize the relationships among characters and to understand in which direction the play will proceed.

The *rising action* of a play presents a series of related events that move toward the *climax*, a defining moment of development, discovery, or disaster. In Shakespeare's *Othello* (1603), the rising action consists of Iago's attempts to ruin Othello, who has recently married Desdemona. Jealous of Othello's success, Iago plots revenge by discrediting his rival Cassio's reputation and encouraging Othello to question Desdemona's loyalty. Each of these events builds on previous ones, increasing the dramatic tension, and the rising action thus escalates to the play's climax when a major change takes place for the central character. In *Othello*, the climax occurs when Othello murders Desdemona, convinced that she has cuckolded him. His anger, pain, and jealously blaze out during the death scene, which culminates from the long string of events that Iago has orchestrated.

Once a play reaches its climax, its remainder addresses the *falling action* and *dénouement*. The falling action marks the point when the past events are made clear and the main story tapers off, leading toward a conclusion. In this part of the play, the playwright dramatizes the fates of central characters and reveals deeper meanings behind events. The final section, the *dénouement* indicates the final state for each character and brings the world back to stasis. In *Tartuffe*, the deceitful Tartuffe is exposed as a hypocrite to Orgon's family when he evicts them from their home during the play's climax; Orgon attempts to flee to avoid legal matters but is caught by Tartuffe, who brings the police with him. This section of the play marks the falling action, the events occurring as a result of the climax. The dénouement follows as the police arrest Tartuffe rather than Orgon, on the orders of the King of France, who abhors hypocrisy. Tartuffe goes to jail and the family is reunited, forever free from this interloper. This particular type of ending, when a significant and unexpected power from outside resolves the play's conflicts, is called a *deus ex machina*, or "god from the machine." This term refers to a plot device in classical drama, in which a god (*deus*) would be lowered from a machine and then resolve all of the plot's difficulties. In contemporary usage, it suggests that an ending is unearned, that the playwright unrealistically resolves the narrative conflict. *Deus ex machina* endings, while typically less convincing than conclusions resulting from the characters' actions, offer playwrights easy solutions to complex and challenging stories.

Although many plays use this five-part plot structure that roughly corresponds to Freytag's pyramid, the sections sometimes blur together. Readers and viewers of plays must watch for these divisions to understand the relationships among events. When the divisions are not clearly demarcated, the audience can ponder how such a presentation affects an understanding of the play. The plot, ultimately, provides the connections among events that are so vital for a play's success.

While the plot tells viewers the events and their causes, its themes elucidate their importance. The *theme* tells the audience how the events of the play connect together to form a controlling idea, and this controlling idea expresses the playwright's attitude toward her subject. Whereas the plot of *Tartuffe* details how Orgon's failure to heed his family's advice leads him to trust the con man and religious hypocrite Tartuffe, and thus nearly to lose his family's property, the play's overarching theme argues that true religious piety does not draw attention to itself. To fully understand how playwrights weave themes into their plots, viewers must consider other narrrative and theatrical elements, such as character, dialogue, and mise-en-scène.

Character and Dialogue

The heart of a play emerges through its characters and their words to one another, for their dialogue defines the characters' personalities and their interrelationships. Most plays feature *principals*, the lead roles. The chief principal role is most often the *protagonist*, around whom the action takes place. Some plays also include an *antagonist*, a character who opposes the protagonist. Returning to previous examples, Orgon and Othello serve as protagonists, whereas Tartuffe and Iago serve as antagonists. Instead of protagonists, some plays feature *antiheroes*, lead characters who exhibit unappealing characteristics, such as selfishness, cowardice, or dishonesty.

Plays also depict characters supporting the protagonist in a variety of other capacities. With *foils*, playwrights construct characters whose personalities and behaviors contrast with those of the protagonists. In Tennessee Williams's *A Streetcar Named Desire* (1947), the fading Southern belle Blanche Dubois cannot adjust to life after her family has lost their fortune, but her sister Stella adapts to her straitened circumstances and marries happily. An initial exchange between the two women highlights their differing viewpoints about Stella's new home:

BLANCHE. Why didn't you tell me, why didn't you write me, honey, why didn't you let me know . . . that you had to live in these conditions?

STELLA. Aren't you being a little intense about it? It's not that bad at all! New Orleans isn't like other cities.

(474)

Stella, the foil, simply shrugs off Blanche's shock, and so this brief bit of dialogue illuminates core differences in their characters. Although foils may have either a positive or negative relationship with protagonists, they highlight the possibilities that protagonists could make other decisions, choose other paths, than they do. Many plays also feature *confidants*, characters to whom protagonists converse directly so that playwrights do not need them to declaim their thoughts exclusively through soliloquies.

Most characters can be described as round or flat. *Round characters*, primarily the protagonist or other lead characters, develop, mature, or achieve some sort of growth or realization over the course of the play, whereas playwrights paint *flat characters* in one dimension. Flat characters may coincide with *character roles*, those who do not take the lead but play an important role in the plot; character roles often contrast with leading roles, such as Lady Wishfort in Congreve's *The Way of the World*, who serves as a comic impediment to the marriage of protagonists Millamant and Mirabell. Other flat characters receive limited stage time and display one primary characteristic, such as unblinking bigotry, romantic idealism, or blind loyalty. A subset of flat characters, *stock characters* embody immediately recognizable stereotypes, such as a "dumb jock" or a "science nerd."

In addition to characters, some plays include narrators or other such figures who explain the unfolding action to the audience. Plays sometimes depict a *chorus*, a character or characters who comment on the action by speaking directly to the audience. This tradition began in the theater of classical Greece, notably in the plays of Sophocles and Aeschylus. In plays from the English Renaissance, such as Christopher Marlowe's *Doctor Faustus*, Shakespeare's *Henry V* and *Romeo and Juliet*, and Thomas Heywood's *A Woman Killed with Kindness*, a chorus figure provides a prologue and often an epilogue as well. The Prologue character of Francis Beaumont's *The Knight of the Burning Pestle* and the Stage-Keeper of Ben Jonson's *Bartholomew Fair* introduce their plays while also interacting with other characters. Such characters clarify the context of the play, often commenting on characters' morality or providing important thematic interpretations. In modern theater, choruses continue to provide playwrights with an important structural device for assessing a play's actions and themes. In Thornton Wilder's *Our Town* (1938), the character of the Stage Manager assumes the chorus role. He introduces the town to the audience and periodically comments on and sometimes participates in the action. Early in the play, after eleven-year-old Joe Crowell and Dr. Gibbs chat, the Stage Manager imparts information about Joe's future:

Want to tell you something about that boy Joe Crowell there. Joe was awful bright—graduated from high school here, head of his class. So he got a scholarship to Massachusetts Tech. Graduated head of his class there, too. It was all wrote up in the Boston paper at the time. Goin' to be a great engineer, Joe was. But the war broke out and he died in France.—All that education for nothing.

(10)

In the role of chorus, or narrator, the Stage Manager benefits from an omniscience that the other characters lack. By telling the audience of Joe's death while the character still lives on stage, the Stage Manager helps viewers interpret Wilder's themes. Such characters as choruses and prologues communicate to the audiences by breaking the theater's *fourth wall*: the imaginary division between the cast and their audience that preserves the illusion of the theater's reality.

Playwrights develop their characters through a variety of means but primarily through *dialogue*, the words they speak to one another. Although stage dialogue is generally more articulate than the conversations of people in everyday life, it varies widely and must represent the voices of an array of characters in a variety of styles. Many early plays were written in verse, combining both poetry and drama. Their highly stylized dialogues create an increased sense of artistry, while also controlling the rhythm of speech, which affects the actual performance of the play. (*For rhyme, blank verse, heroic couplets, see pp. 93–94, 102–03.*) Although most modern playwrights do not compose in verse, analyzing dialogue demands attention to more than the ideas expressed. Not only does the content of the words matter in dialogue, but also the ways in which characters select and articulate their words. Does a character speak in short, direct sentences? Does he create long and convoluted statements? Does she pose questions, deflecting attention to another character? In *Who's Afraid of Virginia Woolf* (1962), Edward Albee depicts the vicious arguments of Martha and George, as they seek to wound each other with their words. In one attack, when Martha is trying to remember a movie's title and George suggests it might be *Chicago*, she responds, "Good grief! Don't you know *anything? Chicago* was a 'thirties musical, starring little Miss Alice *Faye*. Don't you know *anything?*" (157). By stressing certain words in her response, Albee reveals Martha's character to audiences—her impatience and exasperation with George, and her sarcastic retribution for his perceived failures.

The *syntax* of sentences, the ways in which linguistic elements are pieced together to create meaning, can also tell the audience as much about characters as the words they say. In Harold Pinter's *Betrayal* (1978), the central characters' dialogue masks their anxieties. Jerry is afraid his friendship with Robert will be lost because Robert's wife Emma confessed their affair to Robert. As Jerry broaches this painful subject with Robert, he says:

I don't know why she told you. I don't know how she could tell you. I just don't understand. Listen, I know you've got . . . look, I saw her today . . . we had a drink . . . I haven't seen her for . . . she told me, you know, that you're in trouble, both of you . . . and so on. I know that. I mean I'm sorry.

(36)

To demonstrate Jerry's guilt, anxiety, and uncertainty, Pinter sprinkles numerous pauses, represented by ellipses, in this dialogue. Jerry cannot find the right words but nonetheless keeps speaking, unable to complete a sentence because he finds his words ineffective. Also, Jerry focuses his comments on himself and his confusion, which suggests his self-interest: in this short passage, many of the sentences or sentence fragments begin with "I." Eventually, he apologizes, but even then he tempers the apology with the opening words, "I mean." The apology itself, which should be expressed sincerely, tongue-ties Jerry. Combined with the literal meaning of his words, the play's audience gains a deeper understanding of Jerry—self-involved, confused, and uncertain—through the structure of his sentences.

Many characters recite *monologues*, relatively long speeches given by a single character. Eve Ensler's *The Vagina Monologues* (2000) strings together a series of such declamations, in each of which the speaker muses over a key incident of her life relating to issues of gender, sexuality, and her body. A special type of monologue is a *soliloquy*, a speech given by a single character that explores her private thoughts and feelings. Through soliloquies the audience perceives a character's interior musings—those unshared with other characters. Perhaps the most famous soliloquy appears in Shakespeare's *Hamlet* (c. 1601), when Hamlet, lost in grief over his father's death and struggling with his mother's marriage to his uncle, ponders whether life is worth living:

To be, or not to be: that is the question:
Whether 'tis nobler in the mind to suffer
The slings and arrows of outrageous fortune,
Or to take arms against a sea of troubles,
And by opposing end them?

(3.1.55–59)

Characters usually speak soliloquies in private. These speeches, thoughts spoken aloud, enlighten audiences with a more intimate knowledge of the characters. Some characters, instead of delivering a lengthy soliloquy, offer their thoughts to the audience in an *aside*, a brief comment directed to the audience that divulges the character's plans. Even if other characters share the stage with the speaker, an aside is presumed to be unheard by them. When Claudius greets Hamlet—"But now, my cousin Hamlet, and my son"—Hamlet responds in an aside to the audience: "A little more than kin, and less than kind" (1.2.64–65). Hamlet's words would undoubtedly anger his uncle, if he heard them, and thus Shakespeare uses this aside so that audiences recognize Hamlet's distrust for him without the tension between them escalating too quickly. When analyzing the dialogue in a play, it is vital to consider the various ways in which characters speak, to whom they speak, and what is shielded from other characters.

The Physical Stage: Mise-en-Scène and Lighting

When watching a play in a theater, even before the actors enter the stage if the curtain is up, the audience perceives the way the stage is set. The combination of stage set pieces, furniture, decorative objects, and characters in their costumes constitute a play's *mise-en-scène*. These physical elements, in combination with lighting, create an appropriate environment for the characters to interact. Reading a play rather than watching it performed limits its physicality, which comes to life as characters move through and interact with the set.

In most older plays, such as those from the Renaissance, authors provided little guidance on their performance. Most *stage directions*, the physical movements that the playwright indicates for the actors, were limited, mentioning merely a general location and time frame. *Hamlet* begins with these scant directions to set the scene: "*Enter* BARNARDO *and* FRANCISCO, *two sentinels, [meeting]*" (at 1.1.1). Aspects of the setting soon become clear from the dialogue—the time is midnight, the weather is cold—but Shakespeare offers little guidance for setting the details of the stage. (Some of Shakespeare's stage directions are nonetheless memorable, such as the instructions in *Titus Andronicus*, "*Enter a* MESSENGER, *with two heads and a hand*" [at 3.1.233] and in *The Winter's Tale*, "*Exit* [ANTIGONUS] *pursued by a bear*" [at 3.3.58]). Stage directions may also direct the performers on their *blocking*, which involves their movements across the stage, as well as their entrances and exits, as they inhabit their roles.

Many plays since the nineteenth century, though, have incorporated more detailed instructions, allowing directors to construct the playwright's vision more accurately. In *Buried Child* (1978), Sam Shepard describes the scene as follows:

> Day. Old wooden staircase down left with pale, frayed carpet laid down on the steps. The stairs lead off stage left up into the wings with no landing. Up right is an old, dark green sofa with the stuffing coming out in spots. Stage right of the sofa is an upright lamp with a faded yellow shade and a small night table with several small bottles of pills on it.
>
> (11)

The description of the set continues in great detail, leaving little room for creative input from the director or production designer. Such depth of detail ensures that viewers understand from the state of the carpet, sofa, and lamp the sad, dingy, painful world the characters inhabit. The pill bottles on the table are *props* (properties), objects that the actors in a play will hold or use in some way during the course of the play. Like symbols in a poem or novel, props often take on metaphoric meanings.

The actor's costumes should convey key aspects of their characters, and playwrights often detail how their characters should be clothed. In *Ma Rainey's Black Bottom* (1982), August Wilson provides detailed instructions about his title character's clothing as she enters the stage:

> The buzzer sounds. Irvin goes to the door. There is a flurry of commotion as Ma Rainey enters, followed closely by the Policeman, Dussie Mae, and Sylvester. Ma Rainey is a short, heavy woman. She is dressed in a full-length fur coat with matching hat, an emerald-green dress, and several stands of pearls of varying length. Her hair is secured by a headband that matches her dress. Her manner is simple and direct, and she carries herself in a royal fashion.
>
> (576–77)

Wilson's attention to detail—that the headband matches the dress, that the pearls vary in length—paints a picture in the imagination that the play's costumers must match on the stage in order to capture Ma Rainey's queenly bearing. Costumes also provide information about characters' social status, their occupations, their sense of style, and even their morality.

Lighting also affects a play's tone and mood. In most cases, the creative team working on a production takes responsibility for lighting decisions, but playwrights sometimes provide their own directions. In *The Baltimore Waltz* (1992), Paula Vogel writes in a production note prior to first scene, "The lighting should be highly stylized, lush, dark and imaginative, in contrast to the hospital white silence of the last scene" (7). By envisioning the lighting in this way, Vogel evokes a dreamlike atmosphere for the unrealistic actions of her characters. Each element of a play's mise-en-scène assumes additional thematic and narrative meaning, enhancing its construction of an effective and multilayered theatrical experience. Through the combination of these elements—structure, plot, theme, characters, dialogue, mise-en-scène, and lighting—playwrights create an immersive experience for their audiences. They also build from theatrical traditions, particularly those of tragedy, comedy, and drama, which are discussed in this chapter's subsequent section.

Major Theatrical Genres: Tragedy, Comedy, Drama

Plays in general constitute the literary genre of *drama*, with numerous subgenres fostering varied reading and viewing experiences: tragedies aim to make audiences cry, comedies to laugh, and dramas to examine society. Understanding the purposes of these major subgenres of drama allows readers to better contextualize each play they read through its historical development and conventions.

Tragedy

In approximately 335 BCE, Aristotle wrote *Poetics*, in which he defines tragedy. For centuries his definition has helped audiences understand the genre's conventions and effects: "Tragedy, then, is an imitation of an action that is serious, complete, and of a certain magnitude; in language embellished with each kind of artistic ornament, the several kinds being found in separate parts of the play; in the form of action, not of narrative; through pity and fear effecting the proper purgation of these emotions" (6.2, at p. 61). Aristotle's sense that a tragedy must represent "an action that is serious, complete, and of a certain magnitude" suggests that the events depicted must resonate beyond their immediate circle and bear far-reaching consequences for the society as a whole. Thus, the role of the protagonist belongs to a person of significant social standing. In the classical drama of the Greeks, most central characters come from the nobility. Although the protagonist embodies nobility, his basic humanity ensures that he will err in a key aspect of his life. The term *tragic flaw* (or the Greek *hamartia*) refers to the weakness in or the poor decision of the protagonist that leads to his downfall. A common example of hamartia, *hubris* refers to the protagonist's excessive pride, which blinds him to imminent catastrophe.

In addition, Aristotle believed that a tragedy should include "artistic ornament," or elements of "rhythm, 'harmony,' and song" placed at different points of the narrative, suggesting as well that "some parts are rendered through the medium of verse alone, others again with the aid of song" (6.3, at p. 61). The Greek chorus performs some of these musical elements in a tragedy, although this aspect of ornamentation has mostly disappeared from the genre. Also, Aristotle's directive to act out rather than to narrate the action indicates an important distinction between drama and other genres, such as epics. Although a play's chorus might comment on its action, the bulk of the performance is performed as a set of related actions in front of the audience. Finally, Aristotle's belief that tragedy evokes the emotions of pity and fear indicates his sense of the audience's role in tragedy. It is not enough for a play to depict a great man's downfall; instead, audiences themselves experience the tragic consequences of the protagonist's actions. This emotional response catalyzes a *catharsis* within the audience, a psychological purging of these emotions of pity and terror. As a result of catharsis, the audience reenters the world with a sense of relief. According to Aristotle, tragedy allows viewers to experience the horrible events of the play with the protagonist, and, by feeling the intense emotions, move past them. As a critical term, *catharsis* remains extremely difficult to pin down to a specific sense of cause and effect, yet the enduring power of these plays testifies to their inherent ability to draw strong emotions from the events portrayed.

Shakespeare's four major tragedies—*Hamlet* (c. 1601), *Othello* (c. 1603), *King Lear* (c. 1605), and *Macbeth* (1606)—remain the most famous collection of this genre, and they illustrate key aspects of its form. In keeping with Aristotle's theory of tragedy, Shakespeare's four plays stage the fall of powerful men—whether a prince (Hamlet), military hero (Othello and Macbeth), or king (Lear)—due to some weakness or mistake in judgment. Hamlet vacillates and seems almost incapable of action; Othello falls victim to his jealousy, killing his wife Desdemona in a rage; Lear, attempting to preserve his kingdom from future disarray by tending to issues of secession in a timely manner, reacts angrily when perceiving a slight from his daughter Cordelia; and Macbeth, feeling the powerful allure of ambition, succumbs to his wife's encouragement and resorts to violence to facilitate his rise to power. Shakespeare's tragedies end with the stage strewn with dead bodies, which induces catharsis in the audience, with some sense of relief leavening the horror. Despite the deaths of their kings and rulers, the plays end with a brief indication that the regions will return to calm through good rulership: Fortinbras claims the Danish throne in *Hamlet* (5.2.386–90); Lodovico bestows Othello's fortunes to Gratiano in *Othello* (5.2.365–67); Albany declares that Kent and Edgar shall rule in *Lear* (5.3.320–21), and Macduff hails Malcolm as king of Scotland in *Macbeth* (5.9.20–25). Commenting on Renaissance drama, Sir Philip Sidney argues that tragedies teach kings to be good rulers, suggesting that "the high and excellent Tragedy, that openeth the greatest wounds, and showeth forth the ulcers that are covered with tissue; that maketh kings fear to be tyrants, . . . that, with stirring the affects of admiration and commiseration, teacheth the uncertainty of this world" (*Apology for Poetry* 98), and Shakespeare's focus on powerful men in his tragedies adheres to this aspect of the tragic worldview.

Aristotle's definition of tragedy, which Sidney's echoes, remains the single most influential theory of the genre, yet tragic plays have evolved over time. Most notably, many tragedies no longer dramatize major national or political events, instead tackling personal and domestic storylines that affect a family or small community. Norwegian author Henrik Ibsen's *Hedda Gabler* (1890), for instance, offers such an understanding of tragedy removed from Aristotle's definition. The daughter of a general, Hedda Gabler is connected to power but not someone who wields power herself. (While this tragedy is not the first to focus on a female protagonist—Sophocles's *Antigone* did so in the fifth century BCE—most tragic heroes continue to be men.) Hedda marries Jörgen Tesman, a scholar, but after their wedding they settle into a life that Hedda finds boring. When she learns that Ejlert Lövborg, Tesman's rival, has written a new, successful book, Hedda manipulates this recovering alcoholic into drinking again. When Lövborg loses his manuscript, unaware that Tesman picked it up and plans to return it, Hedda lets him believe that the manuscript is irretrievably lost. He confesses his desire to kill himself, and Hedda subtly encourages him:

HEDDA. And what are you going to do, then?

LÖVBORG. Nothing. Only make an end of the whole business. The sooner the better.

HEDDA [*a step nearer*]. Ejlert Lövborg, listen to me. Could you not see to it that—that it is done beautifully?

LÖVBORG. Beautifully? [*Smiling.*] With vineleaves in the hair, as you used to imagine once upon a time—

HEDDA. Ah, not vineleaves. I don't believe in that any more. But beautifully, nevertheless. For once. Good-bye. You must go now, and not come here again.

(344)

Instead of dissuading Lövborg from suicide, Hedda advises him to carry out the final act and even gives him a "souvenir": a pistol to use in the act (344). For Hedda, beauty and enjoyment take precedence over life itself, and her indifference to others leads to Lövborg's death. But it also leads to her own suicide when she learns that Lövborg's suicide was not a moment of beauty but of bloody horror, and that, more importantly, he used her gun to kill himself and it can be linked back to her. Her self-interest and deceit bring about her death. This new type of tragic protagonist lacks the heroic elements of Hamlet, Othello, Macbeth, or Lear, but Hedda reflects the elite of nineteenth century Norwegian society, a moneyed but not necessarily noble class. She is demanding and controls her marriage, for she is concerned with superficial aspects of life. A modern tragedy, *Hedda Gabler* plumbs the psychology of its protagonist to uncover the duplicities of the self in her society.

Tragedy evolved further in the twentieth century, as Arthur Miller explains in his famous essay "Tragedy and the Common Man" (1949). Challenging the idea that tragedies should be populated with kings and nobles, Miller notes that

> the tragic feeling is evoked in us when we are in the presence of a character who is ready to lay down his life, if need be, to secure one thing—his sense of personal dignity. From Orestes to Hamlet, Medea to Macbeth, the underlying struggle is that of the individual attempting to gain his "rightful" position in society.

For Miller, dramatizing the fall of a common man is as appropriate in tragedy as was focusing on the noble man in the tragedy of earlier eras. Miller's most famous play, *Death of a Salesman* (1949), tells of Willy Loman, an unsuccessful traveling salesman who pursues outward signs of achievement such as material goods and likeability. When his boss tires of Willy's poor sales and fires him, Willy begins a downward spiral, refusing job offers from his friend Charley, losing hope, and ultimately taking his own life in the hope that the insurance money can give his son Biff a new start. From his children's youth, Willy encouraged them to believe that he was a great success and could achieve anything, and so he was unable to face his failure in light of his unshakeable faith in the American Dream. Willy's death affects his family but bears no larger consequences for his society. Not even the people he worked with throughout his career attend his funeral: his wife Linda confusedly asks, "But where are all the people he knew?" (137). In its updating of tragedy, *Death of a Salesman* contemplates the loss of self-worth in twentieth-century society and the struggle to find meaning in one's life. From kings on their thrones to everyday Joes struggling to prove themselves, tragedy bespeaks the ultimate frailty of the human condition, reminding readers that all of humanity shares a common fate in the grave.

Comedy

Although Aristotle theorized about comedy as well as tragedy in *Poetics*, only brief snippets of this discussion remain. Despite these gaps in the historical record, it is evident that Aristotle believed comedy differs significantly from tragedy: comedy "consists in some defect or ugliness which is not painful or destructive. To take an obvious example, the comic mask is ugly and distorted, but does not imply pain" (5.1, at p. 59). In many ways, the standard plotlines of comedies and tragedies resemble each other: through a series of events, characters find their worlds turned upside-down. In tragedies, these events lead to catastrophe, but in comedies, the events resolve happily. Literary critic Northrop Frye asserts that "the theme of the comic is the integration of society, which usually takes the form of incorporating a central character into it" (*Anatomy* 43). Furthermore, he adds that this newly integrated society "is frequently signalized by some kind of party or festive ritual, which either appears at the end of the play or is assumed to take place immediately afterward" (163). Such positive resolutions create joy and ease for the audience: because they know from the play's outset that no real pain will come to the characters, they are free to relax and enjoy the story. This understanding of comedy leads to another overarching contrast: tragedies elicit the audience's sorrow, while comedies foster laughter. The roots of this laughter, however, vary depending on the type of comedy depicted on stage. Three prominent theatrical traditions—romantic comedy, comedy of manners, and farce—emphasize different types of humor while also borrowing from one another's comic tropes.

Exceptionally popular since their genesis during the English Renaissance, *romantic comedies* tell the story of a young couple in love who must overcome various hindrances to their union. These difficulties result from the interference of family or of friends, or sometimes from their own misunderstandings. Whatever causes this friction, the play dramatizes how the lovers find their way back to each other by its end. Shakespeare authored many romantic comedies, frequently relying on mistaken and false identities as the center of his humor. *Twelfth Night* (c. 1601) features numerous motifs common to romantic comedies: gender play and crossdressing, as the heroine

Viola dons the appearance of Cesario when shipwrecked on the isle of Illyria; mistaken identities, as the countess Olivia mistakes Viola's brother Sebastian for Cesario and impulsively marries him; unexpected reversals, as Orsino plans to murder Cesario/Viola shortly before he resolves to marry him/her; and shenanigans, as various characters trick the ill-humored Malvolio into believing that Olivia loves him and then lock him in a closet.

Twelfth Night also plays with different forms of humor, including the wit and intellectual humor of Olivia's fool Feste, who embodies the oxymoronic conflation of the "wise fool." Feste proves the necessity of humor and intellect coinciding, such as when he comically and provocatively convinces Olivia that she herself is a fool to mourn her dead brother (1.5.55–74). Shakespeare also plays with low humor with the boorish and unrefined wit of the appropriately named Sir Toby Belch and his friends. This contrast between high and low comic sensibilities, between rarefied wit and crass humor, enlightens various characters' personalities for the audience, who understands them better through the varieties of laughter that they engender.

When Viola contemplates the complications arising from her disguise as Cesario—with Orsino in love with Olivia, who loves Cesario because she is unaware that Cesario is actually Viola—she voices a key comic theme of many romantic comedies:

> My master loves her dearly;
> And I (poor monster) fond as much on him;
> And she (mistaken) seems to dote on me.
> What will become of this? As I am man,
> My state is desperate for my master's love;
> As I am woman (now alas the day!),
> What thriftless sighs shall poor Olivia breathe!
> O time, thou must untangle this, not I:
> It is too hard a knot for me t'untie.
>
> (2.2.33–41)

Viola hopes that time will resolve her difficulties, and she is correct in this assumption. Indeed, Viola does little to effect the play's happy ending, for in most romantic comedies time itself erases the obstacles preventing the lovers' union. In this instance, Orsino happily finds himself in love with the now-female Viola (although she remains dressed as Cesario); Sebastian and Olivia remain married, despite that she wed the wrong man; and it is revealed that Sir Toby has married the clever Maria.

Given their thematic interest in courtship and marriage, many romantic comedies, whether implicitly or explicitly, address issues of gender and sexuality percolating in their era. With *Barefoot in the Park* (1963), Neil Simon offers a more contemporary romantic comedy, one that shares elements of physical comedy and witty repartee with older plays while observing the changing attitudes in twentieth-century relationships. When Corie and Paul

Bratter move into their new home after their honeymoon, their differences in personality spark the play's comedy. Corie adores their imperfect apartment, idealizing it as a reflection of the couple's love. When her mother visits, she points out a critical difference between her daughter and new son-in-law:

> MOTHER. I worry about you two. You're so impulsive. You jump into life. Paul is like me. He looks first. (*She sits down on the suitcase.*)
> CORIE. He doesn't look. He stares. That's the trouble with both of you.
> (35)

Caught up in a spontaneous vision of life, Corie romanticizes love and marriage, while Paul focuses on practical issues, such as the cost of their apartment and planning for their future. Paul and Corie argue about their incompatibility, with Corie pointing out they have "absolutely *nothing* in common," to which Paul replies, "Why? Because I won't walk barefoot in the park in winter?" (95). This argument escalates until Corie demands a divorce and Paul storms out and spends the night outside during winter. In the model of most romantic comedies, Paul and Corie reunite, after his overnight excursion results in her worry and his illness:

> CORIE. . . . I want the old Paul back.
> PAUL. That fuddy duddy?
> CORIE. He's not a fuddy duddy. He's dependable and he's strong and he takes care of me and tells me how much I can spend and protects me from people like you . . . And I just want him to know how much I love him . . . And that I'm going to make everything here exactly the way he wants it.
> (140)

Although Corie's decision to cede her desires to meet her husband's needs (and to let him support her fully) may seem dated to twenty-first-century audiences, the larger concern of the play addresses the couple's reunion, the purpose of a romantic comedy. In his book *Neil Simon*, Robert K. Johnson observes that "Simon celebrates compromise, rather than insisting a position be maintained in all its stark purity. Because this outlook is a traditional one, some people fail to see that it very neatly binds funny lines and funny characters together" (15). Given the focus of romantic comedies on creating unions between lovers, their conclusions often celebrate values of compromise, in which the protagonists adapt themselves to each other's needs.

The *comedy of manners* humorously mocks the behavior and manners of particular social classes, most often the social elite. These plays feature the characters' disruptions of social norms and witty dialogue, known as *repartee* or *badinage*, in which the characters play a verbal game of wits, with their lines humorously building off each other's. The comedy of manners looks underneath the masks worn in polite society, thematically exposing human weaknesses with intelligent and biting wit. They often feature romantic relationships, but these are not a necessity. As with many romantic comedies, the comedy of manners frequently relies on misunderstandings and false appearances.

The comedy of manners became highly popular during the second half of the 1600s, particularly in the work of French playwright Molière, such as his *The Misanthrope, Tartuffe,* and *The School for Wives* (1662). The latter illustrates many of the typical features of the comedy of manners in its story of Agnes, who was raised in a convent by nuns directed to give her only a limited education. Her ward, Arnolphe, believed that keeping her uneducated would make her more likely to marry him when she came of age. Upon leaving the convent, however, Agnes falls in love with Horace, the son of one of Arnolphe's friends. Much of the play's comedy and action result from two misunderstandings: Agnes refers to Arnolphe as Monsieur de la Souche, so neither she nor Horace realize that they know the same person. Also, after a problematic conversation about their relationship, Agnes believes that Arnolphe has agreed to let her marry Horace, while Arnolphe believes she has agreed to marry him. Molière relies on numerous mistakes, communication errors, and the schemes of various characters to create the play's humor, while also criticizing the ways in which the daughters of the elite were (under)educated in his day. Late in the play, Agnes argues with Arnolphe about her desire to marry Horace, and their dialogue reflects the witty banter common in this type of comedy:

> AGNES. Why do you scream?
> ARNOLPHE. Why do you do me wrong?
> AGNES. Just name a single wicked thing I've done!
> ARNOLPHE. Isn't eloping with your lover one?
> ANGES. He wants to marry me. Didn't you say
>   You *have* to marry? Take the sin away?
>   I'm doing what you told me.
> ARNOLPHE. I said so.
>   It's me that you were meant to marry, though!
>   I rather thought I'd dinned that into you.
> AGNES. Perhaps, but frankly—just between us two—
>   You're not my type and *he* is. What's your view
>   Of marriage? Something nasty, something grim.
>   That's *not* the picture that I get from *him*.
>
>   (93)

A staple of the comedy of manners, such clever repartee sparks the comic revelation of the characters' desires. Arnolphe's longstanding plan to create an uneducated and controllable wife backfires, as Agnes instead becomes independent and finds love elsewhere. Indeed, she makes it clear to Arnolphe that she understood that he was manipulating her through her failed education:

AGNES. And what an *education* I've received!
You don't suppose I've ever once believed
That I was anything other than a clot?
(96)

Her "education," unworthy of a girl of her social status, could not constrain her independent spirit. The play exposes the hypocrisies of the upper classes through satiric methods, and it offers a romantic union between Agnes and Horace as well.

During the same period as Molière's *The School for Wives*, and into the eighteenth century, numerous English writers penned comedies of manners. Among these English plays, commonly referred to as Restoration comedies, William Wycherley exposes the hypocrisy of Puritan values in his complexly plotted *The Country Wife* (1675). William Congreve's *The Way of the World* (1700) and Richard Brinsley Sheridan's *The Rivals* (1775) and *The School for Scandal* (1777) stand as the eighteenth century's great achievements in the comedy of manners tradition, with memorable characters engaging in sharp repartee in pursuit of their pleasures. In the late nineteenth and early twentieth centuries, the comedy of manners enjoyed renewed popularity. Oscar Wilde's *The Importance of Being Earnest* and *Lady Windermere's Fan* mercilessly ridicule the pretensions of the late Victorian era. With *Candida* (1898), Irish playwright George Bernard Shaw offers a thoughtful comedy of manners about love and marriage. Noel Coward's *Private Lives* (1930) depicts a divorced couple honeymooning with their new spouses at the same hotel.

Despite the great variety of these plays, written over the course of hundreds of years, they unite in their celebration of style over standard morality. As David Hirst argues of comedies of manners, "Style is all-important in these plays. By style is meant not merely a superficial manner of expression but a definition of behavior. The winners are always those with the most style: the sharpest wits, the subtlest intriguers" (2). Indeed, as Hirst discusses, some critics charge that comedies of manners descend into immorality in their ironic treatment of social mores, but it need not be considered immoral for a play to hold a mirror up to the society it depicts.

Comedies including significant physical antics, exaggerated situations, and/ or crude or sexual jokes, are known as *farces*. Farce is often denigrated in comparison to other forms of humor, as Jessica Davis explains:

As long as it is viewed as existing in symbiosis with "richer" forms of comedy, farce can only be characterized by negatives—the more exaggerated characterizations, the cruder coincidences, and the grosser pieces of joking belong to the farce, while the more sophisticated elements of plot, character, and theme are those of comedy proper.

(6)

Outlandishness is key to farce's appeal, for it pushes harder against propriety than do other comic forms. Joe Orton's *What the Butler Saw* (1969) models this form, focusing on exaggerated situations sparked by sexual desire. When psychiatrist Dr. Prentice decides to seduce a woman applying to be his secretary, he sets off a series of complicated and unlikely events (including cajoling the job applicant to undress during the interview). The play also relies on physical comedy, such as Dr. Prentice hiding the secretarial candidate in his office when his wife arrives. Significantly, the term *farce* can be applied to many comic genres already discussed. Comedies such as *Twelfth Night* and *The Importance of Being Earnest* also employ aspects of farce in their most absurd moments. In an oft-quoted statement on theater, Edward Gordon Craig posits that all plays—not merely comedies—are farcical: "Farce is the essential theatre. Farce refined becomes high comedy: farce brutalized becomes tragedy" (125). Many plays stage unlikely situations, and identifying the ways in which the playwright distills this foundation into a particular form of comedy, or even of tragedy, enlightens how structure influences content, and in turn creates a theatrical experience.

Drama

The term *drama*, as mentioned earlier in this chapter, applies to the genre of plays as a whole, but it also refers to plays focusing on serious subjects using serious styles that lack the devastation or deadly consequences of tragedies. George Bernard Shaw discusses the ineffectiveness of traditional genres of tragedy and comedy in presenting modern life:

> Not only is the tradition of the catastrophe unsuitable to modern studies of life: the tradition of an ending, happy or the reverse, is equally unworkable. The moment the dramatist gives up accidents and catastrophes and takes "slices of life" as his material, he finds himself committed to plays that have no endings. The curtain no longer comes down on a hero slain or married: it comes down when the audience has seen enough of the life presented to it to draw the moral, and must either leave the theatre or miss its last train.
>
> (Preface xv–xvi)

For Shaw, the idea that characters' lives continue past the confines of a play vitally illuminates drama. The real world does not teach conclusions as pat as tragedies and comedies might suggest, and for Shaw and many other playwrights, drama must capture this real world and its moral ambiguity.

Shaw's ideas about drama reflect his commitment to *dramatic realism*, a theatrical genre that depicts the world as it is by attending to the experiences of a broad range of ordinary people and by showcasing situations common to everyday life. Anticipating Shaw's theories of drama, Russian playwright Anton Chekhov consistently muses on themes concerning personal and social failures, as well as the struggle to find meaning in one's life, in his dramas, including *The Cherry Orchard*, *Three Sisters*, and *Uncle Vanya*. In *The Cherry Orchard* (1904), Chekhov presents the story of a wealthy yet severely indebted family who, refusing to act on other options, sells off its estate, with a lovely cherry orchard, to the son of a former serf. The play criticizes the failures of the aristocracy as well as the rise of the new middle class through an intriguing blend of humor coupled with sadness over the loss of identity and place. While the play has been referred to as both a comedy and a tragedy, it more aptly belongs to the realm of drama because it straddles these ostensibly opposed traditions in its dramatization of the absurdity and failings of this specific family. In a wryly comic moment, Firs, an elderly servant who advocates the old system of serfdom, chats with Lopakhin, a wealthy man born in poverty who will eventually buy the estate:

> FIRS. . . . When the slaves were freed, I was already head footman here. I didn't want to be freed. I was head footman. I stayed with my masters . . . (*Pause.*) They were happy then. Why? I don't know. They didn't know themselves.
> LOPAKHIN. Oh, the old days were fine—they could at least flog the peasants then.
> FIRS. (*Not having heard.*) That's right. The peasants took care of the masters, and the masters took care of the peasants. Now everyone goes his own way, and no one understands anything.
>
> (28)

Although the peculiarity of pining for a time of slavery and powerlessness adds to the play's humor, Firs's genuine feelings of loss poignantly capture the disruptions to previous ways of life. This ability to capture a spectrum of emotional experience has made *The Cherry Orchard* one of the most enduring plays of its era.

More recent plays in the school of dramatic realism similarly depict situations which shed light on an array of human experiences and struggles. Lillian Hellman's *The Children's Hour* (1934) tells the story of two women, Karen and Martha, who run a boarding school. When a student begins a rumor that the two teachers are lovers, the ensuing scandal results in many parents removing their children from the school and the smearing of the women's reputations. After losing their school, Martha admits that she does, in fact, have romantic feelings for Karen. Because Karen denies Martha's feelings, saying, "I won't listen to you," and "You're telling yourself a lie. We never thought of each other that way" (79), Martha cannot handle her guilt and commits suicide. The play thematically explores the destruction caused by lies and gossip, as well as the deadly consequences of secrets. The play offers the audience the opportunity to consider the meanings of pain, crisis, truth, lies, and unspoken desires, as Martha and Karen struggle to make the right decisions, and as Karen lives on in a world in which no one intervenes to prevent injustice.

During the first half of the twentieth century, German author Bertolt Brecht and other artists developed *epic theater*, a type of theatrical experience removed from familiar forms of dramatic realism. Brecht explains the central idea of epic theater: "The essential point of the epic theatre is perhaps that it appeals less to the feelings than to the spectator's reason. Instead of sharing an experience the spectator must come to grips with things" (*Brecht on Theatre* 23). In reaction against what he decried as the passivity of audiences to the theater's emotional world, Brecht aimed to create experiences that would shake viewers out of their complacency and force them to confront issues. Brecht used multiple devices to create an *alienation effect* that would make familiar elements unusual and foreign. This process creates *defamiliarization*, the experience of feeling separate from the characters and events of the play. Brecht believed that audience members should not emotionally connect to the characters onstage; this meant that they could better analyze the situations depicted in the play, and thus in life. To achieve this alienation effect and to maintain the audience's awareness that they were watching a play as it was constructed, Brecht used multiple devices and strategies. Actors were encouraged to perform or narrate their characters rather than to emotionally "become" them, creating some distance in the performance. Also, set and costume changes were performed in front of the audience to demonstrate the play's construction of artifice. Plays in the epic theater tradition often interrupt the main action with songs, verse, and jarring visual elements such as slide projections or placards. These effects interrupt viewers' efforts to submerge themselves in the theatrical experience, compelling them to step outside it and consider its themes.

To achieve these effects, Brecht's *Mother Courage and Her Children* (1939) stages numerous songs to emphasize its major themes. Set during the 1600s, the play focuses on wartime profiteers who sacrifice their morality for financial gain. Mother Courage sells her wares during many years of war, and in a brief scene when she travels with her daughter and a chaplain, she comments, "I won't let you spoil my war for me. Destroys the weak, does it? Well, what does peace do for 'em, huh? War feeds its people better" (82). She then sings a song reflecting her problematic attitude to war:

> MOTHER COURAGE. If war don't suit your disposition
>   When victory comes, you will be dead.
>   War is a business proposition:
>   But not with cheese, with steel instead!
>
> (82)

The peculiarity of combining lyrics about the business of war with a lilting melody creates for viewers a chance to listen and deeply ponder Brecht's subject. In fact, no real action occurs in the one-page scene and so its entire purpose is to comment on the theme for the audience. In explaining his goals in epic theater, Brecht comments that the spectator is given the chance to criticize human behavior from a social point of view. . . . The idea is that the spectator should be put in a position where he can make comparisons about everything that influences the way in which human beings behave.

(*Brecht on Theatre* 86)

Brecht sought to create an audience who would act with social and political conscience, and he believed that by coercing his audience to distance themselves from the emotional content of plays, they would become more actively involved in the world.

The playwrights involved in the *Theater of the Absurd* did not share the lofty goals of those involved in epic theater, but they significantly influenced twentieth-century drama. Coming into prominence in France after World War II, the Theater of the Absurd posits that humanity continually devolves into absurdity and that the theater best presents the human condition through art that is itself absurd. Martin Esslin proposes that the main theme of Absurdist plays is "metaphysical anguish at the absurdity of the human condition" (xix), and he further describes the Theater of the Absurd in terms of how it differs from more traditional theater concerned with the same themes. Whereas other plays

present their sense of the irrationality of the human condition in the form of highly lucid and logically constructed reasoning . . . the Theatre of the Absurd strives to express its sense of the senselessness of the human condition and the inadequacy of the rational approach by the open abandonment of rational devices and discursive thought.

(xix–xx)

This perspective results in plays serious in their subject matter yet comic in their staging. Samuel Beckett's *Waiting for Godot* (1953) depicts the story of two men, Vladimir and Estragon, waiting on a rural road for another man, Godot, whom they have never met. The play is comprised entirely of the two men idling the time away: they chat, sleep, play with their hats, consider suicide, and trifle away the hours with only brief interruptions from Pozzo and his slave Lucky. The play ends without Godot's arrival, yet the men do not leave, thus suggesting the futility and meaninglessness of the human condition, as characters lack the necessary depth or motivation that most viewers expect in plays. Other authors such as Jean Genet (*The Maids*, 1949, and *The Balcony*, 1956), Eugène Ionesco (*Rhinoceros*, 1959), Harold Pinter (*The Birthday Party*, 1957), and Tom Stoppard (*Rosencrantz and Guildenstern Are Dead*, 1966) also work in the Theater of the Absurd.

During the latter years of the twentieth century, and into the twenty-first, numerous playwrights have drawn together distinct genres to create blended, hybrid dramatic works. Ntozake Shange describes her *For Colored Girls Who Have Considered Suicide When the Rainbow Is Enuf* (1975) as a "choreopoem," in which a group of women, all named by color (i.e., Lady in Blue), perform a collection of poems. The lines are presented with stage directions, but they are also formatted as poetry. The characters in the play narrate a variety of difficult experiences in the lives of African-American women, including domestic abuse, rape, and abortion. The play concludes with hope when the women come together and recognize their lives lacked something to make them complete. One after another, the women desire a blessing, "a layin on of hands" (60–62). Lady in Red, before the play's conclusion, comments: "i found god in myself / & I loved her / I loved her fiercely" (63). This merger of poetry and drama allows the characters to distill the power and grace of poetry within the communal space of the theater. It is through the women's ability to express pain with this unique poetic language that the play succeeds.

Tony Kushner's *Angels in America* (1991/1992), a play in two parts (*Millennium Approaches* and *Perestroika*), dramatizes the effect of AIDS on the lives of several people during the 1980s. In many ways the play exemplifies the epic reach of dramatic realism, demonstrating the meaning of sexual identity and the challenges of living with AIDS against a vast tableau ranging from earth to heaven. In addition to other plotlines, Louis Ironson, unable to cope with his partner Prior Walter's declining health, abandons him. Several emotionally resonant scenes depict Prior joking about the situation while Louis struggles with his own fears of mortality. In the midst of this realistic framework, Kushner interweaves moments of fantasy, such as when an angel appears to talk to Prior. The stage directions indicate that

> *A sound, like a plummeting meteor, tears down from very, very far above the earth, hurtling at an incredible velocity towards the bedroom; the light seems to be sucked out of the room as the projectile approaches; as the room reaches darkness, we hear a terrifying CRASH as something immense strikes earth; the whole building shudders and a part of the bedroom ceiling, lots of plaster and lathe and wiring, crashes to the floor. And then in a shower of unearthly white light, spreading great opalescent gray-silver wings, the Angel descends into the room and floats above the bed.*

(118)

The contrast between the play's realism and its fantastical moments confronts audiences with the flexible boundaries of art. *Angels in America* also calls for the actors to play multiple roles, drawing attention to the varied performances and the play's metatheatrical strategies. Through the blending of genres and the actors' performing of multiple characters, Kushner questions the boundaries of any type of identity or sexuality.

The concepts of tragedy, comedy, and drama can only begin to cover the vast array of plays and themes, yet understanding these major theatrical genres gives readers a starting point in their analyses and investigations. In many ways, too, these distinctions create artificial boundaries among artworks, for many plays unite the tragic, the comic, and the dramatic to find deeper meanings from their interconnections. Virtually all human life includes moments of the comic (birth, laughter, and love), the tragic (death, loss, and suffering), and the dramatic (misunderstandings and conflict, even with one's family and loved ones). The theater crystallizes such moments for its viewers, speaking to the narrative power of witnessing such events unfold before one's eyes.

2.4 Cinematic Adaptations of Literature

Never could William Shakespeare have imagined that his plays would be transformed into movies, yet cinematic history would lose immeasurably without the many adaptations of his works, including such acclaimed films as Laurence Olivier's *Hamlet* (1948), Kenneth Branagh's *Henry V* (1989), Baz Luhrmann's *Romeo + Juliet* (1996), and John Madden's *Shakespeare in Love* (1998). Indeed, a recent subgenre of Shakespearian film consists of loose adaptations starring young adult leads, such as *Ten Things I Hate about You* (1999, based on *The Taming of the Shrew*), *O* (2001, based on *Othello*), *She's the Man* (2006, based on *Twelfth Night*), and *Warm Bodies* (2013, a zombie flick based on *Romeo and Juliet*). Other esteemed authors whose works are frequently adapted to the screen include Jane Austen, Emily and Charlotte Brontë, Nathaniel Hawthorne, Charles Dickens, and Henry James, but these few names belie the prevalence of adaptation as a narrative strategy for the cinematic arts, in which stories originally composed for readers are reimagined for viewers. Wary of unsure investments, Hollywood studios frequently green-light adaptations of popular novels, expecting their devoted readers to eagerly buy tickets for these films. This strategy often produces winning results, as attested to by the blockbuster status of such recent book and film series as J. K. Rowling's *Harry Potter*, Stephenie Meyer's *Twilight*, and Suzanne Collins's *Hunger Games*.

From Page to Screen: An Overview of Cinematic Adaptations of Literature

Fiction and film are both narrative arts, but they are predicated upon vastly different processes and technologies. Fiction writers typically write alone, whereas numerous artists collaborate to create a film. Fiction writers rely simply on their pens or word processors, whereas cinematic production requires a variety of individuals with specialized skills and technical expertise: the screenwriter, who pens the screenplay; the actors, who embody and give life to the screenwriter's characters; the cinematographer, or director of photography, who controls the camera and takes responsibility for the images shot; the editor, who splices together the footage into the film's final cut; and the director, who envisions and manages the project in its entirety. Hundreds of others, from the costumers to the caterers, are acknowledged for their contributions when the credits roll.

The many differences between fiction and film can be distilled into the difference between words and images: fiction relies on weaving words together into a complete narrative, whereas films unite a string of images, with accompanying dialogue, into a coherent whole. Thus, the process of adapting a novel or other narrative to the screen necessitates that the filmmakers confront the author's words and recalibrate them into an audiovisual medium. Barry Sandler, the screenwriter of *Making Love* (1982), *Crimes of Passion* (1984), and *Knock 'Em Dead* (2013), and who adapted Agatha Christie's *The Mirror Crack'd* (1980), outlines the challenges of transforming another author's story to the screen:

> The challenge of adapting a novel to the screen is to retain the elements of story, character, and tone that make the novel work while creating a filmic structure of protagonist, antagonist, obstacles, and resolution that succeed as a cinematic experience. This may require compressing, combining, or even eliminating elements in the novel to create visual dramatic action and narrative flow that lead from one scene into the next with a constantly building momentum.

As Sandler suggests, adaptation requires a sympathetic understanding of the source text while also recognizing the transformations that must occur to bring it to the screen. His phrase "visual dramatic action" captures the heart of the cinematic experience, for each of these elements—the visuals projected onto the screen, the dramatic structure that creates a compelling narrative, and the actions the characters undertake to advance its plot—must be analyzed separately and complementarily to perceive how the narrative will metamorphose into a new medium.

While novels often span hundreds of pages, most films run between one-and-a-half to two hours, which necessitates that cinematic adaptations compress these narratives' ampler scope. Conversely, many short stories run about twenty pages long, and so screenwriters must devise new scenarios to expand their spare storylines. A rule of thumb for filmmaking proposes that one page of a screenplay translates into one minute of screen time, and so most screenplays consist of about 90 to 120 pages. At the same time, film, as a visual medium, has several advantages over print that counterbalances its paring down of pages. An author might need several paragraphs to describe a setting sufficiently for readers to visualize it, while a film simply shows this image. Authors must capture the ways their characters react to one another and to their experiences through words, but films can depict such moments instantaneously as the camera records a glance, a gesture, or any another such moment that proves again that a picture is worth a thousand words.

Adaptations vary in their fidelity to their source texts, from those adhering to their sources as if page by page, to those straying wildly—promiscuously—from the author's intentions. Nonetheless, when viewing cinematic adaptations of literature, it is important to realize that literature cannot claim an inherent superiority as an artistic medium to cinema, and neither does cinema stand as an inherently superior art form to literature. A frequent criticism of cinematic adaptations condemns them for failing to get the story "right," but as Thomas Leitch argues, such a desire is merely a chimera:

> Fidelity to its source text—whether it is conceived as success in re-creating specific textual details or the effect of the whole—is a hopelessly fallacious measure of a given adaptation's value because it is unattainable, undesirable, and theoretically possible only in a trivial sense.
>
> (161)

Novels cannot be fed through a cinematic filter with a pristinely accurate film resulting. In translating text to image, numerous changes must be made throughout the process of adaptation, and so no story remains unaltered by the process.

Given the vast range of cinematic fidelity to source texts, Geoffrey Wagner proposes a tripartite model for assessing the relationship between an adaptation and the narrative inspiring it:

1   transposition—"a novel is directly given on the screen, with the minimum of apparent interference." (222)
2   commentary—"an original is taken and either purposely or inadvertently altered in some respect. It could also be called a re-emphasis or re-structure." (223)
3   analogy—the analogy "must represent a fairly considerable departure for the sake of making *another* work of art. . . . [A]n analogy generally . . . cannot be indicted as a violation of a literary original since the director has not attempted (or has only minimally attempted) to reproduce the original." (227)

Wagner's model assists spectators in assessing the relationship between an adaptation and its source text, but it should be noted that, as neither literature nor cinema is an inherently superior artistic mode to the other, neither is one of Wagner's modes of transposition, commentary, and analogy essentially superior to the others. Distinguishing among levels of fidelity to a source text nonetheless assists viewers in gauging the narrative effects of these decisions.

The short stories and novels of Truman Capote have been adapted cinematically on numerous occasions, and these adaptions, with their varying artistic objectives, exemplify Wagner's model. In his 1967 film of Capote's masterpiece *In Cold Blood*, Richard Brooks took great care to adhere to the author's vision. One can follow the book with the film in most key scenes, and although Brooks took certain liberties—such as the character of the reporter Jensen, who substitutes for Capote's narrator—his film faithfully captures the consequences of the virtually random slaughter of a family of four in Kansas. Brooks consulted with Capote on the film, and Capote describes how both men sought to adhere to his narrative:

> [W]e both wanted the film to duplicate reality, . . . and to have every scene filmed in its real locale: the house of the Clutter family; the same Kansas variety store where [the killers] bought the rope and tape used to bind their four victims; and certain courthouses, prisons, filling stations, hotel rooms and highways and city streets. . . . A complicated procedure, but the only possible one by which almost all elements of fantasy could be removed and reality thereby achieve its proper reflection.
>
> (*Portraits* 270)

Capote and Brooks concurred that the film must capture the reality depicted in his novel, and so a transpositional adaptation facilitated their joint ambition to maintain the novel's plot and themes as closely as possible.

Cinematic adaptations that take greater liberties with their source texts, which Wagner labels "commentaries," can also succeed as classics in their own right. Capote's novella *Breakfast at Tiffany's* is not a romantic comedy, and his gay narrator expresses no desire to seduce his charming neighbor Holly Golightly. On the contrary, he explicitly states the asexual nature of his affections for her by comparing them to other platonic loves: "For I *was* in love with her. . . . Just as I'd once been in love with my mother's elderly colored cook and a postman who let me follow him on his rounds and a whole family named McKendrick. That category of love generates jealousy, too" (76). It is generally agreed that Capote's gay narrator represents Capote himself, but in Blake Edwards's 1961 film of *Breakfast at Tiffany's*, Capote's narrator becomes a heterosexual author, played by man's man George Peppard, who falls in love with Holly and convinces her to give up her dreams of wealth for happiness with him. Despite this fundamental alteration to the plot, Edwards's film is justly celebrated as one of the defining romantic comedies of Hollywood history. Audrey Hepburn delivers a winsome performance as Capote's Holly, such that her performance defines the character in the popular imagination more than the author's descriptions of her. While one might justly decry the homophobia that led to these alterations between novella and film, the freedom to re-emphasize and restructure the source text in an adaptation of the commentary mode allowed Edwards to bring a new perspective to Capote's tale, in an ultimately winning style.

Still, it must be admitted that the decisions of some filmmakers to adapt a story and change it even more radically—to make the film an analogy of its source text, in Wagner's terms, rather than a transposition or commentary— are perplexing. To continue with examples of adaptations from Truman

Capote's corpus, his comic short story "Children on Their Birthdays" features Miss Bobbit, an irrepressible and amoral child heroine seeking to fulfill her dreams of Hollywood stardom until she dies unexpectedly when hit by bus. The black humor of a dead child, with her dreams and herself quite literally crushed, does not cry out for a cinematic translation, yet in Mark Medoff's 2002 film *Children on Their Birthdays*, the same heroine is recast as the moral guide to her hometown. Furthermore, instead of receiving her comic comeuppance in a head-on collision, she safely boards the bus that whisks her off to Hollywood glory. When confronted by such drastic differences between text and adaptation, viewers often wonder why the filmmakers chose to play so loosely with their sources. Nevertheless, the question that should be asked is not whether the film succeeds in translating its source text to the screen as an accurate representation of its author's themes, but whether the film succeeds or fails in its own right, according to its own terms. Quite simply, not every film that strictly adheres to its source text succeeds; not every film that deviates noticeably from its source text fails. When examining adaptations, viewers should recognize that filmmakers follow their own artistic interests when adapting a novel, and their cinematic aspirations may diverge from the literary themes expressed in their source texts.

Cinematic Vocabulary

Before sitting down to watch a cinematic adaptation, spectators should determine, if possible, which of its many elements they will focus on for their analysis. Indeed, if one is examining the film's dialogue and plot structure, it may be more helpful to read its screenplay before viewing the film. Whether one reads the screenplay or watches the film first, discussing and writing about film requires a critical vocabulary incorporating cinematic terms. As readers of poems, novels, and plays must be able to discuss these literary modes with an apt lexicon for the task, so too must cinephiles employ the proper terminology to capture the aesthetic and dramatic effects of various cinematic technologies.

Novels and films are analogous yet distinct in their creation of fictional worlds, and most follow Gustav Freytag's standard structures of plot construction (*For Freytag's pyramid, see pp. 131–32.*) Further extending the structural comparisons of novels and films, both can be subdivided into chapters. (DVDs typically divide films into chapters, but these divisions are also known as *sequences* in cinematic terms.) Often it is difficult to determine precisely when a sequence begins or ends in a film. Unlike books, which clearly mark chapters with such cues as white space, indentation, and subtitles, films rarely alert viewers to divisions between sequences as the narrative unwinds. Developing the structural analogy between books and films further, as a book's chapters contain paragraphs, film sequences are composed of *scenes*, which consist of several narrative moments united in theme, location, or plot point. As paragraphs are composed of sentences, scenes

Table 2.4.1 Structural Analogy between Books and Films

Novels	Films
Chapters	Sequences
Paragraphs	Scenes
Sentences	Shots
Words	Frames

are composed of *shots*. A *shot* records a scene, or parts of a scene, from the moment that the camera starts until it cuts away to another scene or perspective. Finally, as sentences are composed of words, shots are composed of *frames*. The term *frame* has two interrelated meanings in cinematic analysis: it constitutes the borders of the image filmed, and thus marks off what spectators see from what they cannot see, and it is also a single exposure of a film roll. As literary analysis might focus on the multiple meanings potential in a single word of a poem, a film analysis benefits from detailed consideration of an individual frame.

When viewers pause a DVD, they see one frame in its full complexity and can examine how its various elements unite to convey its narrative and thematic meaning. Some initial questions for analysis include:

- What are the actors wearing, how are they posed, and what are their gestures?
- How is the frame lit, which of its elements are highlighted, and what does the interplay of light and shadow convey?
- What props are used in the frame, how do the actors employ them, and what symbolic meaning might they carry?
- How does the camera's angle contribute to the frame's meaning by positioning the actors and other elements in a particular manner?

Such questions are useful for analyzing a frame of a film, and together they help viewers to read its *mise-en-scène*. As discussed in the previous chapter (*see pp. 162–63*), this French term arises from the world of theater, where it designates the arrangement of the stage for a given production. In cinema, mise-en-scène details the way the space within the frame is filled, including such elements as the actors and their poses, props, lighting, and the camera's perspective on them.

A frame's mise-en-scène is organically connected to its *composition*, which comprises its various visual elements and their interrelationship. In some shots directors aim for *balance*, in which the frame's composition creates aesthetic harmony, with its various elements complementary and symmetrical to one another. Conversely, some shots require that the composition reflect chaos and disorder, and so its various elements are staged to suggest disharmony.

A good strategy for reading frames is to look at the first and last frames of a shot, scene, or sequence, so that one can consider how given frames function within the overarching cinematic narrative. In Billy Wilder's *Double Indemnity* (1944), the apartment of insurance agent Walter Neff reflects his character's sense of orderly behavior and control. Against the wall of his living room is a bare couch and at each end is a small table with a lamp. On the wall above the couch are three evenly spaced framed images. Thus, an early frame from this sequence accentuates the character's ordinary and calm lifestyle. When Phyllis Dietrichson comes to seduce Walter into helping her kill her husband for the insurance payout, she sits on the couch, in shadow just outside the light from one of the lamps, implying that her ideas are immoral and should be hidden from view. When Walter decides, finally, to assist her with the murder, their decision is made in the dark, with one lamp finally turned off and the room's visual balance disrupted. Through its visual cues and compositional imbalance, this frame illustrates the quick dissolution of Neff's morality and his seduction into crime. By analyzing a series of frames from this film, it is apparent that its mise-en-scène and composition enhance its escalating narrative tension. Furthermore, to fully appreciate the effects achieved through mise-en-scène, viewers must ponder the significance of each of its constituent elements to understand how they interrelate.

The Camera and Cinematic Vocabulary

Whereas novelists create aesthetic and emotional effects solely through their words, filmmakers rely on the intersection of word and image, which necessitates the use of cameras. Consequently, much of the critical lexicon of filmmaking refers directly or indirectly to the camera's foundational role in movie-making. Many filmmakers feel passionately about the camera's role in the creative process, such as the Russian documentarian Dziga Vertov, who, in a moment of anthropomorphic exuberance, sings of the camera's versatility and freedom:

> I am kino-eye. I am a mechanical eye. I, a machine, show you the world as only I can see it. Now and forever, I free myself from human immobility. I am in constant motion. I draw near, then away from objects. I crawl under, I climb onto them. I move apace with the muzzle of a galloping horse.

(17)

Vertov's rhapsody celebrates the camera's power to achieve what the human eye cannot accomplish by itself: although both cameras and eyes decipher external visual stimuli into images, eyes cannot capture and relay these images to others, especially images taken from environments inhospitable to human life, from the ocean's depths to outer space.

The camera's placement relative to a shot is referred to as its *angle*. The camera might be placed directly in front of the action being filmed in a fixed position, but livelier shots result from more active camera work. Indeed, many early films feel rather flat due to the camera's static positioning relative to the scene. Once filmmakers realized the camera's position could be moved to create different visual effects, cinematographers began creating deeper compositions by situating their lenses in ways to enhance the film's themes and its depiction of characters and settings. If the camera shoots from above, it is referred to as a *high angle*; if the camera shoots from below, it is a *low angle*. Frequently, high angles make characters appear smaller and thus diminish their stature, whereas low angles make them appear larger and thus more forbidding. In Alfred Hitchcock's classic film *Psycho* (1960), after detective Milton Arbogast, looking for the missing (and unknown to him—dead) Lila Crane, enters the house of Norman Bates and his mother, his suspicions draw him to the staircase. His walk up the stairs is filmed using a high-angle shot, indicating his lack of control and power. Immediately after reaching the top of the stairs, he is stabbed in the chest by Norman's mother and he falls backwards down the stairs, once again filmed from a high angle. By using this dramatic angle in this scene, the film underscores the powerlessness of Arbogast in the insane world of the Bates family. Likewise, in the famous "taunting scene" of *Monty Python and the Holy Grail* (1975), when haughty French guards safely ensconced in a tower mock King Arthur, as he stands below them, the French guards are often shot from low angles to make them appear more powerful, whereas Arthur and his men are often shot from high angles, to accentuate their vulnerability and weakness. While viewers might assume a king should wield more power than guards, the use of contrasting shots from high and low angles assists directors Terry Jones and Terry Gilliam in parodying the legendary British king.

In a *point-of-view shot*, the camera acts as the eyes of a character, and viewers observe the unfolding events through his or her eyes. Typically, a point-of-view shot is established by a prior shot indicating whose perspective viewers will be assuming. In a *reaction shot*, the camera shows a character's response to an interlocutor's statement or to other such unfolding events. In an *establishing shot*, the camera shows viewers where the scene or sequence takes place. If a film's dramatic action occurs in a series of hotel rooms, the director might begin this sequence with an establishing shot of the hotel's exterior. Similar to the establishing shot, a *reestablishing shot* reminds or returns viewers to a setting previously encountered in the narrative.

Shots are also categorized according to the apparent distance between the camera and its subjects. In a *long shot*, the camera captures a wide-angle view, with a vast distance between it and the image filmed. Long shots often convey a film's setting and its characters' relationship to their world, as the shots then move into medium range and closer. *Medium shots* typically capture actors from the waist up. In a *close-up*, the camera focuses intently on an actor or item. Close-ups of actors heighten viewers' emotional connection to the scene: a long shot of a character crying conveys less emotional resonance than a close-up, in which the audience sees each tear trickling down the actor's face. A close-up of an object informs viewers that it bears significance to the narrative. *Extreme close-ups*, or *choke shots*, focus even more intently on the actor or object than do close-ups, further accentuating the moment's narrative importance. In Michel Hazanavicius's *The Artist* (2011), a policeman stops to talk to washed-up silent movie star George Valentin, but Valentin is so distraught that he cannot hear him, which Hazanavicius captures with an extreme close-up of the policeman's moving mouth. Through this jarring image of a talking mouth over an entire screen, Hazanavicius conveys Valentin's mental anguish and further emphasizes the film's thematic treatment of the meaning of speech for stars of silent films.

Another set of shots are named for the objects upon which they are mounted and the kinetic effects that these mechanisms achieve. In a *dolly shot*, the camera is placed on a wheeled cart so that it can move closer to or farther away from a scene, often to boost or to cool its emotional tenor; similarly, in a *tracking shot* the camera is mounted on tracks so that it moves fluidly alongside the dramatic action, allowing viewers to slide along as if they are part of the action. *Crane shots* are captured by mounting the camera on a crane, to gain an aerial perspective on the action, and *aerial shots* are taken from cameras in airplanes or helicopters. As the term implies, *hand-held cameras* are not mounted on any type of dolly or tracking device; the camera crew simply hold them. They imbue films with a more informal style, which can give the appearance that they were created by amateurs. The classic horror film *The Blair Witch Project* (1999) uses hand-held cameras to enhance its quasi-documentary and faux-realist style, as the characters apparently document themselves and their macabre demises. In a *zoom shot*, the camera moves closer to the action filmed, yet the cameraperson achieves this effect through the camera's lenses rather than by moving the camera itself. Like dolly shots, zoom shots bring viewers closer to (zoom-in) or further away (zoom-out) from the scene.

A primary issue to consider with cameras is the temporal length of the *take*, which describes how long the camera films a given shot. *Long takes* are more likely to be used in dramas to capture the emotional resonances of the plot, allowing the actors to engage more deeply in their interactions, whereas *short takes* are more suitable for action films and comedies, which feature quicker pacing. Joe Wright employs a notable long take in his adaptation of *Pride & Prejudice* (2005), starring Keira Knightley. The camera moves from room to room during a ball, pausing briefly to capture bits of conversations, then moving forward to other characters in other rooms. The long take helps viewers understand the size and variety of the party as they wander through it with the camera. Alfred Hitchcock shot all of *Rope* (1948) in long takes, with only eleven shots in the entire film. As a method of creating excitement, Guy Ritchie uses many short takes in *Sherlock Holmes* (2009) during a fight scene that takes place in a warehouse in which a ship is being built. As Robert Downey, Jr.'s Holmes fights the powerhouse Dredger, the chaos and violence of the scene is reinforced through the many short takes suggestive of the fighters' disorientation.

Appropriate lighting is essential for the camera to do its work, as well as for conveying the emotional tenor of a scene, and so cinematographers must ensure that their light sources function both effectively and aesthetically. *Available light*, which is also known as *ambient lighting*, comes from natural sources, whereas *set light* is purposefully designed to achieve the appropriate aesthetic affects for a scene. *Actor light* refers to the ways the actors are foregrounded in a shot, typically through a combination of key and back lighting. Often placed just above the camera and angled toward the actor, *key lighting* is the primary light on a subject. *High-key lighting* delivers full coverage of the subject with little or no shadow, showing the actor or object clearly; *low-key lighting* uses less light, creating shadow to accentuate certain aspects of the subject. *Back lighting* comes from behind the main actors or objects in a scene, offering limited vision of the main objects and showing them mainly in outline. Back lighting can be used to draw attention to serious moments. In *limbo lighting* the light falls only on the actors in a scene, with the setting falling into darkness.

The Editor and Cinematic Vocabulary

When cast and crew finish shooting a screenplay, the project continues for the director and editor, who select the scenes and sequences necessary to build a finished film from the many reels of footage. At this point in the process the editor must decide if some scenes should be cut entirely, perhaps if they do not contribute meaningfully to the narrative's development or if the film is running too long. Most scenes are filmed several times from several angles, and so the editor also chooses which shots best convey the narrative's focus and themes. In putting a film together, editors engage in *cutting*, in which they splice together two pieces of film. The editor's decisions in this regard affect the film's *tempo*, which is also referred to as its *editing pace* or *rhythm*. Broadly speaking, most cutting either maintains continuity, so that a scene builds coherence as it unfolds, or switches to another scene and thus effects a transition in the narrative. In *formal editing*, editors aim for consistency in the length of shots and sequences to create a steady pace for the narrative's flow, but editors might also employ shorter or longer shots to alter the film's pace and emphasize specific moments.

Editors must establish an appropriate logic to their cuts, one consistent with the film's style and genre, so that viewers do not become disoriented. In an *eyeline match*, shots are connected to a character's perspective, such that viewers witness the unfolding events as if through the actor's eyes. Another such editing strategy is the *shot/reverse shot*, also known as the *shot/countershot*, in which, for example, two characters are speaking, and the shot cuts from one person speaking to the person addressed. *Over-the-shoulder shots* assume the perspective of a character, with the camera positioned as if on the actor's shoulder so that the spectator sees, if not directly from the character's eyes, at least from his or her vantage point. Over-the-shoulder shots are frequently used in shots/reverse shots. In *cross-cutting*, which is also known as *intercutting* or *parallel development*, the editor switches between two storylines, which might be occurring simultaneously but in different settings. With a *match cut* the editor links actions so that they appear to be continuous, whereas with a *jump cut* the editor emphasizes the discontinuity between scenes. A brief yet insightful definition of *jump cut* is simply "A cut the audience notices" (Wharton and Grant 82). One of the most famous uses of jump cuts appears in Jean-Luc Godard's *Breathless* (1960). As Michel Poiccard, a small-time crook, drives a stolen car through the French countryside, jump cuts speed up his journey and emphasize the high energy of the main character. More importantly, when Poiccard shoots a police officer who stops him on the road, the jump cuts help viewers understand the confusion and disorientation of this important moment. In a *montage*, the editor links together a series of images or scenes, often to convey an extended process or period of time. While watching sports films, such as John Avildsen's *Rocky* (1976) or Josh Gordon's *Blades of Glory* (2007), viewers would likely find it boring to observe athletes undertaking the necessary training regimen for a competition, but through a montage, the editor conveys the athletes' dedication to their goal while maintaining viewers' interest.

Editors must also consider how to transition from one scene to another. With a *fade-in*, a dark screen brightens and the shot comes into focus; in a *fade-out*, the shot darkens to blackness. A *dissolve* consists of one shot fading out as another emerges, with the two images momentarily sharing the screen. With a *wipe*, the shot flows across the screen—most commonly from left to right but potentially from right to left, or from top to bottom or bottom to top—with the new shot covering the preceding shot. Wipes were common in the first half of the twentieth century; when used in later films, such as George Lucas's *Star Wars* (1977), they often evoke nostalgia for older cinema. When used effectively, fade-ins and fade-outs provide slight pauses in the narrative, whereas dissolves and wipes segue into the following scene immediately; thus, they are effective strategies for slowing or accelerating a film's tempo.

Sound and Cinematic Vocabulary

A film's use of sound further contributes to the efficacy of its storytelling, particularly through its development of acoustic themes and motifs complementary to those of the narrative. The *score* refers to the music playing in a film that remains, for the most part, in the narrative's background. The best film scores create musical motifs that harmonize with the action onscreen, such that the two are forever melded in viewers' memory. Scores also contribute to narrative continuity by aurally cuing viewers to recurrent actions. John Williams, the winner of Academy Awards for scoring *Fiddler on the Roof* (1971), *Jaws* (1975), *Star Wars* (1977), *E. T., The Extra-Terrestrial* (1982), and *Schindler's List* (1993), has created iconic music throughout his career, from the menacing tones of *Jaws* to the rousing chords of *Star Wars*. Despite his status as the preeminent film composer of his era, Williams ponders the importance of music to cinema:

> Anyone interested in film knows that music seems to be an indispensable ingredient for filmmakers. I'm not exactly sure why. We could talk about that for days, but mood, motivation, rhythm, tempo, atmosphere, all these things, characterization and so on—just the practical aspect of sounds between dialogue that need filling up.
>
> (Byrd 417)

Williams's perplexity about music's role in filmmaking is striking, as he candidly admits that the cinema does not inherently need music to convey a story. Nonetheless, the cinematic experience would be immeasurably less satisfying without music, and in some instances a film's fans are likely to hear in their heads the opening notes of the composer's score whenever they think of the film.

Sometimes complementing and sometimes contrasting with the score, *foreground music*, also known as *source music*, includes songs playing in a film to which the characters respond or otherwise acknowledge, such as music at a ball or nightclub, or the songs that a character hears on the radio. Dance films, such as John Badham's disco tragedy *Saturday Night Fever* (1977) and the *Step Up* franchise, employ foreground music for the various scenes in which the characters dance. Many films feature songs, and some of pop music's most enduring melodies exquisitely capture the emotional tenor of the films in which they are featured. Songs may be *diegetic*—in which characters sing them or listen to them as part of the film's unfolding plot— or *extradiegetic*—in which they are performed offscreen. Famous diegetic film songs include Judy Garland's "Over the Rainbow" in *The Wizard of Oz*, Audrey Hepburn's "Moon River" in *Breakfast at Tiffany's*, Kermit the Frog's "The Rainbow Connection" from *The Muppet Movie*, and Jennifer Hudson's show-stopping performance of "And I Am Telling You I'm Not Going" from *Dreamgirls*. Extradiegetic songs often play during a film's opening credits, such as those that famously open the James Bond films, ranging from Shirley Bassey's "Goldfinger" and "Moonraker" to Adele's "Skyfall." Extradiegetic songs also frequently play over montages or other such moments when the narrative action does not require dialogue.

Sound effects comprise any use of sound other than dialogue and music, and they are subdivided into onscreen and offscreen effects. With onscreen effects, viewers see a character engaging in an action—chopping a head of lettuce, starting a car—and the sounds match these actions. With offscreen effects, spectators hear a sound that is not depicted visually and so they must infer its relevance to the narrative action. Horror films often use offscreen sound effects to accelerate the narrative's mystery and growing terror, for the characters, like the viewers, are unsure what is causing these mysterious

noises. In the process of *dubbing*, dialogue and sound effects are synchro-
nized with the film. Some films instead rely on *direct sound*, which is recorded
when a scene is filmed. Tom Hooper's *Les Misérables* (2012), starring Anne
Hathaway, Hugh Jackman, and Russell Crowe, was the first modern musical
that recorded singing as direct sound.

Actors are hired to perform the roles depicted in the screenplay, and their
delivery of the film's *dialogue*—the verbal exchanges, whether bantering or
threatening, expository or revelatory—brings to life the screenwriter's story.
While acting consists primarily of intoning words and expressing corresponding emotions, an actor must also employ gestures, movements, and
reactions in their repertoire of skills—along with such assorted talents as
singing, dancing, dueling, horseback riding, or whatever else the character is called upon to perform. Beyond dialogue, some screenwriters convey
the film's plot development through *voiceover*, in which a narrator and/or
character explains to the spectators the relevance of the actions onscreen or
the character's emotional responses, such as in Billy Wilder's *Sunset Blvd.*
(1950), Ridley Scott's *Blade Runner* (1982), or the television series *Dexter*
(2006–). Some screenwriters consider voiceovers to be an elementary and
overused technique, for they break the classic tenet of creative writing that
one should show but not tell. When voiceovers explain to viewers how a
character is feeling, or why a character reacts as she does, the filmmakers are
trusting neither the actor to convey the proper emotions nor the audience to
interpret the performance.

Correct cinematic terminology is essential for discussing cinematic
adaptations, but simply using these words accurately will not necessarily
advance an interpretation of a film. When employing these terms, it is
also important to consider their effect on the unfolding narrative. That
is to say, it is less interesting to correctly identify a camera angle as shot
from a high or low position as it is to consider how and why the high
angle frames the character in a particular manner at a particular point of
the film. A cinematic lexicon should assist one in assessing the technical
aspects of a film but also in considering how technical decisions achieve
aesthetic effects.

Film Theories: Auteurs, Stars, and Spectators

As literary theories assist readers in formulating interpretations of poems,
novels, and plays, film theories assist spectators in discussing and interpreting a film's meanings. Most films are narrative based, and so many of the
elements of narratological analysis discussed in Chapter 2.2 are applicable
to cinema as well, particularly in relation to film's use of plot structure, point
of view, character, setting, and theme. The various theoretical schools of literary criticism discussed in Chapter 3.2 are also applicable, to some degree
or another, to films. One can analyze a film for its depiction of sexuality, following the precepts of queer theories, or its depiction of race relationships,

following the precepts of postcolonial and critical race theories. These schools of thought can assist viewers in analyzing the ways in which a film creates meaning, yet, at the same time, if one ignores film's critical differences from literature, the resulting analysis cannot as precisely capture the ways in which cinematic technologies communicate to spectators.

The lines between literary and cinematic theories can be slight, and many of these ostensibly separate spheres of interpretation affect each other reciprocally. For example, in her groundbreaking analysis of cinematic depictions of women, Laura Mulvey discusses the ways in which *scopophilia*—the pleasure of gazing—reflects male desires: "In a world ordered by sexual imbalance, pleasure in looking has been split between active/male and passive/female. The determining male gaze projects its fantasy onto the female figure, which is styled accordingly" (19). Countless films prove Mulvey's argument, such as when a camera pans from a woman's feet to her face, luxuriating in her beauty in a manner seldom bestowed upon male characters. In the opening minutes of Garry Marshall's *Pretty Woman* (1990), as prostitute Vivian Ward (played by Julia Roberts) wakes, the camera moves along her body, offering close-ups of her leg, her torso, her arms. Then, as she dresses for work, the camera shoots close-ups of her chest as she puts on clothing, her wrist as she adds bracelets, her foot as she zips her boot, and one eye as she applies makeup. Presenting Vivian entirely in parts, the camera emphasizes her physical beauty before it shows the whole woman. Through this visual introduction, the audience is positioned to see Vivian primarily as a seductive body rather than as a whole, complex person. Mulvey's feminist and psychoanalytic theories about the gendered pleasure of the gaze, although conceived for cinema studies, are relevant to literature as well, such as in the poetic structure of the blazon, in which a male lyric speaker catalogs his female beloved's beauty.

Space limitations preclude the possibility of reformulating the overviews of literary theories in Chapter 3.2 as film theories, but those interested in pursuing further study of film's unique paradigms of these perspectives—from semiotics to genre theory, and all in between—should consider the advantages and limitations of applying literary theories to films and then explore further how these theories shift when discussed in exclusively cinematic terms. For the practical purposes of this guidebook, this chapter focuses on three key areas of film theories—auteur, star, and spectator studies—distinct from literary studies.

Auteur Theories

Auteur theories stress the role of directors in creating films. The French word *auteur* translates as *author*, with this term implicitly comparing film directors to literary authors and thereby suggesting the primacy of their role in creating a film. In his groundbreaking essay on auteur theory, Andrew Sarris outlines three principles of auteur theory:

the first premise of the auteur theory is the technical competence of the director as a criterion of value. A badly directed or an undirected film has no importance in a critical scale of values, but one can make interesting conversation about the subject, the script, the acting, the color, the photography, the editing, the music, the costumes, the décor, and so forth. That is the nature of the medium.

(63–64)

Auteurs must possess basic proficiency with filmmaking to construct coherent pictures, as they are also expected to soar beyond rudimentary techniques into innovative territories. In contrast to the pejorative term *craftsman director*—which refers to directors to whom cinematic projects are entrusted due to their knowledge of the various technologies of filmmaking, rather than for their creative genius—auteurs are celebrated as cinematic artists responsible for a body of groundbreaking work that reformulates the possibilities, themes, and experience of film.

Developing his theories of the auteur, Sarris also proposes that

[t]he second premise of the *auteur* theory is the distinguishable personality of the director as criterion of value. Over a group of films, a director must exhibit certain recurring characteristics of style, which serve as his signature. The way a film looks and moves should have some relationship to the way a director thinks and feels.

(64)

Auteurs create a coherent body of work reflective of their unique sensibilities and style, such that the directors' name serves as a cinematic genre in its own right. Certainly, this is true of many famed directors, even when they share narrative interests with other filmmakers. Despite the frequent forays of Alfred Hitchcock, Martin Scorsese, and Quentin Tarantino into humanity's dark side, viewers would not likely mistake a Tarantino film for one by Hitchcock or Scorsese. Sarris concludes his theorization of auteurs by declaring that

[t]he third and ultimate premise of the *auteur* theory is concerned with interior meaning, the ultimate glory of the cinema as an art. Interior meaning is extrapolated from the tension between a director's personality and his material.

(64)

Although all narratives that auteurs film are unique, they come together as a genre in the fact that a unifying consciousness brought them to the screen, building thematic and stylistic links among them despite their differences.

An auteur analysis typically examines a director's complete corpus and discusses affinities in styles, structures, and themes across this body of work, or it might explore how a particular film within this corpus digresses from the director's typical fare. Proponents of auteur theory lionize certain directors—including such famed figures as Charlie Chaplin, John Ford, Woody Allen, Vittorio de Sica, François Truffaut, Jane Campion, and Kathryn Bigelow—and address how their films, whether made within or outside the Hollywood system, evince their personal investments in a range of stylistic and thematic issues.

The primary limitation of auteur theory is that it diminishes, in favor of directors, the contributions of various artists in the creation of films—the actors, editors, costume designers, cinematographers, composers, and numerous others whose unique contributions leave an indelible mark on the resulting film. Auteur theory also eclipses the fact that many filmmakers work with the same team over many years. Longstanding collaborations between actors and directors allow them to enhance each other's careers, such as John Huston and Humphrey Bogart, Steven Soderbergh and George Clooney, and Tim Burton and Johnny Depp. Martin Scorsese's editor Thelma Schoonmaker has collaborated with him on numerous projects, winning Academy Awards for editing his *Raging Bull* (1980), *The Aviator* (2004), and *The Departed* (2006) over the years of their partnership—in contrast to his single Academy Award for directing. One could cheekily suggest that she is a threefold better editor than he is a director, but nonetheless, with auteur theories, to the director goes the glory. Thus, while auteur theories in some ways encourage viewers to overlook the talents of the director's team, one could enhance the utility of these perspectives by more fully exploring how an auteur's career highlights the contributions of various artists.

Star Theories

Cinematic theories about stars and stardom encourage viewers to examine the ways in which actors create a body of work throughout their careers and how their choices in roles, in a loopback, create their persona. The actors who are cast in a film affect how spectators perceive it, and it is often beneficial to consider which elements of a star's persona match the contours of his or her characters. As much as actors must resist *typecasting*—the perception that they can play only one type of role convincingly—they also benefit from the allure of star personas that cohere with certain roles better than others. As auteur theories posit a director's oeuvre as a distinct body of work, star theories likewise analyze a given performer's career as a discrete cinematic genre, as Richard Dyer explains:

> In certain respects, a set of star vehicles is rather like a film genre such as the Western, the musical or the gangster film. As with genres proper, one can discern across a star's vehicles continuities of iconography (e.g, how they are dressed, made-up and coiffed, performance mannerisms, the setting with which they are associated), visual style (e.g. how they are lit,

photographed, placed within the frame) and structure (e.g. their role in the plot, the function in the film's symbolic pattern). . . . Of course, not all films made by a star are vehicles, but looking at their films in terms of vehicles draws attention to those films that do not "fit," that constitute inflections, exceptions to, subversions of the vehicle pattern and the star image.

(Stars 62)

Thinking of stars as genres unto themselves elucidates the artistic coherency of their careers, as well as the strengths and weaknesses of their individual performances. Stars must become sufficiently famous for their films to become star vehicles, but once they achieve this level of fame and acclaim, their careers thereafter tend to enhance and reinforce their personas. When one thinks of certain iconic stars—Arnold Schwarzenegger, Anne Hathaway, Montgomery Cliff, Meryl Streep, Paul Newman, Katharine Hepburn, Bette Davis, Leonardo DiCaprio—images from their various films coalesce into an overarching view of their performances.

Star theories also illuminate the aspects of an actor's performances that assist them in being cast in various films. For example, which elements of Robert Redford's and Leonardo DiCaprio's star personas make them appropriate choices to play F. Scott Fitzgerald's Great Gatsby, in the eponymous films of 1974, directed by Jack Clayton, and 2013, directed by Baz Luhrmann? Which actor better captures the part? The role of Heathcliff in Emily Brontë's *Wuthering Heights* has been played by, among others, Laurence Olivier (1939), Timothy Dalton (1970), Ralph Fiennes (1992), and Tom Hardy (2009), and it is fascinating to watch how different actors conceive and execute the same role, capturing different nuances of the character, as well as to consider how a particular role fits in within an actor's overarching career. *Cameos*, in which a famous star plays a small role in a film, offer additional opportunities for actors to cement their personas in the public eye, such as Sean Connery's cameo as King Richard the Lionhearted in Kevin Reynolds's *Robin Hood: Prince of Thieves* (1991) and Neil Patrick Harris's cameo as himself in Danny Leiner's *Harold & Kumar Go to White Castle* (2004). (Some directors, including Alfred Hitchcock, Peter Jackson, and Quentin Tarantino, cast themselves in cameos in their films, and in such moments, auteur theories and star theories overlap.) With roles large and small, actors build their persona in the public eye. By maximizing their appeal and range, they ensure themselves of greater career longevity and of a body of work illustrating their talents.

Even when relaxing in comfortable roles aligned with their screen personas, stars' performances cannot be divorced from their acting skills, which necessitates the recognition that cinematic acting differs from theatrical acting. Cinema is more forgiving of mistakes than the theater. A bad take of a film can be reshot endlessly, but actors have only one opportunity to deliver a memorable performance each time they stand on stage. Mel Churcher describes theater acting as a "continual interaction with the other characters," one that unfolds amid the "shared responsibility of teamwork in performance"; additionally, Churcher notes, "Theatre rehearsal allows the freedom for exploration and growth" (20). Film acting, in contrast, often plays for the close-up. The camera can focus on the emotionality of the scéne, thus bringing film spectators closer to the actors than even the audience in a theater's first row. Tom Hanks famously observed that film is a director's medium whereas theater is an actor's medium (Churcher 20). With this statement, he articulates the common perception that a film director's vision elicits the performance desired from the actors, while in the collaborative milieu of theater more discretion is given to the actors to develop their roles throughout the more extended rehearsal period.

Spectator Theories

Film theories also analyze the role of spectators in the construction of cinematic meaning. No two people view a film the same way, yet theories of spectatorship hypothesize how audiences react to a given film or film genre. Robert Stam summarizes five key ways of analyzing film spectatorship. In his first formulation, "the spectator [is] fashioned by the text itself (through focalization, point-of-view conventions, narrative structuring, mise-en-scène)" (231). Directors have a sense of how they wish their films to be interpreted, and their artistic decisions attempt to guide viewers to share in their aesthetic vision. Also, films encourage spectators to assume sympathetic, if not empathetic, relationships with some characters rather than others, with camera angles and other such formal elements contributing to this dynamic. With a proposal complementary to his first, Stam also suggests that "the spectator [is] fashioned by the (diverse and evolving) technical apparatuses" (231). While this statement may seem counterintuitive—for how does a camera used to shoot a scene, or a theater that screens a film, influence its viewers?—the technologies of filmmaking and film distribution play a key role in how audiences respond to a cinematic experience. Theaters with live music playing to accompany silent films, drive-in movie theaters, mall theaters, and IMAX screens attest to the various ways audiences have historically experienced film-going, and evolving technologies construct new relationships between films and spectators. Moreover, films such as Sam Raimi's *The Evil Dead* (1981), Jay Roach's *Austin Powers* (1997), and David Fincher's *Fight Club* (1999) were not blockbuster hits upon their initial cinematic releases, but technologies such as VCR and DVD granted them a second chance to build their audience.

Stam's remaining theories of spectatorship propose that viewers cannot be defined exclusively by a film and its technologies, and respect the audience members for bringing their unique social networks, discourses, and identities to the viewing experience. His third precept of spectatorship asserts that "the spectator [is] fashioned by the institutional contexts of spectatorship (social ritual of moviegoing, classroom analysis, cinémateque)" (231), which recognizes that spectators view movies for various reasons and within various social networks. While most films attempt to appeal to as wide an audience as possible, many are marketed directly to specific audiences: action/adventure movies to young men, romances to women, animation to children. Also, viewers create cult hits out of some films, such as Tod Browning's *Freaks* (1932), Jim Sharman's *The Rocky Horror Picture Show* (1975), and Richard Kelly's *Donnie Darko* (2001). Through this process, audiences construct themselves as unique spectators and these films as unique texts, those enjoyable to a self-selecting set of viewers. In his fourth and fifth precepts, Stam suggests that the "the spectator [is] constituted by ambient discourses and ideologies" and that "the actual spectator [is] embodied, raced, gendered, and historically situated" (231). As Stam moves from the general to the particular, he acknowledges that the communal nature of film spectatorship is complemented by each individual viewing it separately and interpreting it in light of his or her unique identities and experiences. By noting that the spectator of a film is uniquely "embodied, raced, gendered, and historically situated," Stam's theories of spectatorship correlate with literary and cinematic theories addressing race, gender, sexuality, and other markers of personal identity.

Limiting the utility of theories of spectatorship, many fail to acknowledge that viewers do not react uniformly to a given film. Thus, while one may speak of women's relationships with romantic comedies or of gay men's appreciation of musicals, such analysis risks oversimplifying a complex dynamic between viewer and viewed. To ameliorate this potential stereotyping of viewers, Janet Staiger theorizes the possibility of "perverse spectators," those who, quite simply, "don't do what is expected" (37). While film criticism implicitly constructs ideal spectators who consume movies in the manner in which the directors—and possibly, the critics employing traditional theories of spectatorship—would like them to be viewed, the concept of perverse spectatorship cautions filmmakers and critics alike that individual members of the audience bring unique viewpoints to the cinematic experience and that they often reimagine the film in ways suited to their desires rather than to the storyline's sympathies. One of Staiger's examples of such perverse spectatorship reconceptualizes the audience's likely response to John Hughes's classic teen flick *Ferris Bueller's Day Off* (1986). Surely viewers are intended to root for the amiable protagonist Ferris, as played by Matthew Broderick with charming bonhomie, but Staiger proposes instead that viewers might identify with and support his surly sister Jeanie (Jennifer Grey). As Staiger argues, a perverse pleasure arises in rooting for Jeanie, but it is a pleasure nonetheless (115–24). Likewise, the audience is called to support Lester Burnham (Kevin Spacey) in Sam Mendes's *American Beauty* (1999) rather than his adulterous wife Carolyn (Annette Bening), yet viewers could easily find Lester pathetic in his erotic fantasies of young women and root instead for his wife who single-mindedly seeks to improve her life. When discussing film spectatorship, critics must explain precisely how they reached their conclusions about the film's viewers, lest they assume a uniformity of reception not borne out by the various and multiple pleasures potentially arising from the same film.

Film Genres

Cinematic adaptations of literary texts constitute a discrete genre of film. At the same time, many adaptations also fall within the parameters of other film genres, and this brief overview of cinematic genres explores their intersections with literary genres. As critical categories grouping films according to themes, styles, and storylines, genres assist viewers in analyzing a given film in relationship to a wider body of work. The following pages address comedy and romantic comedy, drama, epic, fantasy, film noir, horror and suspense, musicals, science fiction, and Westerns (and Southerns), but this survey is not exhaustive, and other common cinematic genres include action films, war films, gangster films, biopics, caper films, documentaries, parodies, and pornography.

A running thread throughout this analysis of cinematic genres explores how literature and films in particular genres are typically considered aesthetically inferior to dramas. The term *genre fiction* pejoratively denotes science fiction, romance, adventure, espionage, horror, and other such novels because some critics see their adherence to generic conventions as stultifying. Likewise, films in these genres are often viewed as aesthetically inferior to such forms as dramas and epics. With brevity and acumen, Pierre Bourdieu alerts his readers to the ways that aesthetics defines high and low culture and their respective aficionados—"Taste classifies, and it classifies the classifier" (6)—with his words pointing out the cultural effects on individuals for preferring some literary and cinematic forms over others. Cinematic adaptations of genre fiction complicate the blanket denigration of literary and cinematic genres, for numerous celebrated films have been adapted both from literary fiction and from genre fiction. It is not apparent, however, that adaptations from literary fiction are uniformly more successful, whether aesthetically or commercially, than adaptations from genre fiction.

Comedy and Romantic Comedy

Comedies seek to spark laughter from their spectators, and their success or failure in this mission largely determines their appeal. As an expansive form, comedy percolates throughout a range of other cinematic genres, including Westerns (*Blazing Saddles*, *¡Three Amigos!*), horror (*Evil Dead 2*, *Scary Movie*), science fiction (*Spaceballs*, *Men in Black*), and even epics (*It's a Mad, Mad, Mad, Mad World*; *O Brother, Where Art Thou?*). Due to comedy's mutability, Geoff King suggests that it should be seen not as a genre but rather as a cinematic mode: "Comedy is a mode—a manner of presentation—in which a variety of different materials can be approached, rather than any relatively more fixed or localized quality" (2). Even tragedies may depict comic moments—Shakespeare includes a fool in *King Lear* and two clowns in *Hamlet*—and so King's admonition rightly reminds viewers of comedy's role in a range of genres. Consequently, it is prudent to consider the relationship between a given film and the comic tradition from a myriad of perspectives, taking into account that defining a film as a comedy leaves open the possibility of other complementary designations.

Translating comedy from a literary text to a film risks diluting, or even losing, the humor in the process, and some of the greatest comic authors resist cinematic adaptations of their works. Geoffrey Chaucer and Alexander Pope are two of the funniest writers in English literature, but their satires have proven difficult to film, for literary comedy often depends on verbal irony difficult to capture visually. While Chaucer and Pope have faired poorly in their cinematic fortunes, other esteemed comic authors, including William Shakespeare, Jonathan Swift, Jane Austen, Charles Dickens, and Evelyn Waugh, have found great success on the screen, for their plots and humor translate smoothly into a visual medium. Shakespeare's plays, while not written as screenplays, were envisioned with their staging in mind; likewise, Swift's *Gulliver's Travels* calls out for a cinematic translation in the lasting image of his protagonist chained to the ground by a band of tiny Lilliputians. Austen's courtship comedies play on longstanding (and apparently perpetual) anxieties about love and marriage, with the gentle humor of her tone coming across through the dialogue of yesteryear (as in Ang Lee's *Sense and Sensibility*, 1995) or the present (as in Amy Heckerling's *Clueless*, 1995, an adaptation of *Emma*). The disjunctions among the cinematic fates of various comic authors bear witness to the mutable, effervescent, and mercurial nature of comedy, in that it at times resists, and at times flourishes, in the translation from one medium to another.

While cinematic comedy includes numerous subgenres, including screwballs, parodies, and farces, romantic comedies in particular evince strong roots in the literary tradition. Romantic comedies follow their protagonists as they meet, fall in love, encounter obstacles, and then overcome them in marriage—or at least, coupledom. As Leger Grindon observes, this plot structure necessitates little more than two character types: "The conventional characters of romantic comedy are divided into two groups: the lovers and their helpers versus obstacle figures, typically the father or others in authority" (12). Shakespeare's many romantic comedies, including *Twelfth Night* and *As You Like It*, exemplify the form, in which their plucky female protagonists cross-dress to advance their wooing. From its infancy on the Renaissance stage, the romantic comedy now stands as one of Hollywood's most enduring genres, and often a key determinant of an actress's stardom. Doris Day built her career in the 1950s with *Calamity Jane* (1953), *The Pajama Game* (1957), and *Pillow Talk* (1959), as did Julia Roberts in the 1990s with *Pretty Woman* (1990), *My Best Friend's Wedding* (1997), *Runaway Bride*

(1999), and *Notting Hill* (1999), as did Anne Hathaway in the 2000s with *The Princess Diaries* (2001), *Ella Enchanted* (2004), and *Bride Wars* (2009). Romantic comedies point to the ways in which gender influences comedy and comic roles, with women building lasting star images from this comic subgenre.

Drama

Like comedy, drama is such an expansive form that defining it runs the risk of unnecessarily delimiting its field; furthermore, just as any film that leaves the audience laughing can be labeled a comedy, so too can any film with a serious tone be labeled a drama. As with comedies, drama transcends other genres, and subcategories of drama include biopics, war dramas, legal dramas, historical dramas, and romance dramas. More specifically, dramas emphasize character development over plotting; in these films, it is in many ways less important what happens to a character than how the character grows as a result of these events.

In literary terms, *drama* primarily refers to the theatrical world, and this overlap further confuses the meaning of cinematic drama. Many of the plays of the finest theatrical dramatists—Marlowe, Shakespeare, Ibsen, Tennessee Williams—have been adapted to the cinema, and at first blush it would seem a relatively simple matter to transfer a play to the screen. Unlike novels, plays are created to be performed, as the narrative actions of films must likewise be acted. It is nonetheless instructive to follow a cinematic adaptation of a play with the script in hand, so as to notice the many aspects of plot, characterization, and setting that are altered in the transition. Plays must be performed within the physical confines of theaters, whereas films often induce a claustrophobic feeling in the audience if they remain static in their setting. Thus, screenwriters typically rewrite a play's settings and scenes to take advantage of film's freedom of location and motion.

While cinematic drama is an amorphous genre, it is the one that most often receives critical praise. Dramas have won the lion's share of Academy Awards for Best Picture, including numerous adaptations of literary works, such as Cormac McCarthy's *No Country for Old Men*, Michael Ondaatje's *The English Patient*, Alfred Uhry's *Driving Miss Daisy*, Isak Dinesen's *Out of Africa*, and Ken Kesey's *One Flew over the Cuckoo's Nest*. As these few examples show, drama ranges widely in its scope and subject matter, yet is united in the quest of the characters for a deeper sense of personal revelation and understanding.

Epic

In cinema studies, the term *epic* refers to films expansive in scope and spectacle. The American Film Institute (AFI) succinctly defines epics "as a genre of large-scale films set in a cinematic interpretation of the past" and praises David Lean's *Lawrence of Arabia* (1962), William Wyler's *Ben-Hur* (1959), Steven Spielberg's *Schindler's List* (1993), Victor Fleming's *Gone with the Wind* (1939), and Stanley Kubrick's *Spartacus* (1960) as the five finest cinematic epics ("Top 10 Epics"). Although the AFI's definition posits that cinematic epics should be set in the past, science-fiction films set in the future may also claim epic status, such as George Lucas's *Star Wars* franchise and James Cameron's *Avatar* (2009). Notwithstanding whether a particular film is set in the past, present, or future, epic films illustrate humanity tested and then triumphant on a vast scale in struggle against implacable foes. Constantine Santas states that

> an epic serves as the apotheosis of human action, an escape from pedestrianism to an ideal fashioned by tribal struggles. Above all, the epic is a product of the human imagination as it strives to conceptualize the victories of humanity's heroes in the millennia-old and never-ceasing battle between good and evil.
>
> (2)

The scope of cinematic epics invites grand successes and massive failures. Charlton Heston, the star of such epic films as *The Ten Commandments* and *Ben-Hur*, cautions of the genre, "There's a temptingly simple definition of the epic film: It's the easiest kind of picture to make badly" (Elley 1). While Heston speaks with tongue in cheek, he also reveals the simple fact that, on such large-scale projects, which frequently boast casts of thousands and the latest special effects, any number of problems can derail their production. Thus, the chief difficulty in filming epics—the scale of the enterprise—counterbalances their lasting appeal, as these films promise a visual feast of filmmaking. Epics are big pictures in every sense of the phrase, representing Hollywood's efforts to amaze their audiences with over-the-top effects and storylines.

In literature, the term *epic* has a more precise meaning than in cinema. (*For a review of literary epics, see pp. 118–20.*) Thus, although the status of the medieval poem *Beowulf* as a literary epic is unquestioned, few would label its cinematic incarnations as epics in their own right, including Robert Zemeckis's 2007 film starring Ray Winstone (with Angelina Jolie in a surprisingly seductive performance as Grendel's mother) and Graham Baker's 1999 sci-fi version starring Christopher Lambert. Conversely, while the AFI labels *Ben-Hur* and *Gone with the Wind* as cinematic epics, few critics would classify the novels on which these films are based—Lew Wallace's *Ben-Hur: A Tale of the Christ* (1880) and Margaret Mitchell's *Gone with the Wind* (1936)—as literary epics. Despite their many differences, cinematic and literary epics conjointly tell tales of heroism and their protagonists' struggles to achieve their missions, which are often to preserve their civilization from imminent destruction, as they unfold against a vast landscape wracked by struggle.

Fantasy

In fantasy films, the rules of everyday life are forgotten, with characters enjoying experiences beyond the possibilities of the rational world. As Alec Worley explains, "All films require suspension of disbelief to a degree, but fantasy films require the greatest of all, since their currency is the unbelievable" (10). Indeed, while one must suspend disbelief to enjoy most films, given any range of implausible scenarios catalyzing their plots, fantasy films refuse to settle for the banality of reality and instead infuse their environments with the magic and mystery of new worlds. Humans may serve as the protagonists of fantasy films, but viewers are just as likely to discover entirely new races, such as munchkins (L. Frank Baum's *The Wizard of Oz*, as filmed by Victor Fleming, 1939), talking animals (C. S. Lewis's *The Lion, the Witch and the Wardrobe*, as filmed by Andrew Adamson, 2005), or hobbits and orcs (J. R. R. Tolkien's *The Lord of the Rings* trilogy, as filmed by Peter Jackson, 2001, 2002, 2003). Fantasy films may take viewers to such exciting and magical lands as Oz, Narnia, and Middle-earth, as in the films just cited, or they may occur in a non-magical setting, such as Bedford Falls in Frank Capra's *It's a Wonderful Life* (1946) and London in Robert Stevenson's *Mary Poppins* (1964). Frequently, fantasies hint that magical worlds surround blissfully ignorant humans, just as J. K. Rowling's muggles remain ignorant of the wizarding world coexisting with their own.

Like cinematic epics, fantasy films present numerous challenges during shooting, as their creators must construct a credible vision of an alternate reality, often one in which the rules of earthly reality no longer apply. To this end, elaborate sets and special effects are needed to capture the story's magic on the screen. Facing the constraints of filming the impossible, many fantasy movies are animated so that the filmmakers enjoy freer range to create. The celebrated animation studio Pixar, for example, with its string of hits including *Toy Story* (1995), *Finding Nemo* (2003), *The Incredibles* (2004), and *Brave* (2012), traffics exclusively in the realm of fantasy. It should be noted, however, that while animated films can be considered a cinematic genre as well, animation simply refers to a process of filmmaking rather than to a specific narrative structure.

Like much fantasy literature, many fantasy films are denigrated critically because they are viewed as light, escapist fare. Only one fantasy film—Peter Jackson's *The Return of the King*—has won the Academy Award for Best Picture. Dismissed as children's entertainments, fantasy novels and films nonetheless provide some of the most memorable narratives of Western culture, including Lewis Carroll's *Alice in Wonderland*, Carlo Collodi's *Pinocchio*, J. M. Barrie's *Peter and Wendy*, Roald Dahl's *Charlie and the Chocolate*

Factory, and Cressida Cowell's *How to Train Your Dragon*, as well as count-less folk and fairy tales. Indeed, Snow White serves virtually as a miniature genre unto herself, most notably through Walt Disney's classic *Snow White and the Seven Dwarfs* (1937) but also with such modernizations of her story as Rupert Sanders's *Snow White and the Huntsman* (2012) and Tarsem Sin-gh's *Mirror, Mirror* (2012). Resisting the critical impulse to dismiss fantasy literature and films as merely children's entertainments is a necessary inter-vention in the field, for hobbits and orcs may teach readers and spectators as much about the human condition and narrative art as Greeks and Trojans.

Film Noir

Film noir, an American genre that developed in the 1940s, features dark lighting, shady dealings, the criminal underworld, and often a femme fatale employing her seductive wiles to bankroll her future rather than to find her true love. Despite these standard features, noir remains a difficult genre to pinpoint, as Paul Schrader observes:

> [Noir] is not defined, as are the western and gangster genres, by conven-tions of setting and conflict but rather by the more subtle qualities of tone and mood. . . . In general, film noir refers to those Hollywood films of the forties and early fifties that portrayed the world of dark, slick city streets, crime and corruption.
>
> (170)

In some ways noir suggests more a mood than a specific plotline, with dark-ness coloring the characters' ambitions and desires.

While earlier critics dismissed this genre as light entertainment, many noirs now enjoy critical acclaim, particularly such films as John Hus-ton's *The Maltese Falcon* (1941), Otto Preminger's *Laura* (1944), Billy Wilder's *Double Indemnity* (1944), Tay Garnett's *The Postman Always Rings Twice* (1946), and Orson Welles's *The Lady from Shanghai* (1948) and *Touch of Evil* (1958). While noir's birth and heyday were in the 1940s, its legacy resonates in such films as Lawrence Kasdan's *Body Heat* (1981), Paul Verhoeven's *Basic Instinct* (1992), and David Fincher's *The Girl with the Dragon Tattoo* (2011), as well as in many of Joel and Ethan Coen's films, particularly *Blood Simple* (1984), *Fargo* (1996), and *No Country for Old Men* (2007).

Noir's literary roots can be traced to such authors as Raymond Chandler (*The Big Sleep*, *The Long Goodbye*), James Cain (*The Postman Always Rings Twice*, *Mildred Pierce*, and *Double Indemnity*), and Dashiell Hammett (*The Maltese Falcon*). While primarily celebrated as the greatest Southern author of the twentieth century, William Faulkner penned the screenplay of Howard Hawks's *The Big Sleep* (1946) and thus influenced the development of this cinematic genre. Just as film critics initially dismissed noir, literary critics formerly disparaged the novels of Raymond Chandler and Dashiell Hammett, but they are enjoying a new level of appreciation among scholars and readers. Crime fiction and film noir highlight the vagaries of the label of "genre fiction," for this term, so readily applied to a vast body of work, has increasingly been found to denigrate literary and cinematic works of sophistication and insight.

Horror and Suspense

Horror films depict the dissolution of the boundaries between reality and nightmare when monstrous adversaries and supernatural events strip away society's comforting illusions of rationality and civilization. Typically horror films end with the adversary vanquished, the protagonist's sigh of relief, and a promised return to normalcy, but the genre's dark pleasures are sparked by the thrills of upheaval, of environments where a new danger lurks around every corner and even the dead buried in their graves can free themselves to terrorize the living. Ghosts, vampires, monsters, and ghouls populate horror films, and some of their most famous and unvanquishable antagonists—Michael Myers, Jason Voorhies, Freddy Krueger—have entered the popular-culture consciousness as archetypes of unremitting evil.

Horror films feature suspenseful situations in which the protagonists and others are menaced by a monstrous adversary, yet it is helpful to distinguish between horror films and suspense films: a useful, although at times imperfect, distinction proposes that horror stories feature the supernatural whereas suspense films are plausible, if unlikely. Within this rubric, terrifying films including Alfred Hitchcock's *Psycho* (1960), Jonathan Demme's *The Silence of the Lambs* (1991), and James Wan's *Saw* (2004) would be more accurately labeled suspense rather than horror films, for they focus on psychotic killers who are nonetheless bound by the rules of reality. In contrast, such films as William Friedkin's *The Exorcist* (1973), Gore Verbenski's *The Ring* (2002), and Oren Pell's *Paranormal Activity* (2007) fall more comfortably within the realm of horror, for they depict supernatural events beyond the control of ordinary humans.

Although critics frequently condemn horror as a dehumanizing genre that gleefully traffics in suffering and slaughter, Jack Clayton's *The Innocents* (1961), an adaptation of Henry James's *The Turn of the Screw* with a screenplay by Truman Capote, proves the potential of this genre to transcend mere shocks. Bram Stoker's *Dracula* has been adapted numerous times, from Bela Lugosi's iconic portrayal of the role in Tod Browning's 1931 adaptation to Gary Oldman's performance in Francis Ford Coppola's 1992 film. Mary Shelley's *Frankenstein* has generated a rich legacy, including James Whale's classic *Frankenstein* (1931) with Boris Karloff as the monster, Mel Brooks's madcap comedy *Young Frankenstein* (1974), and Tim Burton's animated update *Frankenweenie* (2012). While some deride Stephen King's many novels as formulaic, several have been adapted into mesmerizing classics of the genre, including Brian de Palma's *Carrie* (1976), Stanley Kubrick's *The Shining* (1980), and Rob Reiner's *Misery* (1990).

Musicals

Musicals portray characters who break the boundaries of realism by interjecting song and dance into the dramatic action. In this manner, musicals often inhabit two coexisting narrative levels: one of the characters' reality and the other of their music. Barry Keith Grant suggests that "Film musicals typically present their song-and/or-dance numbers in an imaginary space, even if this space is ostensibly a real location, and contained within a narrative framework" (1). Rick Altman describes this second level of the narrative as "a 'place' of transcendence where time stands still, where contingent concerns are stripped away to reveal the essence of things" (66–67). These formulations capture the ways in which musicals escape the everyday world to a place where song and dance offer liberation, or at least a respite, from the world's pressures.

The roots of musicals trace back to the earliest English literature and drama. It is surely an exaggeration to label Chaucer's *Troilus and Criseyde* a musical, yet Troilus breaks out into song three times in the poem, with these lyric interludes pausing the narrative action to allow him to ponder the meaning of love. Likewise, many of Shakespeare's plays feature songs at key moments, such as when Desdemona sings, "The poor soul sat sighing by a sycamore tree" in *Othello* (4.3.40). These works demonstrate the harmony between narrative and song, in which the story's narrative slows for a moment so that characters may enjoy a brief interlude from their overarching concerns.

Many cinematic musicals are adapted from Broadway shows, yet the route from stage to screen may be circuitous. First filmed in 1988, starring Ricki Lake and the drag queen Divine, John Waters's *Hairspray* was then adapted into a Broadway musical that ran for over 2,000 performances between 2002 and 2009; it returned to the screen in 2007, starring Nikki Blonski, John Travolta, and Zac Ephron. Film musicals with literary roots include *West Side Story* (1961) from Shakespeare's *Romeo and Juliet*, and *Kiss Me Kate* (1953) from his *The Taming of the Shrew*; *Cabaret* (1972) from Christopher Isherwood's *Goodbye to Berlin*; *Oliver!* (1968) from Charles Dickens's *Oliver Twist*; *The Wiz* (1978) from L. Frank Baum's *The Wizard of Oz*; and *Les Misérables* (2012) from Victor Hugo's novel as reconstructed from the Broadway stage. In each of these and other musicals with literary roots, it is intriguing to note the ways in which various songs capture the themes, characters, and storylines of the source text—for in most of these instances, the authors did not envision their characters as so musically inclined.

Science Fiction

Recognizing the challenges of defining his preferred genre, Robert Heinlein, the author of such science fiction classics as *Red Planet* (1949), *Stranger in a Strange Land* (1961), and *Starship Troopers* (1959), proposed:

A handy short definition of almost all science fiction might read: realistic speculation about possible future events, based solidly on adequate knowledge of the real world, past and present, and on a thorough understanding of the nature and significance of the scientific method.

(22)

Like fantasy films, science-fiction films create alternate realities more incredible than the everyday world, but they do so with an eye to the possibilities of a future when technology has solved many of humanity's past problems—while simultaneously creating new challenges. Often—but not always—an optimistic genre, science fiction looks to the future, enabling humanity to consider itself in the present.

A primary criticism of science fiction exposes the genre's tendency to solve narrative difficulties through a miraculous intervention of technology, with a type of plot twist that might be termed a technological *deus ex machina*. (*For this term's use and origins in the theater, see pp. 157–58.*) If a spaceship is hurtling to the fiery embrace of the sun with all systems down and no hope left, the plucky protagonist need only tweak the flux capacitor, or kick into warp drive, or navigate through a quasar field, to save the day. Such criticisms of individual films of the genre are warranted, but they should not be levied against the genre as a whole. Stanley Kubrick's *2001: A Space Odyssey* (1968) proves the power and possibility of science-fiction cinema, as do the *Star Trek* and *Star Wars* series, as these films have stirred the imagination of viewers for over thirty years with little sign of losing their appeal. In contrast, Luigi Cozzi's *Starcrash*, a 1978 rip-off of *Star Wars* starring David Hasselhoff, attests to the genre's camp potential.

Numerous classic science-fiction texts have been adapted for the screen. H. G. Wells's corpus has become a subgenre of science-fiction cinema unto itself, with adaptations of *The Island of Dr. Moreau* starring Burt Lancaster (1977) and Marlon Brando (1996) respectively in the title role. *The War of the Worlds* calls for blockbuster special effects, achieved both in its 1953 and its 2005 adaptations (in addition to the panic induced by Orson Welles's radio broadcast of the story in 1938). Numerous filmmakers have adapted Wells's *The Time Machine*, including George Pal in 1960 and Wells's great-grandson Simon Wells in 2002. Indeed, films featuring time machines and time travel constitute another subgenre of the field, including Richard Donner's *Timeline* (2003) and Steve Pink's comedy *Hot Tub Time Machine* (2010); such films are also heavily influenced by the fantasy genre and the time-travel adventuring of Mark Twain's *A Connecticut Yankee in King Arthur's Court*. Isaac Asimov's novels, including *I, Robot* and *Bicentennial Man*, have also proved ready for adaptation. Some science-fiction films, such as adaptations of Jules Verne's *20,000 Leagues under the Sea* and *Journey to the Center of the Earth*, are designed for children, whereas other works, such as Carl Sagan's *Contact*, combine space exploration with drama that muses over the meaning of the cosmos. The best science fiction films ponder the meaning of human existence in the face of the unknowable.

Westerns (and Southerns)

A uniquely American genre, both cinematically and literarily, Westerns, unlike most other genres, depend on their geography for their narrative action. The frontier played a formative role in the development of the United States and its citizenry, and Westerns reflect the promise and the anxiety of untamed land. For their protagonists, Westerns depict taciturn men reluctant to show their emotions yet with a keen sense of justice. In his classic study of the genre, Will Wright outlines four key plotlines of the genre: a stranger restores order to a lawless town; a character seeks revenge against past injustice; the hero finds himself alienated from his community and must restore its sense of justice; and paid gunfighters unite in their mercenary pursuits, typically realizing the call of justice over money in the end (29–123). Westerns were at the height of their popularity in the 1940s, 1950s, and 1960s. Although they are no longer a dominant box-office draw, the genre remains standard fare among Hollywood offerings, often with films questioning its earlier ethos. In Clint Eastwood's *Unforgiven* (1992), the character Will Munny ponders, "It's a hell of a thing, killing a man. Take away all he's got and all he's ever gonna have," implicitly rejecting the violence the genre often celebrates.

While several novelists of the American West are revered for their literary fiction, including such figures as John Steinbeck, Larry McMurtry, Ken Kesey, and Edward Abbey, the works of authors known primarily for Western plotlines, such as Louis L'Amour and Zane Grey, are denigrated as pulp fiction. L'Amour's and Grey's novels have nonetheless been filmed dozens of times, testifying to the power of their narratives and their appropriateness for cinematic adaptation. In contrast to these more formulaic storylines, numerous Westerns challenge the standard plot scenarios of the genre, such as George Roy Hill's *Butch Cassidy and the Sundance Kid* (1969), Robert Altman's *McCabe and Mrs. Miller* (1971), and Elliot Silverstein's musical comedy *Cat Ballou* (1965). In a similar vein, Ang Lee's *Brokeback Mountain* (2005), based on a short story by Annie Proulx, questions the sexual ideology of the genre by depicting the lives of two gay men in the West.

While the term *Southern* is infrequently used as a genre of cinematic analysis, numerous films set in the U.S. South share themes and storylines that construct them as a distinct body of films. Warren French explains the economic reasons why the "Southern" failed to rival Westerns as a culturally recognizable genre (3–13)—namely, increased production values to cover the cost of the sets. Still, numerous films address the South, the Civil War, and the unique customs of the region. Notable Southerns include Victor Fleming's *Gone with the Wind* (1939), Richard Brooks's *Cat on a Hot Tin Roof* (1958), John Boorman's *Deliverance* (1972), and Tate Taylor's *The Help* (2011). Quentin Tarantino's *Django Unchained* (2012) seamlessly blends the Western and the Southern, taking the Western theme of the outlaw gunfighter striving for mercenary justice and coupling it with the story of a former slave seeking to rescue his beloved from her cruel owner. As with

Westerns and Southerns, other geographic locations suggest certain themes and plotlines reflective of their history and culture. While the term "foreign film" designates many movies in relation to their geography, it tells spectators nothing of the film's plot and only of its country of origin. Geography inflects a movie's storyline, as with most Westerns and Southerns, yet, as with other generic classifications, one must carefully consider how identifying a film as belonging to a genre elucidates its narrative concerns.

* * * *

In sum, cinematic adaptations of literary texts allow readers to see these stories anew, to consider their storylines from another perspective. If spectators simply look for what is lost in the translation from page to screen, they will inevitably find that aspects of the literary work have shifted or were jettisoned altogether. It is more challenging, and often more fruitful, to consider instead both the literature and the film according to their unique merits. As the preceding discussion of genres attests, sometimes weak novels make excellent films, and sometimes esteemed novels lose their magic in cinematic adaptations. The same story can be filmed as a cinematic classic or as a flop, with stars turning in memorable or laughable performances (as evident in Lillian Gish's and Demi Moore's respective turns as Hester Prynne in the 1926 and 1995 adaptations of *The Scarlet Letter*). The mere fact that a film has been adapted from a previously published piece of fiction or play actually tells viewers surprisingly little about it, and so they must approach the film mindful of its past incarnation yet open to its new form.

Unit 3

A Practical Guide to Literary Criticism and Literary Theory

3.1 A Brief Historical Overview of Literary Criticism

When people read and respond to a poem, story, or play—whether by laughing or crying, by pondering its merit or throwing the book across the room—they are engaging in literary criticism. Literary criticism asks readers and authors to consider the various forms of literature and their necessary features, as well as positing why some works resonate over the centuries while others face a shorter shelf-life. It encourages readers to formulate interpretations generated by a text's unique features, while also considering it in relation to a wider field. In contrast to derivative and mundane works, great literature inspires multiple interpretations, as Oscar Wilde proposes in "The Critic as Artist":

> the aesthetic critic rejects these obvious modes of art that have but one message to deliver, and having delivered it become dumb and sterile, and seeks rather for such modes as suggest reverie and mood, and by their imaginative beauty make all interpretations true, and no interpretation final.
>
> (*Complete Works* 1031)

Coursework in literature invites students to act as critics, and thereby to join an ongoing conversation dating back to the earliest narratives. As long as there have been storytellers, their audiences have responded favorably and unfavorably to their tales, and the history of literary criticism details this rich and varied picture.

An early voice of philosophical aesthetics in the Western tradition, Plato tackles a fundamental question of literary criticism in theorizing the utility of literary art. Cautioning against poetry in *The Republic* (c. 380 BCE), Plato argues that, because poetry is a form of imitation, it distances one from the truth:

> painting and imitation as a whole are far from the truth when they produce their work; . . . moreover, imitation keeps company with the part in us that is far from prudence, and is not comrade and friend for any healthy or true purpose.
>
> (286; book 10, 603b)

Had early writers heeded Plato's admonitions, the history of literature would be short indeed, but other philosophers urged their disciples to enjoy literary pastimes. In contrast to his teacher, Aristotle concentrates in his *Poetics* (c. 335 BCE) on the pleasures arising from poetry's ability to mimic reality:

> [T]he instinct of imitation is implanted in man from childhood . . . and no less universal is the pleasure felt in things imitated. We have evidence of this in the facts of experience. Objects which in themselves we view with pain, we delight to contemplate when reproduced with minute fidelity.
>
> (4.2–3, at p. 55)

For Aristotle, the beauty of an image emerges in its ability to convey the truth of what it represents, and the most proficient artists win greater esteem for their ability to recreate life through their art. As Plato's and Aristotle's efforts to distill the purpose of art and poetry indicate, a central strand of literary criticism ponders the broadest of all literary questions: why do artists create, and what is the pleasure and utility arising from their creations?

It is generally acknowledged that authors influence one another through their literature, yet they also influence one another through their literary criticism. In the Middle Ages, the Italian poet Dante Alighieri, author of *The Divine Comedy* and *La Vita Nuova*, advocated that poets should write in their vernacular languages, rather than in Latin, the language of the Christian Church and governmental administration. He puts forth these precepts in his *De Vulgari eloquentia* ("On the eloquence of the vernacular," c. 1302):

> Let us first inquire whether all those who write verse in the vernacular should use this illustrious language; and so far as a superficial considera-tion of the matter goes, it would seem that they should, because every one who writes verse ought to adorn his verse as far as he is able. Where-fore, since nothing affords so great an adornment as the illustrious ver-nacular does, it would seem that every writer of verse ought to employ it.
>
> (170)

By selecting Italian over Latin, Dante defends the essential beauty of his ver-nacular tongue, and his decision bore far-reaching consequences for Eng-lish literature. Following in Dante's footsteps, Geoffrey Chaucer wrote *The Canterbury Tales* (c. 1385–1400) and other works in Middle English, and Dante's influence on the Englishman's decision cannot be discounted. Indeed, it is quite plausible that Chaucer, today celebrated as the Father of English Literature, would have written in Latin rather than English without Dante trailblazing a new path. Although numerous poets from the Middle Ages onward, including such illustrious names as John Gower, John Milton, and Thomas Gray, continued to write poetry in Latin as well as English, Milton joins Dante and Chaucer in advocating the pleasures of vernacular poetry in his *Paradise Regained* (1671):

> Or if I would delight my private hours
> With Music or with Poem, where so soon
> As in our native Language can I find
> That solace?
>
> (Complete Shorter Poems,
book 4, lines 331–34)

This issue of whether poets should write in their native tongues is a rare exception among debates of literary criticism, for it has been decided soundly in favor of the vernacular. For the most part, however, topics of literary criticism are by their nature open to wide-ranging debate and discussion, for one can never definitively conclude most questions of art and aesthetics.

Despite the many centuries between Plato and the English Renaissance, questions concerning poetry's utility and morality persisted. The preeminent literary critic of the sixteenth century, Sir Philip Sidney forcefully argues in *An Apology for Poetry* (c. 1579) for the moral soundness of the poetic arts:

> So that, since the excellencies of it may be so easily and so justly confirmed, and the low-creeping objections so soon trodden down—it not being an art of lies, but of true doctrine; not of effeminateness, but of notable stirring of courage; not of abusing man's wit, but of strengthening man's wit; not banished, but honoured by Plato: let us rather plant more laurels for to engarland the poets' heads . . . than suffer the ill-savoured breath of such wrong-speakers once to blow upon the clear springs of poesy.
>
> (108)

One can deduce from Sidney's passionate words the accusations leveled against poetry in the sixteenth century: that it is a luxurious and idle pastime, ensnaring its writers and readers in a web of lies and unmanly endeavors. Sidney rebuts these charges and suggests instead the virtues of art, yet, whether intentionally or not, he is mistaken on a key point: poetry was not "honoured by Plato," and his citation of the revered philosopher ironically undercuts his argument. Echoing Sidney's claims, Edmund Spenser defends his *Faerie Queene* (c. 1590–1596), declaring that "[t]he general end therefore of all the book is to fashion a gentleman or noble person in virtuous and gentle discipline" ("Letter to Sir Walter Raleigh" 463). Sidney and Spenser are, of course, hardly disinterested commentators on poetry's worth, for in defending poetry as a whole they also defend their individual works.

In addition to discussions of the social merits of literary art, authors and critics also ponder the best styles for their works. During the Renaissance a literary style known as *euphuism* came into fashion, with John Lyly's *Euphues: The Anatomy of Wit* (1578) as the progenitor of this form. Euphuism revels in excess, balancing and counterbalancing phrases and clauses in sentences of impressive length. As Lyly prescribes:

> For as much as every painter that shadoweth a man in all parts giveth every piece his just proportion, so he that deciphereth the qualities of the mind ought as well to show every humour in his kind as the other doth every part in his colour.

(28)

Exhibiting Lyly's zealous fidelity to his maxim, *Euphues* delights, yet often wearies, readers with its arch styling. Some literary fashions fade quickly, however, and in *Timber, or Discoveries* (1640), Ben Jonson advocates a simplicity of style: "a strict and succinct style is that where [the writer] can take away nothing without loss, and that loss to be manifest; the brief style is that which expresseth much in little" (44). He also advises his readers on how best to become an excellent writer—"For a man to write well, there are required three necessaries: to read the best authors, observe the best speakers, and much exercise of his own style" (57)—with the wisdom of his words evident to all who take writing seriously.

In the history of literary criticism, one often sees bursts of interest in certain topics coinciding with the writings of its era. For example, as the eighteenth century witnessed the wit of such masters of the form as Alexander Pope, William Congreve, Oliver Goldsmith, Lady Mary Wortley Montagu, and John Wilmot, Second Earl of Rochester, various critics attempted to define wit, despite the inherent challenge of pinpointing humor's origin and mechanics. John Locke, in *An Essay Concerning Human Understanding* (1690), details the mental agility needed for wit: "For *Wit* lying most in the assemblage of *Ideas*, and putting those together with quickness and variety, wherein can be found any resemblance or congruity, thereby to make up pleasant Pictures, and agreeable Visions in the Fancy" (2.11.2, at p. 156). In his rumination on the topic, entitled "A Discourse Concerning the Original and Progress of Satire" (1693), John Dryden sketches wit as an aggressive yet masterful satiric attack, and muses:

> How easy is it to call [a person] rogue and villain, and that wittily! But how hard to make a man appear a fool, a blockhead, or a knave, without using any of those opprobrious terms! . . . [T]here is still a vast difference betwixt the slovenly butchering of a man, and the fineness of a stroke that separates the head from the body, and leaves it standing in its place.
> (*Dryden: A Selection* 591–92)

In a similar vein, Joseph Addison, in the May 11, 1711, edition of *The Spectator*, quotes Locke's theories of wit, as he then proposes: "In order, therefore, that the resemblance in the ideas be wit, it is necessary that the ideas should not lie too near one another in the nature of things," as he then proceeds with his famed example: "Thus when a poet tells us the bosom of his mistress is as white as snow, there is no wit in the comparison; but when he adds, with a sigh, that it is as cold too, it then grows into wit" (*Essays* 72).

As with most literary terms, wit resists simple categorization, but the efforts of Dryden, Addison, and other theorists assist readers in seeing more clearly how wit differs from such related terms as *humor* and *comedy*, so that they may better discern its function in a range of discourses.

Another primary achievement of eighteenth-century literary criticism was to bolster Shakespeare's reputation as England's greatest playwright. Today it is difficult to conceive the necessity of this task, for his place in the pantheon appears unquestionable—and thus forever unquestioned. Nonetheless, some critics in the decades and centuries following Shakespeare's death criticized his plays harshly, particularly due to such issues as his farcical humor, his melding of storylines featuring characters of differing social classes, and his disregard for the unities of time, place, and action that structured much classical and French drama. In "An Essay of Dramatic Poesy" (1668) John Dryden argues for the breadth of Shakespeare's accomplishments:

> [Shakespeare] was the Man who of all Modern, and perhaps Ancient Poets, had the largest and most comprehensive Soul. . . . Those who accuse him to have wanted learning, give him the greater commendation: he was naturally learn'd; he needed not the Spectacles of Books to read Nature.
>
> (*Poetry, Prose, and Plays* 415)

Dryden's passionate defense of Shakespeare assisted in reclaiming his reputation, yet the grounds of this defense—that Shakespeare was educated by nature rather than by extensive study—can itself be doubted, for it asserts an implausible understanding of the playwright's genius as untainted by formal learning. Samuel Johnson, in the Preface to *The Plays of William Shakespeare* (1765), also sought to restore Shakespeare's luster and pursued this goal by refuting the critical allegation that Shakespeare should have adhered to the unities of time, place, and action:

> To the unities of time and place he has shewn no regard; and perhaps a nearer view of the principles on which they stand will diminish their value and withdraw from them the veneration which . . . they have very generally received, by discovering that they have given more trouble to the poet than pleasure to the auditor.
>
> (*Samuel Johnson* 430)

In contrast, Johnson rightly points out the intelligence of the audience: "The truth is that the spectators are always in their senses, and know, from the first act to the last, that the stage is only a stage, and that the players are only players" (431). Johnson's defense of Shakespeare demonstrates the ways in which strands of literary criticism overlap: because some critics derided Shakespeare's plays for not conforming to expected structural elements, Johnson must question the very foundations of drama as they were understood for centuries to rehabilitate the playwright's reputation. Similar to Dante's defense of the vernacular, Johnson's dismissal of the dramatic unities of time, place, and action has withstood the test of time, and few modern playwrights conform their works to these requirements. The critical task of restoring Shakespeare's reputation nonetheless persisted in subsequent eras, and in his *Biographia Literaria* (1812), Samuel Taylor Coleridge continues the advocacy of Shakespeare voiced by his forebears Dryden and Johnson. Coleridge defends the playwright by characterizing him as a proto-romantic, discerning his "power of so carrying on the eye of the reader as to make him almost lose the consciousness of words . . . and this without exciting any painful or laborious attention . . . but with the sweetness and easy movement of nature" (*Coleridge's Shakespearean Criticism* 1.214).

Because literary criticism reflects the zeitgeist of its era, it is not surprising that Coleridge lauds Shakespeare as a poet of nature or that other romantic critics praise literature that they believe best reflects nature's beauties. Of the major romantic poets, Coleridge was the most prolific as a literary critic, and many of his poems exemplify his aesthetic theories. Foremost, his poem "The Eolian Harp" (1795) stands as a metaphor for romantic poetry in its entirety, for this musical instrument that sounds with the wind's blowing melds the lyrical with the natural:

> And that simplest lute,
> Placed length-ways in the clasping casement, hark!
> How by the desultory breeze caressed,
> Like some coy maid half yielding to her lover,
> It pours such sweet upbraiding . . .
> ("The Eolian Harp," lines 12–16, in
> *Samuel Taylor Coleridge*)

Coleridge's poem dissolves the ostensible boundaries between literature and literary criticism, for it models the precepts he preaches and serves as a vibrant example of this romantic sensibility. In "A Defence of Poetry" (1821), Percy Bysshe Shelley agrees with Coleridge in his view of the poet sounding the natural world. He too uses the metaphor of the Aeolian harp to convey the mystery of poetry's creation:

> Poetry, in a general sense, may be defined to be "the expression of the Imagination": and poetry is connate with the origin of man. Man is an instrument over which a series of external and internal impressions are driven, like the alternations of an ever-changing wind over an Aeolian lyre, which move it by their motion to ever-changing melody.
> (*Shelley's Critical Prose* 3)

For Shelley, nature sparks humanity's creative power, proving the essential connection between the two. In a similar vein, other romantic critics entwine the question of poetry's utility with assessments of nature's power, and Thomas de Quincey sees literature as inspiring humanity to enjoy the fullness of life:

> were it not for the Literature of Power, these ideals would often remain amongst us as mere arid notional forms; whereas, by the creative forces of man put forth in literature, they gain a vernal life of restoration, and germinate into vital activities.
>
> (11.51–95, at 57)

De Quincey's analysis compares humanity nourished by literature to a flower blossoming: an apt image, like the Aeolian harp, that encapsulates the romantic passion for nature as a sublime reflection of human possibility.

As literary critics highlight the chief aesthetic concerns of an era, so too do they help to characterize and promote the literature of various geographies. This strand of criticism is evident in the calls of numerous authors, in the foundational years of the fledgling United States, to foster a distinct American voice. In "The American Scholar" (1837), Ralph Waldo Emerson advocates that his fellow citizens liberate themselves intellectually from European traditions:

> The scholar is that man who must take up into himself all the ability of the time, all the contributions of the past, all the hopes of the future. He must be an university of knowledge. . . . [T]his confidence in the unsearched might of man belongs, by all motives, by all prophecy, by all preparation, to the American Scholar. We have listened too long to the courtly muses of Europe.
>
> (26)

Oliver Wendell Holmes praises Emerson's essay as "Our intellectual Declaration of Independence" (Richard Gray 61), and it profoundly influenced subsequent writers seeking to create a new literary style for America. Among Emerson's acolytes, Walt Whitman echoes his forebear and urges the nation to free itself from European literary traditions:

> You are young, have the perfectest of dialects, a free press, a free government, the world forwarding its best to be with you. As justice has been strictly done to you, from this hour do strict justice to yourself. Strangle the singers who will not sing you loud and strong.
>
> ("Letter to Ralph Waldo Emerson, August 1856" 162)

Emancipating his verse from the European traditions of metrical poetry, Whitman enacted what Emerson preached, and American literature continued to emerge from Europe's shadow.

On the other side of the Atlantic, many Victorian critics, confronting the cultural fallout of an increasingly industrialized landscape, portrayed poetry as a means of spiritual rebirth. Centuries after Sidney and Spenser argued for poetry's core value, Victorian writers praised poetry as a necessary well-spring of human truth. John Stuart Mill characterizes the nature of poetry in simple yet powerful terms—"[t]he truth of poetry is to paint the human soul truly"—because he believes poetry enables an invaluable understanding of the self:

> poetry, which is the delineation of the deeper and more secret work-ings of the human heart, is interesting only to those to whom it recalls what they have felt, or whose imagination it stirs up to conceive what they could feel, or what they might have been able to feel, had their outward circumstances been different. Poetry, when it is really such, is truth.
>
> ("What Is Poetry?" 8)

For Mill, poetry illuminates and enlightens humanity against the degrada-tions of life. It is the quest for truth, one that challenges readers to examine their lives with sympathy and empathy, thereby to feel a connection to humanity and to the self. In a similar vein, Matthew Arnold, the poet of "The Scholar Gypsy" and "Dover Beach," extols, in *Culture and Anarchy* (1868), the "ideal of beauty, of sweetness and light, and a human nature complete on all its sides" (102). This ideal shines through in his definition of poetry: "The best poetry is what we want; the best poetry will be found to have a power of forming, sustaining, and delighting us, as nothing else can" ("Study of Poetry" 5). Walter Pater believes art and culture give meaning to life, as he explains in a series of essays examining Renaissance art and poetry (1868):

> The service of philosophy, of speculative culture, towards the human spirit is to rouse, to startle it to a life of constant and eager observa-tion. . . . To burn always with this hard, gem-like flame, to maintain this ecstasy, is success in life.
>
> (188–89)

Rejecting materialism in favor of passion, Pater proposes a life immersed in art as the necessary antidote for an austerity of the soul. For such Victorian voices as Mill, Arnold, and Pater, art and poetry illuminate one's existence: they demand much of their patrons yet give back even more, for they push one to a deeper comprehension of the human struggle to transcend limita-tions of mind and spirit.

Moving into the modernist sensibilities of the early twentieth century, authors played with literary forms as they also pondered the nature and pur-pose of their endeavors. Joseph Conrad explains, in the preface to his *Nigger of the "Narcissus"* (1897), that novels must speak the truth, for this is how readers come to know the world:

A work that aspires, however humbly, to the condition of art should carry its justification in every line. And art itself may be defined as a single-minded attempt to render the highest kind of justice to the visible universe, by bringing to light the truth, manifold and one, underlying its every aspect.

(145)

A truth that is "manifold and one" is, by its very nature, open to varying interpretations, a sensibility that corresponds with the modernist interest in reinventing narrative forms. One of the chief advocates of modernism's break with the past, T. E. Hulme argues that literature should animate readers with new visions and experiences:

[Poetry] always endeavours to arrest you, and to make you continuously see a physical thing, to prevent you gliding through an abstract process. It chooses fresh epithets and fresh metaphors, not so much because they are new, and we are tired of the old, but because the old cease to convey a physical thing and become abstract counters.

(70)

Hulme's words capture the spirit of much modernist literature in its striving to create new modes of perception. In a complementary yet distinct opinion, Virginia Woolf outlines the ways that insights spring from, quite simply, the world in its entirety, from the awe-inspiring to the mundane:

"The proper stuff of fiction" does not exist; everything is the proper stuff of fiction; whatever one honestly thinks, whatever one honestly feels. . . . All that fiction asks of us is that we should break her and bully her, honour and love her, till she yields to our bidding, for so her youth is perpetually renewed and her sovereignty assured.

("Modern Novels" 36)

Finding inspiration all around her, Woolf advocates an ecumenical outlook that unearths literary worth in every aspect of life, yet one can also see, in her call for renewal, her allegiance to the modernist drive to reimagine literary modes.

Throughout the remainder of the twentieth century and into the beginnings of the twenty-first, various schools of literary criticism have risen to address the nature of reading, writing, and the creation of aesthetic and social meaning. The new critics of the 1930s and 1940s advocated close reading practices, with psychoanalytic approaches employing the insights of Sigmund Freud and other theoreticians of the mind to ponder the ways in which subterranean desires and drives are manifested in literature. In the latter half of the twentieth century, feminist criticism, critical race theories, and queer theories asked readers to examine the ways in gender, race, and sexuality are portrayed—or marginalized—in various texts, thinking through the ways in which cultural privilege erects assumptions about various peoples.

Numerous other critical approaches gaining prominence in the twentieth century, including semiotic, deconstructive, (new) historicist, and cultural studies approaches, testify to the rich pleasures of reading and analyzing literary and other cultural texts, plumbing how they create meaning and how this meaning resonates in the wider society.

While this brief overview of literary criticism addresses some of its prevailing questions in conjunction with the chief authors and theorists of their respective eras, it would be remiss to overlook two primary threads of analysis to which readers frequently return: literary influence and the literary canon. The study of literary influence traces the ways that authors and previous traditions affect the genesis of subsequent literature: how Shakespeare rewrites Chaucer, for example, or how Toni Morrison interweaves Biblical allusions throughout her novels. In "Tradition and the Individual Talent" (1919), T. S. Eliot observes that authors cannot be appreciated solely through their own works, for each author's work resonates with an expanded range of meanings imbued through others' writings, particularly their predecessors:

> No poet, no artist, has his complete meaning alone. His significance, his appreciation is the appreciation of his relation to the dead poets and artists. You cannot value him alone; you must set him, for contrast and comparison, among the dead.
>
> (49)

Imagining authors who create wholly by themselves is rather like imagining children raised alone in the woods: how can language be learned, if the children have no one to teach them? Whereas Eliot's vision of literary influence has a multiplicity of voices uniting in a given author's work, Harold Bloom describes this process in more antagonistic terms:

> *Poetic Influence—when it involves two strong, authentic poets,—always proceeds by a misreading of the prior poet, an act of creative correction that is actually and necessarily a misinterpretation. The history of fruitful poetic influence . . . is a history of anxiety and self-saving caricature, of distortion, or perverse, willful revisionism without which modern poetry as such could not exist.*
>
> (30; italics in original)

Teasing out the relationships between and among authors requires a deep and sympathetic understanding of their respective texts, eras, and styles. One not need agree with Bloom's theory that subsequent authors willfully misinterpret their forebears as they attempt to strike into new territories, yet his point that literary influence involves an encounter with the past reminds readers of the dialectic qualities of authorship, in which writers cannot seal themselves off from all others, for, through the simple act of reading, one's imagination is forever altered.

A particularly fraught question of literary criticism addresses the parameters and utility of a canon—the essential works that one must read to be considered culturally literate. Many authors divulge to their readers, through allusions and other forms of homage, which of their forebears they hold in highest esteem, such as in Chaucer's *House of Fame*, in which he praises the accomplishments of Homer, Statius, Virgil, Ovid, Lucan, and Claudian; or in Samuel Johnson's *The Lives of the English Poets*, in which he praises fifty-two poets, including John Milton, Alexander Pope, Joseph Addison, Jonathan Swift, and Thomas Gray; or in Lemony Snicket's *A Series of Unfortunate Events*, in which the Baudelaire children encounter numerous obstacles during travails that resonate with deeper literary significance. It should be noted as well that literary anthologies and textbooks such as this one participate in forming and perpetuating a literary canon. By including some authors and excluding others in these discussions—many of whom we would like to address but could not due to space limitations and production costs—we shape the contours of the literary canon. Canons, however, are not neutral indices of literary quality, for they also form readers' tastes. In doing so, they become implicated in political questions of which stories best capture that elusive quality of excellent literature, for their representations thus represent the highest cultural good. As Henry Louis Gates, Jr., points out of the canon's historical development and its gaps,

> no women or people of color were ever able to discover the reflection or representation of their images, or hear the resonances of their cultural voices. The return of "the" canon, the high canon of Western masterpieces, represents the return of an order in which my people were the subjugated, the voiceless, the invisible, the unrepresented, and the unrepresentable.
>
> (35)

Gates forcefully condemns the canon for its lack of inclusiveness, a lack that both reflects historical realities yet perpetuates those realities' shadow. One might counter that the problems of the canon could be solved by the creation of complementary canons, yet such a move sidesteps the very purpose of a canon, in that it should unify its readers in a shared cultural and literary history.

As the preceding thumbnail sketch of literary criticism illustrates, readers frequently ponder the relative merits of literature, discussing how and why narratives function, as well as how they affect their readers. Although it is easy to dismiss literary criticism with tired bromides describing critics as failed artists, who, in their disappointments, lash out at others more successful, such a stance neglects the ways in which criticism nurtures deeper and more insightful literary experiences. Furthermore, many of the most perceptive critics also count among the most illustrious authors, and many of these figures explicitly recognize that criticism merits recognition as an art in itself.

Alexander Pope, a poet of extraordinary talent and a critic of extraordinary insight, explains the essential work that literary critics accomplish in *An Essay on Criticism* (1709):

> 'Tis hard to say, if greater want of skill
> Appear in writing or in judging ill;
> But of the two, less dang'rous is th' offense
> To tire our patience than mislead our sense.
>
> (lines 1–4)

Bad writing may bore readers, Pope cautions, but bad criticism hurts readers, directing them away from the glories of the human imagination to pedestrian efforts by mediocre talents. In this light, the history of literary criticism details the efforts of numerous voices over the centuries to bring readers to the best literature through the most discerning of judgments. The pleasure of literature and of literary criticism is that these complementary discourses will never cease, for the pastime of reading and pondering the quality of what one has read remains bounteous in its aesthetic delights.

3.2 Literary Theories and Their Applications

To engage in literary criticism, readers benefit from a variety of interpretive tools that assist them in understanding how various texts function. Without readers, a text has no life, and without a multitude of readers each seeking their own experiences of it, a text would devolve into a singular, static interpretation. As reading theorist Louise Rosenblatt cautions of interpreting poetry, "No one . . . can read a poem for us. If there is indeed a poem and not simply a literal statement, the reader must have the experience, must 'live through' what is being created during the reading" (33). Literature's eternal power arises in its ability to affect each reader individually. Countless readers delight in the works of great poets and authors, yet individual readers interpret each text uniquely, finding special senses and resonances that could never be divulged from a summary.

Theories of literature provide a toolkit for understanding and interpreting poems, novels, plays, and other cultural texts. They assist readers in probing below a text's surface meaning both to gauge its complexities and contradictions and to generate interpretations based on their unique experiences of it. The remainder of this chapter includes concise introductions to these major literary theories, as well as illustrative examples of their utility:

- Close Reading and New Criticism
- Semiotic and Deconstructive Approaches
- (New) Historicist and Cultural Studies Approaches
- Theories of Social Class and Ideology
- Psychoanalytic Approaches
- Gender and Feminist Theories
- Queer Theories
- Postcolonial and Critical Race Theories
- Rhetorical Analysis
- Genre Theories

Each section, after summarizing the main tenets of the perspective under consideration, concludes with potential questions readers can pose of a text to begin generating interpretations. When applied judiciously, literary theories facilitate comprehending, analyzing, and researching a given text, and thus these various theoretical schools facilitate literary pleasure as well.

Close Reading and New Criticism

Read carefully. Pore over the text, catching its nuances. Never skim. While this advice may appear so obvious that it could not constitute a formal approach to literary study, close reading is the wellspring from which all informed interpretations flow. Close reading, also known as explication, necessitates that readers pay keen attention to the formal and aesthetic elements of a text, and the preceding sections of this book have explored the necessary vocabulary and terminology to undertake such readings: rhythm, meter, and types of figurative language for poetry; plot structure, point of view, and character for prose fiction; and dialogue and staging for drama. Besides this essential critical lexicon for analyzing literature, readers must enjoy a vocabulary sufficient for comprehending the range of meanings various words hold. Quite simply, one cannot explicate a text without understanding the words on the page, and so it is essential that readers expand their vocabularies by studying unfamiliar words. A grounding in philology, the study of the historical roots and changing meanings of words, illuminates perceptive close readings, for readers must comprehend, as much as possible, how authors used the words they penned on the page.

Close reading as an interpretive strategy is aligned with new criticism, a school of the 1930s and 1940s associated with such scholars and poets as John Crowe Ransom, Cleanth Brooks, Robert Penn Warren, Allen Tate, I. A. Richards, and William Empson. These critics argued against the biographical and historical approaches to literature current in their day; instead, new critics argued for the necessity of understanding a poem or other piece of literature in and of itself. The difference between these perspectives is summarized in the terms *extrinsic* and *intrinsic criticism*. Extrinsic criticism looks outside a text to consider its relationship to its author, history, and sources, whereas intrinsic criticism looks solely at the text itself. As Cleanth Brooks and Robert Penn Warren argue, "criticism and analysis . . . is ultimately of value *only insofar as it can return readers to the poem itself*—return them, that is, better prepared to experience it more immediately, fully, and, shall we say, innocently" (16). Brooks and Warren's belief that a renewed innocence arises when one more deeply understands a literary text paradoxically captures the sense that a text's continued revelation of its meaning will strike readers freshly upon each subsequent experience.

Foremost in close readings, readers should search for ambiguity, irony, paradox, and symbolism, as well as how these elements function together.

In his classic study *Seven Types of Ambiguity*, William Empson defines ambiguity as "any verbal nuance, however slight, which gives room for alternative reactions to the same piece of language" (1). Whereas journalists and writers of nonfiction eschew ambiguity, in literature this technique opens a text to a plurality of interpretations. Literary texts do not always resolve the issues that they consider; rather than espousing tidy morals, literature more frequently asks readers to weigh the possibilities and pleasure of uncertainty. New critics also proposed that literary texts, despite their ambiguity, should achieve a sense of organic unity, a concept expressed by Brooks and Warren in their description of the poet's craft:

> as he composes, he moves toward his idea—toward his general conception of the poem. At the same time that he is trying to envisage the poem as a whole, he is trying to relate the individual items to that whole. He cannot assemble them in a merely arbitrary fashion; they must bear some relation to each other.
>
> (473)

A primary metaphor for visualizing organic unity compares literary texts to plants. Every plant reflects an organic unity indicative of its species, but its leaves and flowers build an entity unique unto itself, creating a beauty reflective both of its form and of its individuality. Ambiguous yet not arbitrary: for new critics, the evocative interpretive possibilities of ambiguity do not allow for arbitrariness in the writer's artistic decisions, for the organic unity of the text must allow it to stand alone as a work of art.

Because of their keen focus on the text itself, new critics believed that authors are mostly irrelevant to the aesthetic appreciation of their poems, novels, and plays, and they employed the term *intentional fallacy* to refer to the belief that a text reflects the intentions of its author. As W. K. Wimsatt and Monroe Beardsley argue, "the design or intention of the author is neither available nor desirable as a standard for judging the success of a work of literary art" (3). They pithily conclude, "Critical inquiries are not settled by consulting the oracle" (18). New critics also cautioned against the *affective fallacy*, which refers to the belief that a reader's emotional response to a text reflects its value. I. A. Richards tersely warns that "[s]entimentality is a peril" for critical interpretations (14). New critics argued that a work of literature must be experienced without regard for the emotions, and readers must concentrate instead on how it achieves its aesthetic effects.

While close reading skills can be applied to texts of any literary genre, many new critics focused particularly on poetry. In I. A. Richards's and William Empson's divergent readings of Gerard Manley Hopkins's short poem "Spring and Fall" (1880), the poem comes alive through their contradictory interpretations of a key ambiguity:

Margarét, are you grieving
Over Goldengrove unleaving?
Leaves, líke the things of man, you
With your fresh thoughts care for, can you?
Ah! as the heart grows older
It will come to such sights colder
By and by, nor spare a sigh
Though worlds of wanwood leafmeal lie;
And yet you *will* weep and know why.
Now no matter, child, the name:
Sorrow's springs are the same.
Nor mouth had, no, nor mind, expressed
What héart héard of, ghóst guéssed:
It is the blight man was born for,
It is Margaret you mourn for.

The simple phrase "yet you *will* weep" opens up a contrasting array of inter-
pretative possibilities. Richards suggests that "[w]hen 'will' is accentuated
it ceases to be an auxiliary verb and becomes the present tense of the verb
'to will.' She persists in weeping and in demanding the reason for the falling of the leaves" (79–80). In contrast, Empson reads the line and suggests
that "*Will weep* may mean: 'insist upon weeping, now or later,' or 'shall
weep in the future'" (148). These opposing interpretations of the simple
word *will*—does Margaret weep now or in the future?—highlight the power
of strong explications, in which one word shifts an understanding of the
child's sorrow. Readers' vision of Margaret's grief hinges on this ambiguity of *will*, with Richards painting her sorrow as persistently questioning
the reasons behind Nature's transience and with Empson suggesting that
her grief surpasses her current understanding yet that she will mature into
a deeper realization of life's pains. Other elements in this poem that might
elicit close readings include the contradictory images of spring and autumn;
the vegetative symbolism of trees and leaves; the narrator's depiction of
Margaret as a symbol of life; and the ways in which the poem's meter and
rhythm complement its themes.

Many subsequent critical schools, particularly deconstructive and psychoanalytic perspectives, reacted against the formalist approach of new
criticism. Despite these differences in interpretive strategies, and no matter the particular theoretical affiliations a given reader might profess, a
close reading of the text should provide the necessary foundation to support every interpretation of it. One need not agree with the tenets of new
criticism as an interpretive school to benefit from the textual focus available through explication. An interpretation without close reading cannot
marshal the necessary evidence to support its claims, for if a reading is
not grounded in the text that it purports to analyze, upon what then is it
grounded?

Interpretive Questions Based on Close Reading and New Criticism

- What is the text's surface meaning, and what is its secondary meaning?
- What patterns and symbols does the text use repeatedly, and what effect do they achieve?
- What ambiguities, ironies, and paradoxes arise in the text, and how do they create complementary or contrasting interpretations?
- Does the text achieve organic unity, or does it fail to do so? Explain either how the various elements of the text unite into a seamless whole or how they succumb to fragmentation.
- Consider the relationship between form and theme. How does the author's structuring of the text reflect its themes?

Semiotic and Deconstructive Approaches

At its simplest, semiotics comprises the study of signs and symbols in life and in literature. All language is based on signs: letters are grouped together into discrete units to represent words, and words represent all aspects of the intelligible world. If a thought, feeling, or entity does not have a name, discussing it becomes virtually impossible. Ferdinand de Saussure's pioneering work in semiotics differentiates between the sign and signified in a speech act. The *sign* refers to the word itself; the *signified* refers to the entity denoted by the sign. For example, the word *saxophone* is a sign, and a saxophone itself—a musical instrument of the woodwind family—is the signified. Saussure explains that "the process which selects one particular sound-sequence to correspond to one particular idea is completely arbitrary" (111). Despite any etymological and onomatopoeic reasons for words bearing the meanings assigned to them, the relationships among a word's constituent letters, the sounds produced when speaking it, and its meaning are ultimately capricious. Saussure also distinguishes between *parole*, which is the speech and speech codes of a person, and *langue*, which is the speech and speech codes of the person's culture.

Beyond the dyad of the sign and the signified that constitute a word and its referent, language also communicates through connotation; that is to say, a given word can simultaneously denote a specific meaning and connote a related sense. In many ways, the connotations of a sign, which can be described as its conceptual sense, align with Roland Barthes's theories of mythical speech: "Mythical speech is made of a material which has *already* been worked on so as to make it suitable for communication; it is because all the materials of myth (whether pictorial or written) presuppose a signifying consciousness, that one can reason about them while discounting their substance" (*Mythologies* 110). Language never operates in a vacuum, as speakers must negotiate the ways in which words have been used historically to communicate; they in turn communicate with the same semiotic tools, yet in unique situations. To return to the example of *saxophone*, people attach various connotations to saxophones that are implicated within its denotations. Due to its connection to jazz, many people see the saxophone as a "cool" musical instrument and perceive saxophones (and saxophone players) differently to flutes and pianos (and flutists and pianists). The various social connotations assigned to these musical instruments testify to the power of mythologies to imbue words and entities with additional layers of meaning.

Deconstruction questions the correlation between sign and signified, pointing to the multiplicity of potential significations of any given speech act. Particularly through the conceptual and mythological traits of words, language often generates simultaneous yet conflicting senses. Gayatri Spivak summarizes deconstruction as a reading praxis through which readers seek

> [t]o locate the promising marginal text, to disclose the undecidable moment, to pry it loose with the positive lever of the signifier; to reverse the resident hierarchy, only to displace it; to dismantle in order to reconstitute what is always already inscribed.
>
> (lxxvii)

This précis of deconstructive interpretive strategies involves discovery ("to locate," "to disclose") and reformulation ("to reverse," "to dismantle"). Deconstruction requires readers to look beyond the expectation that a sign and its signified will cohere into an organic unit and instead to expect the conceptual and mythological aspects of language to complicate, if not to undercut, such meanings. Spivak cautions as well that, if deconstructive readings merely reinstate an interpretation from the text's margins, they risk mimicking the interpretive strategies that they seek to reframe. From this perspective, a triumphant pleasure arises in deconstruction's ability to "offer a way out of the closure of knowledge" (lxxvii).

At its heart, deconstruction asks readers to ponder the variability of meaning assigned to various words and cultural codes. In Robert Herrick's epigram "Upon Jack and Jill" (1648), the poem's humor arises in Jill's refusal to interpret Jack's words through the interpretive valence he selects:

> When *Jill* complaines to *Jack* for want of meate;
> *Jack* kisses *Jill*, and bids her freely eate:
> *Jill* sayes, of what? sayes *Jack*, on that sweet kisse,
> Which full of Nectar and Ambrosia is,
> The food of Poets; so I thought, sayes *Jill*;
> That makes them looke so lanke, so Ghost-like still.
> Let Poets feed on aire, or what they will;
> Let me feed full, till that I fart, says *Jill*.

Jack encodes a romantic mythology to his kisses, painting them as the only necessary sustenance for lovers. Jill, in contrast, deconstructs his amatory offerings and insists upon an appropriately literal response to her request for food. In this brief poem, Herrick contrasts Jack's and Jill's perspectives, with Jill triumphing as she reconfigures Jack's airy kisses into her own farting. In this masterful reconstruction of symbols, Jill proves that the mythological import attributed to an entity is only so much mythology, which she strips bare through her sharp rejoinder.

Another point to ponder concerning signs and deconstruction is the challenge of interpreting silences. Often a literary text does not answer readers' questions, or authors employ ambiguity to obscure a clear-cut understanding of their (or their characters') motives. As Pierre Macherey explains:

> Yet the unspoken has many other resources; it assigns speech to its exact position, designating its domain. By speech, silence becomes the centre and principle of expression, its vanishing point. Speech eventually has nothing more to tell us: we investigate the silence, for it is the silence that is doing the speaking.
>
> (96)

It is critical to ask what information a story withholds from its readers. For example, Chaucer tells his readers that the Wife of Bath has had five husbands, but it is unclear whether the fifth is still alive when she proclaims, "Yblessed be God that I have wedded five! / Welcome the sixte, whan that evere he shal" (*Wife of Bath's Prologue* lines 44–45). She appears to be searching for her sixth husband, but she never mentions the death of her fifth husband, in contrast to her first four husbands, whom she clearly describes as deceased. Likewise, despite her active sex life and her appreciation of the Christian endorsements of fertility—"God bad [commanded] us for to wexe and mulitplye" (line 28)—Chaucer does not explain whether she has children. Such silences influence readers' understanding of Alison of Bath's character, if only through the fact that such puzzling issues resist resolution and undermine any sense of readers' certainty.

With semiotics positing that the relationship between sign and signified is arbitrary, and with deconstruction further exploring the radical multiplicity of language, some deconstructionists, like the new critics before them, question the necessity of considering the author's role in literary creation. Roland Barthes pronounced in an influential essay "the death of the author" as a topic of literary analysis: "We know now that a text is not a line of words releasing a single 'theological' meaning (the 'message' of the Author-God) but a multi-dimensional space in which a variety of writings, none of them original, blend and clash" (*Image, Music* 146). With this deconstructive notion, Barthes advocates liberating texts from quests for meaning as derived from their authors' agendas. Readers should hesitate, however, to dismiss authors entirely from their analysis. Seán Burke advocates examining the "situated authorship" of a text because its author is *the principle of specificity in a world of texts.* Burke also explains, "far from consolidating the notion of a universal or unitary subject, the retracing of the work to its author is a working-back to historical, cultural and political embeddedness" (202). The tenuous position of the author in deconstructive methodology highlights the necessity for readers to think through the orthodoxies and conflicts of various critical schools and to determine for themselves the relevance of the author for the analysis they are constructing.

Interpretive Questions Based on Semiotic and Deconstructive Approaches

- What disjunctions arise between the text's signifiers and their signifieds? Describe the plurality of possible meanings that arise from these disjunctions.
- Describe the text's primary symbols, and theorize how they signify beyond their surface meanings. How do their connotations and mythologies lead interpretations into new directions?
- How does a character's speech (*parole*) relate to the speech of his or her community (*langue*), and what do these differences in speech reveal to readers about the author's construction of the character?
- What does the text withhold from readers, and how do these silences affect an interpretation of it?
- How is the author relevant to a deconstructive analysis? Would the analysis benefit more from Barthes's theory that the author is dead or from Burke's belief that the text's situated authorship enhances an understanding of its meanings?

(New) Historicist and Cultural Studies Approaches

Historicist approaches to literature consider the cultural moment from which a text emerges. Whereas a close reading or a deconstructive analysis of a poem need not take into account its historical setting, historicist approaches situate texts in their cultural backgrounds, exploring how they reflect or resist the era's zeitgeist. Primary historicist approaches to literature include those of biography, which examines the relevance of authors' lives to their texts; of reception, which investigates how a text was viewed by its contemporary audience; and of historical aesthetics, which considers the text in relation to prevailing cultural and artistic traditions. In sum, historicist approaches seek to understand literature in tandem with its culture: for example, a historicist critic might analyze Chaucer's literature in its context of King Richard II's court, or she might read Dickens's novels through the lens of Victorian science.

The term *new historicism* emerged in the 1980s to inaugurate a critical approach that, like historicism, interprets literature through the context of history, yet new historicists do so by stressing the openness of historical records and the multiplicity of archival sources. Perceptive historicist analysis takes as its foundation that history may guide a literary interpretation, but that history is itself also a narrative. More so, many histories suture over the various ideological conflicts of a period, and thus the old adage that history is written by the winners cautions new historicists to consider the limitations of their sources. They must be aware that history reflects certain perspectives rather than others, and this influences who is heard from a given period. Stephen Greenblatt articulates new historicist tenets in *Renaissance Self-Fashioning: From More to Shakespeare*, his groundbreaking monograph advancing this critical school, in which he advocates that one must examine "the cultural system of meanings that creates specific individuals by governing the passage from abstract potential to concrete historical embodiment." Greenblatt sees literature as part of such a network of cultural meanings and argues that "[l]iterature functions within this system in three interlocking ways: as a manifestation of the concrete behavior of its particular author, as itself the expression of the codes by which behavior is shaped, and as a reflection upon these codes" (3–4). Recognizing that culture is shaped by conflicting and complementary codes of discourse, social structure, governance, and ideology, among others, new historicists engage with history as a contingent yet significant source of a text's construction of meaning.

Following this trajectory of new historicist thought, it is important to realize that the historical periods according to which readers group English, American, and other literatures are in many ways convenient fictions. The eras referred to as medieval, Renaissance, long eighteenth century, Victorian, and modern are retrospective efforts to define periods according to their perceived traditions. In particular, medieval authors never saw themselves as living in the Middle Ages, for they could not know that Renaissance thinkers would describe them as such. And while Elizabeth Barrett Browning surely realized that she wrote during Queen Victoria's reign, she could not have foreseen the ways in which Victorian literature itself would be constructed by future readers, creating a seemingly unified canon from a disparate body of work including, among numerous other texts and various sensibilities, her poetry, Wilkie Collins's sensation novels, and Oscar Wilde's plays. As Claire Colebrook proposes, "New historicism's *ad hoc* procedure of reading, its attention to contiguity and circumstance is perhaps the best strategy literary criticism has produced to disrupt the notions of general interpretive horizons, limits, and justifications" (235). To see a monolithic Victorian era, or any other era, is to create a fantasy that the authors who lived through it would never recognize as their own, and new historicism requires readers to see history in its particularity rather than as a composite. To summarize the distinction between historicist and new historicist approaches, historicism explores how history influenced the creation of a literary text, whereas new historicism sees the interplay of history and the literary text as mutually constitutive.

Closely related to historicist approaches, cultural studies asks readers to consider the ways in which artifacts of popular culture—including comic books, commercials, pulp fiction, blockbuster films, and other such forms—create meaning both within and against other aesthetic discourses. The amorphous divisions between high and low culture, as well as the artistic repercussions of these binaries, stand as a chief line of inquiry for cultural studies because the ostensibly aesthetic reasons for labeling various literary works as high or low art influence how they are received. Still, this is not to suggest that critics in the field of cultural studies uniformly endorse artifacts of popular culture as the aesthetic equivalent of literary art. Richard Hoggart, who, in 1964, founded the Birmingham Centre for Contemporary Cultural Studies, the birthplace of the discipline as a field of scholarly and interpretive inquiry, laments that "Most mass-entertainments are in the end what D. H. Lawrence described as 'anti-life.' They are full of a corrupt brightness, of improper appeals and moral evasions" (277). Such a critique, however, does not hold as its necessary corollary that such popular-culture artifacts therefore do not merit analysis or that all of popular culture is necessarily secondary to other cultural fields.

Raymond Williams's *Culture and Society, 1780–1950*, a foundational text of the field, contrasts working-class culture to elite culture yet argues for their interconnection. For Williams, dialectic opportunities emerge in the crossover between low and high culture: "it is evidently possible both for members of other classes to contribute to the common stock, and for such contributions to be unaffected by or in opposition to the ideas and values of the dominant class" (320). Derogatory views of popular-culture artifacts construe them, sometimes in explicitly Marxist terms, as opiates of the masses. Andrew Ross mentions, as he also counters, the "well-known, conspiratorial view of 'mass culture' as imposed upon a passive populace like so much standardized fodder, doled out to quell unrest and to fuel massive profits" (4). Even if it were uniformly true that consumers of popular culture mindlessly numb themselves with literary pabulum, why would one then exempt these texts from analysis for their conformity or resistance to aesthetic principles and/or ideologies? On the contrary, cultural studies extends its range of analysis beyond the literary and subverts the privileging of high over low art forms, as Chris Rojek zestfully explains:

> treating popular culture seriously impacted against the condescension of elite groups, for the most rarefied of whom, the masses were held to be more or less incapable of generating worthwhile cultural content or form. To declare value in forms of resistance in schooling, to study comics and cartoon characters as signs of knowledge and power . . . was akin to hurling a mixture of salt and pepper in the face of the establishment.
>
> (6)

Positing cultural studies as a form of resistance, Rojek outlines the radical potential of the field, for it fundamentally reimagines the frameworks establishing high versus low art and the power structures latent within these paradigms.

The legend of Robin Hood exemplifies the ways in which new historicist and cultural studies approaches mesh and the insights that may be gleaned from them. Foremost, the ballads of Robin Hood, such as "Robin Hood and the Potter," "Robin Hood and Maid Marian," and "Robin Hood's Birth, Breeding, Valour, and Marriage," arise from folk traditions, and thus are generally viewed as distinct from literary art. It is nonetheless apparent that this folk tradition draws strongly from the literary world of medieval romance and the tales of King Arthur, and that distinguishing between a literary Arthurian tradition and a folk Hoodian tradition oversimplifies their differences. For example, in such romances as *Sir Gawain and the Green Knight*, King Arthur refuses to eat his dinner unless he hears a tale or witnesses a marvel—"Which he had made a point of honor: he would never eat / On such a special day until he had been told / A curious tale about some perilous thing" (Winny, lines 91–93)—and Robin Hood likewise eschews food in preference of adventure in "A Gest of Robyn Hode": "To dyne have I noo lust, / Till that I have som bolde baron, / Or som unkouth gest" (Knight and Ohlgren, lines 22–24). Although Robin Hood is established as a counter-cultural hero in various ballads, he bears himself royally and wins deference from his followers. King Edward marvels at the dedication of Robin's men:

Here is a wonder seemly syght;
Me thynketh, by Goddes pyne [pain],
His men are more at his byddynge
Then my men be at myn.
(lines 1561–64)

Furthermore, Robin's courtesy to ladies—"All wemen werschepyd he" (Knight and Ohlgren, "Robin Hood and the Potter," line 12)—models the chivalric treatment of women expected from knights of the medieval romance tradition. Many esteemed poets have adapted the Robin Hood legend, including Ben Jonson, John Keats, Sir Walter Scott, Thomas Love Peacock, and Alfred, Lord Tennyson, and he has also served as fodder for numerous cinematic adaptations, including *Robin Hood*, starring Douglas Fairbanks and Wallace Beery (1922); *The Adventures of Robin Hood*, starring Errol Flynn, Basil Rathbone, and Olivia de Havilland (1938); *Robin and Marian*, starring Sean Connery and Audrey Hepburn (1976); *Robin Hood: Prince of Thieves*, starring Kevin Costner and Morgan Freeman (1991); and *Robin Hood*, starring Russell Crowe and Cate Blanchett (2010). From this brief overview of the legends of Robin Hood, it is apparent that he participates in folk culture yet that these folk representations draw from literary culture, and that his appearances in literary culture draw from his representations in folk culture. In the cinematic adaptations of his legend, Robin Hood shifts anew for each generation that re-creates him. New historicist and critical studies perspectives keenly attune readers to the ways in which such figures as Robin Hood journey through high and low culture, thereby illuminating and exposing the ideologies from which they spring.[1]

Interpretive Questions Based on (New) Historicist and Cultural Studies Approaches

- In the year (or decade, or century) that the text was written, what events might have influenced its author to depict events in a particular light?
- Does the text belong to high culture or to popular culture? What are the reasons for assigning it to this field?
- How can the text be understood in relation to other artifacts of its culture, including those reflecting such fields as literature, art, music, history, archives, and popular culture?
- How does a high-culture text exhibit affinities with popular culture, and how does a popular-culture text exhibit affinities with high culture? How does the text transgress the boundaries ostensibly separating literary/high and popular/low cultures?
- In what ways can a (new) historicist or cultural studies perspective be combined with other critical schools to generate a deeper understanding of a particular text?

Theories of Social Class and Ideology

Serfs and aristocrats. The proletariat and the bourgeoisie. Poor, rich, and middle class. Although some economic divisions are amorphous—where precisely does the middle class end and the upper class begin?—other social structures are rigidly demarcated: despite the humor of Mark Twain's *The Prince and the Pauper*, few would mistake a commoner for a king. As literature reflects the social conditions of human (and even nonhuman) characters, its characters inhabit class systems as they interact with one another. Social structures, in many ways, make daily life possible. Different people perform different jobs for the smooth functioning of society, and they are rewarded in different ways for their services—or penalized for their lack thereof. Some of the more prominent principles of social and economic organization include capitalism (a free market economy), communism (a government controlled economy), and socialism (a hybrid form, primarily capitalistic but with governmental control of some major industries). Social structures also vary according to historical eras. Vassalage and feudalism no longer organize the political and economic systems of Western Europe, yet these were the predominant social systems of this region in the Middle Ages. While capitalism now appears to be the "natural" economic structure of the Western world, arguments still rage over its format and function, particularly over such issues as the extent of the social safety net afforded to the poor, sick, unemployed, and elderly. To study the class and social structure of a work of literature involves asking probing questions about how the society is organized and for what purpose, and who benefits and who loses from this arrangement.

As Karl Marx and Frederick Engels famously postulated, social class is not a neutral factor in society, for the dominant economic class guides the society as a whole:

In every epoch the ideas of the ruling class are the ruling ideas, that is, the class that is the ruling *material* power of society is at the same time its ruling *intellectual* power. The class having the means of material production has also control over the means of intellectual production, so that it also controls, generally speaking, the ideas of those who lack the means of intellectual production.

(129)

With this powerful explication of the connection between wealth and social consciousness, Marx and Engels argue that economics is not a neutral factor in the creation and maintenance of culture but its overriding rationale: in preserving the benefits of their social class, those who control the means of production also control the nation's ideology.

In sum, a society's ideology comprises its prevailing beliefs that have been naturalized as the correct and proper way for its citizens to interact. Louis Althusser explains that the members of a given society are continuously exposed to its values:

Throughout this schema we observe that the ideological representation of ideology is itself forced to recognize that every "subject" endowed with a "consciousness" and believing in the "ideas" that his "consciousness" inspires in him and freely accepts, must "*act* according to his ideas," must therefore inscribe his own ideas as a free subject in the actions of his material practice. If he does not do so, "that is wicked."

(157)

For Althusser, one's conscience represents not an innate sense of morality but the reflection of society's values, particularly those perpetuating the prevailing order. In effect, ideology builds a culture's collective conscience so that it may replicate prevailing economic and social paradigms. Ideology's power derives from its citizens' belief that contemporary social structures have developed historically and represent the apotheosis of these trends, as well as the sense that the future will continue according to current paradigms.

Because literature cannot spring forth from a vacuum, it participates in the propagation of countless ideological tenets. Every citizen of every culture is exposed to its ideology, which feels as natural(ized) as the air that they breathe, so that all individuals work to propagate their cultures. As Antonio Gramsci argues,

Every historical act cannot but be performed by the "collective man." In other words, this presupposes the attainment of "socio-cultural" unity through which a multiplicity of dispersed individual wills, heterogeneous in their aims, are welded together for the same goal on the basis of an (equal) and common conception of the world.

(*Further Selections* 156)

Indeed, Gramsci sees the hegemonic power of ideology such that the creation of new art becomes almost a paradoxical quest: "To fight for a new art would mean to fight to create new individual artists, which is absurd since artists cannot be created artificially. One must speak of a struggle for a new culture" (*Selections* 98). In Gramsci's view, the governing ideology so prevails throughout a culture that individuals cannot help but to participate in it and thus to reproduce it. Gramsci does speak of the "struggle for a new culture," yet this mammoth task is indeed Herculean due to the sway of ideology in every individual's mind.

With theories of social class and ideology, readers can see more clearly how characters of different social classes interact with one another, as well as how characters of the same social class respond to the benefits or liabilities of their economic status. In "The Ruined Maid" (1866), Thomas Hardy satirizes social-class striving and pretensions, illuminating how two old friends view each other differently when they run into each other after several years. Amelia's friend wonders over Amelia's newfound wealth:

"O 'Melia, my dear, this does everything crown!
Who could have supposed I should meet you in Town?
And whence such fair garments, such prosperi-ty?"—
"O didn't you know I'd been ruined?" said she.

— "You left us in tatters, without shoes or socks,
Tired of digging potatoes, and spudding up docks;
And now you've gay bracelets and bright feathers three!" —
"Yes: that's how we dress when we're ruined," said she.

. . . .

— "I wish I had feathers, a fine sweeping gown,
And a delicate face, and could strut about Town!" —
"My dear — a raw country girl, such as you be,
Cannot quite expect that. You ain't ruined," said she.

(lines 1–8, 21–24)

In this encounter, Amelia's friend marvels at the signs of Amelia's financial success: the fair garments, gay bracelets, and fine sweeping gown that trumpet her ascent in social class. Clearly, Amelia's friend is jealous of Amelia, which reveals the ways in which these former equals have shifted in their ethical perspectives, for Amelia's candid confession that she has been ruined details the moral price she paid for her financial gains. At the same time, Hardy asks his reader to consider who is truly the ruined maid: Amelia, who enjoys the financial perquisites of her fallen state, or Amelia's friend, who has maintained both her chastity and her impoverished condition. Amelia speaks eloquently throughout the poem, but in her final words—"You ain't ruined"—she reverts to the colloquial speech of the lower classes, thereby demonstrating that her newfound airs merely cloak the same woman she was before. The two characters' conflicting economic classes create meaning in Hardy's poem: these women are only intelligible to each other as representatives of their respective social classes, despite their shared status in their early years. The poem thus criticizes the ideologies both of Western capitalism and of Western morality, for the basis of Amelia's success registers exclusively through material possessions, with Amelia's friend blinded by the trappings of wealth. Neither woman seems to realize that financial success cannot guarantee happiness, an ignorance that enables Hardy's blistering denouncement of England's economic structures.

Interpretive Questions Based on Theories of Social Class and Ideology

- How does the text present members of various social classes, and what values are associated with their social classes? Does the text present characters of various social classes in the same manner?
- How are the values of the prevailing economic structure communicated to the society's citizens? How does this system conflict or harmonize with the desires of the characters?
- Describe the cultural ideology of the society portrayed in the text, and consider how various characters adhere to or resist its dominant values.
- Can characters transgress social borders, or are such boundaries impervious? If transgressions are possible, how are the transgressive characters viewed?

Psychoanalytic Approaches

With his theories of the unconscious, Sigmund Freud radically shifted how people view themselves, and his ideas have also affected how readers interpret literature. While many of Freud's theories explaining human behavior can be productively applied to authors and their characters, one should proceed with caution before putting an author or a character on the psychiatrist's couch in the hopes of successfully employing the talking cure. Probing an author through her fiction does not necessarily give insight into her consciousness, and many characters act the way they do for narratological, rather than psychological, reasons. In *Who Framed Roger Rabbit?*, the femme fatale Jessica Rabbit memorably professes, "I'm not bad; I'm just drawn that way," a line that should remind readers that the necessities of plotting often outweigh the need to give a character psychological depth.

Many characters do exhibit psychological depth, however, and psychoanalytic insights can assist readers in teasing out the motivations impelling characters to action. In Freud's view of the unconscious, the *id* represents humanity's drive to satisfy basic instincts, primarily sexual ones, while the *superego* coun-teracts the id by censoring interior desires in consideration of social disciplines. The *ego* balances between the id's impulses and the superego's regulatory influ-ence. *Repression* occurs when the ego redirects desires that the superego denies. These repressed desires cannot be destroyed, however, and they circulate within the individual's unconscious seeking another outlet. Freud proposes that many neurotic symptoms reflect the return of repressed desires, and he further argues that sexual or other desires can be *sublimated* when they cannot be fulfilled. These desires are then redirected to other endeavors, such as art or intellectual passions. More than merely a sign of individual neurosis, repressed and sub-limated desires can achieve positive effects for the individual and society as a whole. Indeed, Freud argues that sublimation provides the backbone to civiliza-tion: "Sublimation of instinct is an especially conspicuous feature of cultural development; it is what makes it possible for higher psychical activities . . . to play such an important part in civilized life" (51).

Freud's theories of dreams offer additional avenues for considering a character's psychology, primarily in the contrast between their *latent* and *manifest* content. To Freud, dreams expose the latent, hidden content of the unconscious, which is made manifest through the images of the dreams themselves. Dreams often involve *displacement*, by which a taboo desire is represented by a more socially acceptable one, and *condensation*, by which several desires coalesce into a single image or activity. Through displacement, condensation, and other such symbolic work, dreams release stifled and otherwise repressed features of the unconscious. The goal of the psycho-analyst, and of readers as well, is to explore the relationship between the manifest and latent content of a dream, unpinning the deeper structures of thought and desire encoded therein.

Despite Freud's perceptive insights into the unconscious, many readers and psychoanalysts dismiss some of Freud's theories as far-fetched. Such concepts as the Oedipal complex, in which the male infant falls in love with his mother and fears that his father will castrate him, and penis envy, in which young girls discover that they do not have penises and redirect their psychosexual energies to future childbirth, have not been confirmed. Many of Freud's ideas nonetheless provide useful metaphors for thinking through the literary structures of various texts and their portrayal of characters' psychological states. That is to say, male infants need not actually have an Oedipal complex for this structure to help readers ponder the psychosexual complexity of Shakespeare's *Hamlet*, in which Hamlet's relationship with his mother Gertrude carries undertones of repressed desire. Likewise, female infants do not need to undergo a period of penis envy for readers to consider how female characters are situated in relation to patriarchal authority that privileges the phallus as its primary signifier.

After Freud, the preeminent psychoanalytic theoretician in literary studies is Jacques Lacan. In Lacan's theory of the *mirror stage*, a baby sees its reflec-tion in a mirror and develops an emerging sense of its self. By recognizing herself in the mirror, the child identifies herself as a whole rather than as a partial and inchoate tangle of arms, legs, chest, and other body parts. This stage coincides with the *imaginary*, in which the individual sees herself in harmony and wholeness. In the realm of the *symbolic*, the child enters into language and learns of absence and difference, in which she must learn of her position in such oppositions as male/female and mother/daughter. Within the symbolic order the phallus is the privileged signifier, as its role in distinguishing between male and female extends beyond biology to the foundations of language and thought. One of Lacan's chief dicta argues that "the unconscious is structured as a function of the symbolic" (12), which suggests that our unconscious desires are sculpted within a symbolic framework of difference. As Saussure's semiotic theories suggest the gulf between signifier and signified, so too does the symbolic order force the child to distinguish between self and other, between representation and symbol. From a Lacanian perspective, the symbolic realm denies the possibility of truly sating desire, for desire, as it were, seeps through the fissures between representation and symbol. As Josiane Paccaud-Huguet explains,

> The function of fantasy is both to give a figure to the Other's desire, and to provide a glimpse at its impossible dead end. The subject in exile is condemned to imagine what the Other wants, and is tempted to respond by a logic of sacrifice which is the neurotic way of giving the Other imaginary consistency.
>
> (285)

The fleeting nature of fantasy, such that it constructs an individual's and an Other's desires amid the murky operations of the unconscious, promises the satisfaction of desire through a sacrifice that can never address any desire's insuperable roots.

When desires hinted at in a text are inscrutable, psychoanalytic theories can illuminate the ways in which they surface and reveal various characters' motivations. In Henry James's *The Turn of the Screw* (1898), the narrator, who serves as a governess, becomes convinced that the ghosts of the former servants Quint and Miss Jessel are haunting her young charges, Flora and Miles. Throughout James's novella it is often unclear whether the governess reports what she sees or what she fantasizes, as in the following passage:

> The apparition had reached the landing half-way up and was therefore on the spot nearest the window, where at sight of me, it stopped short and fixed me exactly as it had fixed me from the tower and from the garden. He knew me as well as I knew him.
>
> (60)

In this dreamlike vision, the governess recalls the locations of her past encounters with this ghost, which register with sexual meaning. The tower, a phallic symbol, represents her repressed desire for sexual penetration, and the garden represents sexuality, fecundity, and reproduction. Also, her ambiguous phrase that "He knew me as well as I knew him" suggests an intimacy with this other, perhaps even a latent desire for the ghost that the governess cannot acknowledge, or even that she projects her desires through the ghost to liberate herself from her Victorian prudery. It is never clear, however, if the ghosts externalize the desires of her own fevered mind or if they are truly malevolent spirits seeking to possess Flora and Miles. At the novella's climax, the governess questions Miles about his transgressions, only then to consider, "for if he *were* innocent, what then on earth was *I*?" (132). James's achievement in *The Turn of the Screw* is that this question is unanswerable, as he invites readers to witness the governess's efforts to save these children—who may not need her interventions. Psychoanalytic theories nonetheless facilitate readers' investigations of these complexities while probing the conscious and unconscious structures at work in literature.

Interpretive Questions Based on Psychoanalytic Approaches

- Using Freud's theory of the id, ego, and superego, examine the ways in which drives and ethics are mediated in the text.
- What drives and desires are repressed in the narrative, and how, when, and why do they surface?
- Does the novel depict any dreams or fantasies, and, if so, how do these dreams reveal the characters' unconscious desires?
- Apply Lacan's theories of the imaginary and symbolic to the text, in order to perceive how various characters are depicted in regard to desires for the self and the other.

Gender and Feminist Theories

In *A Room of One's Own* (1929), Virginia Woolf imagines what life would have been like for Shakespeare's hypothetical sister Judith. Mulling over social conditions for women during the Renaissance, Woolf concludes of this thought experiment that

> what is true in it, so it seemed to me, reviewing the story of Shakespeare's sister as I had made it, is that any woman born with a great gift in the sixteenth century would certainly have gone crazed, shot herself, or ended her days in some lonely cottage outside the village, half witch, half wizard, feared and mocked at.

(49)

For Woolf, Shakespeare's sister represents the inevitable losses accrued as a result of biases against women throughout much of Western history. In regard to literary history, she represents women's repressed artistic genius: the poems and novels never written, the plays never staged, and even the characters stripped of their full humanity. One may think of gender and feminist approaches to literature as metaphorically asking of a text the status of Shakespeare's sister in relation to its authorship, its narrative, and its reception.

In broad historical terms, feminism as a political movement began rather recently. One of the earliest voices of first-wave feminism, Mary Wollstonecraft advocates in *A Vindication of the Rights of Woman* (1792) that "if [women] be moral beings, let them have a chance to become intelligent" (5.136), a modest yet no less revolutionary assertion of women's place in the public sphere. Throughout the nineteenth century, first-wave feminism focused on establishing women's fundamental equality before the law, including voting and property rights, which culminated in the enfranchisement of women in the early twentieth century. Second-wave feminism began in the 1960s to address issues such as reproductive rights and equal treatment in the workforce, and third-wave feminism arose in the 1990s to recognize the plurality of women's lives and experiences. This brief historical trajectory captures the political accomplishments of feminism that radically shifted gender relationships in the Western world. It would nonetheless be remiss to overlook the fact that questions of gender simmer in texts prior to feminism's advent in the late 1700s. The literary tradition of the *querelle des femmes*, or "argument about women," discusses women's moral and ethical worth, and important texts in this genre include Chaucer's *Wife of Bath's Prologue*, Christine de Pizan's *Book of the City of Ladies*, Shakespeare's *The Taming of the Shrew*, and Aemelia Lanyer's *Salve Deus Rex Judeaorum*. It is anachronistic to label the Wife of Bath a feminist, yet it is no less important in understanding her character to assess the ways in which medieval misogynistic traditions influence Chaucer's depiction of her.

A key concept of feminist criticism differentiates between gender and sex. The *genders* of male and female are shaped by the social and cultural expectations accorded to women and men, whereas *sex* is marked by a person's genitalia. In *The Second Sex*, Simone de Beauvoir provocatively posits that "every female human being is not necessarily a woman," as she then suggests that "to be so considered she must share in that mysterious and threatened reality known as femininity" (6). Furthermore, genders are revealed through individuals' performances of femininity and masculinity. As Judith Butler argues, "gender is a kind of persistent impersonation that passes as the real" (x). Because a woman learns to acts like a woman, she is seen and, in effect, becomes a woman. While many Western discourses conflate gender and sex, arguing that women's and men's genders are natural reflections of their biology, feminism questions this assumption, pointing to the ways in which cultures create genders based upon biased interpretations of sexed bodies. Longstanding binaries of feminine and masculine attributes, evident throughout much of Western literature with many persisting today, align men with intellect and women with the body, along with such corollary binaries as active versus passive, rational versus irrational, reasonable versus emotional, temperate versus lustful, and silent versus gossipy.

These stereotypes collapse when women and men are viewed objectively, and the gendered binary positing women as lustful becomes particularly laughable when one looks at the annals of Western art and literature, for they contain numerous examples of women constructed for male pleasure. The countless beloveds of the sonnet tradition picture an ideal woman divorced from any reality, and in "To His Coy Mistress" (c. 1650), Andrew Marvell's lyric speaker exaggerates that he would need eternities to praise his beloved properly—"An hundred years should go to praise / Thine eyes and on thy forehead gaze, / Two hundred to adore each breast" (lines 13–15). Edgar Allan Poe furthers this theme in his troubling assertion that "the death, then, of a beautiful woman is, unquestionably, the most poetical topic in the world—and especially is it beyond doubt that the lips suited for such topic are those of a bereaved lover" ("Philosophy of Composition" 158). Such constructions of women in art as reflections of male desire, as the binary upon which men elevate themselves, stand as the target of much feminist criticism, as in Hélène Cixous's impassioned analysis:

> If woman has always functioned "within" man's discourse, a signifier referring always to the opposing signifier that annihilates its particular energy, puts down or stifles its very different sounds, now it is time for her to displace this "within," explode it, overturn it, grab it, make it hers.
>
> (155)

Subverting and destroying gendered binaries, feminist criticism reorganizes the social order by demanding women's equality.

Aemelia Lanyer's *Salve Deus Rex Judeaorum* (1611) illustrates the strategies authors employ to question longstanding constructions of gender. As a whole, Lanyer's poem argues against misogynist Christian traditions that blame Eve for humanity's expulsion from the Garden of Eden, proposing instead that Pontius Pilate's wife, who urged Pilate to pardon Jesus, should stand as a model of feminine fortitude and wisdom. In the poem's dedication to Anne of Denmark, the queen of James I, Lanyer reformulates the meanings of femininity and masculinity:

> And pardon me (faire Queene) though I presume,
> To doe that which so many better can;
> Not that I Learning to my selfe assume,
> Or that I would compare with any man:
>   But as they are Scholers, and by Art do write,
>   So Nature yeelds my Soule a sad delight.
>
> And since all Arts at first from Nature came,
> That Goodly Creature, Mother of Perfection,
> Whom *Joves* almighty hand at first did frame,
> Taking both her and hers in his protection:
>   Why should not She now grace my barren Muse,
>   And in a Woman all defects excuse.
>
> (lines 145–56)

Lanyer appears to cede that women need not be educated, asserting "Not that I Learning to my selfe assume." She demurs as well that she would not dare compare herself to men due to their superior education. While she appears to endorse the cultural binaries aligning men with art (and thus with learning) and women with nature (and thus with their uneducated status), she then reorders this structure by arguing that all arts descend from nature. Men's superior education, in Lanyer's formulation, derives from a feminized Nature whose fecundity brings forth the educated men who then reject her. Moreover, while Lanyer describes her muse as barren, by the very act of writing she disproves the assumption she appears to support. As Nature is the mother of all arts, so too is Nature the mother of her art, excusing any defects that might arise. In her poem, Lanyer relies on gendered binaries that characterize women and men as separate and unequal, only to dismantle them and force her readers to contemplate anew the assumptions that certain bodies think in certain ways.

Interpretive Questions Based on Gender and Feminist Theories

- How are women and men represented differently in the text, and what cultural values are characterized as female or male?
- How are women's lives depicted within the text's historical framework? Do female characters accede to or subvert their historical era's construction of femininity?
- Which qualities are associated with female protagonists, which qualities are associated with female antagonists, and how do these structures of character complicate the text's depiction of women?
- Describe how the characters perform their gender roles. Which characters perform these roles successfully and which unsuccessfully?
- How is masculinity constructed in the text? Which male characters successfully perform masculinity, and which fail to do so?

Queer Theories

Queer theories developed from gay and lesbian studies, but whereas gay and lesbian studies, by definition, focuses on issues related to homosexuality, queer theories can be applied both to homosexual and to heterosexual characters, as well as to anyone else. The word *queer*, while frequently used in popular parlance as a synonym for *homosexual*, more accurately designates individuals and desires disruptive to cultural codes of sexual normativity. Although it may initially appear paradoxical to use queer theories to analyze heterosexuality, the power of queer theories arises in their ability to question a range of sexualities and desires, not only homosexual ones.

Virtually every major character in a literary text displays some relationship to (sexual) desire, and queer theories provide a valuable tool for teasing out how these desires function to create narrative meaning. Similar to theories of gender and feminism that question longstanding gender roles, queer theories take as their starting point that sexualities are culturally and ideologically constructed and that reactions to a character's sexual desires reveal the ways in which a given culture defines sexuality. Frequently, characters are vilified for expressing illicit desires, while others are extolled for adhering to prevailing codes of sexual and romantic behavior that constitute heteronormativity. The force of heteronormativity is such that other expressions of sexual desire are marginalized and heterosexuality reigns as the only acceptable practice of desire. Adrienne Rich terms this cultural policing of desire *compulsory heterosexuality* and advocates that "heterosexuality, like motherhood, needs to be recognized and studied as a political institution—even, or especially, by those individuals who feel they are, in their personal experience, the precursors of a new social relation between the sexes" (17).

While heteronormativity is a useful concept for analyzing the ways in which modern Western cultures define sexuality, it cannot be used transhistorically without due attention to the sexual paradigms of the period under examination. For example, the sexual codes of ancient Greece as depicted in Plato's *Symposium* differ greatly from those depicted on Shakespeare's stage, which differ greatly from the courtship dynamics of Jane Austen's novels, and so on. Indeed, while homosexual acts appear throughout the historical record, homosexuality as a marker of an individual's identity is a relatively recent phenomenon. Based on his readings of medical discourses of the late nineteenth century, Michel Foucault argues that "Homosexuality appeared as one of the forms of sexuality when it was transposed from the practice of sodomy onto a kind of interior androgyny, a hermaphroditism of the soul. The sodomite had been a temporary aberration; the homosexual was now a species" (43). Foucault's point, which is critical to the work of queer theories, is that homosexual acts prior to these medical discourses did not constitute those who engaged in them as a different class of people. An apropos, although unflattering, comparison would be between homosexuality and theft: a person might steal money and be punished as a thief, but this crime did not necessarily constitute a core factor of his identity. Thieves, after all, may repent, atone, and then "go straight." Following such a homophobic line of reasoning, although people from earlier eras might engage in same-sex eroticism, they could repent for this behavior and reject their ostensibly sinful acts. In line with Foucault's argument about the birth of homosexuality, many critics prefer such terms as *homoerotic* and *same-sex desire* to discuss homosexual acts and actors prior to the late nineteenth century, in order to avoid the potential historical solecism of the term *homosexual*.

Beyond its attention to the sexual desires of the individual, queer theories allow readers to ask deeper questions regarding homosocial groupings. *Homosocial* refers to any group, fellowship, or assembly with a same-sex membership, such as boarding schools, armies, fraternities, sororities, and civic organizations. Homosociality need have no relation to homosexuality; at the same time, queer theories ask readers to analyze the ways in which homosocial traditions respond to homosexuality. Homosocial environments may create a space for ostensibly taboo desires to flourish, or they may police desires rigorously.

Queer theories encourage readers to analyze the circulation of desire in texts, and the *erotic triangle* provides an effective interpretive tool for this task. With this formulation, readers look for a triangular relationship, in which two characters (usually male) pursue the affections of another character (usually female). In many narratives, more attention is paid to the competition between the two men of the erotic triangle than to the pursuit of their mutual beloved. As Eve Sedgwick states in *Between Men: English Literature and Male Homosocial Desire*, the foundational text of queer literary studies, "in any erotic rivalry, the bond that links the two rivals is as intense and potent as the bond that links either of the rivals to the beloved" (21). Such erotic rivalries may not necessarily reveal desire between the two men, but because desire is not limited to the sexual, it behooves readers to consider the ways in which submerged desires surface through such amatory competitions.

Another key concept for investigating literary queerness, the *open secret* probes hidden relationships and other such clandestine affairs and identities. The term *open secret* should collapse into oxymoronic self-contradiction because secrets, by definition, should not be known openly. Open secrets, however, circulate widely throughout a given community, yet all members of this group tacitly agree not to speak of them. Typically, an open secret concerns some transgression of societal norms, but one that, for whatever reason, the society chooses not to enforce. When an open secret becomes truly open, ignoring the "secret" is no longer possible, and penalties and punishments must be enforced. An intriguing historical example of an open secret is Mississippi's taxing of alcoholic beverages in the mid-twentieth century when the state was officially "dry." Most Mississippians knew the law was regularly broken and liquor was consumed, to the extent that government officials taxed the contraband, but it was more palatable to live with this hypocrisy than to admit that the state's citizens were not as abstemious as they collectively proclaimed themselves to be (Mississippi Department of Archives and History).

The story of King Arthur's and Camelot's fall, as told in Sir Thomas Malory's *Le Morte D'Arthur* (c. 1470), illustrates the utility of queer theories in illuminating a narrative of heteroerotic desire, open secrets, and erotic triangles. The Camelot knights know of Guinevere's adulterous relationship with Lancelot, but they accept it as an open secret within the court—one that they acknowledge but never discuss. One day, however, Aggravain demands that the knights defend their king against this betrayal: "I marvel that we all are not ashamed both to see and to know how Sir Lancelot lieth daily and nightly with the queen. We all know well that it is so, and it is shamefully accepted by us all" (693). By speaking openly of Lancelot and Guinevere's affair, Aggravain forces Arthur to take action, despite the fact that, when Arthur learns of their adultery, he dismisses any amatory jealousy he might be expected to feel and instead regrets the impending loss of the Round Table and its homosocial company:

> And much more am I sorry for the loss of my good knights than for the loss of my fair queen; for queens I may have enough, but such a fellowship of good knights shall never be together in any company. . . . Alas, that ever Sir Lancelot and I should be at debate!
>
> (706–07)

While some subsequent tales of Arthur and Guinevere, especially cinematic retellings, portray the lovers as wholly devoted to each other, Malory's version depicts Arthur as knowingly cuckolded yet distraught over the loss of his friend rather than his queen, whom he sees as readily replaceable. This interpretation does not therefore cast Arthur as homosexual, but it does reveal that he prioritizes homosocial bonds over heteroerotic attractions, which necessitates that readers look at this legendary love story anew. Queer theories uncover such insights into the sexual dynamics of texts, encouraging readers to see with fresh eyes the ways in which assumptions of sexual normativity cloak deeper dynamics of desire.

Interpretive Questions Based on Queer Theories

- How does sexual desire function in the text? In the cultural world that the author creates, what are the rules of attraction?
- Which characters are vilified, and which are praised, for their choices in partners?
- How and why are some sexualities coded as suspect while others are coded as laudatory?
- How are homosocial relationships depicted in the text? Who engages in them, what do they gain from them, and do normative or taboo desires circulate in them?
- Trace the narrative's erotic triangles and open secrets, and theorize how they reveal the various characters' expressed and/or enacted desires.

Postcolonial and Critical Race Theories

Postcolonial and critical race theories examine the ways that texts construct relationships among ethnic, racial, and cultural groups while also highlighting power imbalances in the past and present. In Homi K. Bhabha's formulation of the field, "Postcolonial criticism bears witness to the unequal and uneven forces of cultural representation involved in the contest for political and social authority within the modern world order" (190). The history of Western imperialism, writ large, is comprised of encounters between explorers and natives, settlers and the indigenous, in which the conquerors asserted their values as superior to the conquered. The literary record documents such cross-cultural encounters, providing evidence of how the

Western world interacted with a variety of other cultures, and how such issues continue to resonate in today's world.

Postcolonial and critical race theorists pay particular attention to the ways in which dominant cultures envision minority cultures as reflections of their own desires. In *Orientialism*, Edward Said provocatively argues, "The Orient was almost a European invention" (1), as he dismantles Western views of non-Western people as reflective of Western desires rather than Eastern realities. Moreover, Said argues that imperialist discourses facilitate the marginalization of other cultures due to "the hegemony of European ideas about the Orient, themselves reiterating European superiority over Oriental backwardness," for such views "usually overrid[e] the possibility that a more independent, or more skeptical, thinker might have had different views on the matter" (7). Colonialist views include a host of stereotypes delimiting the expected contours of individual behavior, despite the fact that any hint of individualism is effaced through the construction of such stereotypes.

While postcolonial theories focus primarily on the legacy of Western imperialism, critical race theories study the role of skin color in encounters between various peoples and cultures. Obviously, these theories overlap: imperialists' derogatory views of indigenous people coincided with their prejudiced views of these people's pigmentations. In many ways, racism erases history by arguing for trans-historical views of cultures in which external somatic features define their citizens rather than their beliefs, social structures, achievements, artistic traditions, and so on. As Stuart Hall argues:

> [R]acisms also dehistoricize—translating historically specific structures into the timeless language of nature; decomposing classes into individuals and recomposing those disaggregated individuals into the reconstructed unities, the great coherences of new ideological "subjects."
>
> (64)

In Hall's view, racism creates an undifferentiated mass of Others united in skin tone despite their many cultural differences.

One of the guiding concepts of critical race theories concerns the invisibility of whiteness. Because white colonizers invariably viewed their culture and their skin tone as superior, cultural and racial variations from this ostensible norm rendered the colonized as the Others in their own land. Richard Dyer points out that whiteness enables white people to define themselves as arbiters of humanity: "As long as race is something only applied to non-white peoples, as long as white people are not racially seen and named, they/we function as a human norm. Other people are raced, we are just people" (*White* 1). Postcolonial and critical race theories expose this power of whiteness, refusing to accept its de facto status as a universal norm. As Toni Morrison points out of the tension between white and black, "how [Africanism] functioned in . . . the literary imagination is of paramount interest because it may be possible to discover, through a close look at literary 'blackness,' the nature—even the cause—of literary 'whiteness.' What is it *for*?" ("Black Matters" 269). As feminists argue that gender comprises a set of stereotypes associated with the female body, critical race theorists likewise demonstrate how stereotypes become associated with variously raced bodies. In Morrison's provocative questioning of how whiteness functions, she reveals the ways in which bodies are constructed to perform in various ways, with the advancement of literary whiteness often accomplished by the marginalization of other characters.

In many instances, even when white characters enter into marginalized cultures, their whiteness assures their uniqueness and thus their superiority. The experience of "going native," in which a white character assimilates into an indigenous culture and assumes their values and mores, paradoxically confirms the whiteness of the character who experiences this metamorphosis. As Shari Huhndorf argues of "going native" in narratives of American Indians, it is "a means of constructing white identities, naturalizing the conquest, and inscribing various power relations within American culture" (6). Typically, a character who "goes native" remains capable of negotiating between his original and adopted cultures, and even when his original culture is criticized for its abuse of the indigenous, his whiteness allows him the power of social mobility denied to the indigenous characters.

As an anti-slavery novella, Aphra Behn's *Oroonoko: or, The Royal Slave* (1688) questions Eurocentric assumptions about the inferior nature of Africans and their treatment as chattels. While a progressive work of its time, the various contradictions in *Oroonoko* benefit from analyses based on postcolonial and critical race theories. For instance, the narrator praises Oroonoko's beauty, remarking in particular on his black skin: "The most famous Statuary [sculptor] cou'd not form the Figure of a Man more admirably turn'd from Head to Foot. His Face was not of that brown, rusty Black which most of that Nation are, but a perfect Ebony, or polish'd Jett" (43). An irony arises, however, in the narrator's assumption that, although skin tone need not be white to be beautiful, she perceives various shades of black skin hierarchically, preferring Oroonoko's "perfect Ebony" to the brown tones of other Africans. Such a contradiction is also apparent in the narrator's praise of Oroonooko as a universal model of manhood: "I have often seen and convers'd with this great Man, and been a Witness to many of his mighty Actions; and so assure my Reader, the most Illustrious Courts cou'd not have produ'd a braver Man, both for Greatness of Courage and Mind" (43). But while the narrator extols Oroonoko for his exceptionality, arguing that he matches the accomplishments of European courtiers, she also discerns the roots of his greatness in his exposure to Europeans and their customs, including the "*French*-Man of Wit and Learning . . . [who] took a great pleasure to teach Morals, Language, and Science [to Oroonoko]" (43), as well as the English and Spanish traders with whom Oroonoko conversed. By applying postcolonial and critical race theories to Behn's novella, its contradictions emerge and readers see it more clearly in its historical moment.

While Behn's condemnation of slavery sounds loudly throughout her tale of Oroonoko, her construction of her protagonist as such an exceptional figure, one rendered unrepresentative of the many Africans for whom slavery is depicted as a just fate, undercuts her argument. She condemns Oroonoko's slavery as a unique case of injustice that was greater than that of slavery in its entirety, as she also paints Oroonoko himself as endorsing slavery for others: "and that he was asham'd of what he had done, in endeavoring to make those Free, who were by Nature *Slaves*, poor wretched Rogues, fit to be us'd as *Christians* Tools" (90). Postcolonial and critical race theories illuminate the ways in which texts such as *Oroonoko* construct various characters in relation to their culture, ethnicity, and skin tone, all the while highlighting the power imbalances inherent in discriminatory and exploitative views of humans denied their full humanity.

Interpretive Questions Based on Postcolonial and Critical Race Theories

- How does the text describe members of different ethnic and racial groups, and what power imbalances separate them?
- How are ethnic and racial groups presented in the text's construction of its past and present?
- How do members of the same ethnic and racial group view one another, and how does the history of imperialism affect these views?
- How does whiteness function in the text? How is whiteness depicted, and what cultural values does the text associate with whiteness?
- Does a white character "go native"? Does an indigenous character assimilate into Western culture? How do other characters view those who shift between cultural zones?

Rhetorical Analysis

The word *rhetoric* refers to writing and speech used for the explicit purpose of persuasion. In many ways, rhetoric—both the word and the discourses associated with it—is disparaged in contemporary political wrangling. "It's just empty rhetoric," one might hear a pundit say while dismissing a rival's stance on an issue. Indeed, most dictionaries provide secondary definitions of *rhetoric* denoting speeches of insincerity and cant, and so a distrust of rhetoric is encoded in the word itself. Rhetoric, however, is neither intrinsically positive nor negative; it is a tool that can be used honestly or dishonestly, effectively or ineffectively. Aristotle's definition of rhetoric—"the faculty of discovering the possible means of persuasion in reference to any subject whatever" (*"Art" of Rhetoric* 15)—captures its wide-ranging utility. When interpreting a work of literature, readers must carefully distinguish how a given character's rhetoric reflects his or her personality, desires, and objectives. The most effective uses of rhetoric in literature richly unfold the interplay of character, audience, and intention, allowing readers to gauge the power of words intended to persuade.

To conduct a rhetorical analysis, readers must consider the ethos, pathos, logos, time, and place of a given speech act. *Ethos* refers to a speaker's moral character, personal disposition, and ethical core. By examining the speaker's ethos, readers should be able to determine whether they believe his words. Aristotle argues that the "orator persuades by moral character when his speech is delivered in such a manner as to render him worthy of confidence" (17), and the speaker's construction of ethos is of paramount importance in winning the audience's trust. *Pathos* refers to the emotions that a speaker engenders in her auditors. Aristotle observes that the "emotions are all those affections which cause men to change their opinion in regard to their judgments" (173). An effective speaker realizes that emotions often catalyze listeners to agree with his points more effectively than cold facts and figures, and therefore employs pathos to its maximum effect. *Logos* refers to the logical coherency of a given argument. The speaker should support his points with evidence of their truthfulness, citing facts and respected authorities to attest to the validity of his claims. The time and place of the speech act must be considered as well, for they frequently reveal the circumstances motivating the speaker to articulate her concerns.

Most rhetorical analyses address ethos, pathos, logos, time, and place, examining how these five factors interconnect in a given speech act. However, since some speeches rely more heavily on one element over another, the writer of a rhetorical analysis need not expend equal energy detailing each of these constituent elements. For example, consider the rhetorical situation of the closing arguments of a court case in which the accused is clearly guilty. The prosecutor's closing words would likely focus on the logos of the case, honing in on the evidence that conclusively proves the perpetrator's culpability. The defense attorney might try to obfuscate the facts through faulty logic, but, if her client's guilt is readily evident, she might enhance the pathos of her argument to win the judge's sympathy, thus to secure a lighter sentence. Despite their antagonistic positions toward each other, both the prosecutor and the defense attorney would likely present themselves as intelligent, reasonable, and confident professionals in order to project a compelling ethos. In this instance, a rhetorical analysis might focus more on the lawyers' conflicting deployments of pathos and logos, overlooking their similar presentation of an ethos reflective of their occupation.

These five complementary elements of rhetoric are strikingly evident in book 1 of Milton's *Paradise Lost* (1667), in which Satan, after rebelling against God and being cast to hell, rouses his fellow fallen angels to eternal battle. With Satan's soaring rhetoric ringing throughout, this passage is justly acclaimed as one of the finest in the literary tradition. When interpreting *Paradise Lost*, readers must be aware of the ways that Milton builds conflicting perspectives of Satan's ethos, and they should never forget that this former angel committed the ultimate treason by attempting to overthrow

God. Through his words, however, Satan discloses unexpected aspects of his character, which lead readers to question their fundamental assumptions about him. Implacable in his opposition to God's authority, Satan also expresses his optimism for future victories: "We may with more successful hope resolve / To wage by force or guile eternal Warr / Irreconcilable, to our grand Foe" (lines 120–22). In finding hope in the most hopeless of situations, Satan proves himself an optimist and thereby reveals an unexpected side to his character, as he attempts to rouse the spirits of his fellow fallen angels despite the depths to which they have descended.

Milton's Satan continuously expresses his deep concern for his compatriots, and these appeals to pathos strengthen his authority as their leader. His first words in *Paradise Lost*, spoken to his fellow conspirator Beelzebub, stress his affection for this friend: "If thou beest he; But O how fall'n! how chang'd / From him, who in the happy Realms of Light / Cloth'd with transcendent brightness didst out-shine / Myriads though bright" (lines 84–87). Satan also refers to the fallen angels as his "faithful friends" and the "associates and copartners of our loss" (lines 264–65). By stressing his concern for and egalitarian relationship with them, Satan appeals to their sense of camaraderie and loyalty, as he also further establishes his ethos as their leader.

Satan's attempts to infuse logic into his argument descend frequently into spuriousness, yet they testify to his cagy use of rhetoric to build his argument for eternal rebellion against God:

> Here at least
> We shall be free; th' Almighty hath not built
> Here for his envy, will not drive us hence:
> Here we may reign secure, and in my choyce
> To reign is worth ambition though in Hell:
> Better to reign in Hell, then serve in Heav'n.
> (lines 258–63)

Satan's logic is shoddy: within Milton's Christian cosmology, one is never free when separated from God. Nonetheless, it is certainly true that, in creating the foul pits of hell, "th' Almighty hath not built / Here for his envy." Satan then reaches his famous conclusion that it is "Better to reign in Hell, than serve in Heav'n," yet his description of this decision as suited to his own desires misleads his auditors because it overlooks the fact that God expelled him from heaven. He did not choose the location of his eternal suffering, yet he presents it as a desired and logically selected setting to undertake their further efforts to unseat God. The contrast that Satan presents to his audience of the damned—that they may rule over themselves in hell or serve God in heaven—allows him to color their current circumstances as the result of their rational decisions, rather than as the punishment for their failed rebellion.

The time and place of a speech act influence how the speaker's words are received, and effective rhetoricians choose appropriately in this regard to make their arguments, for they want their audience to be wholly receptive to their words. In depicting Satan's rhetorical eloquence, Milton focuses readers' attention on his inspiring words to his comrades, and it is easy to overlook the fact that the speech occurs immediately after his expulsion from heaven and that the dank bowels of hell constitute its setting. This is not to say that Satan (or Milton) camouflages the location of his damnation; on the contrary, Satan accurately describes the scene as a "dreary Plain, forlorn and wilde, / The seat of desolation, voyd of light" (lines 180–81). Still, the majesty of Milton's poetry causes many readers to focus on Satan's lofty eloquence rather than on his shocking disobedience to God. Refusing to paint Satan as a stock character of evil incarnate, Milton enhances the character's appeal to readers through his seductive rhetoric, seeing if they too will fall to his charms. As Stanley Fish argues in his masterful reading of the poem, "Milton's method is to re-create in the mind of the reader (which is, finally, the poem's scene) the drama of the Fall, to make him fall again exactly as Adam did and with Adam's troubled clarity, that is to say, 'not deceived'" (1). Satan's intoxicating words prove the power of rhetoric to ensnare even the savviest of readers, but rhetorical analyses construct a powerful defense. Through these interpretive techniques, readers can examine how various characters attempt to win over both other characters and the readers themselves through words designed to persuade, and thus achieve deeper insights about the author's play with language and character.

Interpretive Questions Based on Rhetorical Analysis

- How does the speaker establishes his/her ethos? Describe whether this ethos is credible.
- How does the speaker's use of pathos generate emotional reactions in his/her audience and in readers, and to what effect?
- How does the speaker use logos and logical reasoning to win support for his/her viewpoint? What are the logical points that uphold it, and what logical inconsistences undermine it?
- Describe the time and place of the speech act, and address how the time and place reflect the speaker's efforts to maximize the persuasiveness of the argument.
- Consider how these elements unite to help readers understand the speaker's goals and his/her audience's reaction to them.

Genre Theories

Genres sort works of literature into categories that assist readers in establishing their expectations for a given text. The three primary divisions of literature are poetry, prose, and drama; these can be divided into numerous subcategories including, but not limited to, epic, sonnet, and ode for poetry; novels, short stories, and essays for prose; and comedy, tragedy, and theater of the absurd for drama. Frederic Jameson notes that an author's use of genre creates a quasi-contractual relationship with readers, emphasizing that "Genres are *institutions,* or social contracts between a writer and a specific public, whose function it is to specify the proper use of a particular cultural artifact" (106). These "genre contracts" establish a basis of authorial meaning and readerly interpretation, but they can also be exploited for playful purposes in which authors subvert their audience's expectations. Authors participate in generic traditions, but they do so with their own unique agendas.

In part due to the prescriptive nature of genres, some readers view them as somewhat inhibitory frameworks: writers and readers must know the rules of genre to play the game of literature. Benedetto Croce humorously captures the common critical frustration with genre as a restrictive and unenlightening interpretive tool: "All books dealing with classification and systems of the arts could be burned without any loss whatsoever" (188). Jacques Derrida agrees with this view of genre as pedantic and antiquated in his essay "The Law of Genre," which begins with his mocking and ironic declaration that "Genres are not to be mixed. I will not mix genres. I repeat: genres are not be mixed. I will not mix them" (223). This is the "law" of genre, but thankfully, as Derrida reveals, it is a law that is not necessarily heeded by authors and artists; one need only parody generic claims of authority to subvert and reduce them to ridiculousness. Furthermore, if genres were inherently conservative modes, all literature would succumb to the formulaic. As overarching patterns of literary art, genres provide a superstructure of creation for authors and of interpretation for readers, yet within an ultimately bounteous and expansive system that solicits its own transgressions.

Tzvetan Todorov's succinct definition of genre—"the historically attested codification of discursive properties" (19)—stresses the historical basis of genres. Literary forms represent poetic and narrative patterns that solidify over time into a recognizable body of forms with shared features, which arise from historically specific cultural discourses and ideologies. The sixteenth century witnessed a vibrant interest in the sonnet tradition, as did the late eighteenth century with the Gothic novel, and the late twentieth and early twenty-first century with graphic novels. By analyzing a text and its genre in relation to its historical moment, readers see with deeper clarity the social conditions stimulating interest in these artistic forms.

Inextricably connected to the historical and social world in which they are created, genres expose the ideological underpinnings of their cultures and the beliefs of the authors. Due to this confluence of generic structure and ideological expression, genres are intertwined with other aspects of their culture, and a fruitful use of genre as an interpretive tool involves combining it with other theoretical perspectives, particularly those of gender, sexuality, race, and social class. As Susan Crane observes of gender and genre,

Gender and genre have phonic and etymological but also more sub-stantial bonds. Both are systems of distinction that are susceptible to hierarchization; both have an informing relation to specific persons and works. They can be conceived as the inspiring potential that generates intelligible identities and texts; they can also become measures that con-strain and evaluate. Gender and genre can make claims to transhistorical permanence, when they ground their claims in nature in the former case and art in the latter, but both categories prove to be subject to negotia-tion as they are mobilized in particular identities and works. Finally the historicity of both categories must be accepted: both are persistent over time but also reperformed and reinterpreted in their every instantiation.

(3)

In this overview of the relationship between gender and genre, Crane con-nects the pair as transhistorical paradigms that reify certain meanings and interpretations through their "informing relation to specific persons and works." Likewise, Simon Gaunt argues in regard to gender and genre "that genres . . . inscribe competing ideologies, that the construction of gender is a crucial element in an ideology, and that the distinct ideologies of . . . genres are predicated in part at least upon distinct constructions of gender" (1). Both Crane and Gaunt consider the ways in which ideology underpins the relationship between gender and genre in literature. Genres communicate cultural meaning by their very presence, and genre criticism fosters investigations into the ways in which genres inform—and misin-form—readers about themselves, their constituent texts, and the social interactions described in them.

The chief utility of genre criticism arises in the clarity it brings to a group of texts, highlighting their connections and their unique features. For exam-ple, an ancient yet vibrant genre of literature is that of the mythic hero. Many narratives adhere to this protean structure, including those of Moses in Exo-dus and J. K. Rowling in her *Harry Potter* novels. Joseph Campbell outlines the standard trajectory of this narrative form:

The standard path of the mythological hero is a magnification of the for-mula represented in the rites of passage: *separation—initiation—return*: which might be named the nuclear unit of the monomyth. *A hero ven-tures forth from the world of common day into a region of supernatural wonder: fabulous forces are there encountered and a decisive victory is won; the hero comes back from this mysterious adventure with the power to bestow boons on his fellow man.*

(30; italics in original)

When analyzing the apparently disparate characters of Moses and Harry Potter through the lens of genre criticism, one sees numerous parallels. Both Moses and Harry Potter are separated from their birth parents and raised as orphans, adopted respectively by the Pharaoh's daughter and Vernon and Petunia Dursley. Both characters receive their call to heroism unexpectedly: Moses through the burning bush, Harry Potter through the unexpected letters from Hogwarts informing him of his admission, and then through Hagrid's rescue of him from the Dursleys. Numerous other plot points link these heroes together.

Campbell also explains that "[t]he composite hero of the monomyth is a personage of exceptional gifts. Frequently he is honored by his society, frequently unrecognized or disdained. He and/or the world in which he finds himself suffers from a symbolical deficiency" (37). Moses's authority becomes evident as God works through him and inflicts the ten plagues upon Egypt, whereas Harry Potter becomes increasingly skilled as a wizard, particularly due to his natural affinity for defensive magic. Both men access supernatural power through totemic items: a rod for Moses, a wand for Harry. Also, Campbell argues that the "the hero of myth [achieves] a world-historical, macrocosmic triumph. . . . [The hero] brings back from his adventure the means for the regeneration of his society as a whole" (38). As Moses frees the Israelites from bondage and leads them to the Promised Land, so too does Harry Potter save the wizarding world from Voldemort and his legion of Death Eaters. Genre criticism allows one to draw insightful parallels between texts, yet it is perhaps more important to see and ponder their disjunctions. Whereas Moses dies before entering the Promised Land, Harry dies only to live again due to his willingness to accept death. These contrastive endings indicate the ultimate malleability of generic traditions and the ways in which writers exploit such possibilities to encode new themes in standard forms. Infusing a gendered analysis with genre criticism, one could also examine the differences in masculinity between these two male characters, as well as noting the relative dearth of females cast as mythic heroes. To employ genre theories fruitfully, readers must seek out overlaps and incongruities, explaining how an author's adherence to and divergence from the typical formulations of a genre create literary meaning.[2]

Interpretive Questions Based on Genre Theories

- What is the text's genre, and what are the typical parameters of this genre?
- To which of the genre's codes does the text adhere, and to which of the codes does it stray? How do these unique variations within the superstructure of the genre create literary meaning?
- How do the genre and the text of this genre relate to their historical moment? Does the text adhere to or resist the ways in which contemporary authors write in this genre?
- How do the genre and the text of this genre reflect cultural expectations of gender, class, race, and sexuality? Does the text adhere to or resist the ways in which contemporary texts of this genre construct these cultural concerns?

A Final Note on Literary Theories

When used effectively, literary theories help readers to ask questions and thus to develop interpretations of texts. Unlike fables, a genre that ends by explicitly stating its moral, most great literature challenges readers to interpret multiple levels of meaning. To probe the significations and contradictions of a text effectively, readers should use the insights of the various schools of interpretation covered in this chapter, but they should never be slaves to them. On the contrary, readers should question the underlying premises of these theories, as well as seeking connections among them that will lead to insights unavailable from a single viewpoint. It is less useful to identify oneself as an adherent of a particular critical school and to follow its tenets single-mindedly than to move nimbly among these many interpretive frameworks, using their various perspectives to develop interpretations true to the text and unique to its reader.

Notes

1 This brief analysis of Robin Hood is drawn from Tison Pugh and Angela Jane Weisl, *Medievalisms* (Abingdon: Routledge, 2013), 64–82. Our thanks to Angela Jane Weisl for allowing us to republish it, in condensed form, in this book.
2 This passage on genre theory has been freely adapted from Tison Pugh, *Queering Medieval Genres* (New York: Palgrave Macmillan, 2004).

Unit 4

A Practical Guide to Writing a Research Essay

4.1 The Research Essay

Throughout their coursework in literary and cultural studies, most students will write numerous research essays. Although instructors assign various other tests and tasks over a semester, many classes culminate with a research project for which students must generate a complex interpretation and analysis of a poem, novel, play, or other cultural text. In contrast to less structured assignments, such as freewriting and response papers, essays allow writers to present their ideas formally and to explicate in detail their interpretations of a literary work. Most essays also incorporate research on their subjects so that authors can demonstrate a deep understanding of the issues raised by their analyses, as well as their understanding of ongoing critical discussions surrounding these topics. Essays are also termed *argumentative writing*, not because they must contentiously assert their positions and vanquish a real or imagined foe, but because they put forth a unique interpretation, or argument, about their subjects.

Many students first learn the rudimentary structure of argumentative writing through the five-paragraph essay. According to this paradigm, an essay begins with an introductory paragraph that includes a thesis statement as its final sentence. Three supporting paragraphs develop and elaborate on this thesis, and a concluding paragraph restates the thesis. The five-paragraph essay provides an excellent introductory structure for learning about writing, but as one's ideas deepen in complexity and sophistication, it no longer suits the ambitions of collegiate and postgraduate writers. The basic structure of the five-paragraph essay is sound, but it must simultaneously be reconceived for higher-level thinking because writers often need more—and sometimes many more—than five paragraphs to convey their ideas. Indeed, as students progress through college and then through their professional lives, they will likely tackle extended forms of the essay, such as theses, dissertations, and books.

The Core Elements of an Essay

Although varying widely in scope and style, all excellent essays consist of an engaging and sophisticated thesis, strong development and support of the thesis, appropriate structuring that unites the essay into a coherent whole, a conclusion that summarizes the author's key argument, and appropriate use of language, grammar, punctuation, and sentence structure. None of these parts reigns above another, and an effective essay cannot succeed in some of these elements while falling short in others. An essay proposing a provocative and compelling thesis might initially interest readers, but if its supporting paragraphs do not adequately develop its argument, then it is built on a foundation of sand. Likewise, if an essay's thesis, supporting paragraphs, structure, and conclusion unite to put forth an intriguing interpretation of a text, but mechanical errors render it incomprehensible or otherwise difficult to decipher, a piece of writing that should be a pleasure to read devolves into a chore.

The *thesis* puts forth the essay's primary argument. In most papers of literary and cultural analysis, it states the author's interpretation of the text(s) under examination. A strong thesis does not merely note a certain aspect of a text (e.g., "Yeats uses striking imagery in his poetry") but formulates an interpretation of how the text creates meaning through its features (e.g., "The striking imagery in Yeats's poetry reimagines the relationship between folklore and literature"). A thesis must make an assertion that other readers would find challenging rather than one that repeats obvious facts about the literary work. A thesis that traffics in bland generalizations cannot build an exciting argument, and writers must take the necessary time to ponder their interpretations of the text to ensure that they attain insights beyond the pedestrian.

Writers typically announce their thesis in the essay's opening paragraph, for the thesis should guide readers throughout the remainder of the essay. Readers cannot readily follow an argument if they are unsure of the author's precise point. Also, whereas the five-paragraph essay teaches that the thesis should be placed as the final sentence of the first paragraph, more sophisticated arguments often require thesis statements that run several sentences long and perhaps require several paragraphs to introduce effectively. Writers should not cram a complex idea into a single sentence; rather, they should explain their ideas clearly and cogently, without concern for whether the thesis statement fits into one, two, or more sentences.

Following the thesis in the essay's introduction, the ensuing paragraphs (and pages) develop and support this argument. The supporting paragraphs of an essay require a logical organization so that readers move from one point to the next with a clear sense of the argument's overall trajectory. Each paragraph should logically lead into the next, helping to develop the essay's argument in increasing depth. To this end, writers must provide smooth transitions between paragraphs, and it is often a good strategy to allude at least peripherally to the ideas of the thesis in these transition sentences. Also, each paragraph should address and explore a single, key idea. Authors should not pack so many ideas into a paragraph that it becomes digressive or otherwise confusing for the reader. (Few readers appreciate paragraphs that carry on for more than a single manuscript page.) Conversely, one-sentence paragraphs should be avoided as well, for, due to their brevity, they cannot develop ideas sufficiently to warrant standing alone.

When developing their interpretations of a literary text in the essay's supporting paragraphs, essayists should assume their readers' familiarity with the literature under consideration. Plot summaries should therefore be avoided, for they unnecessarily digress from the argument at hand. Indeed, plot summaries more undercut than build interpretations, for they merely restate information that readers already know and thus distract from the essayist's points. In contrast, the paragraphs of development and support should examine specific moments in the text that illuminate the essay's thesis, providing only essential background information to situate the context of the quotations. For the most part, essayists quote the text to provide this evidence, with these quotations assisting them to pinpoint particular elements that bolster the argument expressed in the thesis.

Integrating quotations fluently into an essay's supporting paragraphs challenges writers to merge their interpretations with the evidence that the text itself provides. To this end, writers must introduce the speaker of the quotation and explain how his or her words contribute to their overarching arguments. The following examples, focusing on John Kennedy Toole's comic masterpiece *A Confederacy of Dunces* (1980), demonstrate how quotations can be effectively used to illustrate an essayist's points. It is insufficient for a writer to state that Toole achieves a certain effect in his novel; rather, the writer must define this effect and then demonstrate how it functions. By using quotations from the primary text—Toole's novel—the author establishes that Toole depicts his protagonist Ignatius Reilly as a mock Christ figure:

> Although Ignatius's unappealing characteristics should dissever any connection to Jesus and his passive model of suffering masculinity, Mr. Levy realizes "[t]hat Reilly kook had really been worth saving after all. He had saved himself, Miss Trixie, and Mr. Levy, too, in his own kook way" (442). A comic, grotesque, and kooky Christ figure, Ignatius suffers his own stigmata when Miss Trixie "step[s] onto one of Ignatius's outstretched hands" (100).

Simply to assert that the character should be read as a Christ figure would be insufficient. Instead, the writer must demonstrate this interpretation through effective quotations from the text.

Additional research can be used to illuminate the writer's points and thus to bolster the essay's argument. Continuing this example of an essay addressing *A Confederacy of Dunces*, the author further develops this reading of the novel's sexual symbolism by employing the ideas of another scholar:

Ignatius's powerful response to Lana's pornography for teenagers testifies to his stunted sexual development after Rex's death, as well as to the ways in which his literary efforts symbolically register as masturbatory. In his cultural study of masturbation, Thomas Laqueur observes, "The connections between literary practices and masturbation are deep and extensive. Masturbation's evils . . . find parallels in the silent but far-reaching revolution of consciousness that private reading both reflects and helped create" (306). In such a manner, the intense connection between literary study and masturbatory pleasure illuminates Ignatius's desires to find a sexual partner.[1]

When using quotations in their essays, writers must carefully consider the points they are making through these quotations, how to integrate them smoothly into their prose, and then how to transition to the next point of the argument. Writers must also ensure that they present the quotations and ideas of scholars accurately and fairly. A literary essay without quotations can be compared to a court case without evidence: why should jurors believe an unproven argument? Why should an essayist's readers agree with an interpretation that is not anchored in the text and scholarly analyses of it?

Writing a conclusion can challenge even the best of essayists, who often feel that they have said all they have to say on their topics by the time they reach the final paragraph. Thus, for some writers, conclusions appear redundant, if not superfluous. Readers, however, benefit from such a recapitulation of the argument. Conclusions exemplify why writing is so challenging to do well: one must know a topic in sufficient depth to voice an informed opinion and analysis of it, while also explaining it to a knowledgeable reader. Readers, however, should learn new information, or a new interpretation, from essayists, and thus essayists must explain cogently and thoroughly their positions without over-explaining, over-simplifying, or over-complicating their points. It is a delicate balance to seek, and the conclusion, when writers often feel that their endeavors should be finished, mounts these issues anew.

Finally, the language used to express a writer's ideas should be sophisticated and apt but not pedantic or arcane. A vocabulary expressing ideas with stunning clarity and precision should stand as the goal of all essayists. Also, essays should be punctuated perfectly. Every respected artist in any field understands the necessity of flawless technique: a painter must master brushstrokes, as a dancer must master steps, as a writer must master sentence construction. Writers who have never quite determined the difference between a semicolon and a colon, who are unsure where commas belong in complex sentences, and who find themselves flummoxed when contemplating the relative utility of slashes, dashes, and hyphens, must learn these essential rules to communicate their ideas as clearly as possible. Handbooks such as Lynne Truss's *Eats, Shoots and Leaves: The Zero Tolerance Approach to Punctuation* and Karen Elizabeth Gordon's *The Deluxe Transitive Vampire: The Ultimate Handbook of Grammar for the Innocent, the Eager, and the*

Doomed prove that learning punctuation and grammar can be amusing as well as informative.

Research

Research essays in the broad field of literary and cultural studies engage in an ongoing conversation about the meanings, methods, and effects of poems, novels, plays, and other aesthetic texts. To join this conversation effectively, one must digest other readers' interpretations of them. At its heart, literary research entails studying literary texts, the scholarship that analyzes these texts, and additional relevant cultural documents, so that one may voice an informed opinion of their meaning.

A key concept in literary research distinguishes between primary and secondary sources. *Primary sources* comprise the artistic works that serve as the subject of one's research. If a researcher is studying Emily Dickinson's poetry, Dickinson's poems constitute the chief primary source for this project. *Secondary sources* include critical commentary on primary sources. Thus, whereas a collection of Dickinson's poems serves as a primary source, a study such as Alexandra Socarides's *Dickinson Unbound: Paper, Process, Poetics* is a secondary source. In effect, by researching and writing about Dickinson's poetry, an essayist creates another secondary source that will inform readers about Dickinson's literature's value, meaning, creation, or any other of its significant aspects. It should be noted as well that the line between primary and secondary sources, while often clear, can be slight. If one is examining Dickinson's reception in the late twentieth century, various contemporary critical reviews, which would typically be used as secondary sources, in this instance become primary sources.

For students of literary studies, primary sources are typically assigned in their classes—in a Shakespeare class, his plays and poems serve as the chief primary sources for research that students undertake. However, depending on the nature and extent of one's research, additional primary sources may be needed. If one commences a comparative study of the influence of Shakespeare's plays on his contemporary playwrights, these dramas also function as primary sources. Furthermore, primary sources include other artistic or archival materials created for their own intrinsic value rather than to comment on another text. Thus, Renaissance artworks or historical data related to the author's argument about Shakespeare would also serve as primary sources in his or her study.

Despite the wealth of information that the World Wide Web unfolds for all, writers should resist the urge to begin their research for secondary sources with Google and Wikipedia. Google opens up the entire contents of the Web at one's fingertips, and Wikipedia can be productively used to confirm basic facts about authors and their texts. All readers, however, create unique interpretations of literary texts, and no website can summon these interpretations for them. Consequently, rather than combing through the results generated by Google or Wikipedia, researchers benefit by initiating their research through a library's website, preferably that of a research library. In contrast to local public libraries, which stock their collections with resources for the general public, research libraries share a mission to collect and develop resources for academic study. Thus, while both local libraries and research libraries hold extensive materials related to such subjects as literature, film, history, chemistry, and anthropology, a research library devotes its collections to scholarly resources on these subjects, rather than to introductions and overviews.

Students in literature classes are joining an academic community that respects certain research protocols to ensure the quality of interpretation and analysis. Therefore, the lion's share of any essayist's research in secondary sources should focus on locating and examining peer-reviewed research. For research to be published in a peer-reviewed venue, whether as a book, as an article in a journal or on a website, or in any other format, it must be vetted by authorities in the field who agree to its merit. A rigorous process in which respected experts analyze an essayist's claims and conclusions, peer review ensures the quality of essays published by professional associations, academic presses, and other esteemed organizations. In determining the reliability and utility of each source they plan to use for their research, essayists should consider its editorial policies and assess its overall quality. Journals, books, and websites affiliated with universities and professional organizations generally publish stronger material than individual bloggers. The Latin phrase "Caveat emptor" warns consumers to beware of bad deals, and for scholars conducting research both in the library and on the Web, this phrase could be updated to "Caveat lector": let the reader beware of bad information, shoddy interpretations, and dubious claims. The phrase "critical thinking" is bandied about so much in educational circles that it has lost some of its power and meaning, yet the ability to peer through façades—to see that, in some scholarly sources, the emperor wears no clothes—testifies highly to a researcher's ability to improve the field of study.

The websites of many college and university libraries allow researchers to conduct searches from their homepages, but researchers should instead identify specific databases relevant for a particular query and begin with them. A resource of immeasurable utility in literary and cultural studies, the MLA International Bibliography catalogs an extensive range of scholarly research in literary, cinematic, linguistic, folkloric, and other related fields. Other online databases helpful for literary research include the Dictionary of Literary Biography; the Essay and General Literature Index; the Reader's Guide to Periodical Literature; JSTOR; Project Muse; OED: Oxford English Dictionary; and Lit Finder (which includes the databases Poem Finder, Play Finder, and Story Finder). More specialized databases, such as Early English Books Online; the Women Writers' Project, 1500–1800; and the American Periodical Series Online, allow readers access to a wealth of information specific to the various subdisciplines of literary and cultural studies. It is beyond the scope of this brief overview to detail all of the relevant databases and search engines for each subfield of literary studies, but students, who encounter a different subdiscipline in most classes taken throughout their educations, should not allow themselves to feel overwhelmed by this plenitude of resources. Foremost, their instructors can advise them of the various databases available for facilitating research. Also, it is generally acknowledged that librarians' deepest professional pleasure involves helping others to find relevant information and resources. With this in mind, researchers new to a subdiscipline in literary and cultural studies should visit their library's Reference Desk when beginning a project to request assistance in locating various resources for their endeavors.

Building the Essay: Thesis, Research, Outline

A clichéd conundrum ponders whether the chicken or the egg came first, and this riddle's counterpart in literary and cultural studies research asks whether essayists should begin with a thesis or with research. This paradox recognizes that, without a thesis, essayists cannot gather the necessary evidence to build their arguments, for they might simply grasp wildly for any information, no matter how far afield it lies from their actual topic. Conversely, without sufficient reading and critical study in primary and secondary sources, essayists cannot develop their arguments in the first place. One must learn how other scholars have engaged with similar questions if one is to advance, rather than retread, the field. In the quest for a thesis, many researchers initially find themselves flummoxed by this common scholarly quandary.

Given this conflict, many researchers balance their quest for a thesis with their quest for resources to support this thesis, seeking each through the other in a complementary fashion. To develop a thesis through research, writers should first identify an appropriate topic for research and then continually hone this material as it develops into a thesis. An essay's *topic* represents its broad subject matter, whereas a *thesis* represents a unique interpretation within the general field of the topic. For example, a topic might address Michael Chabon's use of comic books in his novel *The Amazing Adventures of Kavalier and Clay* (2000). Once this topic is identified, it is easier for the researcher to begin taking notes and sketching an outline of the argument. In this example, the essayist is now prepared to review Chabon's novel— the primary source—for passages discussing comic books, paying particular attention to recurrent images or thematic patterns accompanying Chabon's depiction of them. The researcher should also employ the MLA International Bibliography and other databases for secondary sources, using such keywords as "Michael Chabon," "comic books," and "*Amazing Adventures of Kavalier and Clay*" in their searches, and realizing that subsequent searches will likely be necessary after honing this topic further. Writers should be open to including source material that challenges their interpretations as well as material that supports it, so that they can provide a thorough and honest representation of the scholarly community's thinking on the specific subject.

Once a researcher has read through the primary source(s) completely and has begun to read widely among the secondary materials, he or she must compile this information into a usable structure through note-taking. An old-fashioned yet highly effective method of note-taking entails scribbling passages from the texts and related thoughts on notecards, but today many people open files on their word processors and type in (or, if working from e-books, cut and paste in) relevant passages. It is of critical importance for these methods of note-taking that they must allow writers to revise their thoughts easily: index cards can be shuffled in a new order, and word-processing documents allow writers the freedom to move around large blocks of text. Whichever method a researcher chooses, it must allow flexibility and adaptability so that the construction of the argument can be easily reimagined.

When researchers discern the hazy beginnings of a thesis, they can begin outlining the essay as a whole. Outlines, even if merely brief sketches, are essential for good writing, for they allow writers to visualize the scope of an entire project and how it will move from the thesis to the conclusion. Some writers create skeletal outlines, noting a phrase or a sentence that advances the argument from its beginning to its end; others put their index cards or word files in a relevant order. Effective organization requires a candid analysis of how the thesis will be supported, and a keen sense for how the argument will proceed from one point to the next. Students new to research essays often wonder how they will select a thesis of sufficient complexity to meet the course requirements for a 1000-word, or 2000-word, or 5000-word (or more) essay. By outlining their ideas as they develop, researchers assist themselves in envisioning the project as a whole and determining a thesis sufficient for the assignment at hand.

An effective method for building an outline involves determining which elements of the primary and secondary sources contribute most meaningfully to the essay's thesis and then organizing them appropriately. Persuasive interpretations of literary texts require apt quotations to illustrate the writer's observation, and so a good rule of thumb for literary analysis proposes that many, if not most, supporting paragraphs of an essay—those other than the introduction and conclusion—should contain at least one quotation from a primary or secondary text. This is a rule of thumb, not a rule, and some paragraphs of a research essay may need to address issues other than ones discussed in the primary or secondary sources, particularly those paragraphs in which authors advance their unique interpretations of the text. Still, if a writer is putting forth an interpretation of a novel but does not quote this novel in a given paragraph, or if a writer is considering the reception of a poem's imagery but does not cite scholars who have addressed this issue, the author should examine how this paragraph contributes to the overarching argument. If a literary essay contains no quotations from the text under examination, it is a clear sign that the author has lost his or her way.

Once an essayist has researched sufficiently to develop a compelling thesis, has taken sufficient notes from primary and secondary sources to support the thesis, and has sketched an outline to guide the argument from thesis to conclusion, all that remains is to write the essay. The outline provides the essay's bones, but it still needs the flesh of writing to bring it to life as a coherent and organic whole. Essayists must pay careful attention to how they segue from one idea to another and articulate these connections and their explications of the text with clear and precise language. When incorporating quotations and other evidence, essayists must fully explain how their evidence supports the essay's thesis and links to other points in their essays. Still, if the author has thoroughly considered the thesis, has undertaken research in primary and secondary sources diligently, and has organized the outline to give a precise map of the interpretation and its development, the final act of writing the essay necessitates simply that one adhere to this plan and bring it to fruition with fluid and graceful prose.

Documenting Sources

The Modern Language Association (MLA) is the preeminent professional organization for literary scholars, and most essays of literary analysis adhere to MLA formatting. This book is documented in MLA style, and so readers may consult it to observe how this documentation style functions. In brief, MLA style employs parenthetical citations within the essay's body and a Works Cited page at its conclusion so that writers may document their sources. Readers interested in the author's subject will likely want to explore further in the field, and thus the Works Cited page, in conjunction with parenthetical citations, allows them to track down the author's sources. The preceding chapters cite an extensive range of primary and secondary sources—poems, plays, novels, films, scholarly studies, websites, and more—with each illustrating how to incorporate primary and secondary sources into an overarching argument.

Parenthetical Citations of Literary Works

Essayists should include in the parenthetical citation only as much information as necessary for the reader to locate this source in consultation with the Works Cited page. For most citations of literary texts, therefore, only the relevant line numbers are needed for poems, the relevant page numbers for novels, and, as applicable, the relevant acts, scenes, and line numbers for plays. In this first example, the author quotes and documents a single line from a poem:

> Derek Walcott concludes "A Far Cry from Africa," in which he wrestles with the continent's colonial traditions and his conflicted relationship to the English language, with a plaintive question, "How can I turn from Africa and live?" (line 33).

The accompanying entry in the Works Cited page for this poem reads as:

> Walcott, Derek. "A Far Cry from Africa." *Selected Poems*. Ed. Edward Baugh. New York: Farrar, Straus & Giroux, 2007. 6. Print.

It is also acceptable to cite the volume of poetry as a whole, particularly when a researcher refers to numerous poems from the same collection. In this case, the entry would read:

> Walcott, Derek. *Selected Poems*. Ed. Edward Baugh. New York: Farrar, Straus & Giroux, 2007. Print.

When citing poetry, writers should determine on an individual basis whether it is necessary to include the word "lines." This book consistently uses "lines" because it cites from a variety of different types of primary sources. On the other hand, if an essayist concentrates solely on the poems of a given poet, the word "lines" would most likely be superfluous. Also, some editions of poems do not number individual lines; in these instances, it is acceptable to provide the page number(s) where the poem is found. When listing a poem by name on the Works Cited page, writers must include the inclusive page numbers from the source in which the poem is found—as the page number 6 indicates in the example of Walcott's "A Far Cry from Africa." If the book has an editor listed on the title page, that name must be included as well.

When quoting from novels, provide the page number of the passage in the parenthetical citation. Because many older novels have been published several times over their lifespans, it is often helpful to include additional information so that readers employing a different edition can nonetheless locate this material, as in the following example:

> Laura Ingalls Wilder concludes her *Little House* series with *These Happy Golden Years*, in which Laura and Almanzo marry. Sidestepping the issue of marital sexuality for her young readers, Wilder depicts instead the couple looking at the offspring of their farm animals, as Almanzo proclaims: "Then let's go look at Lady's big little colt" (288; ch. 33).

The accompanying entry in the Works Cited page for this novel reads as:

> Wilder, Laura Ingalls. *These Happy Golden Years*. 1943. New York: Harper Trophy, 1971. Print.

The addition of "ch. 33" in the parenthetical citation alerts readers not using the edition listed in the Works Cited that they can locate this information in this chapter, regardless of the edition's pagination. Additionally, the first date, 1943, refers to the year of the novel's initial publication; the second date, 1971, refers to the year of the edition's publication.

Many plays, including Shakespeare's, are divided into acts, scenes, and lines, and in providing parenthetical citations, writers should include as much of this information as possible.

After killing his daughter Lavinia at the conclusion of *Titus Andronicus*, Titus compares himself to the Roman centurion Virginius—"I am as woeful as Virginius was / And have a thousand times more cause than he / To do this outrage" (5.3.50–52)—despite that Virginius killed his daughter to protect her from rape, whereas Lavinia has already suffered this violation.

The first number in the parenthetical citation tells the reader the act, the second number refers to the scene, and the concluding numbers refer to the line numbers. The accompanying entry in the Works Cited page for the play reads:

> Shakespeare, William. *The Riverside Shakespeare*. Ed. Blakemore Evans. 2nd ed. Boston: Houghton Mifflin, 1997. Print.

However, many plays are not written in verse, and thus do not indicate the line numbers for each scene. (Indeed, many plays do not enumerate scenes as well.) In these instances, provide as much information as possible, even if it is only the page number:

> In Margaret Edson's *Wit*, Vivian Bearing contemplates the meaning of humor in her life, realizing that she "admired only the studied application of wit, not its spontaneous eruption" (50).

The accompanying entry in the Works Cited page for this play would read:

> Edson, Margaret. *Wit*. New York: Dramatists Play Service, 1999. Print.

Given the great variety of ways in which playwrights structure their works, researchers should ensure that they provide sufficient information to locate the source by respecting each play's unique format.

Books and Book Chapters in the Works Cited

As the preceding examples of parenthetical citations and their accompanying bibliographic entries demonstrate, despite their variations, the basic format for a book in the Works Cited is as follows:

> Last Name, First Name. *Title*. Place of Publication: Publisher, Year of Publication. Medium of Publication.

Following this outline, a standard entry of a book by a single author appears thusly:

> McCrum, Robert. *Globish: How the English Language Became the World's Language*. New York: Norton, 2010. Print.

Common variations on this theme include the following:

- A *book with multiple authors* lists the authors in the order they are listed on the title page, with the first author's name listed last name first, followed by the other authors' names in standard order:

  Hurley, Matthew M., Daniel C. Dennett, and Reginald B. Adams, Jr. *Inside Jokes: Using Humor to Reverse-Engineer the Mind*. Cambridge, Mass.: MIT Press, 2011. Print.

- A *translated book* includes the translator's name after the book's title:

  Roland Barthes. *Mythologies*. Trans. Annette Lavers. New York: Noonday, 1989. Print.

- A *republished book* includes the original date of publication before the publication information of the current edition:

  Woolf, Virginia. *A Room of One's Own*. 1929. Orlando: Harvest, 2005. Print.

- An *edition of a book* includes its edition number and the publication information for the current edition:

  Rosenblatt, Louise. *Literature as Exploration*. 5th ed. New York: Modern Language Association, 1995. Print.

- An *anthology or edited collection* begins with the editor's name (or editors' names) followed by the abbreviation *ed.* (or *eds.*, if two or more) so that it is clear that they have compiled or otherwise edited the book but that they did not write the majority of its text:

  Knight, Stephen, and Thomas Ohlgren, eds. *Robin Hood and Other Outlaw Tales*. Kalamazoo: Medieval Institute Publications, 1997. Print.

- A *book chapter* inserts the chapter title between the author's name and the book title, usually an anthology, and also includes the name of the book's editor and the page numbers of the chapter:

  Schrader, Paul. "Notes on Film Noir." *Film Genre Reader*. Ed. Barry Keith Grant. Austin: U of Texas P, 1986. 169–82. Print.

Note, however, that if the chapter is an untitled preface or introduction, no quotations marks are used around the title.

Some books require combining these formats. For example, a book written by two authors that is subsequently edited would appear as such:

Wordsworth, William, and Samuel Taylor Coleridge. *Wordsworth and Coleridge: Lyrical Ballads*. Ed. R. L. Brett and A. R. Jones. 2nd ed. London: Routledge, 1991. Print.

Note that when multiple editors are listed after the name of the book, *Ed.* is used regardless of the number of editors. The following example includes two authors, a preface, multiple translators, and an edition:

Deleuze, Gilles, and Félix Guattari. *Anti-Oedipus: Capitalism and Schizophre-nia*. Preface by Michel Foucault. Trans. Robert Hurley, Mark Seem, and Helen Lane. 1972. New York: Penguin, 2009. Print.

These examples cover the vast majority of citations necessary for documenting poems, prose fiction, plays, and scholarly sources in print. Once one understands the basic structure guiding the permutations, it is relatively easy to adapt it to unique circumstances.

Periodicals in the Works Cited

Bibliographic entries for periodical articles follow the basic parameters of an entry for a book but with some critical alterations. The standard format for a periodical article displays the following information:

Author's last name, Author's first name. "Article Title." *Title of Source* Volume number. Issue number (Year of volume): Page numbers. Mode of publication.

Following this outline, a standard entry of a single-authored article would appear as:

Leitch, Thomas. "Twelve Fallacies in Contemporary Adaptation Theory." *Criticism* 45.2 (2003): 149–71. Print.

- An *article in a monthly magazine* adheres to the same structure, yet it does not place the year of publication in parentheses, nor does it include volume or issue numbers. Furthermore, if the page numbers of the article are not consecutive and would read something like 118–22, 127–28, 130–31, and 188–90, it is preferable to indicate simply the first page of the article followed by a "+" sign:

Clarke, Gerald. "Bye Society: Capote's Swans." *Vanity Fair* Apr. 1988: 118+. Print.

- An *article in a newspaper or magazine published multiple times during a month* resembles the format of an article in a magazine but includes the precise date of publication:

Greenfeld, Josh. "Truman Capote: The Movie Star?" *New York Times* 28 Dec. 1975: II.1, 17. Print.

Film, Television, and Radio Programs in the Works Cited

Beyond literary texts and secondary sources including scholarly monographs and peer-reviewed articles, researchers in literary and cultural studies often must cite a range of works from the worlds of film, television, and radio. The basic format for a film or video recording is:

Film title. Director's name. Performers' names. Studio, Year. Medium.

Following this outline, a standard entry of a film appears thusly:

> *Breakfast at Tiffany's*. Dir. Blake Edwards. Perf. Audrey Hepburn, George Peppard, and Patricia Neal. Paramount, 1961. Film.

- For a *film released on DVD*, additional information such as the year of DVD release should be included:

> *Breakfast at Tiffany's*. Dir. Blake Edwards. Perf. Audrey Hepburn, George Peppard, and Patricia Neal. 1961. Paramount, 2009. DVD.

- The basic format for *television or radio programs* in the Works Cited page provides the following information:

> "Episode's Title." *Title of Program*. Network. Call letters and city of network affiliate. Date aired. Medium.

Because many television programs are watched through streaming internet services and DVD box sets, the call letters and city of the network affiliate are increasingly irrelevant. Again, give as much information as necessary to direct readers to the source.

> "The Funcooker." *30 Rock*. NBC. 12 Mar. 2009. Television.

Internet Sources in the Works Cited

Citing Web sources can be challenging because no protocols dictate the information that websites must provide about their authors and dates of publication. Foremost, in documenting webpages as scholarly sources, essayists should not cut and paste the URL address of a website into the Works Cited page. Frequently, hosting sites restructure their internal architecture, and so URLs are subject to change. It is also unlikely that someone seeking to read a source on the Web will correctly type in a Web address of one hundred or more characters—or at the very least, she will be quite frustrated by this process. Instead, build the entry for content taken from a standard website from the following skeletal structure:

> Last name, then first name, of author or editor. "Title of Work." *Name of Site*. Version number. Organization or institution that hosts the site, date of source creation. Publication medium. Date of access.

Some of this information may not be available, but fill in as many of these fields as possible. For example:

> "Top 10 Epic." *afi.com*. American Film Institute, n.d. Web. 1 Feb. 2013.

Where there is no publication date provided, you should indicate this by using "N.d." as an abbreviation for "no date given." A good rule of thumb for testing whether sufficient information has been provided to track down a source is to perform a Google search with the key terms of the entry. If the appropriate Web source appears as a result, it is an encouraging sign that readers will enjoy appropriate access to the sources.

Some Web sources require additional content be added to provide more thorough publication information.

- For an *article originally published in print but accessed on a scholarly database*, the researcher should include information about both the original publication and the Web publication:

    Bottomore, Stephen. "Film Museums: A Bibliography." *Film History: An International Journal* 18.3 (2006): 327–49. *Project Muse*. Web. 14 Jun. 2013.

After providing the original print publication details, the name of the scholarly database is included, along with the medium used to access the article and the date of access.

- For a *scholarly journal published only on the Web*, the format follows that of any journal, along with additional Web information:

    Hoff, Ann K. "Googling Allusions: Teaching Eliot to the Net Generation." *The CEA Forum* 38.2 (2009): n. pag. Web. 13 Jun. 2013.

In this case, "n. pag." indicates that this journal does not paginate its articles.

These guidelines address the lion's share of parenthetical citations and Works Cited entries needed for literary and cultural studies essays. For any necessary entry not addressed by these precepts, consult the most recent edition of the *MLA Handbook for Writers of Research Papers*. Another excellent resource for documentation issues, the Purdue Online Writing Lab (owl.english.purdue.edu/owl) provides detailed examples of a variety of issues concerning documentation. No resource can answer every documentation question, however, so it is essential that writers determine the necessary information to use in their parenthetical citations and Works Cited pages so that other scholars can retrace their steps.

Plagiarism

As the preceding section demonstrates, documenting sources in a research essay allows writers to give credit where credit is due, for as a matter of professional courtesy and individual integrity, writers must acknowledge the authors and critics without whom their arguments would not have developed. One's writing should be one's own, and when essayists quote another

writer's ideas, these contributions must be cited. Submitting another scholar's writing as one's own constitutes plagiarism, and, quite simply, it is dishonest and unethical. Stealing is stealing, whether one takes cars, money,
or ideas. And while one can pose vexing philosophical questions about the
morality of theft—is Jean Valjean wrong to steal bread to feed his family in
Victor Hugo's *Les Misérables?*—it certainly will never make anyone smarter
to pass off someone else's words and ideas as his or her own. Moreover,
plagiarists, when caught, must pay severe penalties, including failing the
assignment and/or the class, and even expulsion. Perhaps most importantly,
every time thieves look in the mirror, they see a cheat and a fraud, which is
not a particularly pleasant way to go through life.

The most common form of plagiarism involves copying, or cutting and
pasting, another person's writing and presenting it as one's own. Plagiarism
reminds writers of the importance of punctuation, for many of those accused
of plagiarism plead innocence, claiming that they simply forgot to insert quotation marks before and after the offending material. Readers, however, cannot intuit a writer's intentions. Without the appropriate quotation marks,
the lack of evidence to the contrary points to the writer's guilt. Indeed, a plea
of carelessness fails to mount a compelling defense.

Paraphrasing another writer's ideas without documenting these contributions constitutes plagiarism as well. When essayists rephrase someone else's words, recasting these ideas in new prose but retaining their
essence, they are still plagiarizing. Paraphrasing should be documented as
well as direct quotations, for writers must credit all authors whose work
they use to build their arguments. As the following example demonstrates,
documenting paraphrases adheres to the same formatting as documenting quotations. This example is based on a passage from Lee Edelman's
provocative monograph *No Future: Queer Theory and the Death Drive*:

> [W]e are no more able to conceive of a politics without a fantasy of the future
> than we are able to conceive of a future without the figure of the Child. That
> figural Child alone embodies the citizen as an ideal, entitled to claim full rights
> to its future share in the nation's good, though always at the cost of limiting the
> rights "real" citizens are allowed (11).

If an essayist rewrites this idea, he or she must include an appropriate parenthetical citation and Works Cited entry to document the use of Edelman's ideas:

> DOCUMENTED PARAPHRASE: Lee Edelman discusses how current political
> discourse is shaped by the phantom figure of the Child, an imaginary construct
> that allows people to claim that their actions in the present are designed to
> preserve the future for children, all the while overlooking the consequences of
> their decisions for the culture's current citizens (11).

The Works Cited page would include an entry for this source, regardless of whether it is quoted directly or paraphrased:

Edelman, Lee. *No Future: Queer Theory and the Death Drive*. Durham: Duke UP, 2004. Print.

A plagiarized paraphrase would attempt to pass off Edelman's ideas as the essayist's own, and would therefore not include any citational information:

PLAGIARIZED PARAPHRASE: Current political discourse is shaped by the phantom figure of the Child, an imaginary construct that allows people to claim that their actions in the present are designed to preserve the future for children, all the while overlooking the consequences of their decisions for the culture's current citizens.

Without any mention of Lee Edelman, and without any information about the book from which these ideas are taken, readers would likely, and incorrectly, infer that they belong to the author of the essay rather than to Edelman.

While writers must be careful to document all sources consulted, to paraphrase judiciously, and never to plagiarize, information considered general knowledge falls beyond the requirements of such documentation. General knowledge regarding a literary and cultural studies subject typically includes undisputed facts of authors' careers, such as the publication dates and other basic information about their works. One need not cite any sources to state, "Wallace Stevens, a modernist poet, wrote his famous poem 'Thirteen Ways of Looking at a Blackbird' in 1917." If the essay then discusses how various critics have responded to modernist themes in Stevens's poem, or examines readings of the poem advanced by other scholars, documentation must be included.

Presentations in New Media

Technology continues to evolve rapidly, with new modes of presenting one's research emerging. From PowerPoint presentations to multimedia YouTube videos, from Skype conferences to collaborative writing via Dropbox, the means and methods of pursuing and disseminating one's research expand almost daily. At the same time, everything described in this chapter remains of critical importance for effective communication and research: PowerPoint does not obviate the need for a strong thesis, and a Skype conference does not absolve researchers from the necessary due diligence in covering secondary sources. A solid argument articulated in lucid prose persists as a foundational skill in communication. New technologies will not dispense this need. More than ever, in a world where technology shifts so frequently, researchers need to keep their interpretive skills firmly based in the fundamentals of academic writing: rigorous research, insightful interpretations, and graceful prose.

Notes

1 As discussed in greater detail in the subsequent section of this chapter entitled "Documenting Sources," the accompanying Works Cited page at an essay's conclusion must document all books cited in an essay. The entries for these books would read as follows:

Laqueur, Thomas. *Solitary Sex: A Cultural History of Masturbation*. New York: Zone, 2003. Print.

Toole, John Kennedy. *A Confederacy of Dunces*. Foreword by Walker Percy. 1980. New York: Wings Books, 1996. Print.

4.2 Revising the Research Essay

All Writers Revise

Professional writers consult editors to hone their prose, and students likewise benefit from seeking constructive criticism about their essays before submitting them for grades or other forms of review. Once an essay has been turned in, it cannot be fixed (unless the instructor offers students the opportunity to revise their work). Similarly, once an essay has been published in print, it lives forever, no matter if the author later desires to repudiate it. Given these conditions, all writers must ensure that their work represents their best efforts.

Most colleges and universities host writing centers that assist students, at no charge, with their essays and other writing assignments. Rather than simply showing up at the writing center with essays in hand, writers should maximize the usefulness of these sessions by generating specific questions about their work prior to the meeting. General advice can be helpful, but it is often more instructive for writers to assess their work as objectively as possible and then to ask the writing-center tutors for advice on these topics. Also, instructors and professors at most colleges and universities hold office hours, during which they assist students individually. One of the single best strategies for student success, visiting instructors during office hours allows students to enjoy the benefits of one-on-one instruction. During these sessions, the student and instructor can focus exclusively on the student's writing and ideas.

Some instructors allow students to revise an assignment after it has been graded, and such opportunities to improve one's work should be seized. To make the most of the revision process, students should carefully consider their instructor's feedback, paying particular attention to issues concerning the thesis and the explanation of their argument. Also, writers should resist the urge to correct small grammatical slips and punctuation errors first, for if they are fully responding to the reviewer's comments, they will likely need to rewrite certain sections of the essay altogether. Thus, correcting a comma error in a sentence that needs to be completely rewritten will not substantively improve the essay.

Case Study: Revising an Essay

The following pages demonstrate an essay in two critical stages of production. The first represents a writer's polished draft, with the editor's suggestions for improvement marked throughout. The second represents the writer's response to these suggestions. Analyze the alterations between these drafts carefully, and apply as many of these techniques as possible when writing, and then when revising, an essay.

Devin Snyder
Professor Johnson
English 3311
8 May 2010

According to the Other Woman:
A Formalist Analysis of Anne Sexton's "To My Lover,
Returning to His Wife"

In her poem "To My Lover, Returning to His Wife," Anne Sexton brings to light a situation that is, unfortunately, all too common in today's society. She discusses adultery, but does so from a unique perspective—namely that of the other woman. What's more, she gives the speaker an unexpected role by making her an advocate for the wife. The poet uses contrasting themes—vibrant and weathered, permanent and brief, tangible and intangible—to not only show the differences, but to also point out the ladies' similarities and therefore supplement the speaker's argument that her lover should return to his wife.

In the first stanza of the poem, the speaker sets the tone by complimenting the wife: "She is all there" (21). In other words, the speaker perceives this woman as being complete and sturdy. She also describes her as having been "melted carefully down" for her husband (or the lover, to whom the speaker is talking) and "cast up from [his] one hundred favorite aggies [or marbles]" (21). This statement implies that the wife is finely crafted, made out of marble, something that is solid, dazzling and virtually unbreakable. However, marbles can lose their polish after a time. They can become scratched and tarnished from heavy use. Because the wife is, according to the speaker, made from her husband's "favorite" marbles, it's safe to assume that she's had a lot of wear and tear over the years. So while she is, in the speaker's own words, "exquisite," she isn't without her scuff marks.

It is in this fashion that the speaker describes the wife as both vibrant and weathered. The third line of the second stanza captures this paradox wonderfully by using the metaphor, "Fireworks in the dull middle of February" (21). To begin, fireworks are colorful, explosive, and exciting. They're usually associated with celebrations, July Fourth, New Years and Mardi Gras being the most popular ones. They aren't normally affiliated with February because, with the exception of Groundhog's Day and, of course, Valentine's Day, which is traditionally a lover's holiday, nothing exciting happens. That the wife is portrayed as something beautiful and vibrant in the middle of this dead, frigid month suggests that the woman has her exciting qualities. She adds bursts of bright color to a humdrum existence. At the same time, however, the fireworks metaphor implies that she doesn't present this side of herself very often.

Throughout the essay I've underlined some phrases where you should consider raising your academic diction. You write well, but try to express these ideas more elegantly.

Can you explain these contrasting themes more clearly? Also, are these themes or images? It might be more productive to think about the ways that images build themes.

Poetry should be cited by line number, not page number, where possible.

I see that the phrase "She is all there" implies the woman's completeness, but does it convey as well that she is sturdy? If so, please explain how.

Many finely crafted objects of art are sculpted from marble, but marbles themselves are not "finely crafted"; they are mass produced.

Allow the in-text citation to tell readers to which line of the poem you are referring. Only very rarely should the line number of a poem serve as the subject of a sentence.

The sentence implies that Groundhog's Day is an exciting holiday, but do most people, other than the residents of Punxsutawney, Pennsylvania, see it as such? Concentrate instead on your reading of the significance of Valentine's Day to the poem.

As lovely as they are, fireworks don't last very long—just moments, really—and the occasions on which we use them are sprinkled sparsely throughout the year. So perhaps the wife's vivacious nature only makes itself known on special occasions (like Valentine's Day, for example) and lasts for short periods of time. The point is that she's not like this every day, which could be the reason for her husband's wandering. He's looking outside of his marriage for something it lacks—excitement. But the speaker is quick to remind him that excitement is a rare, precious thing in a relationship that runs deeper than just the occasional affair, and that even *their* relationship will lose its luster over time.

In the third stanza of the poem, the speaker uses specific images to illustrate her argument. She compares herself to a "bright red sloop in the harbor," smoke and "Littleneck clams out of season" (21). All of these things are temporary. The sloop is a shiny new toy; like the wife, it is a childhood dream realized. But unlike the wife and the marbles that represent her, it is free to set sail at any time. It implies that the speaker is available for playtime, but, as she has nothing concrete that would keep her tethered to her lover—like the wedding band that his wife owns—she remains out his of reach. She argues here that she is just momentary, as elusive as a dream and intangible as "smoke [rising] from the car window" (21). Both lack substance, as they can be seen but not touched. The third image, the littleneck clams, represents something that is rare, a delicacy that can only be enjoyed once in a while. This metaphor draws a parallel between the speaker and the wife, because it is similar to the fireworks in stanza two. It suggests that the two women aren't as distinct as the lover may want to believe. While she is bright red and dazzling for now, the speaker essentially states that she won't always be that way. She could very well become the wife in later years, a sobering reality that she's urging her lover to consider.

The next three stanzas describe the things that make the wife more concrete than the speaker and, from the speaker's point of view, make her more of a catch. To begin, the speaker compliments the wife for being the lover's "have to have," someone who "has grown [him his] practical [his] tropical growth" (21). We encounter another paradox in this line, as it places duality on the wife, making her both blasé (practical) and colorful (tropical) at the same time. In addition, by saying that the wife is the lover's "have to have," the speaker is implying that he needs his spouse, both for her practical nature and her rare playful side.

In the last line of the fourth stanza and throughout stanza five, the speaker lists all of the good and practical things the wife has brought to the marriage:

> She sees to the oars and oarlocks for the dinghy,
> has placed wild flowers at the window at breakfast,
> sat by the potter's wheel at midday,
> set forth three children under the moon,
> three cherubs drawn by Michelangelo.
>
> (21)

Italics are rarely necessary for accentuating a point. Let your reading of the poem speak on its own strengths.

Is a sloop temporary? Can you complicate your readings of these images?

Several of the essay's phrasings employ "things," but can you be more specific in your word choice? Look for this issue in other areas of the essay as well.

Avoid idioms and clichés in academic writing.

I understand what you are trying to communicate with the phrase "places duality," but a duality cannot be placed. How can you state this idea more precisely?

There is another boat analogy at the beginning of this section. But unlike the above-mentioned sailboat, which carries romantic connotations, the dinghy isn't nearly as glamorous. It's a lifeboat, something practical and plain. While it isn't as polished as the bright red sloop, which is used for travel and recreation, the dinghy is vital when that sailboat sinks. It saves lives. In the same way, the wife is a vital part of her husband's existence. She sees to the oarlocks and oars, meaning that she steers his life in the right direction and she keeps everything on an even keel. This is why the speaker calls her the lover's "have to have": because she keeps him from sinking. Even if his current relationship with the speaker founders, he will be all right, because he has something solid to hold onto, to keep him anchored down. The speaker, by contrast, is fickle. She could sink out from under him at any time and leave him to drown. There's nothing concrete to keep them together.

Meanwhile, the wife is always with him, as the next three lines signify. She "has placed wild flowers at the window at breakfast, / sat by the potter's wheel at midday, / set forth three children under the moon" (21). Essentially, she's been at her husband's side morning, noon and night, keeping the boat afloat, making life more colorful by decorating it with flowers and adding the practical fixtures to it—the cups, bowls and saucers. Most importantly—or it seems that way because the speaker discusses this point for two stanzas straight—she has given him children, three perfect angels, works of art "drawn by Michelangelo" (21).

Described for ten consecutive lines or two and a half stanzas, the children receive a good portion of the speaker's attention. In fact, she seems more concerned about them than her lover is. In the last couple lines of the sixth stanza, she urges him to notice them. "If you glance up," she says, "the children are there / like delicate balloons resting on the ceiling" (21). The phrase "delicate balloons" indicate that they are fragile, and that they are resting on the ceiling suggests that, while their father is with the speaker, the children are out of his reach. She warns that if he leaves his wife to pursue a permanent relationship with her, he could damage his delicate children and miss out on their upbringing. For their sakes more than anything, the speaker plays advocate for the wife. Her priorities are apparent because, immediately after mentioning the children, she returns her lover's heart and spends the next three stanzas giving him permission to go back to his spouse (22).

The concluding two stanzas of the poem reiterate the speaker's original argument that the wife "is all there" while she, the "luxury" is only a temporary pleasure (21). Her words are simple and blunt:

> She is so naked and singular.
> She is the sum of yourself and your dream.
> Climb her like a monument, step after step.
> She is solid.
> As for me, I am watercolor.
> I wash off.
>
> (22)

"There is" communicates very little to the reader, and the essay employs this phrase a few times. Can you rewrite these sentences with more exciting prose?

"This is why" and "because" communicate the same idea, and thus the sentence suffers from some redundancy in phrasing.

Think about the structure of your argument. The essay quotes these lines of poetry in the preceding paragraph, and then immediately quotes them again. Can you restructure this part of the argument so that you do not repeat yourself?

Is it important that the children are described in ten consecutive lines (rather than nine or eleven)? Such miscellaneous observations detract from your reading of the poem's imagery because they do not meaningfully advance the interpretation.

These last two images are so powerful when contrasted with one another. A monument and a watercolor are both works of art, but while a monument can be climbed as well as admired at a distance, a watercolor can only be looked at, not touched. In addition, watercolor as a medium is almost transparent. Like the smoke in an earlier stanza, the paint lacks any tangible substance. By using this metaphor in relation to herself, the speaker is essentially telling her lover that she is nothing while his wife, by contrast, is everything. In short, she's saying, "You'll get over me, but you can't live without her." This last couplet puts a big, bold period on her argument, giving the lover no room to respond. He'll return to his reliable dinghy and row back to the solid shore while she will set sail for the horizon.

Works Cited

Sexton, Anne. "To My Lover, Returning to His Wife." *Love Poems*. Boston: Houghton Mifflin Company, 1967. 21–22. Print.

Final Comments:

The essay succeeds in deciphering the images of Sexton's "To My Lover, Returning to His Wife" and interpreting them in line with the poem's dramatic action. By paying careful attention to these images, you develop a reading that is sensitive and assured, enlightening your reader to Sexton's deeper themes. To improve the essay, state the thesis more clearly. The thesis is critical to your argument, and so its interpretation of the contrasting images of the wife and the man's lover must be carefully delineated. Also, address the questions concerning some of the interpretations of images in the marginalia, and hone your prose as well, particularly the phrases marked with underlining or marginal comments. As a scholar of Sexton's poetry, you are engaging in a critical discussion with her other readers; as such, the essay should engage with secondary criticism. The essay is quite engaging, and another round of revisions will polish away these few remaining rough edges.

Devin Snyder
Professor Johnson
English 3311
22 May 2010

According to the Other Woman:
A Formalist Analysis of Anne Sexton's "To My Lover,
Returning to His Wife"

In her poem "To My Lover, Returning to His Wife," Anne Sexton discusses adultery from a unique perspective—that of the "other woman." Furthermore, she gives the speaker an unexpected role by making her an advocate for the wife. The poet uses a series of contrasting images to illustrate the differences and similarities between the two women, with the wife primarily depicted as weathered yet permanent and tangible and the speaker depicted as vibrant yet impermanent and intangible. These images supplement the speaker's argument that her lover should return to his wife.

In the first stanza of the poem, the speaker sets the tone by complimenting the wife: "She is all there" (1). With these words, the speaker compliments this woman as complete unto herself. She also describes her as having been "melted carefully down" (2) for her husband (or the lover, to whom the speaker is talking) and "cast up from [his] one hundred favorite aggies" (4). This statement implies that the wife fulfills her husband's childhood aspirations, that she metamorphoses childhood playthings into adult fulfillment. However, marbles lose their polish after a time. They become scratched and tarnished from heavy use. Because the wife is, according to the speaker, made from her husband's "favorite" marbles, she has likely suffered wear and tear over the years. So while she is, in the speaker's own words, "exquisite," she is not without her scuff marks.

As the preceding example demonstrates, the speaker describes the wife as weathered and overused in a series of images, and Sexton builds this paradox when she uses the metaphor, "Fireworks in the dull middle of February" (7). To begin, fireworks are colorful, explosive, and exciting, and they are usually associated with celebrations such as July Fourth, New Year's, and Mardi Gras. They are not normally affiliated with February because, with the exception of Valentine's Day, which is traditionally a lover's holiday, nothing exciting happens. The portrayal of the wife as beautiful and vibrant in the middle of this dead, frigid month suggests that she retains her erotic attraction for her husband. She adds bursts of bright color to a humdrum existence. At the same time, however, this metaphor of fireworks implies that she does not present this side of herself often. As lovely as they are, fireworks do not last long—just moments, really—and the occasions on which we use them are sprinkled sparsely throughout the year. So perhaps the wife only makes her vivacious nature known on special occasions (like Valentine's Day, for example) and for short periods of time. The point is that she is not like this every day, which could be the reason for her husband's wandering. He looks outside of his marriage for the excitement it lacks. But the speaker quickly reminds him that excitement is rare and precious in a relationship that runs deeper than just the occasional affair, and that even their relationship will lose its luster over time.

In the third stanza of the poem, the speaker uses specific images to illustrate her argument. She compares herself to a "bright red sloop in the harbor" (10), to "smoke from the car window" (11), and to "Littleneck clams out of season" (12). These images capture transient pleasures. The sloop is a shiny new toy; like the wife, it is a childhood dream realized. But unlike the wife and the marbles that represent her, it is free to set sail at any time. It implies that the speaker is available for playtime, but, because she has nothing concrete that keeps her tethered to her lover—like the wedding band that his wife owns—she remains out of his reach. She argues here that she is just momentary, as elusive as a dream and intangible as "smoke [rising] from the car window" (11). Both lack substance, as they can be seen but not touched. The third image, the littleneck clams, represents a rare delicacy that can be enjoyed only once in a while. This metaphor draws a parallel between the speaker and the wife, because it is similar to the fireworks in the second stanza. It suggests that the two women are not as distinct as the lover may want to believe. While she is bright red and dazzling for now, the speaker essentially states that she will not always be that way. She could very well become the wife in later years, a sobering reality that she urges her lover to consider.

The next three stanzas depict the wife with more concrete images than are used for the speaker and, from the speaker's point of view, make her more attractive. To begin, the speaker compliments the wife for being the lover's "have to have" (13), someone who "has grown [him his] practical [his] tropical growth" (14). We encounter another paradox in this line, as it dually depicts the wife as blasé (practical) and colorful (tropical). In addition, by saying that the wife is the lover's "have to have," the speaker implies that he needs his spouse, both for her practical nature and for her rare playful side.

The speaker then builds on the poem's nautical imagery by describing the wife's attention to the family's boat: "She sees to the oars and oarlocks for the dinghy" (16). Unlike the above-mentioned sailboat, which carries romantic connotations, the dinghy is not nearly as glamorous. It is a lifeboat, something practical and plain. While it is not as polished as the bright red sloop, which is used for travel and recreation, the dinghy is vital if that sailboat sinks. It saves lives. In the same way, the wife is a vital part of her husband's existence. She sees to the oarlocks and oars, which suggests that she steers his life in the right direction and she keeps everything on an even keel. The speaker calls her the lover's "have to have" (13) because she keeps him from sinking. Even if his current relationship with the speaker founders, he will prosper, because he has something solid to hold onto, to keep him anchored down. The speaker, by contrast, is fickle. She could sink out from under him at any time and leave him to drown. Nothing concrete keeps them together.

The speaker then lists several good and practical accomplishments the wife has brought to the marriage, particularly that she remains with him always, as the next three lines signify. She "has placed wild flowers at the window at breakfast, / sat by the potter's wheel at midday, / set forth three children under the moon" (18–20). Essentially, she has been at her husband's side morning, noon, and night, keeping the boat afloat, making life more colorful by decorating it with flowers and adding the practical fixtures to it—the cups, bowls and saucers. Most importantly—or it seems that way because the speaker discusses this point for two stanzas—she has given him children, three perfect angels, works of art "drawn by Michelangelo" (20). Diana Hume George states that "the mother is the primary symbol of feminine bodiliness in Sexton's poetry" (59), and with this image of maternal fecundity and art, Sexton emphasizes the mother's presence over the lover's ephemerality, despite, paradoxically, that she is so difficult to visualize.

The speaker focuses on the couple's children, paying attention to their needs in the midst of this love affair that threatens their family. In fact, she seems more concerned about them than her lover is, and she urges him to notice them. "If you glance up," she says, "the children are there / like delicate balloons resting on the ceiling" (23–24). The phrase "delicate balloons" indicate that they are fragile, and that they are resting on the ceiling suggests that, while their father is with the speaker, the children remain out of his reach. She warns that if he leaves his wife to pursue a permanent relationship with her, he could damage his delicate children and miss out on their upbringing. For their sake more than anything, the speaker advocates for the wife. Her priorities are apparent because, immediately after mentioning the children, she returns her lover's heart and spends the next three stanzas giving him permission to go back to his spouse.

The concluding stanzas of the poem reiterate the speaker's original argument that the wife "is all there" (1) while she, the "luxury" (10), is only a temporary pleasure. Her words are simple and blunt:

> She is so naked and singular.
> She is the sum of yourself and your dream.
> Climb her like a monument, step after step.
> She is solid.
> As for me, I am watercolor.
> I wash off.
>
> (43–48)

These last two images powerfully contrast with each other. A monument and a watercolor are both works of art, but while a monument can be climbed as well as admired at a distance, a watercolor can only be looked at, not touched. In addition, watercolor as a medium is almost transparent. Like the smoke in an earlier stanza, the paint lacks any tangible substance. By using this metaphor to describe herself, the speaker tells her lover that she is nothing, while his wife, by contrast, is everything. In short, she's saying, "You'll get over me, but you can't live without her." This last couplet emphasizes her argument with emotion, giving the lover no room to respond. He will return to his reliable dinghy and row back to the solid shore while she will set sail for the horizon.

Works Cited

George, Diana Hume. *Oedipus Anne: The Poetry of Anne Sexton*. Urbana: U of Illinois P, 1987. Print.

Sexton, Anne. "To My Lover, Returning to His Wife." *Love Poems*. Boston: Houghton Mifflin Company, 1967. 21–22. Print.

Note the ways in which the author improved various aspects of the already strong draft. The thesis is more clearly defined, and some questions about the interpretations are resolved. The author restructured some supporting paragraphs to move through her ideas more smoothly. Also, the incorporation of a secondary source allows the author to engage more deeply in critical conversations about Sexton's work. Rather than merely correcting a few small writing errors, the author deepened the analysis in key ways, resulting in an essay that more richly plumbs the symbolic meaning of Sexton's poem.

All essayists must concede that no piece of writing ever achieves perfection, but the dignity of the process lies in the aspiration to the unattainable. Surely even the greatest masterpieces of English literature—Chaucer's *The Canterbury Tales*, Milton's *Paradise Lost*—could be improved further, for the infinite range of the English language can never be tamed into a single perfect expression. Through editing and revising, writers aim for a mark of perfection that, ever missed, keeps them improving throughout their careers.

Tips for Self-Editing and Improving Academic Prose

Editing one's prose challenges even the best writers. In effect, writers must learn to read their prose as if they were not the authors so that they can process the words as their readers do. Becoming a proficient editor of one's writing is truly a lifelong endeavor, as even the best prose can be reformulated to express the writer's ideas more cleanly and clearly. Furthermore, the various genres of writing require different styles. Students taking courses in literary studies, creative writing, and technical writing—related yet distinct fields all likely to be hosted by a department of English—need to develop appropriate voices and styles for their various courses.

For writers of research essays, clarity of expression should stand as their primary goal when editing their prose. As William Strunk eloquently affirms in his masterpiece of writing instruction, *The Elements of Style*:

> Vigorous writing is concise. A sentence should contain no unnecessary words, a paragraph no unnecessary sentences, for the same reason that a drawing should have no unnecessary lines and a machine no unnecessary parts. This requires not that the writer make all sentences short or avoid all detail and treat subjects only in outline, but that every word tell.
>
> (Strunk and White xv–xvi)

Strunk's memorable exhortation recognizes that writing must communicate with clarity, concision, and precision. If every word must "tell," as he advocates, words that restate ideas unnecessarily or otherwise clutter sentences with irrelevancies must be edited.

Learning to hear every word "tell," rather than blather, requires keen attention to the precise objective of each sentence. Foremost, novice writers frequently dress up their prose with extraneous phrasings. In the following sentence, the author uses excessive verbiage to convey a simple idea:

In Shakespeare's *Taming of the Shrew*, Kate is further presented as a woman that readers will perceive as short-tempered.

Surely readers do not need to be told that Kate is a female character. Likewise, the phrase "readers will perceive" unnecessarily states an obvious idea. Consequently, this writer would benefit from analyzing the objective of this sentence, for the idea can be expressed more economically as:

In *Taming of the Shrew*, Shakespeare depicts Kate as short-tempered.

Even better, the writer could employ this initial observation about Kate to develop an insight about how the character functions in the play:

In Shakespeare's *Taming of the Shrew*, short-tempered Kate catalyzes the narrative's consideration of unruly women and their tempestuous relationships with men, who ostensibly represent culture and civilization.

Of these examples, the first dallies about in declaring its point, whereas the second condenses the same idea into a tighter phrasing. The third example, the longest of the three, demonstrates that brevity need not be a goal unto itself as much as the expression of a complete and compelling idea. In Strunk's formulation, each word "tells" in the second and third examples, whereas too many words unnecessarily sabotage the first.

Adjectives and adverbs paint pictures in words for readers, and thus they serve an essential function in much creative writing. For analytical essays, however, adjectives and adverbs often distract from the prose's clarity. Consequently, writers should delete adjectives and adverbs that do not contribute meaningfully to their arguments. Consider the following sentence:

Many adaptations of Dickens' novels rewrite his storylines so extensively that the films alter a lot of his original themes and completely change his characters.

The modifiers "a lot of," "original," and "completely" litter the writer's sentences without strengthening the ideas expressed. They also invite readers to ponder the accuracy of the writer's statements. The word *original*, which modifies *themes*, tacitly, and likely unintentionally, suggests that Dickens himself changed many of his themes, for one might assume that these original themes gave way to revised ones in his later drafts. Also, most readers would likely agree with the writer's assertion that cinematic depictions of Dickens's novels change his characters, but do they do so *completely*? Is the character Oliver Twist unrecognizable as Dickens's creation in his film incarnations? The original sentence could be streamlined as such, while also speaking with greater clarity and accuracy:

Many adaptations of Dickens' novels rewrite his storylines so extensively that the films alter his themes and change his characters.

Seemingly innocuous adverbs and adjectives can derail an otherwise persuasive argument when they render a convincing claim untrue.

Concise writing also eschews the passive voice. In active sentences, the subjects perform the action expressed by the verb; in passive sentences, the subject receives the verb's action.

ACTIVE: Quentin Crisp wrote *The Naked Civil Servant*.

PASSIVE: *The Naked Civil Servant* was written by Quentin Crisp.

The active voice construction requires seven words to express this idea, whereas the passive voice construction requires nine. True, this difference of two words may appear insignificant, but such prolixity accumulates noticeably over an entire essay. Indeed, a profusion of passive constructions slows down readers and overcomplicates simple ideas:

PASSIVE: *The Naked Civil Servant* <u>was written</u> by Quentin Crisp, and in it the story <u>is told</u> of how he came out of the closet as a gay man in 1931, when homosexuality <u>was still frowned upon</u> in polite society. (39 words)

Rewriting this sentence in the active voice, and reconfiguring some phrases, allows it to communicate these ideas more directly:

ACTIVE: Quentin Crisp's *The Naked Civil Servant* tells of his coming out of the closet as a gay man in 1931, when polite society still frowned on homosexuality. (27 words)

While the two-word difference between the active and passive voice in the previous example may appear piddling, this example demonstrates how passive constructions accumulate and clog up the clear expression of a writer's ideas.

Excellent writers also understand the importance of an appropriate tone for each piece of writing they undertake. To begin developing an ear for prose, assess the resonance and tenor of words. For instance, the following passage is written in grammatically acceptable English, but it lacks any sort of mellifluousness:

Some words are bad. They say what you want them to say, but they do not say that thing clearly. There is a problem with these words, being that they are unclear.

The same idea can be expressed more economically:

Some words hinder a person's ability to communicate clearly because they create ambiguity in phrasing.

The second passage expresses the same idea as the first passage, but it does so with an apt tone and vocabulary for its message. The first passage reads as if it were spoken English, whereas the second passage captures the same message with a less conversational tone and a more precise vocabulary.

While learning to write well requires diligence with no expectation of shortcuts, weaning oneself from certain crutch words will produce noticeable and ready improvements. Some words tend to degrade the tone of a writer's prose, for they sound more of conversational phrasings than of academic diction. When necessary, restate phrases employing these words: *being*; *I*, *we*, and *you*; *is*, *are*, *was*, *were*, *there is*, and *there are*; *has* and *have*; *seems to* and *serves to*; *thing* and *something*; *this* (as a pronoun); *what*; and any contractions. Certainly, on many occasions these words are essential for communicating one's ideas clearly, but they undermine excellent prose when used excessively and without concern for their potential liabilities. The following precepts are not rules to be followed blindly but strategies to be deployed effectively.

Being

The word "being" only rarely communicates an idea other than an entity's existence. Frequently superfluous to the ideas expressed in a sentence, it can be easily removed.

> EXAMPLE: In John Steinbeck's *Of Mice and Men*, George, being ambitious, wants to buy his own farm, but his friendship with Lennie ultimately makes this dream unachievable.

> IMPROVED: In John Steinbeck's *Of Mice and Men*, George strives to buy his own farm, but his friendship with Lennie ultimately makes this dream unachievable.

In this example, the verb *strives* conveys George's ambitions, rendering the phrase "being ambitious" unnecessary. When tempted to use *being*, writers should seek a more active phrasing to convey their thoughts.

I, We, and You

Academic writing eschews first-person pronouns (*I* and *we*) and second-person pronouns (*you*, both singular and plural). As evident from daily speech, oral communication relies on these words for virtually every human encounter, but written speech differs from speech in key ways, and pronoun usage serves as one such example. For the most part, the pronouns *I* and *we* do not contribute meaningfully to academic writing. Readers understand that, because authors' names are printed at the beginning of their essays, they relay their authors' opinions and assessments.

EXAMPLE: <u>I believe that</u> George Bernard Shaw's depiction of prostitution in *Mrs. Warren's Profession*, while considered frank and shocking to its contemporary audiences, sugarcoats the lives of prostitutes in Victorian England.

IMPROVED: George Bernard Shaw's depiction of prostitution in *Mrs. Warren's Profession*, while considered frank and shocking to its contemporary audiences, sugarcoats the lives of prostitutes in Victorian England.

In a complementary fashion, the pronoun *you* is unnecessary because readers understand that they are interpreting the author's words. Also, when authors tell *you* how *you* should respond to their argument, the prose often feels coercive.

EXAMPLE: Nathaniel Hawthorne reveals Arthur Dimmesdale's secret at the conclusion of *The Scarlet Letter*, which shocks you.

IMPROVED: Nathaniel Hawthorne reveals Arthur Dimmesdale's secret in the shocking conclusion of *The Scarlet Letter*.

Before writing *I*, *we*, and *you*, consider the rhetorical situation at hand and how it differs from conversational English. Writers should only use *I* when it is necessary to highlight their role in penning the text, or to signal that they are moving from an objective analysis to their subjective viewpoints. Also, unless writing with a coauthor, essayists should avoid the pompous affectation of a royal *we*. Carefully consider any use of *you*, and only use it if it is necessary to interject readers into the argument.

Is, Are, Was, Were, There Is, There Are

Rita Mae Brown expresses her distaste for *to be* verbs with passion, acumen, and spunk: "If you want to get your black belt in boredom, load your sentences with variations of the verb *to be*. Granted, sometimes you can't help using them, especially with nonfiction, but at every opportunity knock out *is*, *are*, *was*, etc., and insert something hot" (67). So overused that it communicates little, the word *is* undermines the potential of a writer's prose. Moreover, removing it often encourages writers to state their ideas more concisely.

EXAMPLE: Alan Moore's <u>*The Watchmen* is a graphic novel that plays</u> with multiple levels of narration.

IMPROVED: Alan Moore's <u>graphic novel *The Watchmen* plays</u> with multiple levels of narration.

A corollary benefit of reducing the use of *to be* verbs in one's writing emerges when one rephrases all sentences beginning with *There is* or *There are*. This fluffy construction points out little more than an entity's existence; consequently, it ineffectively builds a writer's ideas.

> EXAMPLE: <u>There is a school of scholars</u> arguing that Shakespeare did not write his plays, and some believe that they were penned by Christopher Marlowe, Francis Bacon, or Edward de Vere.

> IMPROVED: <u>A school of scholars</u> argues that Shakespeare did not write his plays, and some believe that they were penned by Christopher Marlowe, Francis Bacon, or Edward de Vere.

Some ideas must be expressed with an *is*, but limiting oneself to as few as possible in an essay, or editing half of them out of an essay's early drafts, results in livelier prose.

Has, Have

Much like *is* and other forms of *to be*, *has* suffers from such overuse as to convey little meaning other than a general sense of possession or ownership, even when such possession can only be construed in an abstract sense. Opt for a stronger verb to give readers a clearer sense of action.

> EXAMPLE: In many film adaptations of the New Testament gospels, <u>Jesus has an interior conflict</u> with his divine mission—more so than in the gospel accounts, in which <u>he has a deeper understanding</u> of his role.

> IMPROVED: In many film adaptations of the New Testament gospels, <u>Jesus experiences an interior conflict</u> with his divine mission—more so than in the gospel accounts, in which <u>he better understands</u> his role.

This small change results in a stronger sentence, for clean and precise verbs more accurately convey the writer's meaning to readers.

Seems To, Serves To

Does an entity exist if it *seems to* exist? Is an action accomplished if something *serves to* achieve this end? Rarely do these constructions convey meaningful messages to readers, as in the following example:

> EXAMPLE: In Ernest Hemingway's *The Old Man and the Sea*, the fisherman Santiago <u>seems to/serves to represent</u> a Christ figure in the novel's final scenes, as he carries the mast of his boat home.

> IMPROVED: In Ernest Hemingway's *The Old Man and the Sea*, the fisherman Santiago <u>represents</u> a Christ figure in the novel's final scenes, as he carries the mast of his boat home.

Either Santiago represents a Christ figure or he does not. Waffling about with a *seems to/serves to* construction muddies the writer's meaning.

Thing, Something

Because virtually any concrete noun—and many abstract nouns as well—can be referred to as a *thing* or a *something*, these words more often obscure than clarify a writer's meaning. When writers choose words to convey their ideas, they should select specific terms rather than general ones. Few words convey less specificity in meaning than *thing*.

> EXAMPLE: Louise Erdrich discusses these <u>things</u> in her novels, beginning with *Love Medicine*.

> IMPROVED: Louise Erdrich discusses these <u>themes</u> in her novels, beginning with *Love Medicine*.

Also, *things* is often used redundantly to restate ideas already expressed:

> EXAMPLE: <u>These questions are things</u> that the characters of Wilkie Collins's *Armadale* fail to address as the mystery unfolds.

> IMPROVED: The characters of Wilkie Collins's *Armadale* fail to address <u>these questions</u> as the mystery unfolds.

Replace *thing* or a *something* with a word that better communicates the entity that is discussed.

This (as a Pronoun)

Writers should use "this" in their essays only when a noun immediately follows it. When a noun does not follow "this," readers often find themselves confused by the writer's assumption that they will understand what "this" signifies.

> EXAMPLE: Susanna Clarke's *Jonathan Strange and Mr. Norrell* obscures <u>this</u>, thus asking her readers to determine the line between magic and morality for each of them.

> IMPROVED: Susanna Clarke's *Jonathan Strange and Mr. Norrell* obscures <u>her characters' motivations</u>, thus asking her readers to determine the line between magic and morality for each of them.

Also, much like the empty phrase *there is*, *this is* ineffectually advances a writer's ideas.

> EXAMPLE: <u>This is the pivotal moment</u> of Chaucer's *Book of the Duchess*, when the narrator realizes that the Man in Black's beloved has died.

IMPROVED: <u>At this pivotal moment</u> of Chaucer's *Book of the Duchess*, the narrator realizes that the Man in Black's beloved has died.

Again, attuning oneself to words such as *this* does not necessitate that one never use them, but simply that one use them mindfully so that they do not obfuscate the idea expressed.

What

Because *what* is primarily used as an interrogative pronoun in questions, removing it from sentences often results in clearer and more succinct phrasings.

> EXAMPLE: <u>What *Jane Eyre* asks readers to consider</u> is the limits to female agency in Victorian England.

> IMPROVED: <u>*Jane Eyre* asks readers to consider</u> the limits to female agency in Victorian England.

Another reason to avoid *what* in academic writing is that it often introduces rhetorical questions. In academic essays, however, writers bear the responsibility to put forth interpretations of texts, not to query their readers on their opinions.

> EXAMPLE: What is Bertha Mason's motive for burning down Rochester's manor?

> IMPROVED: While readers may assume Bertha Mason burns down Rochester's manor due to her insanity, Brontë subtly suggests a reason behind this apparent act of madness.

Moreover, rhetorical questions often give the appearance that writers have not sufficiently thought through their ideas, that they are developing the argument as they write rather than constructing it with an overarching view of its points. For these reasons, be wary of *what*.

Any Contractions

More appropriate for conversations than for writing, contractions carry a light and informal tone. Thus, rewriting them into their standard forms raises the tenor of one's writing. This precept of academic writing, while somewhat old-fashioned, reminds writers to seek a precise diction in their prose, and so it is worth pondering the benefits and liabilities of employing contractions in an essay.

> EXAMPLE: Art Spiegelman's graphic novel *Maus* rewrites the story of the Holocaust from the perspective of mice, but some readers <u>don't approve</u> of recasting this horrific human tragedy as a beast fable.

IMPROVED: Art Spiegelman's graphic novel *Maus* rewrites the story of the Holocaust from the perspective of mice, but some readers <u>do not approve</u> of recasting this horrific human tragedy as a beast fable.

Writing out contractions into standard English requires little work beyond an eye for detail and steady attention to one's phrasings.

Before submitting an essay for review, writers should use the search function of their word processors to locate these various words and phrases, and they should consider editing sentences in which they appear, in order to express their ideas more clearly and precisely. At the same time, one must recognize that guidelines for writing well should not be mistaken for laws. George Orwell, in his influential essay "Politics and the English Language," concludes with the admonition, "Break any of these rules sooner than say anything outright barbarous" (966). We heartily agree with this advice, and our readers will find that, on occasion and as necessary, we have excused ourselves from these precepts throughout this book. Still, we did so knowingly, after multiple rounds of revision, during which we determined that some sentences would communicate their ideas more clearly with an *is*, or with one or two modifiers more than absolutely essential to convey a point, or through a passive construction, or, as in this sentence, with the pronoun *we*. The preceding suggestions can improve the rhythm, flow, and clarity of a writer's prose, but they must be used judiciously, and no guideline can substitute for developing one's own ear for expression.

To this end, writers must always keep reading, for only by reading will they enhance their sensitivity to and appreciation for pitch-perfect phrasing and well-turned constructions. By voraciously reading literature and scholarly essays, by paying attention to how authors craft their sentences and move from one idea to the next, and by noticing how they explain the miniscule details of their overarching themes and arguments, readers develop a mental storehouse of styles and techniques that they can adapt to their own purposes. One hopes that, in choosing to study literature, students are following a passionate interest in the subject and that reading others' writing, both literary and analytical, offers them one of the greatest pleasures in their lives. A pleasure, indeed, yet writing is also a challenging task: it is difficult to do, and more difficult to do well. Words dance about in writers' heads, yet the right ones hold back. Ideas coalesce and then dissolve, and only by continually rebuilding and reorganizing will the structure hold. Still, when writing captures one's ideas fluently and elegantly, few pleasures offer greater rewards.

Works Cited

Achebe, Chinua. *Things Fall Apart*. 1958. New York: Anchor-Doubleday, 1994. Print.

Addison, Joseph. *Essays in Criticism and Literary Theory*. Ed. John Loftis. Northbrook, Illinois: AHM, 1975. Print.

Addison, Joseph, and Sir Richard Steele. *The Spectator*. Ed. Gregory Smith. London: Dent, 1964. Print.

Albee, Edward. *The Collected Plays of Edward Albee, 1958–1965*. New York: Overlook Duckworth, 2004. Print.

Allende, Isabel. *The House of the Spirits*. 1982. Trans. Magda Bogin. Toronto: Bantam, 1986. Print.

Althusser, Louis. *"Lenin and Philosophy" and Other Essays*. Trans. Ben Brewster. London: NLB, 1971. Print.

Altman, Rick. *The American Film Musical*. Bloomington: Indiana UP, 1987. Print.

Arberry, A. J., ed. *Persian Poems: An Anthology of Verse Translations*. London: Everyman's Library-Dent, 1964. Print.

Aristotle. *The "Art" of Rhetoric*. Ed. and trans. John Henry Freese. Cambridge: Harvard UP, 1982. Print.

——. *Poetics*. Trans. S. H. Butcher. Intro. Francis Fergusson. New York: Hill & Wang, 1961. Print.

Arnold, Matthew. *Culture and Anarchy*. Ed. R. H. Super. 1868. Ann Arbor: U of Michigan P, 1965. Print.

——. *Matthew Arnold*. Ed. Miriam Allott and Robert Super. Oxford: Oxford UP, 1986. Print.

——. "The Study of Poetry." *Essays in Criticism*. London: Macmillan, 1888. 1–55. Print.

Auden, W. H. *Collected Poems*. Ed. Edward Mendelson. New York: Random House, 1976. Print.

Auden, W. H., and John Garrett, eds. *The Poet's Tongue*. 1935. London: Bell & Sons, 1971. Print.

Austen, Jane. "Letter to James Edward Austen, 16 Dec. 1816." *Jane Austen's Letters*. Ed. Deirdre Le Faye. 3rd ed. Oxford: Oxford UP, 1995. 323. Print.

——. *Pride and Prejudice*. Ed. Pat Rogers. 1813. Cambridge: Cambridge UP, 2006. Print.

Auster, Paul. *Leviathan*. New York: Penguin, 1992. Print.

Bakhtin, Mikhail. *The Dialogic Imagination: Four Essays*. Trans. Caryl Emerson and Michael Holquist. Austin: U of Texas P, 1981. Print.

Baraka, Amiri. *Selected Poetry of Amiri Baraka/LeRoi Jones*. New York: William Morrow, 1979. Print.

Barnes, Julian. *A History of the World in 10½ Chapters*. New York: Vintage-Random, 1989. Print.

Barth, John. *Lost in the Funhouse: Fiction for Print, Tape, Live Voice*. New York: Anchor-Random, 1988. Print.

Barthelme, Donald. *Sixty Stories*. New York: Putnam's, 1981. Print.

——. *Snow White*. New York: Scribner, 1967. Print.

Barthes, Roland. *Image, Music, Text*. Trans. Stephen Heath. New York: Hill & Wang, 1977. Print.

——. *Mythologies*. Trans. Annette Lavers. New York: Noonday Press, 1989. Print.

Beauvoir, Simone de. "Introduction to *The Second Sex*." *French Feminism Reader*. Ed. Kelly Oliver. Lanham: Rowman & Littlefield, 2000. 6–20. Print.

Bede. *Baedae Historia Ecclesiastica Gentis Anglorum* [Bede's *Ecclesiastical History of the English People*]. *Historical Works*. Trans. J. E. King. 2 vols. Cambridge: Harvard UP, 1930. Print.

Behn, Aphra. *Oroonoko; or, The Royal Slave*. Ed. Catherine Gallagher. Boston: Bedford/St. Martin's, 2000. Print.

Bhabha, Homi K. "The Postcolonial and the Postmodern." *The Cultural Studies Reader*. Ed. Simon During. 2nd ed. London: Routledge, 1999. 189–208. Print.

Bishop, Elizabeth. *Poems*. New York: Farrar, Straus & Giroux, 2011. Print.

Blake, William. *The Complete Poems*. Ed. Alicia Ostriker. London: Penguin, 1988. Print.

——. *Jerusalem*. London: Trianon Press, 1952. Print.

Bloom, Harold. *The Anxiety of Influence: A Theory of Poetry*. 2nd ed. New York: Oxford UP, 1997. Print.

Borges, Jorge Luis. *Ficciones*. Trans. Anthony Bonner. New York: Grove, 1962. Print.

Boswell, James. *Life of Johnson*. Ed. R. W. Chapman. Oxford: Oxford UP, 1980. Print.

Bourdieu, Pierre. *Distinction: A Social Critique of the Judgment of Taste*. Trans. Richard Nice. Cambridge: Harvard UP, 1984. Print.

Bradford, Richard. *The Novel Now: Contemporary British Fiction*. Malden, Mass.: Blackwell, 2007. Print.

Brecht, Bertolt. *Brecht on Theatre: The Development of an Aesthetic*. Ed. and trans. John Willett. New York: Hill & Wang, 1994. Print.

——. *Mother Courage and Her Children*. Trans. Eric Bentley. New York: Grove Weidenfeld, 1966. Print.

Breton, André. *Nadja*. Trans. Richard Howard. New York: Grove; London: Evergreen, 1960. Print.

Brewster, Scott. *Lyric*. London: Routledge, 2009. Print.

Brontë, Emily. *The Poems of Emily Brontë*. Ed. Derek Roper with Edward Chitham. Oxford: Clarendon, 1995. Print.

Brooks, Cleanth, and Robert Penn Warren, eds. *Understanding Poetry*. 4th ed. 1938. Fort Worth: Harcourt Brace, 1978. Print.

Brown, Rita Mae. *Starting from Scratch: A Different Kind of Writer's Manual*. Toronto: Bantam, 1988. Print.

Browning, Elizabeth Barrett. *"Aurora Leigh" and Other Poems*. Ed. Cora Kaplan. London: Women's Press, 1977. Print.

——. *Selected Poems*. Ed. Margaret Forster. Baltimore: Johns Hopkins UP, 1988. Print.

Burke, Seán. *The Death and Return of the Author: Criticism and Subjectivity in Barthes, Foucault, and Derrida*. 2nd ed. Edinburgh: Edinburgh UP, 1998. Print.

Burns, Robert. *The Best Laid Schemes: Selected Poetry and Prose of Robert Burns*. Ed. Robert Crawford and Christopher MacLachlan. Princeton: Princeton UP, 2009. Print.

Butler, Judith. *Gender Trouble: Feminism and the Subversion of Identity*. New York: Routledge, 1990. Print.

Byrd, Craig. "Interview with John Williams." *Celluloid Symphonies: Texts and Contexts in Film Music History*. Ed. Julie Hubbert. Berkeley: U of California P, 2011. 414–22. Print.

Byron, George Gordon, Lord. *Byron: The Poetical Works*. Ed. Frederick Page. Corrected by John Jump. Oxford: Oxford UP, 1987. Print.

Calvino, Italo. *If on a Winter's Night a Traveler*. 1979. Trans. William Weaver. San Diego: Harvest-Harcourt, 1981. Print.

Campbell, Joseph. *The Hero with a Thousand Faces*. Princeton: Princeton UP, 1949. Print.

Camus, Albert. *The Stranger*. Trans. Stuart Gilbert. New York: Knopf, 1946. Print.

Capote, Truman. *"Breakfast at Tiffany's" and Three Stories*. 1958. New York: Vintage, 1993. Print.

——. *Portraits and Observations: The Essays of Truman Capote*. New York: Modern Library, 2008. Print.

Carew, Thomas. *The Poems of Thomas Carew*. Ed. Rhodes Dunlap. Oxford: Clarendon, 1964. Print.

Carretta, Vincent. "Olaudah Equiano or Gustavus Vassa? New Light on an Eighteenth-Century Question of Identity." *Slavery & Abolition: A Journal of Slave and Post-Slave Studies* 20.3 (1999): 96–105. Print.

Castiglione, Baldesar. *The Book of the Courtier*. Trans. Charles Singleton. Garden City, NY: Anchor-Doubleday, 1959. Print.

Caws, Mary Ann. *Surrealism and the Literary Imagination: A Study of Breton and Bachelard*. The Hague: Mouton, 1966. Print.

Cervantes Saavedra, Miguel de. *Don Quixote of La Mancha*. Trans. Walter Starkie. New York: Signet Classic, 1964. Print.

Chaucer, Geoffrey. *The Riverside Chaucer*. Ed. Larry Benson. 3rd ed. Boston: Houghton Mifflin, 1987. Print.

Chbosky, Stephen. *The Perks of Being a Wallflower*. New York: Gallery Books, 1999. Print.

Chekhov, Anton. *The Cherry Orchard*. Trans. Jean-Claude van Itallie. New York: Dramatists Play Service, 1995. Print.

Child, Francis James, ed. *The English and Scottish Popular Ballads*. New York: Cooper Square, 1965. Print.

Churcher, Mel. *Acting for Film: Truth 24 Times a Second*. London: Virgin, 2003. Print.

Cixous, Hélène. Excerpt from *Sorties*. *A Critical and Cultural Theory Reader*. Ed. Antony Easthope and Kate McGowan. Toronto: U of Toronto P, 1992. 146–57. Print.

Coetzee, J. M. *Waiting for the Barbarians*. New York: Penguin, 1982. Print.

Colebrook, Claire. *New Literary Histories: New Historicism and Contemporary Criticism*. Manchester: Manchester UP, 1997. Print.

Coleridge, Samuel Taylor. *Coleridge's Shakespearean Criticism*. Ed. Thomas Middleton Raysor. Cambridge: Harvard UP, 1930. Print.

——. *The Collected Works of Samuel Taylor Coleridge: Table Talk*. Ed. Kathleen Coburn. Vol. 14. Princeton: Princeton UP, 1990. Print.

——. *Samuel Taylor Coleridge*. Ed. H. J. Jackson. Oxford: Oxford UP, 1985. Print.

Columbus, Christopher. *The Journal of Christopher Columbus*. Trans. Cecil Jane. New York: Bonanza Books, 1989.

Confucius. *The Analects of Confucius*. Trans. Simon Leys. New York: Norton, 1997. Print.

Congreve, William. *The Way of the World*. Ed. Henry Ten Eyck Perry. Northbrook, Illinois: AHM Publishing, 1951. Print.

Conrad, Joseph. *The Nigger of the "Narcissus."* Ed. Robert Kimbrough. 1897. New York: Norton, 1979. Print.

Crabbe, George. *The Complete Poetical Works*. Ed. Norma Dalrymple-Champneys and Arthur Pollard. Oxford: Clarendon, 1988. Print.

Craig, Edward Gordon. *Index to the Story of My Days*. London: Hulton, 1957.

Crane, Susan. *Gender and Romance in Chaucer's "Canterbury Tales."* Princeton: Princeton UP, 1994. Print.

Crèvecoeur, J. Hector St. John de. *Letters from an American Farmer and Sketches of Eighteenth-Century America*. New York: Penguin, 1981. Print.

Croce, Benedetto. *Aesthetic as Science of Expression and General Linguistic*. Trans. Douglas Ainslie. London: Macmillan, 1922. Print.

Crystal, David. *The Cambridge Encyclopedia of the English Language*. Cambridge: Cambridge UP, 1995. Print.

Cullen, Countee. *On These I Stand: An Anthology of the Best Poems of Countee Cullen*. New York: Harper, 1947. Print.

Daiches, David. *The Novel and the Modern World*. Rev. ed. Chicago: U of Chicago P, 1984. Print.

Dante. Excerpt from *De Vulgari eloquentia*. *Medieval Literary Criticism: Translations and Interpretations*. Ed. O. B. Hardison, Alex Preminger, Kevin Kerrane, and Leon Golden. New York: Frederick Ungar, 1974. 145–86. Print.

Davis, Jessica. *Farce*. London: Methuen, 1978. Print.

de Grazia, Sebastian, ed. *Masters of Chinese Political Thought: From the Beginnings to the Han Dynasty*. New York: Viking, 1973. Print.

De Quincey, Thomas. *De Quincey's Collected Writings*. Ed. David Masson. 1890. New York: AMS, 1968. Print.

Derrida, Jacques. *Acts of Literature*. Ed. Derek Attridge. London: Routledge, 1992. Print.

Díaz, Junot. *Drown*. New York: Riverhead, 1996. Print.

Dickens, Charles. *David Copperfield*. 1850. New York: Macmillan, 1962. Print.

——. *Oliver Twist*. 1838. New York: Norton, 1993. Print.

Dickinson, Emily. *The Poems of Emily Dickinson*. Ed. Thomas H. Johnson. Cambridge: Belknap, 1979. Print.

Donne, John. *The Complete English Poems*. Ed. A. J. Smith. New York: St. Martin's, 1974. Print.

——. *Devotions upon Emergent Occasions*. Cambridge: Cambridge UP, 1923. Print.

Dostoevsky, Feodor. *Crime and Punishment*. Ed. George Gibian. Trans. Jessie Coulson. 2nd ed. New York: Norton, 1975. Print.

Douglas, Keith. *The Complete Poems*. Ed. Desmond Graham. 3rd ed. Oxford: Oxford UP, 1998.

Doyle, Arthur Conan. *A Study in Scarlet*. Ed. Owen Dudley Edwards. World's Classics. Oxford: Oxford UP, 1994. Print.

Dreiser, Theodore. "True Art Speaks Plainly." *Sister Carrie*. Ed. Donald Pizer. 1900. New York: Norton, 2006. 469–70. Print.

Dryden, John. *Dryden: A Selection*. Ed. John Conaghan. London: Methuen, 1978. Print.

——. *Poetry, Prose, and Plays*. Ed. Douglas Grant. Cambridge: Harvard UP, 1967. Print.

Dunbar, Paul Laurence. *Selected Poems*. Ed. Herbert Woodward Martin. New York: Penguin, 2004. Print.

Dyer, Richard. *Stars*. London: British Film Institute, 1998. Print.

——. *White*. London: Routledge, 1997. Print.

Edelman, Lee. *No Future: Queer Theory and the Death Drive*. Durham: Duke UP, 2004. Print.

Edson, Margaret. *Wit*. New York: Dramatists Play Service, 1999. Print.

Edwards, Jonathan. *Jonathan Edwards: Basic Writings*. Ed. Ola Elizabeth Winslow. New York: Signet Classic-New American Library, 1966. Print.

Eliot, T. S. *Collected Poems, 1909–1962*. San Diego: Harcourt Brace Jovanovich, 1963. Print.

——. "Tradition and the Individual Talent." *The Sacred Wood: Essays on Poetry and Criticism*. 1920. London: Methuen, 1967. 47–59. Print.

Elizabeth I, Queen. *Collected Works*. Ed. Leah Marcus, Janel Mueller, and Mary Beth Rose. Chicago: U of Chicago P, 2000. Print.

Elley, Derek. *The Epic Film: Myth and History*. London: Routledge & Kegan Paul, 1984. Print.

Emerson, Ralph Waldo. *Emerson: Political Writings*. Ed. Kenneth Sacks. Cambridge: Cambridge UP, 2008. Print.

——. "The Poet." *Ralph Waldo Emerson Texts*. Web. 6 Aug. 2012.

Empson, William. *Seven Types of Ambiguity*. 1936. New York: New Directions, 1966. Print.

The Epic of Gilgamesh. Trans. N. K. Sandars. Rev. ed. London: Penguin, 1972. Print.

Essed, Philomena, and David Theo Goldberg, eds. *Race Critical Theories*. Malden, Mass: Blackwell, 2002. Print.

Esslin, Martin. *The Theatre of the Absurd*. Garden City, NY: Anchor-Doubleday, 1961. Print.

Euripides. *"Medea" and Other Plays*. Trans. Philip Vellacott. London: Penguin, 1963. Print.

Fern, Fanny. *"Ruth Hall" and Other Writings*. Ed. Joyce Warren. New Brunswick: Rutgers UP, 1986. Print.

Fielding, Henry. *Joseph Andrews*. Ed. Martin Battestin. Middletown, Conn.: Wesleyan UP, 1967. Print.

Finch, Anne, Countess of Winchilsea. *Selected Poems of Anne Finch, Countess of Winchilsea*. Ed. Katharine Rogers. New York: Frederick Ungar, 1979. Print.

Fish, Stanley. *Surprised by Sin: The Reader in "Paradise Lost."* London: Macmillan, 1967. Print.

Fitzgerald, F. Scott. *The Great Gatsby*. 1925. New York: Scribner's, 1953. Print.

Ford, Patrick, trans. *"The Mabinogi" and Other Medieval Welsh Tales*. Berkeley: U of California P, 1977. Print.

Forster, E. M. *Aspects of the Novel*. 1927. San Diego: Harvest-Harcourt, 1955. Print.

——. *Howards End*. Ed. Paul B. Armstrong. New York: Norton, 1998. Print.

Foucault, Michel. *The History of Sexuality, Vol 1*. Trans. Robert Hurley. 1978. New York: Vintage, 1990. Print.

Franklin, Benjamin [Richard Saunders]. *Poor Richard, 1935. An Almanack For the Year of Christ 1935. The Papers of Benjamin Franklin*. Vol. 2. Ed. Leonard W. Labaree. New Haven: Yale UP, 1960. 3–12. Print.

French, Warren, ed. *The South on Film*. Jackson: UP of Mississippi, 1981. Print.

Freud, Sigmund. *Civilization and Its Discontents*. Trans. James Strachey. New York: Norton, 1989. Print.

Freytag, Gustav. *Technique of the Drama: An Exposition of Dramatic Composition and Art*. Trans. Elias J. MacEwan. 2nd ed. 1863. Chicago: Griggs, 1896. Print.

Frost, Robert. *Complete Poems of Robert Frost, 1949*. New York: Henry Holt, 1949. Print.

Frye, Northrop. *Anatomy of Criticism: Four Essays*. 1957. Princeton: Oxford UP, 1990. Print.

——. "Approaching the Lyric." *Lyric Poetry: Beyond New Criticism*. Ed. Chaviva Hosek and Patricia Parker. Ithaca: Cornell UP, 1985. 31–37. Print.

García Márquez, Gabriel. *Love in the Time of Cholera*. Trans. Edith Grossman. 1985. New York: Knopf, 1989. Print.

——. *One Hundred Years of Solitude*. 1967. Trans. Gregory Rabassa. New York: Avon, 1971. Print.

Gates, Jr., Henry Louis. *Loose Canons: Notes on the Culture Wars*. Oxford: Oxford UP, 1992. Print.

Gaunt, Simon. *Gender and Genre in Medieval French Literature*. Cambridge: Cambridge UP, 1995. Print.

Gay, John. *"The Beggar's Opera" and Companion Pieces*. Ed. C. F. Burgess. Northbrook, Illinois: AHM Publishing, 1966. Print.

George, Diana Hume. *Oedipus Anne: The Poetry of Anne Sexton*. Urbana: U of Illinois P, 1987. Print.

Gilman, Charlotte Perkins. *"The Yellow Wall-Paper" and Other Stories*. Ed. Robert Shulman. Oxford: Oxford UP, 1995. Print.

Ginsberg, Allen. *"Howl" and Other Poems*. San Francisco: City Lights Books, 1959. Print.

Gogol, Nikolai. *"The Overcoat" and Other Tales of Good and Evil*. Trans. David Magarshack. New York: Norton, 1957. Print.

Gordon, Karen Elizabeth. *The Deluxe Transitive Vampire: The Ultimate Handbook of Grammar for the Innocent, the Eager, and the Doomed*. New York: Pantheon, 1993. Print.

Gramsci, Antonio. *Further Selections from the Prison Notebooks*. Ed. and trans. Derek Boothman. Minneapolis: U of Minnesota P, 1995. Print.

——. *Selections from Cultural Writings*. Ed. David Forgacs and Geoffrey Nowell-Smith. Trans. William Boelhower. Cambridge: Harvard UP, 1985. Print.

Grant, Barry Keith. *The Hollywood Film Musical*. Malden, Mass.: Wiley-Blackwell, 2012. Print.

Gray, Richard. *A Brief History of American Literature*. West Sussex: Wiley-Blackwell, 2011. Print.

Gray, Thomas. *The Complete Poems of Thomas Gray*. Ed. H. W. Starr and J. R. Hendrickson. Oxford: Clarendon, 1966. Print.

Greenblatt, Stephen. *Renaissance Self-Fashioning: From More to Shakespeare*. 1980. Chicago: U of Chicago P, 2005. Print.

Grindon, Leger. *The Hollywood Romantic Comedy: Conventions, History, Controversies*. Malden, Mass.: Wiley-Blackwell, 2011. Print.

Hall, Stuart. "Race, Articulation, and Societies Structured in Dominance." Essed and Goldberg 38–68.

Hardy, Thomas. *Selected Poems of Thomas Hardy*. Ed. John Crowe Ransom. New York: Collier, 1961. Print.

Hawthorne, Nathaniel. *The House of the Seven Gables*. Columbus: Ohio State UP, 1965. Print.

——. *Nathaniel Hawthorne's Tales*. Ed. James McIntosh. New York: Norton, 2013. Print.

Heaney, Seamus. *Opened Ground: Selected Poems, 1966–1996*. New York: Farrar, Straus, & Giroux, 1998. Print.

Heath-Stubbs, John. *The Ode*. Oxford: Oxford UP, 1969. Print.

Heinlein, Robert A. "Science Fiction: Its Nature, Faults and Virtues." *The Science Fiction Novel: Imagination and Social Criticism*. Ed. Basil Davenport. Chicago: Advent Publishers, 1959. 14–48. Print.

Hellman, Lillian. *Six Plays*. New York: Modern Library, 1960. Print.

Herbert, George. *George Herbert: Verse and Prose*. Great Britain: SPCK, 2002. Print.

Herrick, Robert. *The Complete Poetry of Robert Herrick*. Ed. J. Max Patrick. New York: Norton, 1968. Print.

Hesiod. *Works of Hesiod and the Homeric Hymns*. Trans. Daryl Hine. Chicago: U of Chicago P, 2005. Print.

Hijuelos, Oscar. *The Mambo Kings Play Songs of Love*. New York: Farrar, Straus, & Giroux, 1989. Print.

Hirst, David. *Comedy of Manners*. London: Methuen, 1979. Print.

Hoggart, Richard. *The Use of Literacy: Changing Patterns in English Mass Culture*. 1957. Boston: Beacon, 1966. Print.

Homer. *The Iliad*. Trans. Richard Lattimore. Chicago: U of Chicago P, 1961. Print.

Hopkins, Gerard Manley. *Gerard Manley Hopkins*. Ed. Catherine Phillips. Oxford: Oxford UP, 1986. Print.

Hughes, Langston. *Selected Poems of Langston Hughes*. New York: Vintage-Random, 1974. Print.

Hughes, Ted. *New Selected Poems*. New York: Harper & Row, 1982. Print.

Huhndorf, Shari. *Going Native: Indians in the American Cultural Imagination*. Ithaca, NY: Cornell UP, 2001. Print.

Hulme, T. E. *The Collected Writings of T. E. Hulme*. Ed. Karen Csengeri. Oxford: Clarendon, 1994. Print.

Ibsen, Henrik. *"Hedda Gabler" and Other Plays*. Trans. Una Ellis-Fermor. Harmondsworth, Eng.: Penguin, 1980. Print.

I Ching: Book of Changes. Trans. James Legge. New York: Causeway Books, 1973. Print.

Ishiguro, Kazuo. *The Remains of the Day*. 1989. New York: Knopf, 1993. Print.

James, Henry. *The Turn of the Screw*. 1898. New York: Modern Library, 1930. Print.

Jameson, Frederic. *The Political Unconscious: Narrative as a Socially Symbolic Act*. Ithaca: Cornell UP, 1981. Print.

Johnson, Robert K. *Neil Simon*. Boston: Twayne, 1983. Print.

Johnson, Samuel. *Samuel Johnson*. Ed. Donald Greene. Oxford: Oxford UP, 1984. Print.

Jonson, Ben. *The Complete Poetry of Ben Jonson*. Ed. William B. Hunter. New York: New York UP, 1963. Print.

——. *Timber, or Discoveries*. Ed. Ralph S. Walker. Westport, Conn.: Greenwood, 1976. Print.

Joyce, James. *A Portrait of the Artist as a Young Man*. 1916. New York: Penguin, 1964. Print.

Julian of Norwich. *Showings*. Trans. Edmund Colledge and James Walsh. Mahwah, NJ: Paulist Press, 1978. Print.

Kafka, Franz. *The Metamorphosis*. Trans. and ed. Stanley Corngold. New York: Norton, 1996. Print.

Keats, John. *John Keats*. Ed. Elizabeth Cook. Oxford: Oxford UP, 1990. Print.

Kelly, Brigit Pegeen. *Song*. Brockport, NY: BOA Editions, 1995. Print.

Kempe, Margery. *The Book of Margery Kempe*. Ed. Sanford Brown Meech. London: Early English Text Society, 1997. Print.

Khayyam, Omar. *The Ruba'iyat*. Trans. Ahmad Saidi. Berkeley: Asian Humanities P, 1991. Print.

King, Florence. *With Charity toward None: A Fond Look at Misanthropy*. New York: St. Martin's, 1992. Print.

King, Geoff. *Film Comedy*. London: Wallflower, 2002. Print.

Kinnell, Galway. *Mortal Acts, Mortal Words*. Boston: Houghton Mifflin, 1980. Print.

Kipling, Rudyard. *The Collected Works of Rudyard Kipling*. New York: AMS Press, 1970. Print.

Klaeber, F., ed. *Beowulf*. 3rd ed. Lexington, Mass.: Heath, 1950. Print.

Knight, Stephen, and Thomas Ohlgren, eds. *Robin Hood and Other Outlaw Tales*. Kalamazoo: Medieval Institute Publications, 1997. Print.

Kushner, Tony. *Angels in America, Part I: Millennium Approaches*. New York: Theatre Communications Group, 1993. Print.

Kyd, Thomas. *The Spanish Tragedy*. Ed. Thomas W. Ross. Berkeley: U of California P, 1968. Print.

Lacan, Jacques. *The Seminar of Jacques Lacan: Book VII, The Ethics of Psychoanalysis, 1959–1960*. Ed. Jacques-Alain Miller. Trans. Dennis Porter. New York: Norton, 1992. Print.

Langland, William. *The Vision of Piers Plowman: A Critical Edition of the B-Text Based on Trinity College Cambridge MS B.15.17*. Ed. A. V. C. Schmidt. 2nd ed. London: Everyman, 1995. Print.

Lanyer, Aemelia. *The Poems of Aemilia Lanyer*. Ed. Susanne Woods. New York: Oxford UP, 1993. Print.

Lao Tsu. *Tao Te Ching*. Trans. Gia-Fu Feng and Jane English. New York: Vintage-Random, 1989. Print.

Laqueur, Thomas. *Solitary Sex: A Cultural History of Masturbation*. New York: Zone, 2003. Print.

Larkin, Philip. *Collected Poems*. Ed. Anthony Thwaite. London: Farrar, Straus & Giroux and The Marvell Press, 1999. Print.

Lawrence, D. H. *Lady Chatterley's Lover*. 1928. New York: Modern Library, 1959. Print.

Leitch, Thomas. "Twelve Fallacies in Contemporary Adaptation Theory." *Criticism* 45.2 (2003): 149–71. Print.

Lerer, Seth. *Inventing English: A Portable History of the Language.* New York: Columbia UP, 2007. Print.

Lichtenstadter, Ilse. *Introduction to Classical Arabic Literature: With Selections from Representative Works in English Translation.* New York: Twayne, 1974. Print.

Liuzza, R. M., trans. *Beowulf: A New Verse Translation.* Ontario: Broadview, 2000. Print.

Locke, John. *An Essay Concerning Human Understanding.* Ed. Peter Nidditch. Oxford: Clarendon, 1975. Print.

Longfellow, Henry Wadsworth. *Evangeline: A Tale of Acadie.* Ed. Bruce Fergusson. Halifax, N.S.: Nimbus, 1951. Print.

Lovelace, Richard. *The Poems of Richard Lovelace.* Ed. C. H. Wilkinson. Oxford: Clarendon, 1953. Print.

Lowell, Amy. *Pictures of the Floating World.* New York: Macmillan, 1919. Print.

Lyly, John. *Euphues: The Anatomy of Wit and Euphues and His England.* Ed. Leah Scragg. Manchester: Manchester UP, 2003. Print.

Macherey, Pierre. *A Theory of Literary Production.* Trans. Geoffrey Wall. 1966. London: Routledge, 2006. Print.

Machiavelli, Niccolò. *The Prince.* Ed. Quentin Skinner and Russell Price. Cambridge: Cambridge UP, 1988. Print.

MacIntyre, C. F., trans. *French Symbolist Poetry.* Berkeley: U of California P, 1958. Print.

Malory, Sir Thomas. *Le Morte D'Arthur.* Ed. and trans. R. M. Lumiansky. New York: Collier, 1982. Print.

Mann, Thomas. *Death in Venice.* Trans. and ed. Clayton Koelb. 1912. New York: Norton, 1994. Print.

Mariani, Paul. *Gerard Manley Hopkins: A Life.* New York: Viking, 2008. Print.

Marinetti, F. T. "The Founding and Manifesto of Futurism." Trans. Robert Brain, R. W. Flint, J. C. Higgitt, and Caroline Tisdall. *Documents of Twentieth-Century Art: Futurist Manifestos.* Ed. Umbro Apollonio. New York: Viking, 1973. 19–24. Rpt. in *ItalianFuturism.org.* N.d. Web. 3 Jun. 2013.

Marlowe, Christopher. *The Complete Poems and Translations.* Ed. Stephen Orgel. New York: Penguin, 2007. Print.

——. *Tamburlaine, Parts I and II, Doctor Faustus, A- and B-Texts, The Jew of Malta, Edward II.* Ed. David Bevington and Eric Rasmussen. Oxford: Clarendon, 1995. Print.

Martel, Yann. *Life of Pi.* Orlando: Harcourt-Harvest, 2001. Print.

Martin, Reginald. "The Black Arts Movement." *The Oxford Companion to Women's Writing in the United States.* Ed. Cathy Davidson and Linda Wagner-Martin. Oxford: Oxford UP, 1995. 119–22. Print.

Marvell, Andrew. *The Poems of Andrew Marvell.* Ed. Nigel Smith. Rev. ed. London: Pearson Longman, 2007. Print.

Marx, Karl, and Frederick Engels. Selections from *The German Ideology. Karl Marx: Selected Writings.* Ed. Lawrence H. Simon. Indianapolis: Hackett, 1994. 102–57. Print.

McCrum, Robert. *Globish: How the English Language Became the World's Language.* New York: Norton, 2010. Print.

McKay, Claude. *Harlem Shadows: The Poems of Claude McKay.* New York: Harcourt, 1922. Print.

Melville, Herman. *Selected Poems.* Ed. Robert Faggen. New York: Penguin, 2006. Print.

Mill, John Stuart. *On Liberty*. Ed. Stefan Collini. Cambridge: Cambridge UP, 1989. Print.

——. "What Is Poetry?" *Essays on Poetry*. Ed. Parvin Sharpless. Columbia: U of South Carolina P, 1976. 3–22. Print.

Miller, Arthur. *Death of a Salesman*. 1949. New York: Viking Press, 1968. Print.

——. "Tragedy and the Common Man." *New York Times* 27 Feb. 1949: n. pag. *New York Times*. Web. 4 Jun. 2013.

Milton, John. *Complete Shorter Poems*. Ed. Stella Revard. Malden, Mass.: Wiley-Blackwell, 2009. Print.

——. *Lycidas*. Ed. Scott Elledge. New York: Harper & Row, 1966. Print.

——. *Paradise Lost*. Ed. Barbara Lewalski. Malden, Mass.: Blackwell, 2007. Print.

Mississippi Department of Archives and History. "Black Market Tax Data, 1955–1981." *Mississippi Archives Online Catalog*. Web. 4 Dec. 2012.

Modern Language Association. *MLA Handbook for Writers of Research Papers*. 7th ed. 1977. New York: MLA, 2009. Print.

Molière. *The School for Wives*. Trans. Ranjit Bolt. London: Oberon Books, 1997. Print.

——. *Tartuffe*. Trans. Richard Wilbur. New York: Dramatists Play Service, 1991. Print.

Montaigne, Michel de. *Essays*. Trans. J. M. Cohen. London: Penguin, 1958. Print.

Moore, Clement. *Poems*. New York: Bartlett & Welford, 1844. Print.

Morrison, Toni. *Beloved*. New York: Plume-Penguin, 1987. Print.

——. "Black Matters." Essed and Goldberg 265–82.

Mulvey, Laura. *Visual and Other Pleasures*. Bloomington: Indiana UP, 1989. Print.

Newman, John Henry, Cardinal. *The Idea of a University*. Garden City, NY: Image, 1959. Print.

Newton, Isaac. *Papers and Letters on Natural Philosophy*. Ed. Bernard Cohen. 2nd ed. Cambridge: Harvard UP, 1978. Print.

Ngũgĩ wa Thiong'o. "The Language of African Literature." *Decolonising the Mind: The Politics of Language in African Literature*. London: James Currey; Nairobi: Heinemann Kenya; Portsmouth: Heinemann; Harare: Zimbabwe Publishing, 1986. 4–33. Print.

O'Connor, Flannery. *The Complete Stories*. New York: Farrar, Straus & Giroux, 1988. Print.

O'Donnell, Daniel, ed. *Caedmon's Hymn: A Multi-Media Study, Edition, and Archive*. Cambridge: Brewer, 2005. Print and CD-ROM.

Olds, Sharon. *The Dead and the Living*. New York: Knopf, 1984. Print.

Orwell, George. *Essays*. Ed. John Carey. 1968. New York: Knopf, 2002. Print.

Owen, Wilfred. *Selected Poetry and Prose*. Ed. Jennifer Breen. London: Routledge, 1988. Print.

Oxford English Dictionary. 2nd ed. Oxford: Clarendon, 1989. Print.

Paccaud-Huguet, Josiane. "Psychoanalysis after Freud." *Literary Theory and Criticism*. Ed. Patricia Waugh. Oxford: Oxford UP, 2006. 280–97. Print.

Paine, Thomas. *The Essential Thomas Paine*. Ed. Sidney Hook. New York: Mentor, 1969. Print.

Pater, Walter. *The Renaissance: Studies in Art and Poetry*. Ed. Donald L. Hill. Berkeley: U of California P, 1908. Print.

Paz, Octavio. *Configurations*. Trans. Muriel Rukeyser. New York: New Directions, 1971. Print.

Peschel, Enid Rhodes. Introduction. *Four French Symbolist Poets: Baudelaire, Rimbaud, Verlaine, Mallarmé.* By Charles Baudelaire, Arthur Rimbaud, Paul Verlaine, and Stéphane Mallarmé. Trans. Peschel. Athens: Ohio State U, 1981. 1–65. Print.

Petrarch. *Selected Sonnets, Odes, and Letters.* Ed. Thomas Goddard Bergin. Arlington Heights, IL: Harlan Davidson, 1966. Print.

Pindar. *The Odes of Pindar.* Trans. C. M. Bowra. Harmondsworth: Penguin, 1969. Print.

Pinter, Harold. *Betrayal.* New York: Grove Press, 1978. Print.

Pirandello, Luigi. *Pirandello's Major Plays.* Trans. Eric Bentley. Evanston: Northwestern UP, 1991. Print.

Plath, Sylvia. *Ariel.* New York: HarperPerennial, 1965. Print.

Plato. *The Republic of Plato.* Trans. Allan Bloom. New York: Basic Books, 1991. Print.

Poe, Edgar Allan. *The Collected Tales and Poems of Edgar Allan Poe.* New York: Modern Library, 1992. Print.

——. "The Philosophy of Composition (1846)." *Selections from the Critical Writings of Edgar Allan Poe.* Ed. F. C. Prescott. New York: Gordian, 1981. 150–66. Print.

Pope, Alexander. *"The Rape of the Lock" and Other Major Writings.* Ed. Leo Damrosch. London: Penguin, 2011. Print.

Pound, Ezra. "A Retrospect." *Literary Essays of Ezra Pound.* Ed. T. S. Eliot. New York: New Directions, 1935. 3–14. Print.

——. *Selected Poems.* New Edition. New York: New Directions, 1957. Print.

Pound, Omar S., ed. and trans. *Arabic and Persian Poems in English.* New York: New Directions, 1970. Print.

Proust, Marcel. *Remembrance of Things Past.* Trans. C. K. Moncrieff and Terence Kilmartin. Vol. 1. New York: Random House, 1981. Print.

The Purdue Online Writing Lab. Purdue University, 1995–2011. Web. 4 May 2013.

Pushkin, Alexander. *Eugene Oneguine [Onegin]: A Romance of Russian Life in Verse.* Trans. [Henry] Spalding. London: Macmillan, 1881. *Project Gutenberg.* Web. 24 May 2013.

Rich, Adrienne. "Compulsory Heterosexuality and Lesbian Existence." *Journal of Women's History* 15.3 (2003): 11–48. Print.

Richards, I. A. *Practical Criticism: A Study of Literary Judgment.* 1929. New Brunswick: Transaction, 2004. Print.

Rojek, Chris. *Cultural Studies.* Cambridge: Polity, 2007. Print.

Rosenblatt, Louise. *Literature as Exploration.* 5th ed. 1938. New York: Modern Language Association, 1995. Print.

Ross, Andrew. *No Respect: Intellectuals and Popular Culture.* New York: Routledge, 1989. Print.

Rossetti, Christina. *Poems and Prose.* Ed. Jan Marsh. London: Dent, 1994. Print.

Rúmí, Maulána Jalálu-'D-Dín Muhammad I. *Masnavi I Ma'Navi: Teachings of Rumi.* Trans. E. H. Whinfield. London: Octagon, 1979. Print.

Rushdie, Salman. *Imaginary Homelands: Essays and Criticism, 1981–1999.* London: Granta, 1991. Print.

Ruskin, John. *Modern Painters.* Ed. David Barrie. New York: Knopf, 1987. Print.

Said, Edward. *Orientalism.* New York: Vintage, 1979. Print.

Salih, Tayeb. *Season of Migration to the North.* 1966. Trans. Denys Johnson-Davies. New York: New York Review Books, 2009. Print.

Salinger, J. D. *The Catcher in the Rye.* 1951. New York: Back Bay, 2010. Print.

Sandler, Barry. Message to Tison Pugh. 18 Jan. 2013. E-mail.

Santas, Constantine. *The Epic in Film: From Myth to Blockbuster.* Lanham, Maryland: Rowman & Littlefield, 2008. Print.

Sappho. *Poems and Fragments.* Trans. Guy Davenport. Ann Arbor: U of Michigan P, 1965. Print.

Sarris, Andrew. Excerpt from "Notes on the Auteur Theory in 1962." *Theories of Authorship: A Reader.* Ed. J. Caughie. London: Routledge & Kegan Paul, with the British Film Institute, 1981. 62–65. Print.

Saussure, Ferdinand de. *Course in General Linguistics.* Ed. Charles Bally and Albert Sechehaye. Trans. Roy Harris. La Salle, Illinois: Open Court, 1972. Print.

Schelling, Felix. *The English Lyric.* 1913. Port Washington, NY: Kennikat, 1967. Print.

Schrader, Paul. "Notes on Film Noir." *Film Genre Reader.* Ed. Barry Keith Grant. Austin: U of Texas P, 1986. 169–82. Print.

Sedgwick, Eve Kosofsky. *Between Men: English Literature and Male Homosocial Desire.* New York: Columbia UP, 1985. Print.

Sexton, Anne. *The Complete Poems.* Boston: Houghton Mifflin, 1981. Print.

Shakespeare, William. *The Riverside Shakespeare.* Ed. Blakemore Evans. 2nd ed. Boston: Houghton Mifflin, 1997. Print.

Shange, Ntozake. *For Colored Girls Who Have Considered Suicide When the Rainbow Is Enuf.* New York: Collier, 1989. Print.

Shaw, George Bernard. *Major Barbara.* Ed. Nicholas Grene. 1907. London: Methuen Drama, 2008. Print.

——. Preface. *Three Plays by Brieux.* By Eugene Brieux. 6th ed. New York: Brentano's, 1913. vii–liv.

Shelley, Percy Bysshe. *The Complete Poems of Percy Bysshe Shelley.* New York: Modern Library, 1994. Print.

——. *Shelley's Critical Prose.* Ed. Bruce McElderry. Lincoln: U of Nebraska P, 1967. Print.

Shepard, Sam. *"Buried Child" and "Seduced & Suicide in B$^\flat$."* New York: Urizen, 1979. Print.

Sidney, Sir Philip. *An Apology for Poetry, or The Defence of Poesy.* Ed. Geoffrey Shepherd. Manchester: Manchester UP, 2002. Print.

——. *Astrophil and Stella. Sir Philip Sidney: Selected Poetry and Prose.* Ed. Robert Kimbrough. 2nd ed. Madison: U of Wisconsin P, 1983. 159–240. Print.

Simmons, Ernest J. *Chekhov: A Biography.* Boston: Little, Brown, 1962. Print.

Simon, Neil. *Barefoot in the Park.* 1963. New York: Random House, 1964. Print.

Sinfield, Alan. *Dramatic Monologue.* London: Methuen, 1977. Print.

Sitwell, Edith. *Fire of the Mind.* Ed. Elizabeth Salter and Allanah Harper. London: Michael Joseph, 1976. Print.

Smith, Bessie. "Empty Bed Blues." *Bessie Smith: The Collection.* New York: Columbia Records, 1989. CD.

Smith, Charlotte. *The Poems of Charlotte Smith.* Ed. Stuart Curran. New York: Oxford UP, 1993. Print.

Smith, Stevie. *The Collected Poems of Stevie Smith.* New York: Oxford UP, 1976. Print.

Sone, Monica. *Nisei Daughter.* 1953. Seattle: U of Washington P, 1991. Print.

Southwell, Robert. *The Poems of Robert Southwell, S. J.* Ed. James H. McDonald and Nancy Pollard Brown. Oxford: Clarendon, 1967. Print.

Soyinka, Wole. *Death and the King's Horseman.* Ed. Simon Gikandi. New York: Norton, 2003. Print.

Spenser, Edmund. *The Faerie Queene.* Ed. Thomas Roche. London: Penguin, 1978. Print.

——. "Letter to Sir Walter Raleigh." *Literary Criticism: Plato to Dryden.* Ed. Allan Gilbert. Detroit: Wayne State UP, 1962. 462–65. Print.

——. *The Shorter Poems.* Ed. Richard McCabe. London: Penguin, 1999. Print.

Spivak, Gayatri Chakravorty. Translator's Preface. *Of Grammatology.* By Jacques Derrida. Trans. Gayatri Chakravorty Spivak. Baltimore: Johns Hopkins UP, 1997. ix–xc. Print.

Staiger, Janet. *Perverse Spectators: The Practices of Film Reception.* New York: New York UP, 2000. Print.

Stam, Robert. *Film Theory: An Introduction.* Malden, Mass.: Blackwell, 2000. Print.

Strand, Mark. *Selected Poems.* New York: Atheneum, 1980. Print.

Strunk, William, Jr., and E. B. White. *The Elements of Style.* 4th ed. Boston: Allyn & Bacon, 2000. Print.

Suckling, Sir John. "Out upon It!" *The New Oxford Book of English Verse, 1250–1950.* Ed. Helen Gardner. Oxford: Oxford UP, 1989. 305. Print.

Surrey, Henry Howard, Earl of. *Poems.* Ed. Emrys Jones. Oxford: Clarendon, 1964. Print.

Tabachnick, Stephen, ed. *Teaching the Graphic Novel.* New York: Modern Language Association, 2009. Print.

Tennyson, Alfred, Lord. *Idylls of the King.* Ed. J. M. Gray. London: Penguin, 1996. Print.

——. *Selected Poems.* Ed. Christopher Ricks. London: Penguin, 2007. Print.

Thomas, Dylan. *Dylan Thomas: Selected Poems, 1934–1952.* New York: New Directions, 2003. Print.

Thomson, R. L., ed. *Pwyll Pendeuic Dyuet.* Dublin: Dublin Institute for Advanced Studies, 1986. Print.

Todorov, Tzvetan. *Genres in Discourse.* Trans. Catherine Porter. Cambridge: Cambridge UP, 1990. Print.

Tolkien, J. R. R., and E. V. Gordon, eds. *Sir Gawain and the Green Knight.* 2nd ed. Ed. Norman Davis. Oxford: Clarendon, 1967. Print.

Tolstoy, Leo. *Anna Karenina.* Trans. Constance Garnett. *Project Gutenberg.* Web. 25 May 2013.

Toole, John Kennedy. *A Confederacy of Dunces.* Foreword by Walker Percy. 1980. New York: Wings Books, 1996. Print.

"Top 10 Epics." *afi.com.* American Film Institute, n.d. Web. 1 Feb. 2013.

Truss, Lynne. *Eats, Shoots and Leaves: The Zero Tolerance Approach to Punctuation.* New York: Gotham, 2003. Print.

Tuttleton, James. *The Novel of Manners in America.* Chapel Hill: U of North Carolina P, 1972. Print.

Unforgiven. Dir. Clint Eastwood. Perf. Clint Eastwood, Gene Hackman, and Morgan Freeman. Warner Bros., 1992. Film.

Vertov, Dziga. *Kino-Eye: The Writing of Dziga Vertov.* Ed. Annette Michelson. Trans. Kevin O'Brien. Berkeley: U of California P, 1984. Print.

Vogel, Paula. *The Baltimore Waltz*. New York: Dramatists Play Service, 1992. Print.

Wagner, Geoffrey. *The Novel and the Cinema*. Rutherford, N.J.: Fairleigh Dickinson UP, 1975. Print.

Walcott, Derek. *Selected Poems*. Ed. Edward Baugh. New York: Farrar, Straus & Giroux, 2007. Print.

Webster, John. *The Works of John Webster, Volume 1: The White Devil and The Duchess of Malfi*. Ed. David Gunby, David Carnegie, Antony Hammond, and Doreen DelVecchio. Cambridge: Cambridge UP, 1995. Print.

Wharton, David, and Jeremy Grant. *Teaching Auteur Study*. London: British Film Institute, 2005. Print.

Wheatley, Phillis. *The Poems of Phillis Wheatley*. Ed. Julian Mason. Chapel Hill: U of North Carolina P, 1989. Print.

Whitman, Walt. *Leaves of Grass: A Textual Variorum of the Printed Poems*. Ed. Sculley Bradley, Harold Blodgett, Arthur Golden, and William White. Vol. 1. New York: New York UP, 1980. Print.

——. "Letter to Ralph Waldo Emerson, August 1856." *Leaves of Grass: 150th Anniversary Edition*. Ed. David S. Reynolds. Oxford: Oxford UP, 2005. 161–67. Print.

Who Framed Roger Rabbit? Dir. Robert Zemeckis. Perf. Bob Hoskins, Kathleen Turner, and Christopher Lloyd. Touchstone, 1988. Film.

Wigglesworth, Michael. "The Day of Doom." *The Day of Doom: Or, a Description of the Great and Last Judgment. With a Short Discourse about Eternity*. London: W. G. for John Sims, 1673. 1–67. *Early English Books Online*. Web. 5 Jun. 2013.

Wilde, Oscar. *Complete Works of Oscar Wilde*. Ed. Vyvyan Holland. New York: Harper & Row, 1989. Print.

——. *The Importance of Being Earnest: A Reconstructive Critical Edition of the Text of the First Production, St. James's Theatre, 1895*. Ed. Joseph Donohue. Gerrards Cross: Colin Smythe, 1995. Print.

Wilder, Laura Ingalls. *These Happy Golden Years*. 1943. New York: Harper Trophy, 1971. Print.

Wilder, Thornton. *Our Town: A Play in Three Acts*. 1938. New York: Harper & Row, 1957. Print.

William of Nassyngton. *Speculum Vitae: An Edition of British Museum Manuscript Royal 17C. viii*. Ed. John Smeltz. Diss. Duquesne University, 1977. Print.

Williams, Raymond. *Culture and Society, 1780–1950*. London: Chattus & Windus, 1958. Print.

Williams, Tennessee. *Tennessee Williams: Plays, 1937–1955*. New York: Library of America, 2000. Print.

Wilson, August. *Ma Rainey's Black Bottom. Black Drama in America: An Anthology*. Ed. Darin Turner. 2nd ed. Washington, D.C.: Howard UP, 1994. 553–613. Print.

Wimsatt, W. K., and Monroe Beardsley. "The Intentional Fallacy." *The Verbal Icon: Studies in the Meaning of Poetry*. By W. K. Wimsatt. 1954. Lexington: UP of Kentucky, 1982. 3–18. Print.

Winny, James, ed. and trans. *Sir Gawain and the Green Knight*. Ontario: Broadview, 1992. Print.

Wollstonecraft, Mary. *The Works of Mary Wollstonecraft*. Ed. Janet Todd and Marilyn Butler. New York: New York UP, 1989. Print.

Woolf, Virginia. "Modern Novels." *The Essays of Virginia Woolf, Volume 3: 1919–1924*. Ed. Andrew McNeillie. San Diego: Harcourt Brace Jovanovich, 1988. 30–37. Print.

——. *A Room of One's Own.* 1929. Orlando: Harvest, 2005. Print.

——. *To the Lighthouse.* Ed. Mark Hussey. 1927. Orlando: Harvest, 2005. Print.

Wordsworth, William, and Samuel Taylor Coleridge. *Wordsworth and Coleridge: Lyrical Ballads.* Ed. R. L. Brett and A. R. Jones. 2nd ed. London: Routledge, 1991. Print.

Worley, Alec. *Empires of the Imagination: A Critical Survey of Fantasy Cinema from Georges Méliès to "The Lord of the Rings."* Jefferson, NC: McFarland, 2005. Print.

Wright, Will. *Six-Guns and Society: A Structural Study of the Western.* Berkeley: U of California P, 1975. Print.

Wroth, Mary. *The Poems of Lady Mary Wroth.* Ed. Josephine A. Roberts. Baton Rouge: Louisiana State UP, 1983. Print.

Wyatt, Sir Thomas. *Selected Poems.* Ed. Hardiman Scott. New York: Routledge, 2003. Print.

Yeats, William Butler. *Yeats's Poetry, Drama, and Prose.* Ed. James Pethica. New York: Norton, 2000. Print.

Index

Abbey, Edward 206
abstract words 143
accent 97–105
Achebe, Chinua 37, 83–84
acts 155
Adam Bede 31
adaptation (cinematic) 180–82
Addison, Joseph 24, 214–15
Adonais 27, 118
Adventures of Huckleberry Finn,
  The 50, 148
Aelfric 14
Aeneid 118
aerial shot 186
Aeschylus 67
affective fallacy 225
Al-Khansā' 71
Al-Qays, Imra' 71
Al-Shanfarā 70–71
Albee, Edward 155, 160
Alcott, Louisa May 47
Aldington, Richard 104
Alfred, King 15
alienation effect 174
All My Sons 61–62
allegory 146
Allende, Isabel 88
alliteration 95
allusion 108
Althusser, Louis 235
Altman, Rick 204
Amado, Jorge 88
Amazing Adventures of Kavalier and Clay,
  The 265
ambiguity 225
American Dictionary of the English
  Language, An 8
American Scholar, The 47, 217
Amis, Kingsley 35
Amis, Martin 37
Amoretti 17–18, 128
Analects 69–70
anapest 97, 99–100
Angels in America 62, 176

angle 184–85
Anna Karenina 78
Annabel Lee 47, 99
Annunciation, The
antagonist 158
antecedent action 156–57
antihero 158
Apollinaire, Guillaume 80
Apology for Poetry, An 213
Apology for the Life of Mrs. Shamela
  Andrews, An 23–24
Arcadia 18, 125
argumentative writing 259
Aristophanes 67
Aristotle 68, 164, 167, 212, 249–50
Arnold, Matthew 116–17, 218
As I Lay Dying 55
As You Like It 18, 121, 125, 198
Ashbery, John 58
aside 161–62
assonance 94
Astrophil and Stella 18, 128
Aubade (Edith Sitwell) 114
Aubade (Philip Larkin) 35, 114
aubade 114
Auden, W. H. 34, 118, 128
Aurora Leigh 30
Austen, Jane 10, 28, 150
Auster, Paul 135
auteur theories 191–93
Autumn 106
Awakening, The 51–52

badinage 169
Bakhtin, Mikhail 146
balance (cinematic) 183
ballad 114–16
Ballad of Reading Gaol, The 100
ballad stanza 115
Ballad upon a Wedding, A 121
Baltimore Waltz, The 62, 163
Balzac, Honoré de 151
Baraka, Amiri 58–59
Barchester Towers 32

Bard, The 24
Barefoot in the Park 168–69
Barlow, Joel 44
Barlowe, Arthur 40
Barnes, Djuna 55–56
Barnes, Julian 37, 142, 143
Barth, John 60–61, 147
Barthelme, Donald 60, 144, 153
Barthes, Roland 227, 229
Bartholomew Fair 19, 159
Bartlett, Neil 37
Baudelaire, Charles 79
Beardsley, Monroe 225
Beat Poets 57–58
Beaumont, Francis 18, 159
Beauvoir, Simone de 81, 241
Beckett, Samuel 36, 175
Bede 4, 13
Beggar's Opera, The 24
Behn, Aphra 22, 23, 248–49
Belle Dame sans Merci, La 27–28, 115
Bells, The 97
Beloved 61, 143
Beowulf 5, 14, 95, 118, 200
Berryman, John 58
Betrayal 160–61
Bhabha, Homi K. 246
Big Sea, The 54
bildungsroman 32, 147–49
Bishop, Elizabeth 102, 118
Black Art 58–59
Black Arts Movement 58–59
Black Mountain poets 58
Blackberry Eating 107
Blake, William 25
blank verse 94, 102–03
Bleak House 32
Blessed Damozel, The 31
blocking 162
Bloom, Harold 220
Boccaccio 15, 74
Bonny Barbara Allan 115
Book of Margery Kempe 16
Book of Songs, The 68–69
Book of the Courtier, The 74, 75
Book of the Duchess 117
Borges, Jorge Luis 87
Boswell, James 23
Bourdieu, Pierre 197
Bradford, Richard 153
Bradford, William 40
Bradstreet, Anne 41
Break, Break, Break 112
Breakfast at Tiffany's (film) 181
Breathless 188
Brecht, Bertolt 81–82, 174–75
Breton, André 80
Brontë, Charlotte 31, 148
Brontë, Emily 31, 112, 118, 130
Brooke, Rupert 34

Brooks, Cleanth 224–25
Brooks, Richard 181–82
Brown, Rita Mae 292
Brown, William Hill 44–45
Browning, Elizabeth Barrett 30, 116, 128
Browning, Robert 30, 114, 116
Brut 15
Bryant, William Cullen 48
Budgell, Eustace 24
Bukowski, Charles 109
Bunyan, John 23
Buried Child 162
Burke, Edmund 25
Burke, Seán 229–30
Burne-Jones, Edward 31
Burney, Fanny 24
Burning Babe, The 108–09
Burns, Robert 26
Burroughs, William S. 57
Butler, Judith 241
Butler, Samuel 22, 109
Byatt, A. S. 37
Byron, George Gordon, Lord 26–27, 120

Cabeza de Vaca, Álvar Núñez 39–40, 42
Caedmon and *Caedmon's Hymn* 13
caesura 105
Cain, James 202
Calvino, Italo 136, 154
Campbell, Joseph 254–55
Camus, Albert 81
Can You Forgive Her? 32
canon 221
Canonization, The 19
Canterbury Tales, The 6, 15, 31, 101, 108, 212
Canterville Ghost, The 9
Capote, Truman 59–60, 180–82, 203
captivity narrative 41–42
Carew, Thomas 111, 113, 118
Carmen Deo Nostro 20
carmen figuratum 101
carpe diem 19–20
Cary, Elizabeth 18
Casas, Bartolomé de las 39
Cash, Johnny 116
Cask of Amontillado, The 46–47, 132
Castiglione, Baldesar 74
Castle of Otranto, The 28
Cat on a Hot Tin Roof 62
catastrophe 131–32, 156
Catcher in the Rye, The 144
catharsis 164
Cather, Willa 52
Causley, Charles 34
Cavalier poetry 19–20
Caxton, William 16–17
Celtic languages 3–4
Cervantes, Miguel de 23, 75–76, 146
Chabon, Michael 265

Champlain, Samuel de 40
Chandler, Raymond 202–03
character 137–39, 158–62; flat character
    159; round character 159; stock character
    159
character role 159
characterization through action, description,
    and dialogue 137–39
Charge of the Light Brigade, The 100
Charlotte Temple 45
Chaucer, Geoffrey 6, 17, 22, 94, 96, 101,
    108, 114, 117, 125–26, 198, 204, 212,
    225
Chbosky, Stephen 148
Chekhov, Anton 79, 157, 172–73
Cherry Orchard, The 173
Chestnutt, Charles 50, 51
Child, Francis James 114
Childe Harold's Pilgrimage 27
Children on Their Birthdays 182
Children's Hour, The 173
Chopin, Kate 51–52
chorus 159
Chrétien de Troyes 15, 125
Churcher, Mel 194–95
Churchill, Caryl 36
Circus Animals' Desertion, The 34
Cixous, Hélène 242
Clarissa, or the History of a Young Lady 23,
    147
climax 131–32, 156
close reading 224–27
close-up/extreme close-up 185–86
code-switching 10
Coetzee, J. M. 85–86
Colebrook, Claire 231
Coleridge, Samuel Taylor 26, 115, 117, 124,
    216
Collar, The 107
Collins, Wilkie 32
Collins, William 24
Columbus, Christopher 38–39
comedy 167–72, 197–99
comedy of manners 169–71
coming-of-age novel 147–49
Common Sense 43
"Commonwealth Literature" Does Not Exist
    11
Complaint to Venus 94
complication 131–32, 156
composition (cinematic) 183
concrete words 143
condensation 238
Confederacy of Dunces, A 261–62
confessional poetry 58
confidant 159
conflicts, external vs. internal 131
Confucius 69–70
Congreve, William 24, 102, 123, 159, 171
Conjure Woman, The 50

*Connecticut Yankee in King Arthur's Court,
    A* 126, 205
connotation 143
Conrad, Joseph 35, 135, 218–19
consonance 95
Cooper, James Fenimore 45–46
Coover, Robert 60, 154
Coquette: Or, the History of Eliza Wharton
    45, 147
Corso, Gregory 57
Cortázar, Julio 88
Cortés, Hernán 40
Country of the Pointed Firs, The 50
Country Wife, The 24, 171
Coward, Noel 171
Cowley, Abraham 123
Crabbe, George 24, 125
Craig, Edward Gordon 172
Crane, Stephen 51
Crane, Susan 253–54
Crashaw, Richard 20
Creeley, Robert 58
Crèvecoeur, J. Hector St. John de 43
Crime and Punishment 78–79
Crisis, The 43
Critic as Artist, The 211
critical race theories 246–49
Crito 68
Croce, Benedetto 253
Crucible, The 62
Cry of the Children, The 30
Crystal, David 11
Cullen, Countee 53–54
cultural studies 230–34
cutting and cross-cutting 187–88
Cymbeline 114

dactyl 97, 100
Daddy 58
Daiches, David 151–52
Daisy Miller 150–51
Dante Alighieri 15, 74, 116, 212
Darwin, Charles 29
David Copperfield 32, 134–35, 148
Davis, Jessica 171
Day of Doom, The 41
De Quincey, Thomas 217
De Vulgari eloquentia 212
Dead, The 36
Death and the King's Horseman 84–85
Death in Venice 82
Death of a Salesman 62, 166–67
Death of Bessie Smith, The 155
deconstructive theory 227–30
defamiliarization 174
Defence of Guinevere, The 31
Defence of Poetry, A 216
Defoe, Daniel 23
Delaney, Shelagh 36
DeLillo, Don 62–63, 149

denotation 143
dénouement 131–32, 156–57
Derrida, Jacques 253
Desert Places 53
Desire 72–73
deus ex machina 158, 205
Devil on the Cross 84
Devotions upon Emergent Occasions 19
dialect 6–7
dialogue 160–62, 190
Díaz, Junot 11
Dickens, Charles 31–32, 134–35, 145, 148, 154
Dickinson, Emily 47, 48–49, 94–95, 263
diction 142–43
dictionaries 8–9
Dictionary of the English Language 8
diegetic/extradiegetic sound 189
Digging 35
Discourse Concerning the Original and Progress of Satire, A 22, 214
Discourse on the Pindaric Ode 123
displacement 238
dissolve 188
Divorce Tracts, The 20
Do Not Go Gentle into That Good Night 34
Doctor Faustus 18, 103, 159
documenting sources 267–75
dolly shot 186
Don Juan 27, 120
Don Quixote 23, 75–76, 146
Donne, John 19, 114, 116, 118, 120
Dos Passos, John 55–56
Dostoevsky, Fyodor 78–79, 151
Double Indemnity 184
Douglas, Keith 34–35
Douglass, Frederick 44, 47–48
Dover Beach 116–17, 218
Doyle, Arthur Conan 138–39
Dracula 147, 203
drama 163–64, 172–77, 199
dramatic monologue 116–17
dramatic realism 172–73
Dream of the Rood, The 14
Dreiser, Theodore 52, 151
Dryden, John 22, 96–97, 214–15
dubbing 190
Dubliners 36
Duchess of Malfi, The 18, 103
Duffy, Carol Ann 116
Dulce et Decorum Est 34–35
Dunbar, Paul Laurence 10, 50, 51
Duncan, Robert 58
Dunn, Douglas 35
Dyer, Richard 193–94, 247

Early Modern English 8, 10
Easter Wings 101
Eastwood, Clint 206
Eating Poetry 128

Ecclesiastical History of the English People 4, 13
Edelman, Lee 274–75
editing pace 187
editing tips 288–91
Edson, Margaret 269
Edwards, Blake 181
Edwards, Jonathan 42
elegy 14, 111–12, 117–18
Elegy upon the Death of the Dean of Paul's Dr. John Donne, An 111, 113, 118
Elegy Written in a Country Churchyard 24, 118
Eliot, George 31, 37, 141
Eliot, T. S. 53, 56, 108, 111, 116, 220
Elizabeth I, Queen 17, 19, 110
Ellis, Bret Easton 142
Ellison, Ralph 59
Emancipation 10
Emerson, Ralph Waldo 47, 217
Emily Bronte (poem) 118
Emma 28
Empson, William 224, 225–26
Empty Bed Blues 107
end-stopped line 105
Engels, Frederick 234–35
English language 3–12
enjambed line 105
Eolian Harp, The 26, 216
epic 118–20, 199–201
Epic of Gilgamesh, The 64, 118
epic simile 119
epic theater 82, 174–75
epistolary novel 147
epithalamion 18, 120–21
Epithalamion (Edmund Spenser) 18, 120
Epithalamion Made at Lincoln's End 120–21
Equiano, Olaudah 44
Erdrich, Louise 61
erotic triangle 245
Essay Concerning Human Understanding, An 21, 214
Essay of Dramatic Poesy, An 22, 215
Essay on Criticism, An 22, 222
Esslin, Martin 175
establishing shot/re-establishing shot 185
ethos 250
Eugene Onegin 76–77
Euphues: The Anatomy of Wit 213–14
Euripides 67–68
Evangeline: A Tale of Acadie 48, 100
Eve of St. Agnes 27–28
Exeter Book 14
existentialism 81
exposition 131–32, 156
eyeline match 187

fade-in/fade-out 188
Faerie Queen, The 18, 119, 126, 213
falling action 131–32, 156–57

fantasy 201–02
Far Cry from Africa, A 267–68
farce 171–72
Faulkner, William 55, 59, 134, 152, 202
feminine ending 102
feminist theory 240–43
Ferlinghetti, Lawrence 57, 63
Fern, Fanny 136–37
Ferris Bueller's Day Off 196
Ficciones 87
Fielding, Helen 37
Fielding, Henry 23–24, 119–20
figurative language 108–11, 145
film noir 202–03
Finch, Anne, Countess of Winchilsea 122
Fireside Poets 48
Fish, Stanley 252
Fitzgerald, F. Scott 55, 135
flashback 130–31
Flea, The 19, 116
Fletcher, John 18
foil 158
*For Colored Girls Who Have Considered
   Suicide When the Rainbow Is Enuf*
   175–76
Ford, John 18
foreshadowing 157
formal editing 187
Forster, E. M. 35, 129–30
Foster, Hannah Webster 45, 147
Foucault, Michel 244
fourth wall 160
frame 183
frame tale 130
Frankenstein, or The Modern Prometheus
   28, 203
Franklin, Benjamin 42
free verse 104–05
Freeman, Mary E. Wilkins 50, 51
French, Warren 206
Freneau, Philip 44
Freud, Sigmund 33, 152, 219, 237–38
Freytag, Gustav, and Freytag's pyramid
   131–32, 156–58, 182
Frost, Robert 53
Frye, Northrop 121, 167
Fuentes, Carlos 88
Futurism and Futurist Manifesto 83

Gallantry 35
Game 144
García Márquez, Gabriel 87–88, 133
Gates, Henry Louis, Jr. 221
Gaunt, Simon 254
Gawain-Poet 15, 117
Gay, John 24
gender theory 240–43
Genet, Jean 175
genre 113–14, 252–55
genre fiction 197

Geoffrey of Monmouth 15
Gilman, Charlotte Perkins 140–41
Ginsberg, Allen 49, 57
Giovanni, Nikki 59
Globish 11
Goblin Market and Other Poems 31
Goethe, Johann 147–48
Gogol, Nikolai 77–78
Goldsmith, Oliver 24, 125
Good Man Is Hard to Find, A 60, 131
Good Morrow, The 19
Gordimer, Nadine 85–86
Gordon, Karen Elizabeth 262
Gottfried von Strassburg 15
Gower, John 16, 212
Gramsci, Antonio 235–36
Grant, Barry Keith 204
Grapes of Wrath, The 56
graphic novel 154
Graves, Robert 34
Gray, Thomas 24–25, 118, 212
Great Awakening 42
Great Expectations 32, 148
Great Gatsby, The 55, 135, 145
Great Vowel Shift 7–8
Greenblatt, Stephen 231
Grey, Zane 206
Grimald, Nicholas 17
Grimm, Jacob and Wilhelm 114
Grindon, Leger 198
Gulliver's Travels 22, 198
Gunn, Thom 35
Gurney, Ivor 34
Gutenberg, Johann 16
gutter 154

H. D. [Hilda Doolittle] 104
Hāfiz of Shiraz 72–73
hagiography 14
Hall, Stuart 247
hamartia 164
Hamlet 157, 161–62, 165, 198, 238
Hammett, Dashiell 202–03
Hand That Signed the Paper, The 109
hand-held camera 186
Hansberry, Lorraine 61
Hard Times 32
Hardy, Thomas 35, 118, 236–37
Harlem Renaissance 53–54
Harper, Michael S. 59
Harris, Joel Chandler 50
Harry Potter 37, 131, 148, 178
Hawthorne, Nathaniel 46, 126, 133
Haywood, Eliza 24
Heaney, Seamus 35
Heart of Darkness 135
Hedda Gabler 165–66
Heinlein, Robert 204–05
Hellman, Lillian 61, 173
Hemingway, Ernest 55

Her Kind 122
Herbert, George 20, 101, 107
heroic couplet 102
Herrick, Robert 19–20, 98, 107, 120, 228–29
Hesiod 65–66
Heston, Charlton 200
heteronormativity 244
high angle 185
Hijuelos, Oscar 139–40
Hirst, David 171
His Farewell to Sack 20
historical novel 149
historicism 230–34
History of Rasselas, Prince of Abyssinia 22
History of the Kings of Britain 15
History of the World in 10½ Chapters, A 37, 142, 143
Hitchcock, Alfred 185, 186, 192, 194, 203
Hoggart, Richard 232
Hollinghurst, Alan 37
Holmes, Oliver Wendell, Sr. 48, 217
Holy Sonnets 19
Homer 65, 119
Hopkins, Gerard Manley 30, 103–04, 121, 225–26
horror 203
Hosseini, Khaled 148
House of Fame 221
House of Life, The 31
House of the Seven Gables, The 46, 126
House of the Spirits, The 88
Housman, A. E. 34
Howard, Henry, Earl of Surrey 17, 102–03
Howards End 35
Howells, William Dean 51, 151
Howl 57
hubris 164
Hudibras 22
Hughes, Langston 53–54, 115, 116
Hughes, Ted 35, 118
Huhndorf, Shari 248
Hulme, T. E. 219
Hunt, William Holman 31
Hurston, Zora Neale 53–54
Hwang, David Henry 62
Hymn to the Evening, An 93–94

I Ching 69
I Find No Peace 126–27
I Sing the Body Electric 49
I Wonder as I Wander 95
I, Too 54
I'm Happiest When Most Away 112
iamb 97–98
iambic pentameter 101–03
Ibsen, Henrik 165–66
id, ego, and superego 237–38
Idea of a University, The 29
Ideal Husband, An 32

Idylls of the King 30, 125
If on a Winter's Night a Traveler 136
Iliad, The 65, 118, 120
image 106–08
Imagism 52–53
Importance of Being Earnest, The 32, 171
In a Station of the Metro 52–53
In Cold Blood 60, 180–81
in medias res 156
In Memoriam A. H. H. 30, 118
In Praise of Limestone 34
Incidents in the Life of a Slave Girl 44, 48
Inferno 116
Inge, William 61
intentional fallacy 225
Interesting Narrative of the Life of Olaudah Equiano, or Gustavus Vassa, the African, The 44
Interpretation of Dreams, The 33
introduction 131–32, 156
Invisible Man 59
Ionesco, Eugène 175
Irving, Washington 45
Ishiguro, Kazuo 135
Ivanhoe 28, 149

Jacobs, Harriet 44, 48
James, Henry 50–51, 134, 150, 151, 203, 239–40
Jameson, Frederic 253
Jamie, Kathleen 35
Jane Eyre 31, 148
Jefferson, Thomas 43
Jemison, Mary 41
Jerusalem 25–26
Jewett, Sarah Orne 50, 51
Johnson, Robert K. 169
Johnson, Samuel 8, 22–23, 24, 215–16
Jones, LeRoi *see* Baraka, Amiri
Jonson, Ben 18–19, 22, 99, 103, 120, 123, 159, 214
Joseph Andrews 119
Joyce, James 36, 134, 148, 152
Julian of Norwich 16
jump cut 188
Jungle Book 32
Junius manuscript 14

Kafka, Franz 81–82, 130
Keats, John 27–28, 115, 124
Kelly, Brigit Pegeen 107
Kelmscott Chaucer 31
Kempe, Margery 16
Kerouac, Jack 57–58
Kesey, Ken 206
Khayyam, Omar 71–72
King Lear 18, 105, 165, 198
King, Florence 94
King, Geoff 197–98
King, Stephen 203–04
Kingston, Maxine Hong 61

Kinnell, Galway 107
Kipling, Rudyard 32, 116
Knight, Etheridge 59
Kramer, Larry 62
künstlerroman 148
Kushner, Tony 62, 176
Kyd, Thomas 18, 108

L'Amour, Louis 206
La Salle, Robert de 40
LaBute, Neil 63
Lacan, Jacques 238–39
Lady Chatterley's Lover 36
Lady Windemere's Fan 32, 171
Lake Poets 26
Lament for a Brother 71
Lamia 28
Lâmîyat al-'Arab 70–71
Langland, William 15, 146
langue 227
Lanval 15
Lanyer, Aemelia 242–43
Lao Tzu 70
Laqueur, Thomas 262
Larkin, Philip 35, 114
Last of the Mohicans, The 46
Late Speech with My Brother 59
Lawrence, D. H. 35–36
Layamon 15
Le Roman de Brut 15
Leatherstocking Tales 45–46
Leaves of Grass 48–49, 104
Lee, Harper 59–60, 142
Legend of Sleepy Hollow, The 45
Lehman, David 63
Leitch, Thomas 180
Lermontov, Mikhail 77
Less Than Zero 142
Lessing, Doris 37
Letters from an American Farmer 43
Levertov, Denise 58
Leviathan 135
Lewis, C. S.
Lewis, Matthew 28
Libra 149
Life of Pi 145
Life of Samuel Johnson, L.L.D., The 23
lighting 187
Lines Written a Few Miles above Tintern
    Abbey 26
Lion, the Witch, and the Wardrobe, The 146
literary criticism 211–22
literary influence 220
literary theories 223–56
Little Brown Baby 10
Little Dorrit 32
local color 50
Lochhead, Liz 35
Locke, Alain 53
Locke, John 21, 214

logos 250
London, Jack 52, 140
long shot 185
long take 186
Longfellow, Henry Wadsworth 48, 100
Lord Randall 115
Lorde, Audre 59
Lost in the Funhouse 60–61
Lost Leader, The 30
Love in the Time of Cholera 87, 133
Love Song of J. Alfred Prufrock, The 53,
    110–11, 116
Lovelace, Richard 19–20, 113
low angle 185
Lowell, Amy 106
Lowell, James Russell 48
Lowell, Robert 58, 116, 118
Lucasta 20
Lycidas 20, 109, 118
Lydgate, John 15
Lyly, John 213–14
Lynching, The 54
lyric 121–22
Lyrical Ballads 26, 115

Ma Rainey's Black Bottom 163
Mac Flecknoe 22
Macbeth 99, 165
Macherey, Pierre 229
Machiavelli, Niccolò 74–75
Maggie: A Girl of the Streets 51
magical realism 87–88
Mahfouz, Naguib 86
Major Barbara 33
Mallarmé, Stèphane 79
Malory, Sir Thomas 15, 17, 126, 245–46
Mambo Kings Play Songs of Love, The
    139–40
Man Who Would Be King, The 32
Manfred 27
Mann, Thomas 81–82
Marie de France 15
Marinetti, F. T. 83
Marlowe, Christopher 18, 103, 124, 159
Married State, A 20
Martel, Yann 145
Marvell, Andrew 21, 125, 242
Marx, Karl 234–35
masculine ending 102
Masnavi 72
masque 18–19
Matar, Hisham 86
Mather, Cotton 40
McClure, Michael 57
McCrum, Robert 11
McCullers, Carson 59–60
McEwan, Ian 37
McInerney, Jay 63
McKay, Claude 53–54
McMurtry, Larry 206

McNally, Terrence 62
McTeague 51
Medea 67–68
medium shot 185
Melville, Herman 46, 50, 95–96, 145
Merchant of Venice, The 101
Meredith, George 128
metafiction 60–61
Metamorphosis, The 81, 130
metaphor 108–09
meter 97–105
metonymy 109–10
Middle English 5–7
Middlemarch 31
Mill, John Stuart 29, 218
Millais, John Everett 31
Millay, Edna St. Vincent 128
Miller, Arthur 61–62, 166–67
Milner, Ron 59
Milton, John 20, 94, 109, 118–19, 212, 250–52
mirror stage 238–39
mise-en-scène 162–63, 183
Mistral, Gabriela 88
MLA documentation style 267–73
MLA International Bibliography 264–65
Moby-Dick; or, The Whale 46, 145
Model of Christian Charity, A 40
Modern English 10
modern novel 151–52
Modern Painters 29
modernism 52, 79
Modest Proposal, A 22
Molière 156, 170–71
Moll Flanders 23
monologue 161
Mont Blanc 27
montage 188
Montagu, Lady Mary Wortley 22
Montaigne, Michel de 75
Monty Python and the Holy Grail 185
Moonlight 79–80
Moonstone, The 32
Moore, Clement 99
Moore, Marianne 53
morality play 16
Morgan, Edwin 35
Morris, William 31
Morrison, Toni 61, 143, 247–48
Morte D'Arthur, Le 15, 75, 126, 245–46
Mother Courage and Her Children 82, 174
motif 142, 188
Movement, the 35
Mrs Warren's Profession 32
Mrs. Dalloway 36
Mulvey, Laura 191
Murray, James A. H. 9
music: foreground music 189; score 188–89; source music 189
musicals 204

My Last Duchess 30, 116
mystery play 16

Nabokov, Vladimir 60
Nadja 80
Naipaul, V. S. 37
narration: first-person narration 133–37; second-person point of view 136–37; third-person narration 133–34, 136–37
narrative conflict 131
Narrative of the Captivity and Restoration of Mrs. Mary Rowlandson, A 41
Narrative of the Life of Frederick Douglass, An American Slave 44, 48
Narrative of the Life of Mrs. Mary Jemison 41
naturalism 49–50, 51–52
Neruda, Pablo 88
new criticism 224–27
new historicism 230–34
new media 275
New Negro: An Interpretation, The 53
New York School 58
Newman, John Henry, Cardinal 29
Newton, Sir Isaac 21
Ngũgĩ wa Thiong'o 84
Nigger of the "Narcissus," The 218–19
Nightwood 55–56
Nisei Daughter 138
Nocturnal Reverie, A 122
nonfiction novel 129
Norris, Frank 51
Northanger Abbey 28
Nose, The 77–78
Not Waving But Drowning 34
Not without Laughter 54
Notes on the State of Virginia 43
novel of manners 150–51
novella 129
novel 129–54
Nowell Codex 14

O'Brien, Tim 61
O'Casey, Sean 36
O'Connor, Flannery 59–60, 131
O'Hara, Frank 58
O'Neill, Eugene 56
Occom, Samson 43–44
ode 123–24; Horatian ode 123; Pindaric ode 66–67, 123
Ode on a Grecian Urn 27, 124
Ode on Intimations of Immortality from Recollections of Early Childhood 124
Ode on Melancholy 27, 124
Ode to a Nightingale 27, 124
Ode to Evening 24
Ode to Himself 123
Odets, Clifford 61
Odyssey, The 65, 118–19, 120, 152
Oedipal complex 238

Of Plymouth Plantation 40
Old English 5
Olds, Sharon 59
Oliver Twist 32, 145, 204
Olson, Charles 58
Olympian IV 66–67
On Books 75
On Liberty 29
On Monsieur's Departure 17, 110
On the Road 57–58
One Art 102
One Hundred Years of Solitude 87–88
online databases 264–65
onomatopoeia 96–97
open secret 245
Origin of Species, The 29
Oroonoko, or The Royal Slave 23, 248–49
Orton, Joe 172
Orwell, George 296
Osborne, John 36
Othello 157, 165, 204
Other Voices, Other Rooms 60
Our Town 56, 159–60
Out upon It! 20
outlines 265–67
over-the-shoulder shot 187
Owen, Wilfred 34
Oxford English Dictionary 9
oxymoron 110

Paccaud-Huguet, Josiane 239
Paine, Thomas 25, 43
Pamela, or Virtue Rewarded 23, 147
Pamphilia to Amphilanthus 18, 112–13, 128
Paradise Lost 20, 94, 118–19, 250–52
Paradise Regained 212–13
paradox 110
paraphrasing 274–75
Parliament of Fowls 96
parole 227
Parton, Dolly 108, 116
Passionate Shepherd to His Love, The 124
pastiche 153
pastoral 124–25
Pastoral Care 15
pastoral elegy 118
Pater, Walter 218
pathos 250
Paton, Alan 85–86
Paul Revere's Ride 48
Paz, Octavio 88–89
Pearl 15, 117–18
Percy, Thomas, Bishop 114
Perks of Being a Wallflower, The 148–49
Petrarch, Francesco 15, 17, 73–74
Philips, Ambrose 24
Philips, Katherine 20
Pied Beauty 103–04
Pierre Menard, Author of Don Quixote 87
Piers Plowman 15, 95, 146

Pike 35
Pilgrim's Progress, The 23
Pinter, Harold 36, 160–61, 175
Pirandello, Luigi 82–83
plagiarism 273–75
Plath, Sylvia 58
Plato 68, 211–12, 244
Plays of William Shakespeare, The 215–16
plot and plot structure 129–32
Poe, Edgar Allan 46–47, 50, 97, 99, 132, 133
Poet, The 47
Poet's Tongue, The 34
poetic line 97–105
Poetics 68, 164, 167, 212
poetry 93–128
point of view 132–37; limited omniscient 133–34; omniscient 133
point-of-view shot 185
Politics and the English Language 296
Poor Richard's Almanack 42
Pope, Alexander 22, 116, 119–20, 125, 198, 221–22
Portrait of a Lady, The 50, 134
Portrait of the Artist as a Young Man, A 148
postcolonial theories 246–49
postmodern novel 152–53
postmodernism 56–57
Pound, Ezra 49, 52–53, 104, 115, 116
Power of Sympathy, The 44–45
Pre-Raphaelite Brotherhood 31
Preface to *Fables Ancient and Modern*, The 22
Pretty 106
Pretty Woman 191
Pride and Prejudice 10, 28, 150
primary sources 263–67
Prince, The 74–75
principals 158
Prometheus Unbound 27
props 163
prose fiction 129–54
protagonist 158
Proust, Marcel 80–81
Psycho 185, 203
psychoanalytic theory 237–40
Puig, Manuel 88
Pullman, Philip 120
Purcell, Henry 22
Pushkin, Alexander 76–77
Pwyll Pendeuic Dyuet 3
Pynchon, Thomas 60

qasīdahs 70–71
Queen and Huntress 99
queer theories 243–46
querelle des femmes 241
quotations (in research essays) 261
Qur'an 71

Radcliffe, Anne 28
Rain 71

Rambler 24
Ransom, John Crowe 224
Rape of the Lock, The 22, 119
Raven, The 47
reaction shot 185
realism 49–50; psychological realism 50–51
realistic novel 151
Red Badge of Courage, The 51
Red, Red Rose, A 26, 108
Reed, Henry 34
Reed, Ishmael 60, 153
Relacíon de Alvar Núñez Cabeza de Vaca, La 39–40
Remains of the Day, The 135
Remembrance of Things Past 80–81
repartee 24, 169
repetition 143
repression 238
Republic, The 211
Resistance to Civil Government 47
Retrospect, A 104
return 131–32, 156
Revelation 72
revising 277–88
Rhetoric 68, 249–50
rhetorical analysis 249–52
rhyme 93–94
rhythm 97–105
Rich, Adrienne 59, 244
Richard II 18
Richard III 101
Richards, I. A. 224–26
Richardson, Samuel 23, 147
Rights of Man 25
Rimbaud, Arthur 79
Rime of the Ancient Mariner 26, 115
Rip Van Winkle 45
rising action 131–32, 156–57
Rivals, The 24, 171
Rob Roy 28, 149
Robin Hood (legends and films of) 115, 233
Robinson Crusoe 23
Rojek, Chris 232
romance 15, 125–26
romantic comedy 167–69, 197–99
Romeo and Juliet 110, 159, 204
Room of One's Own, A 240
Rosenblatt, Louise 223
Rosencrantz and Guildenstern Are Dead 36, 175
Ross, Andrew 232
Rossetti, Christina 31, 95, 115
Rossetti, Dante Gabriel 31
Rowlandson, Mary 41
Rowling, J. K. 37, 131, 148, 178, 201, 254–55
Rowson, Susanna 45
Ruba'iyat, The 71–72
Ruined Maid, The 236–37
Rūmī, Jalāl al-Dīn 72

Runaway Slave at Pilgrim's Point, The 30, 116
Rushdie, Salman 11, 37
Ruskin, John 29
Ruth Hall 137–38

Said, Edward 247
Sailing to Byzantium 33–34
Salih, Tayeb 86
Salinger, J. D. 144
Salve Deus Rex Judeaorum 242–43
Sanchez, Sonia 59
Sandler, Barry 179
Santas, Constantine 200
Sappho 66
Sarris, Andrew 191–92
Sartre, Jean-Paul 81
Sassoon, Siegfried 34
Satanic School 26–27
Satanic Verses, The 37
Saussure, Ferdinand de 227
Scarlet Letter, The 46
scene 182–83
Schelling, Felix 121
School for Scandal, The 24, 171
School for Wives, The 170–71
Schrader, Paul 202
Schuyler, James 58
science fiction 204–05
scopophilia 191
Scorsese, Martin 192, 193
Scott, Sir Walter 28, 114, 149
Seafarer 14, 117
Season of Migration to the North 86
Second Coming, The, 110
Second Sex, The 81, 241
Second Shepherds' Play 16, 125
secondary sources 263–67
Sedgwick, Eve 245
semiotics 227–30
sentimental novel 45
Sermon Preached at the Execution of Moses Paul 43–44
setting 139–41
Sexton, Anne 58, 122, 278–88
Shakespeare, William 18, 22, 99, 101, 105, 110, 114, 120, 125, 157, 159, 161, 165, 167–68, 178, 198, 204, 215–16, 263, 268–69
Shange, Ntozake 175–76
Shaw, George Bernard 32–33, 171, 172
Shelley, Mary 28, 203
Shelley, Percy Bysshe 26–27, 118, 124, 216
Shepard, Sam 162
Shepheardes Calendar, The 118, 125
Sheridan, Richard Brinsley 24, 171
Shiloh 95–96
short story 129
short take 186
shot 182–83, 185–86; shot/reverse shot 187

Showings 16
Sidney, Sir Philip 18, 125, 128, 165, 213
Silko, Leslie Marmon 61
simile 108–09, 145
Simon, Neil 168–69
Sinfield, Alan 116
Sinners in the Hands of an Angry God 42
Sir Gawain and the Green Knight 7, 15, 75, 95, 125, 233
Sir Patrick Spens 115
situational irony 112–13
Sitwell, Edith 114
Six Characters in Search of an Author 82–83
Sketch of His Own Character 25
slave narrative 44
Sleepers, The 104
Smith, Bessie 107
Smith, Charlotte 127
Smith, John 40
Smith, Stevie 34, 106, 114
Smith, Zadie 37
Smollett, Tobias 24
Snow White 153
Snyder, Gary 57
social class and ideology 234–37
soliloquy 161
Sone, Monica 138
Song (Brigit Pegeen Kelly) 107
Song (Christina Rossetti) 95
Song for St. Cecilia's Day, A 96–97
Song of Roland 118
Songs and Sonnets 19
Songs of Innocence and Experience 25
sonnet 17, 126–28; sonnet sequence 128
Sonnets from the Portuguese 30, 128
Sophocles 67, 165
Sound and the Fury, The 55, 152
sound effects (cinematic) 189–90
sounds (poetic) 93–97
southern gothic 59–60
Southerns 206–07
Southey, Robert 26
Southwell, Robert 108–09
Soyinka, Wole 84–85
Spanish Tragedy, The 18, 108
Spark, Muriel 37
spectator theories 195–97
Spectator, The 24, 214
Spenser, Edmund 17–18, 118, 119, 120, 125–26, 128, 213
Spiegelman, Art 61, 154
Spivak, Gayatri 228
spondee 97, 100
Spring and Fall 225–26
sprung rhythm 103–04
stage directions 162
Staiger, Janet 196
Stam, Robert 195–96
star theories 193–95

Star Wars 188, 200, 205
Steele, Sir Richard 24
Stein, Gertrude 53
Steinbeck, John 55–56, 206
Sterne, Laurence 24, 133
Stevens, Wallace 53, 275
Stevenson, Robert Louis 32
Stoker, Bram 147, 203
Stoppard, Tom 36, 175
Stowe, Harriet Beecher 48
Strand, Mark 128
Strange Case of Dr. Jekyll and Mr. Hyde, The 32
Stranger, The 81
stream of consciousness 134
Streetcar Named Desire, A 62, 158–59
Strunk, William 288
Study in Scarlet, A 138–39
style 142–46
sublimation 238
Suckling, Sir John 19–20, 121
Sufi poets 72–73
Sun Stone 88–89
Sunne Rising, The 114
surrealism 80
suspense 203
suspension of disbelief 133
Swift, Jonathan 22, 198
Symbolism 79–80
symbols 107–08, 145–46
synecdoche 109
syntax 144

Tabachnick, Stephen 154
take 186
Tam o' Shanter 26
Tao Te Ching 70
Tarantino, Quentin 192, 194, 206
Tartuffe 156–57, 170
Tate, Allen 224
Tatler, The 24
Technique of the Drama 131–32
Temple, The 20
Tennent, Gilbert 42
Tennyson, Alfred, Lord 29–30, 100, 112, 116, 118
Thackeray, William Makepeace 31
The Brain—is wider than the Sky 49
Theater of the Absurd 36, 175
Their Eyes Were Watching God 54
theme 141–42, 158
Theogony 65–66
There Is No Natural Religion 25
These Happy Golden Years 268
thesis statement 260, 265–66
Things Fall Apart 37, 83–84
Third Part of Henry VI, The 101
Thomas, Dylan 34, 109
Thomson, James 24, 125

Thoreau, Henry David 47
Thousand and One Nights, The 73
Timber, or Discoveries 214
Timon of Athens 110
Titus Andronicus 162, 269
To Althea, from Prison 20, 113
To an Athlete Dying Young 34
To Build a Fire 140
To His Coy Mistress 21, 242
To His Excellency, George Washington 44
To John Donne 19
To Kill a Mockingbird 60, 142
To My Lover, Returning to
  His Wife 278–88
To the Immortal Memory and Friendship of
  That Noble Pair, Sir Lucius Cary and Sir
  Henry Morison 123
To the Lighthouse 36, 134
To the Memory of My Beloved, the Author,
  Mr. William Shakespeare: And What He
  Hath Left Us 103
To the Moon 127
To the Noblest and Best of Ladies, the
  Countess of Denbigh 20
To the Virgins, to Make Much of Time 20
To Wordsworth 27
Todorov, Tzvetan 253
Tolkien, J. R. R. 37
Tolstoy, Leo 77, 151
Tom Jones 24
tone 142–46
Toole, John Kennedy 261–62
topic 265
Tottel's Miscellany 17
tracking shot 186
Tradition and the Individual Talent 220
tragedy 164–67
Tragedy and the Common Man 166
tragic flaw 164
transcendentalism 47
Tristam Shandy 24, 134
trochee 97, 99
Trollope, Anthony 31–32
Turgenev, Ivan 78
Turn of the Screw, The 51, 203, 239–40
Tuttleton, James 150
Twain, Mark 50, 126, 148, 151, 205
Twelfth Night 101, 167–68, 172, 198
Two Noble Kinsmen, The 101
typecasting 193

U. S. A. 56
Ulysses 36, 152
*Uncle Tom's Cabin; or, Life among the
  Lowly* 48
Unforgiven 206
unreliable narrator 135
Updike, John 62
Upon His Departure Hence 98

Upon Jack and Jill 228–29
Upon the Double Murder of King Charles 20
Upon the Nipples of Julia's Breast 20

Vagina Monologues, The 161
Valéry, Paul 79
Vanity Fair 31
Vanity of Human Wishes, The 22–23
Vargas Llosa, Mario 88
Vaughan, Henry 20
Vercelli Book 14
Verlaine, Paul 79–80
Vertov, Dziga 184
Village, The 24, 125
Villette 31
Vindication of the Rights of Men, A 25
Vindication of the Rights of Woman, A 25,
  241
Vine, The 107
Virgil 15, 17, 124
Visit from St. Nicholas, A 99
Vogel, Paula 62, 163
voice 111–14
voiceover 190
Vonnegut, Kurt 60

Wace 15
Wagner, Geoffrey 180
Waiting for Godot 36, 175
Waiting for the Barbarians 85–86
Wakefield Master 16, 125
Walcott, Derek 267–68
Walden 47
Walker, Alice 147
Walpole, Horace 28
Wanderer, The 14, 117
Warren, Robert Penn 224–25
Wasteland, The 53, 108
Waverley Novels 28, 149
Way of the World, The 24, 102, 159, 171
We never know how high we are 94–95
Webster, John 18, 103
Webster, Noah 8
Weldon, Fay 37
Welles, Orson 62
Wells, H. G. 205
Welty, Eudora 59–60
Westerns 206
Wharton, Edith 52
What the Butler Saw 172
Wheatley, Phillis 44, 93
When I Was One-and-Twenty 34
White Man's Burden, The 32
White, T. H. 126
Whitefield, George 42, 44
Whitman, Walt 47, 48–49, 104, 217
Whittier, John Greenleaf 48
Who's Afraid of Virginia Woolf 160
Wife of Bath's Prologue 8, 229, 241

Wife's Lament, The 14, 117
Wigglesworth, Michael 41
Wilde, Oscar 9, 32, 100, 171, 211
Wilder, Laura Ingalls 268
Wilder, Thornton 56, 159–60
Wilhelm Meister's Apprenticeship 147–48
William of Nassyngton 6
Williams, John 188–89
Williams, Raymond 232
Williams, Tennessee 61–62, 155, 158–59
Williams, William Carlos 53
Wilmot, John, Second Earl of Rochester 22
Wilson, August 163
Wimsatt, W. K. 225
Windhover, The 30
Winter's Tale, The 18, 162
Winterson, Jeanette 37, 148
Winthrop, John 40
wipe 188
Wise Blood 60
Wit 269
Wollstonecraft, Mary 25, 241
Woman in White, The 32
Woolf, Virginia 36, 56, 134, 219, 240

Wordsworth, Dorothy 26
Wordsworth, William 26, 115, 124, 125
Works and Days 65–66
Works Cited: books and book chapters
    267–71; film, television, and radio
    271–72; Internet sources 272–73;
    periodicals 271
Worley, Alec 201
Wright, Richard 59
Wright, Will 206
Wroth, Mary 18, 112–13, 128
Wulfstan 14
Wuthering Heights 31, 130
Wyatt, Sir Thomas, the Elder 17, 126–27
Wycherley, William 24, 171
Wynette, Tammy 116

Yeats, William Butler 33–34, 110, 115, 118
Yellow Wallpaper, The 140
Yet Do I Marvel 54
Young Goodman Brown 46, 133
Ysrael 11

zoom shot 186